When Baghdad Ruled
the Muslim World

When Baghdad Ruled the Muslim World

The Rise and Fall of Islam's Greatest Dynasty

HUGH KENNEDY

Da Capo Press
A Member of the Perseus Books Group

To Hilary, Xana, Katharine, Alice and James,
with love and thanks for everything

Cataloging-in-Publication data for this book is available
from the Library of Congress.

First Da Capo Press edition 2005
First Da Capo Press paperback edition 2006
Published by arrangement with Weidenfeld & Nicholson.
First published in the United Kingdom as *The Court of the Caliphs*.
ISBN-10: 0-306-81480-3
ISBN-13: 978-0-306-81480-8

Published by Da Capo Press
A Member of the Perseus Books Group
www.dacapopress.com

Da Capo Press books are available at special discounts for bulk purchases in the
U.S. by corporations, institutions, and other organizations.
For more information, please contact the Special Markets Department at the
Perseus Books Group, 11 Cambridge Center, Cambridge, MA 02142,
or call (800) 255-1514 or (617) 252-5298, or e-mail
special.markets@perseusbooks.com.

3 4 5 6 7 8 9—08

Contents

Acknowledgements

It is a pleasure to acknowledge help and support from many colleagues and friends. I must first thank Judith Herrin who first suggested my name to Georgina Capel. It was Georgina's encouragement and support which persuaded me to undertake a book I had not previously thought of writing. I would also like to thank the team at Weidenfeld and Nicolson, especially Penny Gardiner whose editorial skills and enthusiasm helped so much, and Tom Graves for his work on the illustrations. I owe a great debt of gratitude to the translators of Tabari's *History*, whose readings have so often guided me through the text, to Julia Bray for fresh and witty translations of Arabic poetry, and Letizia Osti, who has helped me with her great understanding of classical Arabic prose and tenth-century court culture. I am very grateful to Rebecca Foote for sharing information about her excavations in Humayma and to Georgina Herrmann for making it possible for me to visit Merv. My thanks are also due to Helen and Robert Irwin for hospitality in London and long hours of fruitful conversation about aspects of orientalism. And finally my family who have, as ever, supported my absences, and absent-mindedness, with tolerance and good grace and to whom this book is lovingly dedicated.

Illustrations

Map list

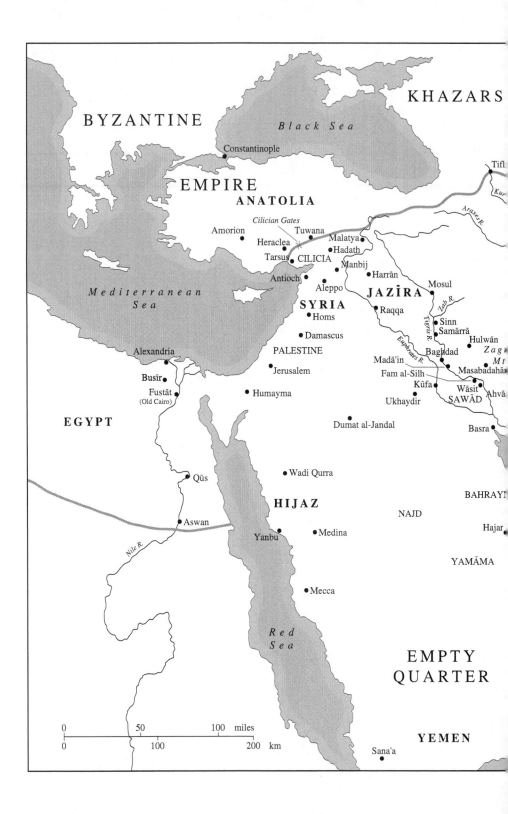

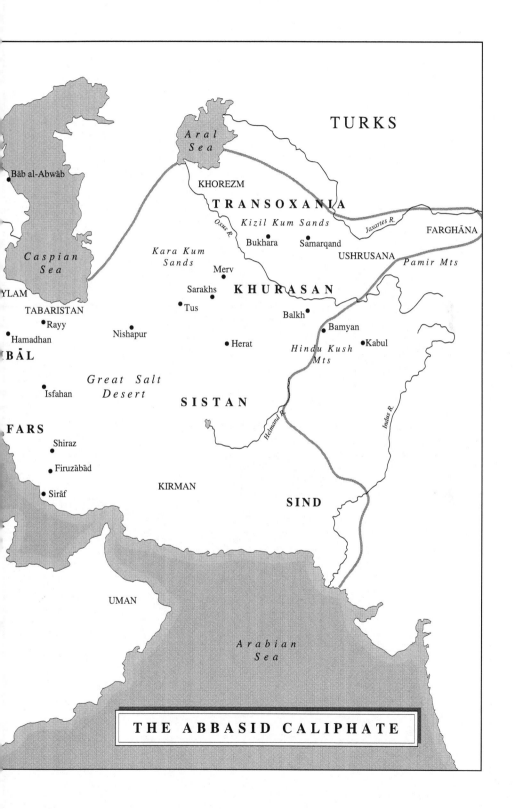

THE ABBASID CALIPHATE

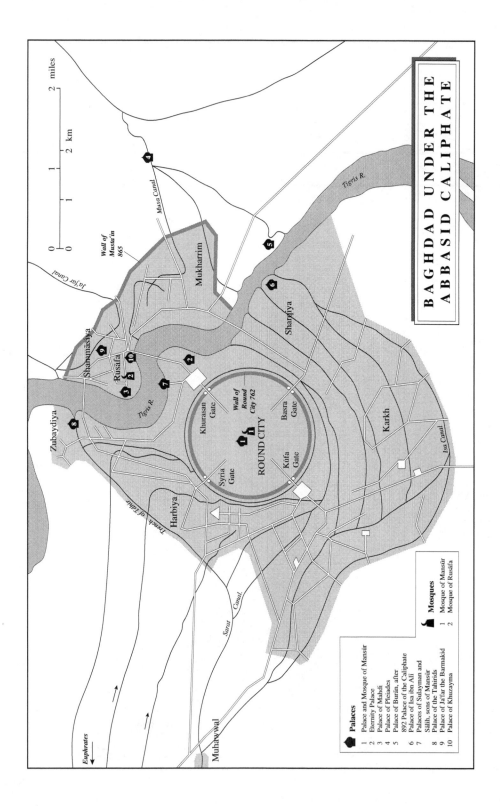

BAGHDAD UNDER THE ABBASID CALIPHATE

Euphrates

Muhawwal

Sarat Canal

Trench of Tahir

Harbiya

ROUND CITY

Syria Gate

Khurasan Gate

Wall of Round City 762

Kufa Gate

Basra Gate

Karkh

Isa Canal

Zubaydiya

8

Shammasiya

Tigris R.

9
Rusafa
2
3
10
2
7

Mukharrim

Ja'far Canal

Wall of Musta'in 865

Musa Canal

4

5

6

Sharqiya

Tigris R.

0   1   2 km

0   1   2 miles

Palaces

1 Palace and Mosque of Mansūr
2 Eternity Palace
3 Palace of Mahdi
4 Palace of Pleiades
5 Palace of Burān, after 892 Palace of the Caliphate
6 Palace of Isa ibn Ali
7 Palaces of Sulayman and Sāḥ, sons of Mansūr
8 Palace of the Tahirids
9 Palace of Ja'far the Barmakid
10 Palace of Khuzayma

Mosques

1 Mosque of Mansūr
2 Mosque of Rusāfa

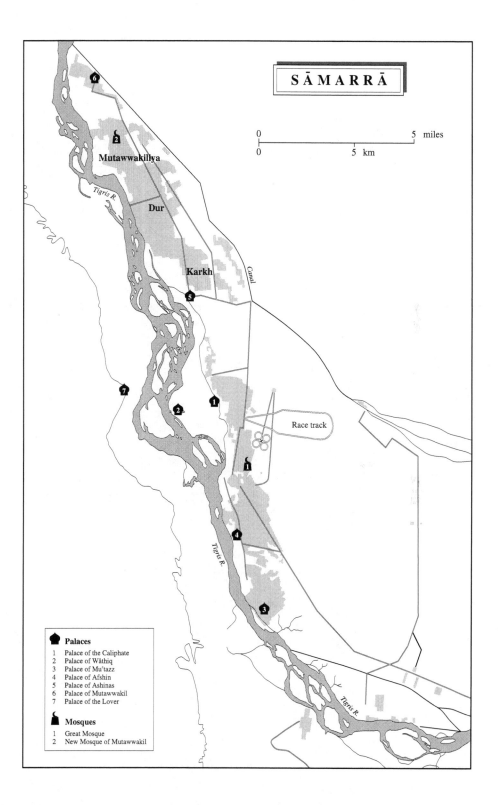

SĀMARRĀ

0   5 miles
0   5 km

Tigris R.

Mutawakiliya

Dur

Karkh

Canal

Race track

Tigris R.

Tigris R.

Palaces

1   Palace of the Caliphate
2   Palace of Wāthiq
3   Palace of Muʿtazz
4   Palace of Afshin
5   Palace of Ashinas
6   Palace of Mutawwakil
7   Palace of the Lover

Mosques

1   Great Mosque
2   New Mosque of Mutawwakil

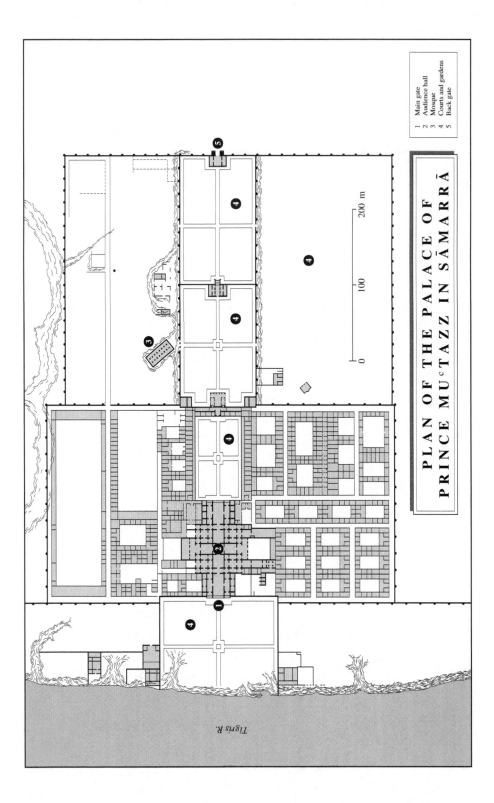

Tigris R.

**PLAN OF THE PALACE OF
PRINCE MUᶜTAZZ IN SĀMARRĀ**

1 Main gate
2 Audience hall
3 Mosque
4 Courts and gardens
5 Back gate

0   100   200 m

The Abbasid Caliphs

reigning caliphs are numbered with dates of accession

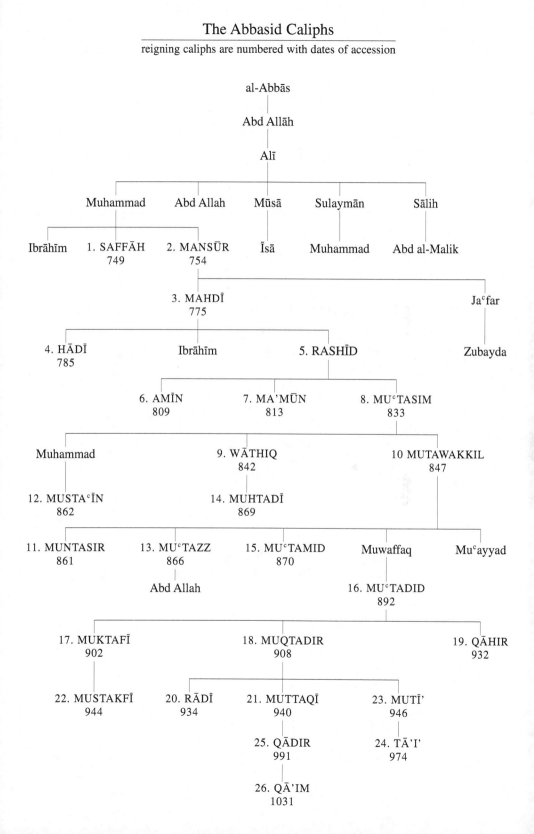

Timeline

632   Death of the Prophet Muhammad
632–61   Rightly Guided Caliphs (Rāshidūn)
661–750   Umayyad caliphs
750   Saffāh
751   Muslim armies defeat Chinese at battle of Talas
           (Kazakhstan)
751   Pepin, first Carolingian monarch, crowned king of the
           Franks
752   Foundation of Rashtrakuta kingdom in south and central
           India
754   Mansūr
758–96   Offa, king of Mercia
762   Foundation of Baghdad
775   Mahdi
785   Hādī
786   Hārūn al-Rashīd
789   Death of Khayzurān
793   Vikings sack Lindisfarne monastery
800   Coronation of Charlemagne, foundation of the Holy Roman
           Empire
802   Foundation of Angkor in Cambodia
803   Fall of the Barmakids
809   Amīn
813   Ma'mūn
814   Death of Charlemagne
811–19   Great Abbasid Civil War
812–13   First siege of Baghdad
831   Death of Zubayda
833   Mu‘tasim

836	Caliphate moves to Sāmarrā
838	Sack of Amorion
840	Trial and execution of Afshīn
842	Wāthiq
845	Death of Abd Allah ibn Tāhir in Khurasan
846	Conspiracy of Ahmad ibn Nasr in Baghdad
847	Mutawwakil
849	Execution of Ītākh
860	First Viking attack on Constantinople
861	Muntasir
862	Musta°īn
865	Second siege of Baghdad
866	Mu°tazz
869	Muhtadi
869–83	Rebellion of the Zanj in southern Iraq
870	Mu°tamid
871–99	Alfred the Great, king of England
882	Kiev becomes capital of the Rus
885–6	Viking siege of Paris
892	Mu°tadid
892	Caliphate returns to Baghdad
893	Death of author Ibn Abi Tāhir
902	Muktafi
907	Fall of Tang dynasty in China
908	Muqtadir
911	Rollo founds Duchy of Normandy
923	Death of the historian Tabari
932	Qāhir
934–40	Rādi
935	Ibn Rā'iq takes over as Amir of Amirs

Foreword

From the revolution of 750 that brought the dynasty to power until its collapse in the 930s and 940s the Abbasid caliphate* was by far the greatest political power in the Islamic world. But it was more than that; it was the continuation of that universal caliphate which had been established by Abu Bakr and his supporters immediately after the death of the Prophet Muhammad in 632, which was to continue in different guises and in different places down to the abdication of the last Ottoman caliph in 1925. In later centuries the caliphs were often purely ornamental figures with no power and little status, but in the three hundred years after 632 caliphs, first the four 'Rightly Guided' caliphs, then from 661 the Umayyads and finally from 750 the Abbasids, exercised real power and leadership over the Muslim people. They embodied the unity of the Muslim community or *umma*. The court of the caliph established the style for all Muslim rulers, and the administrative systems they set up served as a model for all successor regimes.

This book is intended to tell the story of the Abbasid caliphs and their court in the two centuries that constituted their golden age. I use the word 'story' deliberately. I have written a determinedly narrative history that concentrates on people and events. This is not because longer-term changes and social and economic factors are unimportant; clearly they are, and I have written about them elsewhere. But in the concern to make the history of the Islamic Middle

* The term 'caliph' (Ar. *Khalīfa*) is short for the Caliph or Deputy of God (Ar. *Khalīfat Allāh*), which became the normal designation of the ruler of the Muslim community in the generation that followed the Prophet's death in 632. The ruler was more formally known as Commander of the Faithful (Ar. *Amīr al-Mu'minīn).* The word 'sultan' is used in the Arabic texts of the period to mean 'the authorities' or 'the government' in the abstract. It is not until the eleventh century that it is used as a personal title for rulers who were not caliphs, in the same way that the abstract noun 'majesty' becomes a personal title in English.

East scientific and academically respectable we, and I mean here the small community of scholars who work on these subjects, have distrusted and avoided narrative, mere storytelling. In doing so, we have done ourselves and our subject no favours. For people coming from outside our specialized world we have made our field difficult, problematic and, yes, rather dull.

We have also in a sense betrayed our sources, for the Arabic chronicles on which our reconstructions of the past depend use narrative and anecdote throughout to make points and illuminate personalities. The Abbasid bureaucracy certainly produced large quantities of documents, first on papyrus and then, from the end of the eighth century onward, on paper. However, virtually all of these are lost beyond hope of recovery. We must rely largely on the literary sources to reconstruct the history of this civilization and much of this literature is narrative in form. And what narratives! There is straightforward recounting of events – military campaigns, for example, though these are seldom as simple as they appear at first glance. There are funny stories, tragic stories, stories that seem to be inconsequential musings, stories whose real meaning now escapes us. If we want to discover how an army was recruited, how taxes were collected, how a room was decorated or what sort of a man Hārūn al-Rashīd really was, it is to these narratives and anecdotes that we must turn. The issue of the reliability of these stories, whether they are really 'true', is a complex one. On certain key events, the unexpected death of the Caliph Hādī in 786, for example, we have different accounts that appear to contradict each other; but they are all contemporary or near contemporary, and all reflect what some people thought had happened or what they thought ought to have happened. So this book is full of stories; and I make no apology for this, for I am following, humbly and falteringly, in the steps of the great Arab historians of the ninth and tenth centuries.

This is not the place for a full-scale discussion of early Islamic history writing, for this has been excellently done by scholars better qualified than I.[1] It is, however, important to introduce some of the writers on whom I have drawn.

Muhammad ibn Jarīr al-Tabari came, as his name suggests, from the province of Tabaristān at the south end of the Caspian Sea. He was of Iranian origin but also a pious Muslim steeped in Arabic history and tradition. He worked mostly in Baghdad in the second half of the ninth century and was thus contemporary with many of the events described in this book. He was broadly supportive of the Abbasid regime, but he was not a court historian, dependent on favour and patronage. He lived off the revenues of his estates in Tabaristān, which were brought to him each year by pilgrims from his native land passing through. He lived an austere life and does not seem to have married or had children, and he played no active part in politics. He was pious and shared the distrust of the bourgeoisie for common people. He believed in order and hierarchy.

He was a man of truly astonishing industry. His great *History of the Prophets and Kings* has recently been translated into English. It runs to thirty-eight printed volumes, each of well over two hundred pages, perhaps ten thousand pages in all. And this was by no means the limit of his endeavours: he also wrote a commentary on the Koran which is not much shorter. Both the commentary and the *History* have remained the classic works on their subject. Tabari is particularly valuable as a historian because he incorporated earlier works, whether whole books or fragmentary accounts, almost verbatim. This was not plagiarism, since he did not try to claim the credit and made it quite clear what he was doing. In some ways Tabari's *History* is more like a whole library than a conventional book, but the fact that he preserves this material means that we can come close to many original voices and eyewitness accounts. The *History* forms the foundation of this work, just as it has been the foundation of all other works on the early history of Islam.

Abu'l-Faraj al-Isfahāni (d. 967) (the man from Isfahan) was, despite his name, of Arabic origin; indeed, he was a descendant of the Umayyad caliphs who had ruled before the coming of the Abbasids in 750. He was not, however, a propagandist for the old dynasty and his political sympathies lay rather with the descendants of Alī. He wrote a melancholy but very scholarly account of the deaths of members of the house of Alī at the hands of the Abbasid authorities. It is, however, his great *Book of Songs* which I have mostly drawn on for this work. Like Tabari's *History*, this is vast: it has never been translated into English but the Arabic editions all run to more than twenty full-length volumes. Tabari's work is not without its lighter touches, but it is largely concerned with the weighty matter of politics and warfare. Isfahāni was interested in songs, singers and poets. Though certainly scholarly, the work is altogether more light-hearted, and he preserves numerous anecdotes, some informative, some funny, some scabrous, which open a window on the everyday life of the period. Like Tabari, he is careful to preserve verbatim narratives and credit his sources, and through him we can approach the writings of ninth-century writers like Ibn Abi Tāhir, even when the bulk of their original work has been lost.

The other major work on the history of the Abbasids was Masᶜūdī's *Meadows of Gold*. This is a general history of the Islamic world covering much the same ground as Tabari's *History*, but it is in many ways a more polished and literary production. It combines historical narrative with engaging stories about court life and culture. In a way, its more literary style makes it less vivid than the cruder verbatim narratives that Tabari gives us and, on occasion, Masᶜūdī's narratives seem to reflect the perceptions of his own time rather than those of the earlier Abbasid period. But Masᶜūdī is still a great read. There is an English translation of those parts of *The Meadows of Gold* which deal with the Abbasids. The translation is abridged but lively and reliable, and is probably the best introduction to the Arabic historical tradition for the non-specialist.

I have used many other sources for details and insights and specialists will find them in the endnotes and the Bibliography.

This book is not a general history of the Abbasid caliphate. It focuses on the caliphs and their court and court life. There are few tales from the provinces. I am aware that I have not discussed huge areas of the cultural life of the period. I have neglected the developments in Islamic law and theology in the period which laid the foundations for the study of these subjects ever since. It was in this period too that the traditions of the Prophet were collected and evaluated, and I have not given space to this process. With few exceptions, these worthy enterprises were not the products of court culture or the recreations of caliphs. They came rather from the sober and industrious bourgeoisie of Baghdad and other cities, whose lifestyles were in many ways the antithesis of the glamorous but sometimes morally dubious world of the court. My discussions of the poetry and literature of the Abbasid period are illustrative, not comprehensive; they consider this art as part of a wider court culture and concentrate as much on the lives of the writers as on their work.

I am aware that the more austere and learned of my colleagues will think this book frivolous. With its concentration on dramatic events, striking personalities and the trivia of everyday life, it may seem to go against many recent trends in historical writing. But I make no apology for trying to introduce a wider audience to the pace, excitement, glamour, fear and danger of Abbasid court life.

I am equally aware that some Muslim readers may feel that this is in some ways a disrespectful account of the glorious days of the Abbasids. The caliphs and their advisers are not treated with undue reverence. The book contains its fair share of, to put it bluntly, booze and sex. The fact that wine was widely and generally drunk may be especially distasteful to the pious. However, there is nothing here which is not in the original Arabic sources. The writers of the ninth and tenth centuries knew that their rulers had their fair share of human frailties and they were quite happy to describe them. To produce a sanitized and whitewashed version of history does no service to our understanding of the caliphate. So this account reflects the rich variety of human nature; the brave and loyal, the shrewd and calculating, the cruel and corrupt and the foolish and besotted are all here.

In some places too the language may be surprising. Arab authors of the period, including the pious Tabari, were not inhibited about using coarse and direct language in a way that later authors may have felt embarrassed about. When the great thirteenth-century historian Ibn al-Athīr was writing his epitome of Tabari's history he was amazed that Tabari, 'pious man that he was', could reproduce the scabrous poem about the caliph Amīn's sexual proclivities, and he contented himself with quoting a couple of fairly innocent lines. But, as the ninth-century cultural critic Jāhiz wrote, 'Some people who affect asceticism and self denial are uneasy and embarrassed when cunt, cock and fucking are mentioned but most men you find like that are without knowledge, honour, nobility or dignity.'[2] I have certainly not played up these features of the narrative, but nor have I attempted to bury them in 'the decent obscurity of a dead language', for they are an integral feature of this lively and robust culture.

This book is an attempt to introduce the rich history and culture of the period, and the men and women who made it, to a non-specialist audience. The Abbasid caliphate in the eighth and ninth centuries was as central and pivotal to world history as the Roman Empire was in the first and second. Like the Roman Empire too, its legacy was to influence politics and the development of society for generations to come. Yet the characters and events of the golden age of the caliphate are largely unknown beyond, and often within, the confines of the Muslim world. I hope this book will go a little way towards making the world of the Abbasid caliphs a part of the world-view of educated people in the way in which the world of ancient Greece and Rome already is.

A NOTE ON TRANSLITERATION AND NAMES

The non-Arab reader of this work will encounter many strange and unusual names which may well seem off-putting and unmemorable. I have tried to make the names as simple as possible but I know that problems will still remain.

There are now standard and acceptable ways of transliterating Arabic letters into Roman script. I have not adopted any of these in their entirety. For a non-Arabist, it is not very helpful to be able to distinguish between the two types of *h* or *s* or *t*, and readers who do know the language will be aware of these anyhow. Arabic has both long and short vowels and these I have indicated in most cases. It does seem to me to be helpful to know that the name of the caliph Rashīd is pronounced Rasheed not Raashid. Put simply *ā* is pronounced as a long aa, *ī* as an ee and *ū* as an oo, and the stress falls on these long syllables.

I have also marked the Arabic letter *ayn* as ^c when it comes in the middle of words. The *ayn* is a consonant peculiar to Arabic whose pronunciation can only be learned by imitation. It is perhaps most helpful to think of it as a gutteral prolongation of the previous vowel. The symbol ' (Arabic *hamza*) is a simple glottal stop.

The names themselves can be divided into certain groups. Abbasid caliphs had a given name from birth but, like popes, were given official titles when they succeeded to the throne, and it is by these official titles that they are usually known. From the time of Mu^ctasim these titles were almost always active participles beginning in Mu, which gives a certain uniformity to the titulature.

The given names of individuals were sometimes biblical in origin: Ibrāhīm is Abraham, Ishāq is Isaac, Yūsuf is Joseph, Mūsā is Moses, Hārūn is Aaron, Yahya is John and Īsā is Jesus. Some names, such as Muhammad and Alī, had purely Islamic religious connotations.

There were also names describing the holder as a slave *(abd)* of God in any of His names, most commonly Abd Allah, but also Abd al-Malik (the slave of the king).

Men were also named after their fathers, thus Ibn Fulān (Fulān meaning 'so and so'), or after their sons, thus Abu Fulān. We also find men called Ibn Abi Fulān, 'son of the father of so and so'. Women were known as Bint Fulān, 'daughter of so and so', or, more commonly as Umm Fulān, 'mother of so and so'.

However, many names, especially non-Arabic names of Turkish soldiers in the ninth and tenth centuries, are one-off examples and sometimes, because of the vagaries of Arabic orthography, we cannot be at all certain what they meant or how they were pronounced.

COINS, WEIGHTS AND MEASURES

There were two principal coins in circulation in the Abbasid period. The most valuable was the gold *dīnār*, a small coin about a centimetre in diameter. Along with this was the larger *dirham*, a thin silver coin slightly over 2 centimetres in diameter and weighing about 3 grams. All the coins bore inscriptions but, except on rare occasions, no images. The relationship between the two was not constant, but in the ninth century there were about twenty *dirham*s to the *dīnār*. Coins were usually weighed not counted, and the *dīnār* was often a unit of account rather than an actual coin. In the eighth century there were copper coins called *dāniq*s, but these seem to have gone out of circulation by the mid-ninth.

The main unit of weight was the *ratl* (from the Greek *litron* or pound). This varied greatly from one part of the Islamic world to another but in Iraq in the ninth century it was usually about 400 grams or slightly less than a pound avoirdupois.

Short lengths were measured in cubits *(dhirā)*, each about half a metre. Longer distances were measured in *mīl*s (Roman miles) or the Persian *farsakh* (Parsang).

I have given most measurements in modern equivalents and they are, needless to say, approximate.

I

Revolution

In about the year 720, a wandering perfume seller was doing the rounds of the small villages in the semi-desert areas of southern Jordan. It was an out-of-the way area, a land of small farming villages and Bedouin encampments, far from the centres of power in Damascus 400 kilometres to the north or Medina 640 kilometres to the south-east. There was nothing unusual about his appearance and he became accepted as a feature of local life. This is just what he intended, for Bukayr ibn Mahān was a man with a mission that went far beyond scraping a living as a wandering pedlar in this remote part of the Muslim world. To begin with he was a man of some wealth in his native Kūfa in southern Iraq. He had travelled widely, serving as a volunteer in the Muslim armies conquering the mountainous area of Jurjān at the southern end of the Caspian Sea and visiting Khurasan, the vast wild province of north-east Iran which marked the limits of the Muslim world in central Asia. Just before he left home, he heard that his brother had died in distant Sind (southern Pakistan), leaving a considerable fortune, and he was urged to go there to secure his inheritance. He refused, having more important things on his mind.

Travel does not seem to have been difficult for a man in his position. The Muslim empire, which had been ruled by the Umayyad dynasty since 661, had few internal frontiers. While Coptic Christians bound to their native Egyptian soil were obliged to wear lead seals around their necks and carry written passports if they wished to move from one town to another, Bukayr was a Muslim, a member, if only a humble one, of the new Muslim ruling class, and no one looked askance when he crossed from Iraq to the Syrian capital at Damascus, bought a donkey, loaded it up with perfumes and set off south.

When he had spent enough time in the area to be accepted as a simple salesman, Bukayr came to the settlement at Humayma. He asked where he could stay and was directed to the guest house. Here he took off his disguise and his travelling clothes and began his real business. Humayma today is a sand-blown ruin in the scorching plains of southern Jordan, known as the Hisma. It is only a day's journey from the palm-fringed Red Sea and Aqaba, but no sea breezes reach this far inland. The surrounding mountains are stony and barren, while in the distance, on the south-eastern horizon, through the shimmering heat haze, the sudden and dramatic peaks of the Mountains of Rum appear, startlingly spiky at the end of the flat, sandy plain.

Nowadays Humayma is uninhabited, but in ancient times it looked very different. The Nabataeans, builders of Petra, had created a settlement here. Using the careful techniques of water harvesting, gathering the run-off from the winter rains in cisterns, they had made agriculture possible. Under Roman rule the settlement had flourished, churches were built and a bath house established, in itself a minor miracle of hydraulic engineering in this wasteland.

Bukayr had not come all this way to admire the irrigation. He had come to see the owner of the principal house in Humayma. Muhammad ibn Alī led the life of a quiet country gentleman. He had an orchard of some three hundred fruit trees, probably mostly olives, which he tended in person, and to which he retired to pray. His house consisted of a series of single-storey rooms surrounding a roughly rectangular courtyard. In the middle of the east wall lay an entrance to the whole complex. A few yards to the south-east there was a small mosque, with a conspicuous prayer niche pointing towards Mecca, and it was to this mosque that the male members of the family would retire to eat shared meals and discuss religion and the affairs of the day. The house had none of the grandeur of the palaces of the ruling Umayyad family, with their fine stonework and rich decoration, but some of the rooms were covered with frescos to make the plaster look like marble and there was furniture with deco-rated ivory plaques, though people would mostly have sat and slept on mats and *farsh*, those padded fabrics, a combination of mattress and pillow, which are so typical a feature of traditional Arab domestic life.

To all outward appearances, Muhammad ibn Alī was simply a pious and retiring landowner, but he had one attribute which made him very special indeed as far as Bukayr was concerned: he was a member of the Family of the Prophet Muhammad. Muhammad himself had died some ninety years before Bukayr began his travels. His own status as Messenger of God had been unchallenged, but he had left little guidance as to how the Muslim community should be led after his death. Dispute began even as his body was being washed and prepared for burial. His companions, led by Abu Bakr and Umar, who had been with him since the early days in Mecca, felt that they had the vision and experience to guide the Muslim community and were its natural leaders. Others, especially the people of the city of Medina, which Muhammad had made his home and base of operations during the last ten years of his life, were less certain and hoped that the Prophet's own Family might take the lead. Muhammad had no surviving son but he had left an adult daughter, Fātima. In the approved local manner, she had married her first cousin, Alī ibn Abī Tālib. Together they had two sons, Hasan and Husayn, the Prophet's grandchildren, whom he had loved dearly and dandled on his knee. In the event, the Companions won the struggle, though Alī did have a brief and troubled reign as caliph from 656 to 661. The Family of the Prophet remained a focus of opposition as power passed to the Umayyad caliphs of Damascus. Their status among the pious was only enhanced when Husayn and his immediate family were killed by the troops of the Umayyad caliph Yazīd in 680, an event still commemorated with extended displays of popular grief and self-flagellation in Iran and other Shiite lands.

The Family of the Prophet remained the last great hope of all those, old Muslims and new converts alike, who felt that the Islamic state represented by the Umayyads (who were not members of the Prophet's Family) had betrayed the ideals of Islam, or, more prosaically, had not brought them the prosperity and status they felt they were due: 'If only', the argument went, 'we could restore the rule of the Family of the Prophet, inequity and evil would be banished for ever.' Such people became loosely known as the Shia, or party, of Alī.

But Muhammad ibn Alī, squire of Humayma, was not a descendant of Muhammad or of Alī. His ancestor had been Abbās, the Prophet's paternal uncle. In some ways Abbās was a prestigious figure: the paternal uncle played a central role in the life of the extended family and Abbās had protected his nephew against his enemies in the early years of struggle. But in other ways the inheritance was more problematic; there was no getting away from the fact that Abbās had never become a Muslim and would now be burning in hell. Besides, descent from the Prophet's uncle could never have the same status; he could not claim to have his blood running in his veins.

So in many ways, Muhammad ibn Alī was an unlikely figure for Bukayr to be interested in. Bukayr himself came from the sprawling garrison town of Kūfa, in Iraq, strategically founded by the Muslim conquerors at the place where the irrigated Sawād (Black Land) of the Iraqi alluvium bordered on the north-eastern margins of the Arabian deserts. Most Kūfans hated the Umayyads, who had reduced their city to the status of a provincial town and sent arrogant and overbearing Syrian soldiers to rule over them. There was a long tradition of devotion to the Family of the Prophet which occasionally showed itself in doomed attempts at rebellion. Bukayr belonged to a small cell of political activists, probably no more than thirty strong. He believed in the claims of the Family but decided not to give his allegiance to any of Muhammad's direct descendants. He may have wished to control his own movement rather than being part of someone else's.

He had sought out Muhammad ibn Alī to offer him his allegiance and persuade him to take an active role in politics. He had not come empty handed. He and his companions had collected 190 gold *dīnār*s, and one of the women had sent a gold ring and a robe she had woven with her own hand.[1] During his stay in Humayma, Bukayr constantly reminded his host of his position as a member of the Family of the Prophet and wondered why he kept himself in retirement in this remote village when many people in the Islamic world were looking for leadership from the Family. He himself had travelled widely and had spoken to many such people. He especially remembered an Iranian Muslim who had said to him (in Persian), 'I never saw a more useless people than the Arabs. When their Prophet, on whom be peace, died, they handed over his authority to someone who was from a completely different family.' And Bukayr described how the Persian had wept for the sadness of the situation, and he himself had been unable to restrain his tears.

In this highly charged emotional atmosphere, Bukayr persuaded Muhammad to leave his desert retreat and the two left Humayma and went to Damascus. Here they were to part, Muhammad ibn Alī going north to fight as a *ghāzi*, or warrior, in the Holy War on the Byzantine frontier, while Bukayr was to head east to Iraq. Before they parted, they made arrangements to keep in touch, and finally, in a dramatic gesture, Bukayr took Muhammad's hand and formally pledged allegiance to him as leader of the Muslims, the first man ever to swear an oath of fealty to a member of the Abbasid family. Then Muhammad warned Bukayr to keep what had happened secret, but the latter just laughed and said, 'I'm not that stupid' and left to continue his journey.[2]

This account comes from a history of the Abbasid movement compiled by an unknown author in the years after the family had become rulers of the caliphate and, like the stories of the origins of any great political movement, it has become embroidered with myth and legend. Neither Muhammad nor Bukayr lived to see the triumph of the conspiracy they had begun at Humayma. However, the kernel of the story certainly rings true: a small group of activists in Kūfa made contact with the Abbasids in Humayma and urged them to tap into the sentiment in favour of the Family of the Prophet in Khurasan.

Khurasan stretched from the great deserts of central Persia way beyond the frontiers of modern Iran as far as the borders of China. It was an area of dramatic geographical contrasts. Rich oasis cities such as Bukhara, Samarqand and Nishapur were separated by vast tracts of scrubby sandy steppe. The mighty River Oxus flowing from the Pamir mountains, along the northern frontier of what is now Afghanistan, carved its majestic way between the Kara Kum (Black Sand) and Kizil Kum (Red Sand) deserts until it fanned out through the oasis delta of Khorezm and reached the Aral Sea. Beyond the deserts and oases loomed the great mountains of the Pamir and Hindu Kush (Indian Slayer) ranges, on whose lower slopes there were villages and castles where men still preserved ancient customs and beliefs that had vanished from the flat lands and were ruled by princes of proud and ancient lineages.

The varied landscapes were inhabited by an equally varied population. There were Iranians, settled in the towns and villages, especially in the west; there were Soghdian merchants, who for centuries had managed the commerce of Bukhara and Samarqand and sent caravans far into the wastes of central Asia and beyond to China, the original silk road; there were Turkish nomads who roamed the steppes of Kazakhstan and the mountains of Kyrgyzstan, ferociously hardy folk who lived on their ponies and who were masters of the art of mounted archery, the most difficult and the most deadly form of mounted warfare. The area also had a native aristocracy of Iranian or Turkish origin. Sometimes these were rulers of oasis settlements like the lords of Bukhara, but more often their power was based in mountain castles and strongholds. To the south-east of Samarqand rose the steep Fan mountains which sheltered the principality of Ushrusana, whose hereditary kings, the Afshīns, resisted any attempt by the Muslims to tamper with their ancient traditions and ways.

The princely courts preserved an aristocratic culture. Songs and poems based on ancient Iranian stories were recited by wandering poets, a literary tradition that was to form the basis of the Shāhnāma, the Persian national epic composed around the year 1000. Here were told the tales of the old kings, of Jamshīd and Kay Khusraw, and the mighty hero Rustam, whose slaying of his own son Sohrab by the banks of the Oxus is one of the world's great tragic stories, made famous in the English reading world by the Victorian poet Matthew Arnold. The lifestyle of these lords is portrayed in wall paintings and on silver dishes. We see them feasting and drinking, hunting on horseback, processing on elephants. With their long gowns and far-eastern features they were very different from the Arab Muslims. Their rich aristocratic culture was to have a marked influence on the Abbasid court.

Into this medley of languages and people the Arab Muslims had irrupted from 650 onward. Arab tribes had fanned out through the lowlands, establishing themselves in villages and the steppe lands. They faced stiff resistance from Turks and Iranians alike: more Arabs were drafted in from Iraq and this remote area on the north-east fringes of the caliphate soon became one of the most heavily Islamized areas outside Arabia and the Fertile Crescent. The Arab conquerors might rule the lowland cities, but they had to make difficult compromises with the Turkish nomads and the Iranian princes. As often happens, the conquerors were profoundly influenced by the customs and language of those they conquered and intermarried with. In Khurasan there emerged an Arab–Iranian elite, Muslim in religion but in many cases Persian in speech and lifestyle.

The capital of this province was the ancient city of Merv. It lies in an immense desolate plain, fiercely hot in the summer and often bitterly cold in winter. There is virtually no rainfall and the city exists, now as then, because of the River Murghāb, which flows north from the Afghan hills to create an inland delta. Here crops of all sorts flourished; it was an early centre of cotton and linen production and was famed above all for its wonderful melons which were cut in strips, dried and exported as far away as Iraq. Called Margiana by Alexander the Great, it was already well established by the time he conquered it in 329 BC. When the Arabs arrived in 650 they found a vast rectangular town, enclosed by high mud brick walls, not the neat, vertical walls of classical Greek and Roman fortifications but the huge sloping ramparts of inner Asia. These were crowned with fired brick walls with galleries and interval towers. On one side lay a massive oval citadel, constructed on the same vast scale in mud brick, which was more than a thousand years old at the time of conquest.

Merv had been the frontier outpost of the Sasanian Persian kings in this area, and the Arabs made it their base. It was from here that annual expeditions set out to subdue and plunder the rich oases of Transoxania (the lands beyond the Oxus), and it was to Merv that the booty was taken back and sold. It was here that the Arab soldiers were paid and here that they spent their money. Merchants and men looking for work flooded in from other parts of Khurasan and soon there were quarters of Bukharans, Soghdians and men from remote Tukharistan on the upper Oxus. The lord of Bukhara maintained a town house there in order to liaise with the Arab authorities. A steel industry sprang up to cope with the demand for military equipment. The city soon spilled out beyond the ancient walls to form new fashionable quarters along the Majān canal to the west. It was here that the new Government House was situated, and it was in a dwelling here that the first supporters of the Abbasids had gathered to dye their robes black as a sign of allegiance to their chosen dynasty. The very house was still being shown as a tourist attraction to visitors two centuries later.[3]

It was among the Muslims of this developing metropolis that the first Abbasid missionaries, sent from Iraq, found their recruits. As in many Third World cities today, the rapid growth of Merv led to great disparities of wealth and status. Many Muslims, both Arab immigrants and newly converted locals, felt that the Umayyad caliphs of Damascus, twenty days' journey to the west, were very distant, even for the fastest messenger. The local governors they appointed often seemed to disregard the interests of pious and humble Muslims in the province. The Abbasid missionaries who began to come into the area soon after Bukayr's visit to Humayma had a simple message: if all Muslims were to support a chosen member of the Family of the Prophet (they were careful not to specify the Abbasids so as to be as inclusive as possible), then the rule of the Umayyads could be overthrown, a truly Islamic state established and the interests of all Muslims safeguarded.

The Abbasid missionaries set up a clandestine network of supporters. There were many difficulties and tensions between the original nucleus in Iraq, the Abbasid family and their growing army of supporters in Khurasan, but the movement held together and gathered in strength. More supporters from different areas and social classes were recruited. The efforts of the Umayyad governors to root them out were brutal but ineffective. Finally, in the early summer of 747, the black banners of the Abbasids were openly raised in one of the villages of the Merv oasis. The revolution had begun.

The revolutionary movement gathered support from many sections of society. Arabs and non-Arabs alike were attracted by the charisma of the House of the Prophet. The details were left deliberately vague, but the simple message of Islamic revival was as potent then as it is now. The military leader of the new movement was not a member of the Abbasid family, nor one of the circle of conspirators at Kūfa, but a mysterious figure called Abu Muslim. In Abbasid times there was much speculation about his origins. His name, 'father of Muslim', clearly a pseudonym, gave nothing away. He was probably of lowly origin, perhaps an ex-slave, who made himself indispensable as a clandestine link between the Kūfa circle and their supporters in Khurasan. He readily assumed command of the movement, arousing a passionate devotion among many of its supporters but brutally purging anyone, including some of the original supporters of the Abbasids, who got in his way. Perhaps every revolutionary movement needs a ruthless enforcer if it is to survive after the initial euphoria of seizing power: Abu Muslim certainly played this role for the Abbasids, and it was said that he had killed sixty thousand people in cold blood during his period in power.[4] The figures may well be exaggerated but the implication is clear: Abu Muslim was not a man to be trifled with.

While revolution raged in Merv, the Abbasid family remained out of the way at Humayma. This was either because the Kūfa group, now, after Bukayr's death, led by a man called Abu Salama, did not want to risk bringing them into the centre of affairs, or because they wanted to keep control of the movement for themselves. But even here the Umayyad regime was rapidly catching up with them. One day an Umayyad agent appeared in Humayma, asking for Ibrāhīm, who had emerged as Muhammad ibn Alī's successor. He was uncer-emoniously arrested and taken away to the caliph Marwān in Harran, far to the north, where the last Umayyad caliph had made his base. Here he was soon executed in prison. The surviving Abbasids knew that they had to move swiftly. Fourteen men and their followers left Humayma never to return. They crossed to Iraq by the remote southern route through the desert oasis of Dūmat al-Jandal[5] to avoid the authorities and arrived in Kūfa exhausted and penniless: they could not even find the 100 *dīnār*s they needed to pay the camel-drivers they had hired.[6] They were put up secretly by their local sup-porters at a safe house and ordered not to go out. The Umayyads may have been on the defensive but they were still dangerous.

Meanwhile Abu Muslim had secured his position in Merv and sent his armies to the west. In a string of brilliant victories they rolled up the Umayyad forces in Iran and soon they were descending into the plains of Iraq and approaching Kūfa itself. In the city a coup was organized by an Abbasid sympathizer and soon the revolutionary troops had taken the city. There was still no sign of the Abbasids in whose cause they had fought. Enquiries were made among the local people, the safe house was discovered and a group of Khurasanis swore allegiance to their new leader, Abū'l-Abbās, who took the title of Saffāh. It was not a good moment for Abu Salama and the Kūfa group: they had hoped to stage-manage all this themselves or even, their enemies alleged, to install a member of the House of Alī as their caliph. Abu Salama rushed to make his apologies. For the moment both the Abbasid family and their followers savoured victory. The new caliph, although suffering from fever, appeared before the people in the mosque. He made a speech justifying their rebellion, before retiring, leaving the stage to his more eloquent uncle Dāwud. Then people in Kūfa, both natives and soldiers of the army of Khurasan, filed past to pledge their loyalty to the new caliph and the new dynasty. There was no ceremony of coronation in Islam. Instead the people came to affirm their allegiance by taking the hand of the new caliph or his representative and swearing an oath. In early Abbasid times this was a public ceremony conducted in the main mosque of the capital city and lasting several days. In later and more secretive times the oath was taken rapidly in the palace by small groups of soldiers and bureaucrats, and the wider Muslim community was simply informed of what had happened.

The triumph in Kūfa was soon followed by more victories. The Umayyad caliph himself led his armies against the forces of the Abbasids, led by Saffāh's uncle Abd Allah. The two forces met in a battle on the River Zab, south of Mosul in northern Iraq, in February 750. Marwān was an experienced general and many of his Syrian supporters were hardened by years of experience fighting the Byzantines in the bleak mountains of Anatolia. But the Khurasanis too were tried and tested by warfare on the north-east frontiers of the Muslim world, and they were buoyed up by the experience of victories over other Umayyad armies on their way through Iran and during the fall of Kūfa. Using a tactic that their Syrian opponents had developed, they formed a spear wall, kneeling in line of battle with the points of their lances directed at the enemy. The Umayyad cavalry charged but the spear wall held. Marwān and his army fled, many being drowned in the river, swollen by winter rains, as they scrambled to get away. The last Umayyad caliph was driven first from northern Iraq and then south through Syria, past Harran, which he had made his base, past Damascus, the traditional capital of his dynasty. The Syrian armies were broken, their land wasted by earthquake and pestilence, and nowhere were the people able to mount a strong resistance. He fled on and on before the Khurasani troops, until in August they caught up with him in the small town of Busīr in the Egyptian delta. Here he was killed in a short, sharp battle. The Abbasid era had begun.

II

Mansūr and his Legacy

The oaths of allegiance taken in the mosque at Kūfa marked the formal inauguration of the new dynasty, the battle on the River Zab had broken Umayyad military power, and the death of Marwān meant the end of their hold over the caliphate.

The position of the new dynasty was still very precarious. No members of the family had fought in the revolutionary armies and the new caliph himself was a complete unknown, with neither reputation nor following to support him. True, the Khurasani army and the Kūfans had sworn allegiance to him as caliph, but the overwhelming majority of the Muslims had not supported the Abbasids. Would the putsch in Kūfa be the prelude to the break-up of the Muslim empire? Even among those who longed for the rule of the Family of the Prophet, the majority expected to see a descendant of Alī and Fātima as their leader and inspiration, not the obscure offspring of the Prophet's unbelieving uncle Abbās. The supporters gathered in Kūfa may have pledged their allegiance, but would they allow the new caliphs real power, or simply use them as puppets, to give a veneer of legitimacy to their own rule? Triumph was rapidly followed by doubt and fear.

The post-revolutionary struggle began almost immediately. As with both the French and Russian revolutions, the leading protagonists soon turned on each other. The first to go was Abu Salama, leader of the Kūfa group, whose slowness to acknowledge the Abbasid was his undoing. One evening he was summoned to the caliph's residence to receive a robe of honour. He stayed much of the night talking, but when he walked home alone through the deserted streets he was set upon and done to death. The authorities said that he had been killed by terrorists from the Kharijite movement, who rejected Umayyad and Abbasid caliphs alike, but everyone knew that this was disinformation to cover up the role of the Khurasani military, who distrusted Abu Salama's ambitions.[1]

Saffāh, the first of the Abbasid caliphs, reigned only a short while before dying of natural causes in June 754. He seems to have been in his early thirties, but his health may have been weak since his accession as caliph, and there was no suggestion of foul play. He had survived as caliph, but his short reign had solved none of the underlying problems of legitimacy and power which threatened the new regime.

He was succeeded by his brother, Abu Jaᶜfar, called Mansūr, the Victorious, the most remarkable individual in the whole story of the Abbasids. It is very difficult to reconstruct the character of a figure who died more than 1,200 years ago and medieval sources seldom discuss character in the way modern biographers would wish. In the case of Mansūr, however, the old Arabic tradition presents a portrait that is consistent and rings true. This picture does not take the form of an extended description but rather a series of vignettes, of short stories and anecdotes illustrating a quirky and difficult but at the same time very impressive personality whose idiosyncrasies could by turns be either comic or terrifying depending on the position of the narrator.

We have no painted portraits of Mansūr, or of any other figures from this period, but we have several descriptions. He was tall and thin with brown, weather-beaten skin, but what struck observers most was the fineness and thinness of his beard.[2] A strong bushy beard was an essential attribute of the manliness of the Muslim male. Mansūr's failed to match up to the stereotype: when he wept while preaching in the mosque* his beard was so thin that his tears flowed down to the ground. His hair too was fine and dyed with saffron (when it began to go grey) because it could not take the henna most people used. His anger was terrible, but usually controlled and deliberate. He was often thoughtful and would sit or squat for long periods of time, brooding and wily, scratching and poking at the ground with a cane or rod as he tried to work out what should be done,[3] or biting his index finger as he thought how to frame a pronouncement.[4]

Mansūr was a political operator of genius. A shrewd judge of men,

---

* Unashamed public weeping was considered a natural and appropriate way of expressing emotion in the early Islamic world, just as it was in medieval Europe. The history of changing attitudes to weeping tells us much about perceptions of masculinity through the ages.

he knew exactly who could be bought and who could not and how to play one potential enemy off against another. He was not a great general – indeed, he seems never to have led an army in person, but he could and did use military force when necessary. He had not been born to ease and luxury. He was brought up on the family estate at Humayma and in his early years had travelled extensively, at one time joining an unsuccessful rebellion against the Umayyads in the rugged Zagros mountains of western Iran. When he became caliph several people from very modest backgrounds who had done him favours or given him hospitality came to his court to ask for rewards. One, called Azhar, with whom he had stayed during his wanderings, pushed his luck too far: on his first visit he was given 4,000 dirhams to pay off his debts and celebrate the marriage of his son and told not to come back and make any more requests. Azhar soon reappeared, saying that he had come to wish the caliph well, and again he was given money and told not to come back, either to request money or offer good wishes. When Azhar appeared a third time, he claimed he had come to learn a prayer he had heard the caliph say. 'Don't bother,' the caliph replied, 'for it was not answered. I was praying God to spare me from your demands but He did not do it.'[5]

Mansūr was a genuinely if conventionally pious man, praying regularly. No wine was served at his table, as the famous doctor, Bukhtīshu, found out to his chagrin. As he was a Christian there was no religious objection to the doctor's drinking, and he claimed he never took food without wine. At the caliph's table, however, he had to drink Tigris water, which, tactfully, he pronounced to be as good if not better a drink.[6] Mansūr also disapproved of music. One of his intimate servants, a Turk called Hammād, told the story[7] of how he had been with the caliph when they heard a noise in another part of the palace. Hammād was sent to investigate and found one of the eunuchs sitting down with the slave girls and playing the tunbur or mandolin. He reported back to his master, who then asked, rather in the manner of the famous British judge who claimed not to know who the Beatles were, what a tunbur was. Hammād described one and, on being further questioned, said that he had seen them in Khurasan before he entered the caliph's service. Then the caliph called for his sandals and walked stealthily towards the unsuspecting revellers. When he burst in they scattered in panic, but the eunuch was caught. The caliph ordered that the instrument be broken over his head and that he himself should be taken away and sold in the common slave market.

Another side of his character comes across in an anecdote recounted by one of the court servants, Salām al-Abrash (the Speckled). Later, when he was a senior member of the administration, Salām remembered how, as a young page, he and a companion used to wait for the caliph when he left the domestic area and went to appear in public. He recalled that in private Mansūr was friendly and easygoing, very tolerant of young boys' games and noise. When he went to hold audience, and put on his official robes, his whole demeanour changed and his eye reddened. One day when he returned, the pages were waiting for him as usual in the corridor and the caliph said to Salām, 'My boy, if you see I have put on my robes, or just returned from holding audience, then be sure that none of you comes near me in case I do him a mischief.'[8]

Mansūr was also a great preacher. Eloquence was always highly esteemed among the Arabs, and Mansūr was the only caliph of the dynasty who had a reputation for great public oratory. In the mosque at Friday prayers he would exhort the audience to live pious lives and justify his rule in person. He had a ready response to the hecklers who occasionally dared to challenge him.[9] Later caliphs were to abandon this public performance of monarchy, but in Mansūr's time the caliph could be seen and heard by anyone who came to Friday prayers in the great mosque of the capital.

He was a systematic, even obsessive, administrator. His day[10] began well before dawn, when he would rise and go to his private oratory. When the sun rose he would join his household for prayers before going to the *īwān** to take his place for the morning audience, which was the most important and public part of the day's work. After a midday siesta[11] the afternoons were spent in relaxed conversation with members of his family. When evening prayers were finished he would go through his correspondence and discuss affairs with his advisers before retiring at around ten o'clock.**

His attention to detail during the work on his new capital at Baghdad was typical of the man. The caliph was a stickler for costs

---

* Known as an *ivān* in Persian, this open arched hall was a characteristic feature of ancient architecture, adopted by the Muslims and much used in Islamic architecture down to the present day.
** 'when a third of the night had passed'.

and must have driven his builders to distraction by constant interference. When he saw a feature he liked he demanded that it be repeated, but more cheaply. For one vault, he added up the cost of all the bricks and plaster, making the workmen come to him and say exactly how much material they would use. When one builder said he could not produce an accurate estimate, the caliph said he would help:

> He sent for the fired brick and plaster needed for the vault. He then began to add up all the materials that were going to be needed. He stayed with them for the next day and a half until the work was finished. When it was finished, he sent for Musayyab [the project manager] and told him to pay the man for his labour and materials. The builder was given five dirhams but the caliph thought this was excessive and kept on at Musayyab until he reduced it by one dirham. Then he scrutinised the estimates for all the other vaults and compared them with the one he already knew about for comparison. Musayyab was forced to return more than six hundred thousand dirhams he already had in hand to the caliph and he was not allowed to leave the palace until he had done so.[12]

Much of his time was spent reading and evaluating intelligence reports. He relied heavily on an organization called the *barīd*. This is usually translated as 'post', but though it did carry official correspondence its remit ran much wider. The agents of the *barīd* operated in every city and district a sort of alternative government structure, reporting directly to the caliph on the behaviour of the governor, the *qādī* or judge and such mundane but important matters as the movement of prices of essential commodities. Any disturbances or problems would be reported to the ruler immediately.[13] Mansūr placed the highest value on good intelligence and regarded the agents of the *barīd* as one of the pillars of his regime.[14]

His love of system extended in more sinister directions. A woman called Jamra, who had been Mansūr's perfumer and knew some of the darker secrets of the palace, told a chilling story which could have come out of one of the more gruesome episodes of the *Arabian Nights*.[15] Before he left on the pilgrimage to Mecca on which he died, he gave instructions of a very particular sort to his daughter-in-law, Rīta, wife of his son and heir Mahdi, who was at that time in Iran.

He gave her the keys to all his storerooms but there was one she was only to open when she was absolutely sure of his death. Even then only she or her husband were allowed to go in. When he heard that his father had died, Mahdi hurried to Baghdad to claim his inheritance and Rīta told him about the key to the special store. The young couple then went to open the store. They found themselves in a vast and cavernous vaulted chamber in which were laid out the bodies of all the members of the Family of Alī whom he had executed, no doubt well mummified in the dry Mesopotamian air. There were a large number of all ages, from infants to old men. In the ear of each corpse was a label, carefully inscribed with the name and genealogy of the victim. Why the dead caliph had preserved this macabre collection is not at all clear. Perhaps he wanted to remind himself that these potential challengers to his throne really were dead, or perhaps he could not come up with a way of burying them without the danger of their tombs becoming centres of popular devotion. Mahdi, who hoped to be able to heal the rift with the Alids (the direct descendants of Alī and Fātima, and hence of Muhammad himself), was horrified by what he saw. He ordered that the corpses be removed secretly and buried in a common grave, and a shop was constructed over the site.

But it was his meanness which really passed down into history and legend. Probably in his own lifetime, and certainly after his death, he was known as Abu'l-dawāniq, the father of pennies, because he counted them all. It is true that he could be generous to members of his family and devoted servants, but the Arab historians loved to make the contrast between the mean old father and his generous and easygoing son, Mahdi. Two anecdotes are typical. In one[16] a slave girl called Khālisa, who was a maid to Mahdi's concubine,* later wife, Khayzurān, goes to visit the caliph because he has toothache. When he heard her voice he told her to come in and she saw him holding his head in his hands. For some time he said nothing but eventually he asked her, 'Khālisa, how much money do you have?' and she replied that she had a thousand *dīnār*s. Then he told her to put her hand on his head and swear to it, so she had to confess that she actually had ten thousand *dīnār*s. 'Bring them to me,' he ordered. When she returned to Mahdi and Khayzurān, he kicked her in a

---

* Jāhiz, writing almost a century later, remembered Khālisa as one of the women who had been allowed to mingle freely with men in the old days (*Qiyān*).

good-natured way and said, 'Why on earth did you go to see him? There's nothing wrong with his teeth. I asked him for some money yesterday and he's pretending to be ill. You'd better take the money to him.' She did as she was told, and the next day, when Mahdi went to see his father, the old caliph reproved him for asking for money when one of his slave girls had so much.

In another anecdote[17] Mansūr lays out all sorts of worn-out garments to give to his son, and when the latter arrives he finds his father working on patching them. Mahdi laughs and says that people will make jokes about his meanness, but the caliph replies, perhaps remembering the poverty of his youth and seeking to remind his son, who had only known wealth and prosperity, of it, that winter is coming and they will need clothes for the household and children. Mahdi simply laughs and says that he will take care of it. 'As you like,' the old man replies. In another story, Mahdi visited his father dressed in a new black robe. As he got up to go, the old man's gaze followed him, full of love and admiration for his handsome, easy-going son. As he walked through the portico, Mahdi tripped on his sword and tore the robe. Picking himself up, he carried on as if nothing had happened. His father pulled him up short, reproaching him with taking God's blessings for granted. Mahdi then returned to apologize.[18]

When Mansūr succeeded his brother in the summer of 754, the position of the new dynasty was far from secure. His rule was immediately challenged by his own uncle, Abd Allah. Mansūr also realized that he could not really be effective ruler of the caliphate as long as Abu Muslim continued to rule Khurasan and much of the rest of Iran as his own domain. Then there was the latent threat posed by the House of Alī and their numerous supporters. Despite all the attempts of Abbasid propaganda, many people felt that the Family of Alī, being direct descendants of the Prophet, had a better claim to the caliphate than the Abbasids. Inevitably, too, there were many who felt that the revolution had simply not delivered the just Islamic society they had hoped for. Some time, somewhere, there would be an attempt at violent change.

The first challenge to Mansūr's rule came from within his own family, from his uncle Abd Allah. There was no system of primogeniture in Islam, or even a general acceptance that the new caliph should be one of his predecessor's children. Saffāh had boys of his own but they were still young, and he nominated his brother Mansūr as his heir. Despite this, his uncle, as one of the senior men of the family, had a good claim to be considered its leader. Furthermore, as he was fond of pointing out, it was he who had taken his life into his hands and led the Abbasid army against the Umayyad forces at the battle of the Zab. His claim was a strong one. When Saffāh died in June 754, Mansūr was away on pilgrimage in Arabia and Abd Allah resolved to seize his chance.

He was just about to embark on a summer campaign against the Byzantines and had with him an army of Khurasani troops. He had also recruited a substantial body of Syrian soldiers. Most of these were men who had supported Marwān and the Umayyads. Now disbanded and unemployed, they were keen to find a military role again. When he received the letter informing him of Saffāh's death, Abd Allah gathered his army commanders, Syrians and Khurasanis alike, and announced that he was claiming the caliphate. No one seems to have objected.

Meanwhile Mansūr, now returned from pilgrimage, worked hard to persuade Abu Muslim, who had been with him on the pilgrimage, to lead the Khurasanis against his uncle. Eventually, with some misgivings, Abu Muslim agreed. When the armies confronted each other at the ancient city of Nisibin, west of Mosul, tensions among Abd Allah's followers began to rise. He himself was suspicious of his Khurasani followers, fearing that they would join their fellow countrymen and go over to Abu Muslim. The Syrians, who, only four years before, had been defeated by Abd Allah at the battle of the Zab, became uneasy about his leadership. Abu Muslim said he had no quarrel with Abd Allah but had simply been sent as governor of Syria. Immediately the Syrians thought there was a plot and that Abu Muslim would ravage their homeland while they were stuck at Nisibin. Abd Allah's hastily gathered coalition began to disintegrate in suspicion and recrimination. The Khurasanis joined Abu Muslim, the Syrians went home, and he himself was forced to flee along the desert road to distant Basra, where his brother Sulaymān took him in and offered him refuge. The threat was over, and Abu Muslim had performed his last service for the dynasty.

For Mansūr, Abu Muslim was now the near and present danger. As long as he remained in power, the caliph was not really a monarch in his own lands. On the other hand Abu Muslim was in a very strong position. He commanded the hearts and minds of many in eastern Iran, including some who secretly or openly wanted to drive out all the Arabs, reject Islam and restore the old Sasanian dispensation. Furthermore there were moral issues: the Abbasids owed a huge amount to Abu Muslim, who had, after all, first raised the black banners in their name and organized the armies that had brought them to power. His brother Saffāh and other members of the family advised caution, but Mansūr, more ruthless and clear sighted, knew he had to act.

And a good, perhaps the only, opportunity now presented itself. Abu Muslim had come west to Iraq to see for himself how the new regime was working, leaving many of his most loyal supporters at garrisons on the long road through Iran. Mansūr knew this was a chance that could not be missed, but it would not be easy. After the victory over Abd Allah ibn Alī, Abu Muslim decided to return to his base in Khurasan, refusing an invitation to visit the caliph. He and his Iranian advisers knew that the caliph's summons could be a trap. And yet, against his better judgement, he changed his mind. Men he trusted kept arriving from the caliph, bringing with them warm invitations, and he could hardly bring himself to believe that the caliph could do him any harm after all his services to the dynasty.

And so the drama was played out like some theatrical tragedy.[19] Many times Abu Muslim hesitated and many times he could have changed his mind and gone back to the security of Iran. When he arrived to see the caliph, who was staying simply in a tent in a temporary capital near Kūfa, all seemed well. We have a number of supposedly eyewitness accounts of what happened next although, as is often the case with eyewitness accounts, even of quite recent events, they frequently disagree on details. One man who was certainly there was Mansūr's chief secretary or vizier, Abu Ayyūb al-Muryānī. Abu Ayyūb knew what his master was plotting and he was a very worried man indeed. He knew that Abu Muslim's followers would be enraged and that they would be unlikely to spare Mansūr or anyone connected with him. At the same time, he could not talk the caliph out of it.

Abu Muslim arrived in the camp one evening and came to the tent. Before he arrived, Mansūr told Abu Ayyūb that he wanted to have him killed as soon as he appeared, but Abu Ayyūb urged caution, saying that his followers would immediately and violently avenge him. In reality, as he admitted, Abu Ayyūb was terrified, and still hoped that the problem would be solved some other way. So when Abu Muslim did arrive, the caliph, sitting simply on a prayer mat on the floor of his tent, restricted himself to pleasantries, suggesting that Abu Muslim take a bath to relax after the long journey.

The next morning the caliph was in a foul mood, cursing the hapless Abu Ayyūb for being so cautious. Abu Muslim was due to come to see him later in the morning, so he called a few of his most trusted guards. He asked the commander[20] whether he would do anything he ordered. The commander naturally agreed. Then he went on, 'Would you kill Abu Muslim?' There was a long pause during which the commander stared at the ground. 'What's the matter?' Abu Ayyūb asked. 'Why aren't you answering?' Finally the commander replied in a low voice that yes, he would do it.

The stage was now set for the execution, but the caliph was taking no chances. He sent Abu Ayyūb out into the camp to see what the mood was. On his way he met Abu Muslim, who smiled and greeted him. It was the last time Abu Ayyūb saw him alive. Abu Muslim had spent the early part of the morning visiting a friend, a second cousin of the caliph's called Īsā ibn Mūsā, but Īsā stayed behind to wash before coming to court, so Abu Muslim entered alone. The caliph himself later told Abu Ayyūb what had happened. It had all been over very quickly. As Abu Muslim stood before him, the caliph had started to abuse him and then, at a pre-arranged signal, the clap of his hands, the guards rushed at him and cut him down; then, on their master's order, they cut his throat. The body was wrapped up in a cloak and left in the corner of the tent.

The deed had been done but the dead man's followers and friends could still prove dangerous. When Īsā ibn Mūsā arrived he asked after Abu Muslim. 'He's rolled up over there,' the caliph replied, pointing to the corpse in the corner. The shocked Īsā replied with the traditional Arab words of resignation: 'We are from God and to him we return.' An elaborate charade was devised to allay suspicions.[21] It was given out that Abu Muslim was staying with the caliph. Another section was added to his tent and carpets and cushions were brought to furnish it. Meanwhile his body was quietly dumped in the Tigris, so he had no known grave. The next day the news was out. Mansūr sent magnificent presents to Abu Muslim's senior commanders and sooner or later most of them accepted his offers and entered his service. But many of his humbler followers went away saying, 'We have sold our master for pieces of silver.'[22]

The murder of Abu Muslim was an immense gamble. Both politically and morally, the caliph was taking an enormous risk. He knew this, but he also knew that without asserting his authority he could never be the real sovereign of the Muslim world. He demonstrated all his clear-sightedness and ruthlessness. He had calculated right. There was sporadic resistance from the troops Abu Muslim had left on the Khurasan road, but it was defeated. The memory of Abu Muslim lingered on among many in eastern Iran, as a symbol of what might have been, and his achievements became the subject of epic poetry and legend.

After the death of Abu Muslim, Mansūr could devote himself to consolidating his hold over his vast domains. The next few years were comparatively uneventful, and the caliph began making preparations for the establishment of a new permanent capital at Baghdad. Meanwhile, his eldest son, now given the royal title of Mahdi, was sent off to Iran to act as viceroy and to gain experience of government. He established his own court at Rayy (just south of modern Tehran), from where he could keep an eye on the affairs of Khurasan to the east.

There was one problem, however, which continued to nag at the caliph's mind. He knew there were descendants of Alī and Fātima who had never accepted the Abbasids' right to rule in the name of the Family of the Prophet. He also knew that they could count on considerable popular support, especially in Iraq. The government Mansūr had set up looked very much like the Umayyad one it replaced, but with different people in charge. Those who wanted a more charismatic religious leadership were bound to be disappointed. The problem for the caliph was that he could not be sure which one of the many descendants of the Prophet would rise to take up the challenge, and where they would do it.

Mansūr tried to deploy both carrot and stick. He wanted the members of the Family to be safely at court receiving state benefits: here he could keep an eye on them. Many of them accepted his blandishments and opted for the comfortable life. However, by 756, soon after the beginning of his reign, he was anxiously aware that two younger members of the family, Muhammad ibn Abd Allah and his brother Ibrāhīm, had disappeared.

The rebellion of Muhammad, known as al-Nafs al-Zākiya ('The Pure Soul'), and his brother Ibrāhīm was one of the defining moments of the history of the Abbasid caliphate. We know a lot about it, or more exactly we are told a lot about it, by authors who are by and large sympathetic to Muhammad.[23] As usual with Arabic sources of this period we are presented not with a continuous narrative but with a number of vignettes, chosen to illustrate some aspect of character or the course of events. Despite the fragmentary and clearly partisan nature of the sources, we can build up a vivid picture of the rebellion and the hopes and fears of participants on each side. The image of the righteous man, taking up arms against hopeless odds, apparently sensing right from the beginning that he was doomed but fearless in embracing martyrdom, is an immensely potent one.

Muhammad the Pure Soul himself was a big, burly, rather ungainly man with a very dark complexion and a pronounced stammer.[24] Whenever he mounted the wooden pulpit in the mosque, one spectator remembered, the whole thing shook. At the same time, he inspired great devotion among his supporters. He very clearly sought to follow the path of his ancestor, the Prophet Muhammad, whose name he also shared. He was also strikingly mild and generous in his behaviour: Riyāh, the Abbasid governor of Medina who was responsible for much of the persecution his family suffered, was simply imprisoned and would have survived if one of Muhammad's over-enthusiastic followers had not murdered him at the moment when his rebellion was being crushed.[25] Even the officer who led the pursuing Abbasid forces when Muhammad's baby son died was only imprisoned and survived the whole experience. He remained easygoing and approachable even after he had taken control of Medina: one man remembered how, when he was a boy of fifteen, 'we came to him when people had gathered around gazing at him. No one was kept away from him. I got up close to him so I could see him and got a good look at him. He was on a horse and wearing a white quilted tunic and a white turban, a broad-chested man with small-pox scars on his face.'[26] It was very different from the security-conscious environment Abbasid caliphs lived in.

As his sobriquet, the Pure Soul, may suggest, Muhammad was at the same time a romantic and rather naive character. In the hard world of realpolitik, Medina was no place to raise a rebellion. It was

far too distant from the centres of wealth and power. It was dependent for its food supply on imports from Egypt, which could easily be
cut off. But for Muhammad Medina was the only place to start to
recreate the Islamic state the Prophet had originally built up. It was a
dream that flew in the face of contemporary reality, but Muhammad
was an idealist for whom symbols carried more weight than
practicalities.

Enquiries in Medina (where they, like many members of the
Family, lived) met with the response that the Muhammad and his
brother had gone hunting and could not be found. In fact they wan-
dered extensively through the Muslim world, moving from one safe
house to another, and trying to avoid Mansūr's agents. In the end
Muhammad returned to the Hijaz, around the city of Medina, where
he knew the territory and could count on a network of sympathizers.
He had some near-escapes. On one occasion he was hiding in a
ravine near Yanbu to the north of Medina when he was surprised by
government forces and had to flee through the barren mountains. He
had with him a concubine who had just given birth to a young son,
but the baby fell from her arms and was dashed to pieces on the
rocks.[27] On another occasion he pretended to be a simple Bedouin,
bending over between the supporting posts of a well while the
Abbasid governor road by.[28] Once, with a friend called Uthmān, he
was walking to a mosque in Medina when he saw the governor
approaching. Uthmān thought the game was up but Muhammad
said, 'Keep moving!' Uthmān kept on walking, 'though', as he said
later, 'my feet would hardly carry me'. Muhammad sat down with his
back to the road with his cloak over his face and the governor passed
by, thinking that he was a woman who did not want her face to be
seen.[29]

So Muhammad played a cat-and-mouse game with the authorities
while he waited to make his move. He wanted to allow his brother
Ibrāhīm time to build up support in Iraq so that they could launch a
simultaneous strike, but a change in Abbasid policy drove him to
premature action. In March 762, Mansūr himself came to Medina to
make the pilgrimage and to supervise the search for Muhammad.
Pressure was put on anyone who may have known where he was.
One Medinan notable, Ziyād ibn Ubayd Allah, was woken in the
middle of the night by the sound of men trying to break into his
house. It is a well-known strategy of security forces everywhere to

arrest their suspects in the early hours of the morning when they are
at their most vulnerable. Ziyād emerged from his bedroom wearing
nothing but a waist wrapper and woke his slaves and eunuchs, who
were sleeping in the portico, and told them not to say anything. After
a while the men left, but they soon returned with an iron battering
ram and began to break down the door. At this point Ziyād opened
the gate before the whole house was destroyed and was frog-marched
('like an ostrich' is the Arabic expression) down to the governor's
palace, where the caliph was staying. In the antechamber to the
domed room where the caliph sat, he was met by the chamberlain,
Rabī, who upbraided him for causing so much trouble. Then the
curtain was drawn back. The chamber was lit by candles in the
corners with servants by each of them. In the gloom Ziyād could pick
out the caliph, squatting on his heels on a carpet, with neither a
cushion nor a prayer rug to make him comfortable. His head was
bent forward and he was poking at the ground with an iron rod. Rabī
told Ziyād that the caliph had been like this all night. He stood there
for what seemed like hours before finally the caliph raised his head
and snapped, 'Where are Muhammad and Ibrāhīm, you son of a
bitch?' Then he lowered his head and went on scratching with his
rod. Finally he repeated his question, adding, 'May God kill me if I
don't kill you!' Ziyād managed to keep his nerve and explained to the
caliph that his threats to kill them had scared them away. 'Get out!'
said the caliph, and Ziyād left, relieved no doubt to be alive and
untortured.[30]

The caliph then ordered that all Muhammad's male relations,
including his elderly father, should be arrested and taken to Iraq.
They were summoned to the mosque by the governor and a blacksmith was called to make fetters for them. They travelled the long
desert road in litters, shackled at the neck and foot. Some of them
were beaten up, all were publicly humiliated.[31] While they were confined, Muhammad's mother, Hind, contrived to visit his father (the
women were never arrested and seem to have been allowed freedom
of movement) with a message from their son that he was prepared to
give himself up to spare the old man, but he urged his son to remain
in hiding and carry on the work of recruiting supporters.[32]

The original plan of the two brothers was that they would coordi-
nate their rebellions in Medina and Basra and divide the Abbasid
forces, but the persecution of his family and the ever present threat of

arrest drove him to take action prematurely. On the night of 23 September 762 he led his followers to take over the Mosque of the Prophet in Medina. Wearing a yellow robe and a yellow *qalansūwa* (tall round hat), he proclaimed himself caliph and urged his followers not to kill anyone. The governor's palace, which was connected with the mosque, was barred against them, but they set fire to the connecting door and one man laid his shield down so that they could cross the embers. The governor's retinue fled, and he himself was spotted in one of the wooden lattice-work windows of the upper floor. He was brought down and imprisoned.[33] No one had been killed.

Medina was soon in the hands of the rebels. The news reached the caliph quickly. A man from Medina rode the 1,100 odd kilometres to Kūfa, where Mansūr was, in nine days. Arriving at night, he demanded loudly to be let in. Rabī the chamberlain protested that it was far too late, but the man insisted and ended up by telling the caliph about the Pure Soul's rebellion and who was with him. He was generously rewarded for bringing the caliph what was essentially good news.[34] When Mansūr asked the opinion of an old Syrian soldier who had fought many campaigns with the Umayyad caliph Marwān, he replied, 'Praise God! he has begun his rebellion in a place where there is no money, no men, no weapons and no fodder. Send someone you trust to Wadi Qurra [on the road north from Medina] to stop provisions coming from Syria and he will starve where he is.'[35] Mansūr immediately sent a small but well equipped army under the command of his cousin, Īsā ibn Mūsā, to cross the desert and retake the city.

More realistic people in Medina realized that the city was not a good place to base a bid for power and resisted the popular enthusiasm and kept their distance.[36] As the Abbasid forces approached, Muhammad's supporters urged him to go to Egypt, where he would find supplies and support, or leave for the desert and throw in his lot with the Banu Sulaym Bedouin, who had more horses than any other tribe in western Arabia. The Pure Soul resisted: his ancestor and inspiration, the Prophet, had dug a trench to defend Medina from his enemies and he would follow his example.[37] The trench became a symbol. He rode out to the site in his white robe and belt and began digging with his own hands. When he found some mud bricks from the Prophet's original trench, his followers said, 'God is most great! This is the trench of your grandfather the Prophet of God.'[38]

This almost apocalyptic enthusiasm did not survive the reality of war. As the Abbasid forces advanced towards the city Muhammad went out to meet them with a vast crowd of Medinans. When the enemy came nearer, he said, with typical generosity, that any of them who wished to flee were absolved from their oaths of allegiance. A few left and the stream became a torrent as the crowds returned to the city and threw away their arms. Īsā and his men made short work of the trench, taking doors from a nearby house, putting them across it and going over with their horses. On 6 December Muhummad the Pure Soul, with a handful of raggedly equipped followers, was left to face the armoured might of the Abbasid troops. By the evening it was all over. Muhammad is said to have refused all suggestions that he should flee or go into hiding. One man who claimed to be an eyewitness spoke of him fighting bravely with the Prophet's sword, just as Hamza, the Prophet's uncle, had done at the battle of the first trench. 'He was not injured until a man shot him with an arrow. I can see it now, blue steel and red blood. Then the horses rode at us and he took a stand by the side of a wall…death came on him there.'[39] As the battle ended and the Abbasid troops entered the city, it was said that a rainstorm the like of which no one could remember burst on the city.[40] Muhammad's head was taken to Mansūr, who put it on a silver dish and had it publicly displayed.[41] His family were allowed to bury his body. His brother Ibrāhīm did rebel in Basra, too late to distract the Abbasid forces, and he in turn was killed in battle.

With the defeat of the Álid revolts of 762, Mansūr had overcome the main challenges that had faced him when he became caliph eight years before. He had established the Abbasid caliphate on a solid foundation with a paid professional army of mostly Khurasani soldiers and an efficient tax system to collect the money to pay for them. Not everyone approved. Many Muslims felt alienated and disfranchised, resentful that the community of believers had become an empire like those that had come before. But stability and growing prosperity, at least in Baghdad, must have convinced many waverers to tolerate the new regime. Mansūr devoted himself to the consolidation of power and the administrative systems he established at this time were to have a profound influence, not just on later Abbasid caliphs but on successor states right down to modern times.

Mansūr's success owed much to the members of his extended family, and throughout the eighth century the wider royal family were among the most important supporters of the caliphs. The revolution that had brought the Abbasids to power was not launched in the name of one individual but rather of the whole family, and the slogans used proclaimed only that the new ruler would be a 'Chosen one from the Family of the Prophet'. In the event, as we have seen, first Saffāh and then in 754 Mansūr emerged as rulers, but it was only natural that they would share their new-found fortune among their kin; indeed, their kin would have objected most vigorously if they had not.

The family was very extensive. Saffāh and Mansūr were sons of Muhammad ibn Alī, who had owned the estate at Humayma. They had four brothers of whom two had died before the revolution; neither of the other two made a major impact on politics or court life. Much more significant was the role of Mansūr's uncles, Muhammad's brothers: as older-generation males they expected to play a major role in government. As far as we know there were seven of them still living at the time of the revolution, though one, Dāwud, died very soon after. Many of them were forceful personalities who expected to be treated with respect. They were very different in age and one of them, Abd al-Samad, was much younger than his nephew Mansūr, and in fact survived into the reign of his great-great-nephew Hārūn. At times too they formed a powerful pressure group to safeguard the interests of any one of them who had fallen into disfavour.[42] Mansūr, though naturally cautious with money, treated his uncles very generously: perhaps their seniority in the family made him nervous.

The uncles were very powerful but they were not often to be found around the palace. Dāwud died before the Abbasids had really become established and Abd Allah was kept under house arrest as a result of his ill-advised attempt to secure the caliphate after the death of Saffāh. To execute a member of the royal family like a commoner rebel would undermine the status of them all, and the uncles closed ranks to protect him. Stories were told of how the caliph tried to dispose of him by causing houses to fall on him 'accidentally', and when he did die, in 765, it was widely believed that he had been murdered.[43]

Other brothers were allowed to establish courts of their own in the provinces. The most powerful of these was Sālih, who established his family's power in Syria. Here he inherited many of the properties that had been owned by members of the Umayyad family and, indeed, he married the widow of the last Umayyad caliph, Marwān: it was said that his son, Abd al-Malik, who inherited much of his power and was a major figure in the politics of Hārūn's reign, was really an Umayyad by descent, but then Abd al-Malik had many enemies at court who disliked his old-fashioned austerity and conservatism and his disputed parentage may have been no more than malicious gossip. The family spent most of their time on their Syrian estates, in the suburbs of Aleppo and at Manbij north-east of Aleppo, where Abd al-Malik built a magnificent castle which Hārūn coveted. Until the end of the eighth century the family remained linked to the caliphal branch of the Abbasid family by marriage, but by the ninth century they had established themselves as a landowning family in northern Syria, conscious no doubt of their illustrious descent but no longer members of the caliph's court.

Of the other brothers, Sulaymān was established in Basra, where he acquired vast wealth and properties which were eventually inherited by his son Muhammad, while Mansūr's nephew, Īsā ibn Mūsā, set up his court in Kūfa. Ismāᶜīl established a branch of the family in Mosul, where they built a market, mosque and bath house – in fact established their own quarter in the city. They too became part of the local urban upper class but lost all contact with the caliph's court. The only uncles who seem to have remained at court were Īsā and Abd al-Samad, who was very young and something of the black sheep of the family.

Īsā had had a promising political career at one time. Immediately after the revolution, he had been sent to take over Fars in south-west Iran in the name of the Abbasids. However, Abu Muslim, based in Khurasan, felt that this was in his sphere of influence and sent his own man, a tough and experienced soldier.[44] Faced with this ruthless rival, Īsā was lucky to get away with his life. In return he promised that he would never accept a governorate again and never draw his sword except in the holy war. And he was as good as his word. Instead, unlike his brothers, he remained at court. He was a favourite of both Saffāh and Mansūr, and when Baghdad was founded he became a major property owner in the new city. He was the first member of the Abbasid family after the caliph himself to build a palace there. He dug a new canal which was named after him and which joined the Tigris at the port where the river boats left for

Wasit and Basra. The position of his palace, overlooking the river, was certainly delightful, but it could also prove hazardous: shortly before his death there was a disastrous fire among the ships in the port. Many people were burned to death and the boats and all their contents were lost.[45] Īsā also dug canals and built water mills on his estates in the suburbs. Until his death in the spring of 780,[46] he remained at court as an elder statesman. He was one of the very few men who could tackle Mansūr in one of his rages, and a number of young men remembered him with gratitude for interventions that saved their lives.[47] He does not seem to have had the same close relationship with Mahdi and, despite his gout, spent more and more of his time on the Byzantine frontier, fighting the infidel.

The generation of Mansūr's children did not have the same opportunities to establish their own sub-dynasties. Apart from his son and heir Mahdi, the caliph had eleven other sons.[48] Few of them led charmed lives. Five seem to have died young without starting families of their own, one died when he broke his neck falling off his horse while leading the pilgrimage in 789, and another was killed when, for reasons that are not explained, he was jumping from one rooftop to another and fell between the buildings. The survivors were sometimes appointed to lead the pilgrimage, a privilege of the ruling family under the Abbasids, and were given short periods as provincial governors. Unlike the earlier generation, they remained firmly based in Baghdad and some were active at court. Three of them, Jaʿfar, Sālih and Sulaymān, all built impressive palaces on the western banks of the Tigris, close to the Eternity Palace where the caliphs lived most of the time. Jaʿfar also owned real estate and a river port in the area. Known as Jaʿfar the Elder, to distinguish him from a younger sibling who was born after his early death, he maintained his own household in Baghdad and patronized poets, although, of course, the real stars gravitated to the court of the caliph himself, where the major rewards were to be had. He is presented in the sources as a rather credulous, simple man who might easily be led astray. He was subject to fits and came to believe at one stage that he was bewitched by a woman of the jinn and intended to marry her.[49] He died before his father in 767,[50] and was the first person to be buried in the newly established cemetery of the Quraysh. Two of his children were important members of Hārūn's court. His son, Īsā, was a close friend of the caliph's and often used to be his partner in the camel litter, one travelling on either side of the hump, on journeys, though since he was a rather stout man, stones or weights had to be put in Hārūn's side to make it balance. His closeness to the caliph meant that he was an important source of court gossip and a go-between in court circles.[51] He served as governor of Basra and the Gulf provinces for a while but was never a political figure of major importance.[52] His sister Zubayda, on the other hand, became Hārūn's favourite wife and a woman of immense power and influence.

In the following generation, Mahdi had seven sons, including the caliphs Hādī and Hārūn. The other brothers were more active in affairs of state than their uncles, Mansūr's sons, had been: Ubayd Allah was governor of the notoriously difficult frontier province of Armenia[53] and the more tranquil one of Egypt. He was subsequently given large landed estates in the fertile region of Ahwaz to cultivate[54] and had a riverside palace on the East Bank of the Tigris in Baghdad.[55] His brother Mansūr fought in Hārūn's armies against the Byzantines and played a major role in the politics of Iraq during the great Abbasid civil war while a third brother, Ibrāhīm, branched out in a completely different direction and became one of the most celebrated poets of his generation.

The cadet members of the Abbasid family emerged during the latter part of Mansūr's reign and through the time of Mahdi and Hārūn as an important social group around the court. With their riverside palaces in Baghdad, clustering around the caliphal residences, they were among the wealthiest members of court society. They had their own households, with their chamberlains and boon companions, a sort of miniature version of the caliph's own court.[56] And they tried to pretend that the singers they patronized were the best that money could buy. The sources repeatedly return to the theme that the lifestyle of these gilded youths was in marked contrast with the austerity of the older generation. Mansūr and Mahdi are both described as trying to keep singers away from their vulnerable and easily led children while the *jeunesse dorée* themselves were eager for the latest fashions in music and song. Men like Īsā ibn Alī in the older generation and Īsā ibn Ja'far ibn Mansūr in the younger may have been political lightweights but they were important generators of court culture, norms and mores.

The day-to-day management of the court was in the hands of palace servants who ranged from the chamberlain down to the humble sweepers and cleaners. There were always young pageboys hanging around waiting to be sent on errands. Many of these were slaves or freedmen (ex-slaves). As time went on, more and more of them were eunuchs. Eunuchs had been a part of the court life of the Sasanians and many important figures at the courts of contemporary Byzantine emperors were eunuchs. The Umayyad caliphs had rarely employed eunuchs but as the Abbasid court expanded and became more settled they formed a larger and growing segment of court society until, at the beginning of the tenth century, even the army commander Mu'nis was a eunuch.

At the head of this hierarchy of servants was the chamberlain, in charge of the day-to-day running of the court. He was the man who managed the public audiences and, most important of all, he was the man who controlled access to the caliph. Without his cooperation it was very difficult to see the ruler and make those personal contacts that were so vital for successful advancement. For virtually the entire early Abbasid period, the office of chamberlain was filled by Rabī ibn Yūnus and his son Fadl.

Rabī's origins could hardly have been less propitious. His father Yūnus came from a family of modest means living in the Hijaz near Medina. As a young man Yūnus had got one of his father's slave girls pregnant but then vigorously denied his paternity. The young child was sold to another family and given some education but he misbehaved himself in some way (we are not told how) and was sent to a desert estate belonging to the family to spend his days minding a water-wheel. It was not the obvious road to advancement. However, he was soon sold on and was eventually purchased by the governor of Medina, one of Mansūr's numerous relatives. Along the way he acquired a good literary education and, at least according to the Book of Songs, it was his aptitude for Arabic poetry which drew him to the attention of the caliph.[57]

Rabī started life as a slave, but Mansūr had granted him his liberty. He then became a *mawla* of the caliph. This word has a variety of different meanings in Arabic but in this context it means a freedman. Being the caliph's *mawla* gave Rabī an identity that his own upbringing had not provided and attached him firmly to the ruling dynasty. He became in turn a *mawla* of Mansūr, Mahdi and Hādī. His son and heir, Fadl, who of course had never been a slave, is also described as Hārūn's *mawla* and, at the end of his life, when the structure of the early Abbasid court had been torn apart by civil war, he is described as the last of the *mawlas*.[58] There were many other *mawlas* in the caliph's service, some in very menial jobs, others as high-profile personal attendants or administrators. They formed a powerful pressure group at court, sometimes coming into conflict with the military and the secretaries and very concerned to maintain their privileges and status. Rabī and his son were the effective leaders of this group.

By the time of the foundation of Baghdad in 762, Rabī was one of Mansūr's most trusted servants. He was given a large tract of land south of the city where the great markets of Karkh were established. He supervised the building of the *sūq*s but the cost of construction was paid by his master. He was then given a further piece of real estate to build his own houses on.[59] Probably more as master of works than as architect he built the Eternity Palace, down by the Tigris, which became a favourite residence of Mansūr and his successors.

Rabī had made a killing out of real estate and property development in the boom city of Baghdad but it was his role at court which ensured his place in history. Numerous stories show him allowing or denying access to the caliph. When he wanted to undermine one of the caliph's viziers who he saw as a rival, he allowed the man's enemies to visit the caliph on the quiet and spread malicious rumours.[60]

His greatest triumph was ensuring the peaceful accession of Mahdi as caliph when Mansūr died on pilgrimage in the autumn of 775. After his services at the time of the succession, Mahdi, not surprisingly, kept him on as chamberlain. Rabī was clearly an intelligent and forceful man. He was also dour and unflamboyant. He seldom patronized poets or held salons for writers and intellectuals as did the Barmakids (of whom we shall hear more later) and one gets the impression that he disapproved of the more frivolous aspects of Mahdi's court. Both he and his master Mansūr were men whose early lives had been tough and they felt the next generation had little experience of the world outside the privileged environment of the court.[61] His loyalty to Mansūr and the dynasty was unquestioned, but he could be cruel and vindictive to rivals who he felt were trying to undermine him or not treating him with proper respect. When Mahdi's first vizier insulted him by keeping him waiting when he visited and then making him sit on an ordinary carpet, not a prayer rug, he set about destroying him. Finding nothing he could use against the vizier himself, he attacked the man's wayward son, accusing him of heresy (*zandaqa*) and staging a horrendous scene at court. The young man was questioned on his knowledge of the Koran and, when his ignorance had been thoroughly demonstrated, he was condemned as an unbeliever. Then the father was called upon not just to disown his son but to execute him in person. When he could not bring himself to do this, his fate was sealed: he was removed from office and driven from court.[62] The world of court intrigue was not for the faint-hearted.

The succession of Mahdi's son Hādī as caliph in 785 was Rabī's last service to the dynasty he had served so well, and he died of natural causes the same year. His son Fadl inherited much of his status at court, and Hādī is said to have appointed him as chamberlain because he had managed to find the rogue poet Ibn Jāmi, who had been banished by Mahdi as a bad influence, and bring him to court.[63] Hārūn put him in charge of his personal seal,[64] though he does not seem to have acquired the office of chamberlain until 795.[65] Like his father before him, he was one of the most powerful people at court and was able to control access to the caliph; if you wanted to attend one of Hārūn's audiences, you had to keep in with Fadl ibn Rabī.[66] If Hārūn wanted to have someone brought to him secretly or to organize a test for someone he suspected of disloyalty, Fadl could be relied on to carry this out.[67] He was also jailer to high-status prisoners.[68] In many of the anecdotes of Hārūn's court he appears as the foil to the Barmakids. Like his father he has the image of being hard-headed, practical and somewhat unimaginative, though he is said to have written 'a little' poetry[69] (but so did almost everyone else at the time). Like his father too he was doggedly loyal to the dynasty and was present at Hārūn's death in 809 as his father had been present at Mansūr's.[70]

There were a large number of more shadowy figures at court who performed a sort of Rosencrantz and Guildenstern role in events, often appearing at crucial moments but never holding centre stage for any length of time. We have already come across Salām al-Abrash (the Speckled) as a young page, waiting on Mansūr when he returned from the public audience. He is said to have been a eunuch, and this enabled him to visit parts of the palace and the domestic quarters that were forbidden to whole men.[71] At the same time, his gender status did not prevent him from acting in the public sphere. As an adult, he was appointed to organize the *mazālim* sessions,[72] where the public could bring complaints about maladministration to the caliph, and he certainly helped individual petitioners. He was Mahdi's drinking companion and the caliph ordered him to flog poets with whom he was displeased.[73] As with many courtiers, his career had its low points – he was arrested by Hārūn when he became caliph, perhaps because he had been close to his dead brother Hādī, but he had certainly recovered the caliph's trust by 803 when he was appointed to take charge of the house and possessions of Yahya the Barmakid after that family's fall from grace. He arrived to find that the curtains had already been taken down and the goods collected for removal, Yahya observing disconsolately that this was like the coming of the Last Hour.[74]

In the chronicles of the time, Salām appears as a bit player with no more than a walk-on part every now and again. Things looked very different for those outside the charmed circle of court life.[75] When the penniless poet Ibn Jāmi arrived in Baghdad, without either money or contacts, he made his way to one of the mosques. Here, tired and hungry, he sat down and watched as all the other worshippers left to return to their homes. Finally there was one man left, praying. Behind him was a retinue of servants and slaves waiting patiently until he had finished his devotions. The man took his time, but when he had finished he caught sight of Ibn Jāmi and began to ask him who he was and where he came from. The chance encounter led to an invitation to the palace and Ibn Jāmi's rise to fame and fortune. The man with the retinue was none other than Salām al-Abrash. To the struggling poet he was a figure of wealth and power beyond anything he had come into contact before. Though he had begun life as a slave, he now had a household of his own; indeed, one of his cooks, Ītākh, later became a famous general in the time of the caliph Muᶜtasim.[76] But he was more than that: he was the man who could make the vital introductions, could open the doors that led to fame and fortune.

Salām also had another, rather unexpected, side to his character. He is recorded as one of the earliest men to translate Greek scientific texts into Arabic, perhaps under the patronage of the Barmakid family. This suggests that he may have been of Greek origin, a boy captured during the frontier wars between the Muslims and Byzantines.[77]

Under Mansūr the Abbasid caliphate rapidly developed an impressive bureaucracy. Unlike any contemporary state in the Christian West, the caliphate had a staff of salaried professional clerks (*kuttab*) who kept records of income and expenditure and lists of those who served in the army and their rates of pay. Furthermore, the clerks who worked in the offices (*dīwāns*)* were all laymen: while there was a certain overlap, the clerks of the bureaucracy were an entirely different group from the religious scholars or *ulamā*. In a process not unknown in our day, the bureaucracy expanded even as the frontiers of the empire contracted, and by the beginning of the tenth century, against a background of chaos and disintegration, one of the clerks, Qudāma ibn Jaᶜfar (d. 948), produced a manual of administration which described the whole apparatus in exhaustive detail at the very moment of its disintegration. It also developed its own sense of identity and *esprit de corps*; another clerk, Jahshiyāri (d. 922), wrote a history of the development of the bureaucracy, celebrating its achievements and its heroes.

Caliphs, as well as governors and other important figures in the state all had their own secretaries, who would compose and write their letters according to the exacting standards of diplomatic form which had become established by the end of the eighth century. This was not because caliphs and their main lieutenants were illiterate. On the contrary, it was most unlikely that a caliph would be unable to read and write (another striking contrast to the Western tradition in which few monarchs were able to read before the thirteenth century) and many were highly educated. It was rather because the writing of official documents became increasingly formal and full of protocol: doing it correctly was a task for professionals.

The expansion of bureaucracy, and of general literacy, was facilitated by the appearance of a new form of writing material, paper. Until the early Abbasid period documents had been produced on papyrus, imported from Egypt, while books had been written on parchment, that is animal skins. Paper, made from rags (almost all

---

* The word *dīwān* has been inherited by most European languages, but in two quite different ways. In its meaning of a government office, it becomes *dohana* in the administration of Norman Sicily in the twelfth century, and from there becomes the *dogana* of Italian and the *douane* of French, both meaning customs. In addition to office, it also meant the bench on which the officials sat, and it is this meaning, in the Persian pronunciation of *divan*, which has entered English, signifying a bed without headboards. The word also means a collection of poetry, and was adopted by Goethe in the title of his *West-Östliche Divan*.

paper before the nineteenth century was made of textiles rather than wood-pulp), was both cheaper and more efficient than either of these two. Paper had been invented centuries before in China and, according to a later Arabic tradition, the technology passed to the Muslim world when a group of Chinese paper-makers were captured in a battle with Arab forces at Talas in Kazakhstan in 751. As it stands, the story is almost certainly a myth, but paper began to be used in the Abbasid administration in the reign of Mansūr. By the ninth century, paper-making had become efficient and cheap: the vast literary output of the Abbasid period would have been inconceivable without the arrival of this new writing material.

Umayyad caliphs had had secretaries, and under the early Abbasids this office developed into the office of vizier (*wazīr*). The viziers became the chief advisers of the caliphs on political matters and also the heads of the civil service. As such they were important figures at court. Mansūr's first vizier was a man called Abu Ayyūb al-Muryānī, from a village of Muryān in Khuzistan. He had originally worked as a secretary in the Umayyad administration but was shrewd enough to attract the attention of Mansūr soon after the Abbasid revolution. He quickly became one of the caliph's closest advisers whose competence went far beyond the simple writing of letters. It was Abu Ayyūb who advised Mansūr on how to lure Abu Muslim to court so that he could be isolated and executed. He was with Mansūr when he chose the site of Baghdad, and he was in charge of distributing land in one quarter of the city.[78] He and his family became immensely wealthy and acquired enormous estates in the Basra area and in his homeland of Khuzistan. In doing so they made many enemies: ordinary people came to regard them as grasping and oppressive, especially when they speculated in grain prices in time of famine.[79] Their underlings were notorious for taking bribes.[80] They also made the mistake of alienating Khālid the Barmakid, who was a potential rival for the post of vizier.[81] Nemesis came suddenly in 770. One of their clerks, a man called Abān ibn Sadaqa, accused them of corruption. Rabī used his position as chamberlain to make sure that the caliph got to hear of the allegations. Without warning or trial, the vizier and his brother, Khālid, were arrested. They both died in prison and the next year the caliph ordered an executioner to take Khālid's sons, to cut off their hands and feet and then behead them.

The property confiscated from the vizier and his family was vast, both in terms of landed estates and cash. The office really had been a licence to print money. But it was also extremely insecure. With enemies at court and too many dubious business dealings behind them, the vizier and his family could be swept away in an instant on the orders of the caliph. It was the first time this was to happen under the Abbasids, but it was far from being the last.

The history of the administration and much of the court life of the early Abbasid period is dominated by the Barmakids. Alone of the numerous clerks and civil servants of the era, their name was immortalized in the *Arabian Nights*, where Jaᶜfar the Barmakid appears as Hārūn's faithful companion in adventure; their name has even passed into the *Oxford English Dictionary*.* For Nizam al-Mulk (d. 1092), the great vizier of the Saljuk sultans, writing three centuries later, the Barmakids were the viziers par excellence, renowned alike for their aristocratic Persian ancestry and their political shrewdness.[82] The Barmakids were the richest and most famous family in Baghdad after the Abbasids themselves, and their name is forever associated with the city, but their origins lay far to the east.

They came from Balkh in the fertile valley of the Oxus river in what is now northern Afghanistan. Balkh, now little more than a ruin-field of shapeless heaps of mud, was one of the great cities of Asia in antiquity and the early Middle Ages. Capital of the Greek kingdom of Bactria after the break-up of Alexander's empire, it had subsequently been ruled by a Buddhist dynasty called the Kushans, and it was in the first centuries BC that Buddhism became firmly established. In neighbouring Bamyan the two great Buddhas still stood as memorials of the rich culture of this period until their recent destruction by the Taliban regime. Balkh was typical of the multicultural cities the Arabs found in central Asia. The city itself was enclosed by a great mud-brick wall, and looking south from the ramparts you could see across the startlingly green fields of the irrigated plain to the steep, barren foothills of the Hindu Kush mountains, rising with dramatic suddenness from the flat lands. In this plain the eye could pick out the great stupa of the Nawbahar Buddhist shrine,

---

* The expression Barmecide feast, meaning a 'feast' at which there is no food, derives from a story in the *Arabian Nights*, where a member of the Barmakid family teases a sponger by inviting him to a meal and pretending that there is nothing to eat. The first recorded use in English dates from 1713.

the spiritual centre of the oasis. It was also a centre of pilgrimage for Buddhists from many lands, and a Muslim source compares it to Mecca. The temple was vastly wealthy and owned extensive properties, the people who worked them being described as its slaves.

The Barmakid family were hereditary guardians of the great shrine and enjoyed both wealth and status as a result. The name Barmak was a hereditary title and, though it was abandoned as a first name after the family became Muslim, they remained known as Barmakids (Ar. *Barāmika*). They married into the royal families of the mountain kingdoms of the upper Oxus valley: Khālid ibn Barmak's mother was a princess from Saghanian in modern Tajikistan. However, for reasons we can only guess at, they decided to convert to Islam and, like many non-Arab Muslims in eastern Iran, threw in their lot with the Abbasids. Khālid ibn Barmak, the leader of the family at the time, was soon prominent among the leaders of the revolution. He had special responsibility for the division of the money collected and the payment of the troops:[83] perhaps his family background in managing great estates had suited him for this.

Thereafter he made his career in the court and the bureaucracy. There is no record that he ever returned to Balkh and the Nawbahar temple disappears from the historical record. Instead, Khālid became the great financial administrator of the early Abbasid caliphate. This position brought new rewards. Khālid was among those who advised Mansūr on the layout of Baghdad, and when the development spread to the east bank of the Tigris there were properties, palaces and markets for Khālid and his children as well as estates in the Basra area.

As well as skill in financial administration, he also appears to have had links to old Persian interests. He enjoyed two short periods as a provincial governor, in Fars, which had been the centre of the Sasanian empire and where old Persian customs were still entrenched, and Tabaristān. Tabaristān, the mountainous area at the southern end of the Caspian Sea, was a region that had hardly been penetrated by the Arab invasions and where old traditions lingered on. When he was governor, Khālid is said to have worked wonders and discovered the treasure of the old Persian kings which they brought to this mountainous refuge when fleeing the Arab invasions. He established new markets and, as a sign of respect, the local people are said to have decorated their shields with his portrait, a very un-Islamic thing to do.

This connection with the old Persian heritage is emphasized by the story of the arch of Kisra (Chosroes). To the south of Baghdad lay the old Persian capital, usually known in the West by the Greek name of Cteisphon but referred to in the Arabic sources simply as 'the cities' (al-Mada'in). The site was dominated by the great arch of the *iwān* which had been erected by Chosroes II. This huge brick span was much wider than anything Abbasid builders could attempt. It stood as mute testimony to the superiority of ancient culture. According to a story that bears all the hallmarks of literary fabrication, Mansūr was determined to destroy the arch and use the materials in his new city but Khālid argued that its existence as an uninhabited ruin demonstrated the superiority of Islam and the monument was saved for posterity.[84] The great span can still be admired today.

Even for a courtier as widely respected as Khālid, life could never be entirely secure. The caliph could sometimes turn very nasty, and to be a victim of this *ira regis* could imperil all a man's achievements and indeed life itself. Khālid's son Yahya tells us a story[85] which illustrates all the insecurities of the time and how great men tried to protect themselves against the revolutions of the wheel of fortune. Mansūr had become suspicious of Khālid's wealth and, without notice, demanded the immense sum of 3,000,000 *dirham*s from him. Even Khālid did not possess such resources, and he suspected that the caliph was simply out to destroy him. In this dire emergency, he turned to the men he optimistically referred to as his 'brothers' at court. He sent his son Yahya, then a young man, round to their palaces to ask for loans. Khālid's friends came from the ranks of the household officials, men such as Sālih, whose formal title was Keeper of the Prayer Rug *(Sāhib al-Musalla)*, but whose responsibilities extended to such chores as keeping the water cisterns in working order for the caliph's pilgrimage to Mecca and selling papyrus from the treasury which was surplus to requirements.[86] He had also been responsible for allocating properties on the east bank of the Tigris in Baghdad. He had kept a generous share for himself and used it to develop commercial premises.[87]

Sālih and the others agreed to help out: after all, no one could tell when their turn would come and when they would need friends.

However, many did so surreptitiously, refusing to see Yahya and sending money on afterwards; it would not have been wise to be too openly friendly with a man who might soon be completely disgraced. The most problematic interview Yahya had was with a man called Umāra ibn Hamza. Like Sālih, Umāra was a court functionary of modest social origins who had become immensely wealthy as a result of his palace connections. Described as one-eyed and misshapen, his generosity was equalled only by his pride.[88] He was known to be a difficult man and Yahya was not encouraged by his first response. When he called on Umāra, who must have known why he had come, he found him sitting in the courtyard of his house, facing the wall. He did not turn to look at Yahya and contented himself with asking him how his father was in an unenthusiastic way. Yahya explained his mission but Umāra made no reply. Yahya felt that the walls were closing in on him and that the earth was about to swallow him up, but he kept on with his speech. Finally Umāra replied dismissively that he would do what he could and Yahya was sent away, cursing Umāra quietly for his arrogance and pride. No sooner had he returned to his father and told him the story than Umāra's messenger appeared with 100,000 *dirham*s.

Eventually there were only 300,000 *dirham*s left to collect, but the deadline was fast approaching. Yahya was crossing the bridge of boats over the Tigris in Baghdad when he passed a fortune teller who had a crow that he claimed could tell the future. The man shouted out, 'the chick can tell you!' Yahya passed on, sunk in anxious thought, but the man ran after him, grabbed his bridle and told him that God would dispel his anxieties and that he would be passing that way tomorrow with a banner in his hand. Yahya promised the man 5,000 *dirham*s if this was true and went on, never imagining that it would be. Meanwhile, at court, news had come that the Kurds had overrun the area around Mosul and the caliph was looking around for someone to deal with the problem. The commander of the guard, Musayyab, who was a friend of Khālid's, recommended that he be appointed. So the next day Yahya and his father did indeed pass the fortune teller with the banner for Mosul before them and the fortune teller got his money.

The story tells us much about the insecurity of court life but also about the importance of networking. Khālid survived because he had a group of friends who, no doubt often for selfish motives, were prepared to help him out with money or recommendations. The wretched vizier Abu Ayyūb had lacked these contacts and his career had ended miserably.

Khālid died in 780 after returning from an expedition with the young prince Hārūn against the Byzantines. His son Yahya had already established for himself a major place in the administration, and indeed something of the father's status may have been due to the reputation of the son: Mansūr joked that whereas most men begat sons, Yahya had begotten a father.[89]

Yahya ibn Khālid dominates the history of the Abbasid court during the reign of Mahdi and much of that of Hārūn. Yet it is difficult to form a clear idea of his talents and achievements. Many of the stories about his life read more like exemplars written to show how a good minister and bureaucrat should behave and what he should accomplish, rather than as a historical record. Yahya's reputation was idealized by subsequent generations of secretaries who held him up as a model, and it is through their eyes that we see their hero. Despite these reservations, the accounts are important because they show us how an ideal courtier and administrator was supposed to behave, and what accomplishments he should display.

The key to his success was a relationship with the royal family which was much more intimate than that enjoyed by most bureaucrats, and shrewd networking among other members of the administration. The close association with the royal family seems to have come about as much by accident as anything. Mansūr had appointed Khālid governor of mountainous Tabaristān, where he served for seven years. While he was there, he appointed his son Yahya, still quite a young man, as his representative in the city of Rayy to the south. In 758 Mansūr sent his son Mahdi to Rayy to act as his viceroy in Khurasan and the east, and Yahya naturally entered his service. The connection is said to have become more intimate. When Hārūn was born to Mahdi and his favourite Khayzurān, Yahya's wife, Zubayda bint Munīr, took to breast-feeding the infant Abbasid while Khayzurān returned the favour to Yahya's own son, Fadl, born the year before.[90] There seems to be no parallel for this foster relationship in the history of the Abbasid family, and why the Barmakids should have been so honoured, if indeed they were, is not clear. It may simply have been a friendship between two young mothers posted to a strange city. Whatever the circumstances, the story is symbolic of the close relationship that developed between Yahya and the young Hārūn.

This relationship was confirmed when the young Hārūn was sent on an expedition against the Byzantines in 780. It was effectively his first independent command and he was young and inexperienced. His father, the caliph Mahdi, appointed Yahya to accompany him. He was given control of the expenses, the secretariat and all the administration of the army. Rabī ibn Yūnus was also sent with the army, and Hārūn used to consult them both on all matters. This cemented the close relationship between Yahya and Rabī, which meant that the chamberlain, who had quarrelled with earlier viziers, was able to work closely with Yahya at crucial moments. Fortunately the expedition was a success, if only a fairly limited one. The small Byzantine border fortress of Samalu was conquered, the army returned in triumph and Yahya's status was confirmed.[91]

Throughout the rest of Mahdi's reign, Yahya acted as a father figure to Hārūn. The accession of Hādī as caliph in 785 posed a major threat to his position. Hādī resented Hārūn's position as heir apparent and wanted to replace him with his own son. Yahya could see this as a clear threat to his influence: if Hārūn lost his place in the succession, his father figure would have no role and no patronage to offer. Along with Khayzurān, whom he had known since the old days in Rayy, and Rabī he tried to protect Hārūn's interests. Typically, where Khayzurān was hostile to her eldest son, Yahya attempted to mediate, urging Hādī to be patient with his younger brother and Hārūn to stand up to Hādī's threats.

The turn of the wheel of fortune which now put Hārūn on the throne, virtually unopposed, meant that Yahya was the effective ruler of the caliphate. From Hārūn's accession in 786 until the dramatic fall of the Barmakids in 803, Yahya and his sons, the solid Fadl and more glamorous Jaᶜfar, dominated the caliph's court. In 794 we are told, 'Hārūn handed over all his affairs to Yahya the Barmakid.'[92]

Yahya emerges as the omni-competent fixer. In a whole genre of stories, men approach him to say that the estate next door to the one they own in the Sawad of Iraq has suddenly come on the market but they do not have the cash to buy it.[93] The great man says he will see what he can do, and when they reach home the money has already been provided. Another story shows him helping a stressed-out colleague, Alī, in the office. The man complained that he had so many petitions that he could not handle them: 'My slippers and sleeves were stuffed with them.' Yahya invited him to relax with him, they had some drinks together and washed and, while his colleague slept, Yahya dealt with all the papers, determining which were important and signing them all. The next day Alī went to meet the petitioners with a sinking heart, afraid to face them and admit that he had not done the work. When the papers arrived, he found that they were all completed for him.[94] We all need colleagues like Yahya the Barmakid sometimes.

Yahya was also impatient with inefficiency. Although he was responsible for the letters that were sent out from the caliph, the caliph's private seal was held, at least for a time, by another official, Abu'l-Abbās al-Tūsi. Yahya was irritated by Abu'l-Abbās's slowness in doing his job and the delays this caused. He complained to the caliph Hārūn who gave him permission to bypass the seal holder and order his own secretaries to dispatch letters directly.[95]

Yahya was in many ways the public face of Abbasid government. He and his sons Fadl and Jaʿfar would sit every day to receive petitions; 'they stayed into nightfall, looking into the affairs of the people and their needs. No one was refused admission and the curtain was never drawn on them'.[96] It was to his door that the masses of petitioners would come. Every morning they would be waiting for him on the bench outside the gate of his house, and every day he would give them a friendly and cheerful greeting.

Another vignette shows Yahya taking action in an emergency. The caliph Hārūn is away on one of his hunting expeditions and the Tigris is in flood in Baghdad. Everyone is amazed by the power of the water. We see Yahya, leading the army commanders, sending them to areas threatened with flooding and ordering the building of dykes to protect them.[97]

We also find him as a progressive landlord. He is said to have spent 20 million *dirham*s on digging a canal which came to be known as Abu'l-Jund (father of the army) because the immense yields of the newly cultivated lands were used to pay military salaries. He arranged that supplies of wheat should be sent from Egypt to the Holy Cities of Mecca and Medina, where many descendants of the Emigrants and Helpers lived as pensioners of the state.[98] Everyone regarded this as a pious and meritorious act.

Apart from his bureaucratic skills, Yahya played an important role as a patron of culture. Poets certainly wrote verses in his praise and he was (predictably and conventionally) generous to them. He is said to have written a small amount of poetry himself, but it does not seem to have been of great distinction; his claims to originality lay in his patronage of scientific literature. He is refuted to have been the first man to take an interest in the translation of Ptolemy's *Almagest* into Arabic, but the project seems to have run into difficulties because there was a shortage of skilled translators.[99] He commissioned a book on the prism. Perhaps because of the eastern background of his own family, he also took a keen interest in Indian culture. He is said to have sent a man to the subcontinent to bring back plants used in Indian medicine and information about Indian religions which forms the basis of accounts given in later Arabic texts.[100] He paid an Indian scholar called Manka to translate an Indian medical book (which the Arabic text calls the Book of Sasard) into Arabic.[101] This broad range of interests marked Yahya and his circle out from the more conventional bureaucrats and courtiers. They were also very influential; the image of the bureaucrat as patron of science, begun as far as we can see by Yahya, was to bear fruit in the next century when the pupils of the Barmakids ran the administration and were among the main patrons of the translation of Greek science into Arabic.

The Abbasid dynasty came to power on the back of a military revolution. It was the armies of the Muslims of Khurasan which defeated the forces of the Umayyads and swept the new dynasty to power in 750. In the end, it was military power which underpinned the authority of the dynasty, and Mansūr was careful to develop an effective military machine. It was only to be expected that the military leaders who achieved this would occupy a major position in the court of the caliphs.

The total number of troops in the Abbasid armies in the late eighth century was probably around 100,000. It is interesting to compare this with the army of the eastern Roman empire in the sixth century, which probably numbered between 90,000 and 150,000 regular troops, though of course the Abbasid army was scattered over a much larger area. In 762, when Mansūr faced the rebellion of the Alid Ibrāhīm, brother of Muhammad the Pure Soul, there were 30,000 troops under the command of his son and heir Mahdi in Rayy, 40,000 in Tunisia, where there had been trouble among the local Berbers, and just 4,000 who had been sent to Medina to fight Muhammad the Pure Soul. The caliph had only 1,000 men with him and was forced to recruit soldiers from Syria as quickly as he could. We know there were also garrisons in Azerbayjān, in Mosul, and perhaps 25,000 on the Byzantine frontier. All these were paid, or were supposed to be paid, a monthly wage, but many of them, like Ottoman janissaries, must have had jobs and small businesses in the area in which they lived as well. After the foundation of Baghdad, substantial numbers of troops were settled in the city. It became their home, and they and their descendants formed a substantial element in the population of the new metropolis.

They inhabited quarters to the north and west of the Round City, away from the commercial districts to the south. Here the great families of the Abbasid military had their compounds: Hasan ibn Qahtaba, son of the first military leader of the revolution, had a small quarter (*rabad*) which contained his house and the houses of his family leading into a side street (*darb*) called after him.[102] His colleague, Musayyab ibn Zuhayr, chief of police for many years, had a house just outside the Kūfa Gate of the Round City, which had its own private mosque with a tall minaret.[103] Other soldiers lived in more modest quarters, and there were whole sections of the city inhabited by soldiers from the far north-east of the empire, with groups from Merv, Balkh, Bukhara and other areas of Transoxania settled together in this city of immigrants.[104]

Most of the soldiers lived and worked in a different world from the court and court society, but there were always soldiers around the court.[105] On one occasion, towards the end of his reign, Mansūr conducted a formal review. He convened an assembly on the banks of the Tigris just south of Baghdad and ordered his family and court to wear arms. He himself appeared in a coat of mail, a black *qalansūwa* and a helmet.[106] However, this was obviously an unusual event, and military dress was not normally worn at court.

There were two elite groups among the military who had much closer links with the caliph. These were the guard (*haras*) and the police (*shurta*). The difference between the two units is not always clear but the guard were probably confined to looking after the security of the caliph (and disposing of his victims) whereas the police had a wider role in keeping the peace in Baghdad and elsewhere.

At the foundation of the city of Baghdad, the guard were given quarters near the caliph's own palace. In the heart of the Round City, there was an open court. In this court lay the palace, the Golden Gate and the mosque. The only other buildings in this area were quarters for the guard. Near by were two large porticoes, roofs supported on columns made of fired brick and gypsum where the commanders of the guard and police would sit. They also functioned as overspill prayer halls for the mosque.[107] Guards were also stationed at the four gates to the Round City. Each gate is said to have had a detachment of a thousand men with their own commanders; they had rooms in the arcades that flanked the entrance passageways.[108]

The guard was maintained throughout the early Abbasid period, but we have little information about their appearance or functions. They must have been stationed at the entrance to royal palaces and been in attendance at formal receptions. Before Baghdad was built, when Mansūr was living in a tented encampment, he had guards on hand, for it was the guard he called on to kill Abu Muslim when he appeared. When Mansūr was attacked by members of a fanatical sect called the Rāwandiya in 758/9, and was in serious personal danger, the commander of the guard went out to negotiate with the rebels. As he was returning, he was shot from behind by an arrow and died a few days later. As an unusual mark of respect, the caliph led the funeral prayers for him in person and stayed until the body was buried. The office was then passed to the dead man's brother.[109] The commander of the guard also acted as a messenger between visitors and the caliph: one senior military commander (Hasan ibn Qahtaba) is described as coming to see the caliph and finding the commander of the guard's son sitting on the *farsh* his father used at the entrance to the royal quarters and leaving a message with him.[110] Later the guard are described as being armed with maces when they attended court, but we have no idea what sort of uniform, if any, they wore.[111]

Mansūr reigned for another twelve years after the end of the Pure Soul's rebellion in 762. These years were largely peaceful, and the caliph was able to devote quite a lot of time and resources to building operations. The work on the Round City of Baghdad was largely finished by the end of 766, only four years after the project was begun.[112] Two years later, in 768, he embarked on a major expansion of the metropolis. His son and heir Mahdi had returned from Iran, and Mansūr wanted to establish him in his own palace and give him the opportunities for patronage and rewarding his supporters which he had created on the west bank. A whole new city, with its own mosque and royal palace, was now created on the east bank. Members of the Abbasid inner circle, like the Barmakid family, soon acquired property on both sides of the river. Bridges of boats were built to connect the two sides. These bridges, of small boats tied side by side with a wooden walkway over the top, were the normal way of spanning the Tigris right up to the twentieth century, when masonry and concrete bridges became possible. The city on the east bank, sometimes called Rusafa, was the beginning of the east bank settlement that was to be centre of the city in medieval and early modern times.

In 771 the caliph visited Syria and Jerusalem, and during this journey he settled on the site of yet another new city. This was just outside the ancient city of Raqqa on the Euphrates, now in Syria. The next year he sent his son Mahdi to begin the construction, and he is said to have made it on the same plan as Baghdad with the same gates and walls and towers. The outline of Abbasid Raqqa still survives. It is not a round city but is 'D'-shaped. Its walls and towers, now standing to the height of three or four metres, may suggest how Baghdad was designed. The city was intended to be a forward base for the Abbasid army for launching campaigns on the Byzantine frontier and, probably, in case of unrest in Syria. With its easy river communications to Baghdad, it became a favourite residence of later caliphs, especially Hārūn al-Rashīd.

In the summer of 775, Mansūr set out on the pilgrimage to Mecca. He had been before in 765 and 770, but this time increasing illness may have given added urgency to his plans. He was probably 63 years old and his health was not as robust as it had been. Like many Muslims, he would have believed in the spiritual benefits of dying in the holy precinct. Most of the important figures in the state went with him, including his faithful chamberlain Rabī and the young Mūsā, son of his heir Mahdi and later to be caliph himself with the title of Hādī. Mahdi was left in Baghdad to run the government.

As the long journey progessed, Mansūr became increasingly unwell. In one of those stories which illustrate how close up and personal life was even for the grandest people, we are told how Mansūr's camel was watched from a distance by a member of the family of Alī, who had reason to fear the caliph's anger. He saw the camel move to the side of the track and kneel. The caliph got out of his litter and

defecated by the roadside. Then he got back beside Rabī and continued the tiring journey. When the coast was clear, the observer, who
had a doctor with him, went over to where the caliph had squatted
and looked at the place where he had relieved himself. The doctor
who was with him had no doubts: 'I have seen the bowel movements
of a man who has not long to live.'[113] No wonder caliphs of later generations preferred to live in the seclusion of their palaces, where you
could have a quiet crap without some busybody coming along to peer
at the results.

Everyone in the expedition had known that the caliph was seriously ill. He himself was desperate to enter the Haram area around
Mecca and to die on holy ground. When he came to the first halt
inside sacred territory, the end was clearly near. He died at sunrise on
21 October 775. He was probably in his early sixties. By the standards
of the Abbasid family this made him an old man. Despite, or perhaps
because of, the fact that they could call on the most famous physicians of their day, all the other Abbasid caliphs, even the famous
Hārūn al-Rashīd, were dead before they reached fifty.

Only Rabī and a few personal servants were with him, and Rabī
knew he had to act decisively. To buy himself time, he forbade the
women to start mourning and kept his master's death secret. The
camp was alive with rumours. According to Rabī's own version of
events, when the caliph died he had the corpse propped up on a
couch behind a thin curtain. Then the leading members of the
Abbasid family were called in and renewed their oaths of allegiance
to the heir apparent, Mahdi, imagining that the old man was still
alive. Only when this was done did Rabī announce that he was in fact
dead already.[114]

Alī al-Nawfali, a distant relative of the royal family whose writings
give us quite a lot of gossipy detail about court life, tells[115] how Rabī
assembled all the main figures at court in a large tent. In the place of
honour by the pole sat Mahdi's son Mūsā. The tent began to get very
full with men sitting cross-legged on the floor. Everyone was won-
dering what was going to happen. Nawfali was sitting next to a
prominent member of the Alid family, so close that their thighs were
touching. 'Do you think the Man is dead?' his neighbour whispered.
'I don't think so,' Nawfali answered (after all, nobody wants to
prophesy the death of a monarch), 'but he may be very ill or uncon-
scious.' Just then one of the black servants came into the tent and

began to bewail the death of his master, scattering ashes on his own head. Everyone got up and rushed towards the caliph's private tent but they were pushed back by the servants. Then Rabī persuaded everyone to sit down quietly again. He read out a scroll which he claimed was the caliph's last testament, written 'on my last day in this world and my first in the next', but which Nawfali thought had been made up by Rabī, in which he decreed that everyone should take an oath of allegiance to Mahdi. When he had finished reading, and before anyone had a chance to start any discussion or raise any objection, Rabī began to lead the most important figures at court by the hand, one by one, to the young Prince Mūsā; they took his hand to pledge their allegiance to his father. The crisis was over and Mahdi's accession was now assured.

The new caliph, a tall, thin man with curly hair, was now in his early thirties. Mahdi already had considerable political experience as viceroy of Khurasan during his father's lifetime, and his urban development on the east side of Baghdad had enabled him to reward his followers well. It was here, in the Rusafa quarter, that he built the palace in which he usually lived. The Arabic sources paint a picture of an engaging and easygoing man, unpretentious and generous, in marked contrast to his stern and calculating father. Although he had been born shortly before the revolution, he had been brought up in comfort and privilege. He loved poetry and the company of women.

At the same time Mahdi was genuinely pious, and is shown as a just righter of wrongs. He preached in the mosque[116] and sat in the *mazālim* court to answer petitions. He made continuous and largely successful efforts to reconcile members of the Family of Alī to Abbasid rule and to be generous to them and their supporters. He was also a great builder and restorer of mosques. In 776, immediately after his accession, he built a big new mosque at Rusafa[117] and others were enlarged at Basra and Mecca.[118] He began a campaign to restore mosques to their simple, ancient condition, ordering that pulpits should be reduced in height and that *maqsūra* should be done away with. The *maqsūra* was an enclosure designed to provide a private, protected area in the mosque for the governor or other important personages. Its existence was an affront to many of the pious, who believed that all Muslims should be treated equally in the house of prayer: Mahdi was responding to these popular sentiments. He demonstrated his religious commitment in other ways. His sons were sent on expeditions against the unbelievers, Hārūn against the Byzantines and Hādī against those who refused to accept the authority of the caliph in Jurjān, at the south-east corner of the Caspian Sea. The caliph ordered a maritime expedition to western India, which set out from Basra. A city in Gujarat was captured and the daughter of the king brought back among the booty, but the returning expedition was laid waste by storms and scurvy on the inhospitable southern shores of Iran and many of the Muslims perished.

We catch a more personal glimpse of Mahdi in a story about the caliph on a hunting expedition (he was a great hunter: it was to be, literally, the death of him). He is alone with a single companion and they come across a peasant who has a reed hut and a vegetable garden. Feeling hungry, the caliph asks, 'Have you anything to eat?'

The man replies that he has a stew made of salt fish and some barley bread. 'If you have some oil, that would be perfect,' the caliph goes on.

'Yes, I have oil.'

'And leeks too?'

So the man goes to his vegetable patch and brings back herbs and leeks and onions, all good peasant food but not the normal fare of caliphs. When the caliph and his companion have eaten well, Mahdi asks his companion to improvise a poem, which he does, making fun of their simple host. The caliph reproves him and changes the verse to make it complimentary. Then they leave and return to their camp and the caliph orders 20,000 *dirham*s, a vast sum, for the peasant.[119] The theme of the caliph and the peasant is a common one, and the whole incident may well be fictitious, but it is still interesting. The picture of the caliph hunting in the countryside with just one attendant, no guards, no servants, no picnic, is a striking one, and also brings out once again the vast gulf that separated the lifestyles of the caliph and his courtiers from those of his humbler subjects.

Mahdi's reign was not without its problems. There were rebellions by local chiefs in Khurasan. The swift rise and even swifter fall of his favourite and vizier Ya°qūb ibn Dāwud showed once more the precarious situation of chief administrators whose power was entirely dependent on the caliph. Overall, however, Mahdi continued and consolidated the achievements of his great father Mansūr during a reign of modest but all too brief success.

III

Hārūn al-Rashīd:
the Golden Prime

Hārūn al-Rashīd is undoubtedly the most famous of the Abbasid caliphs. He may not have been the most gifted, the most learned or the most politically astute of his dynasty, but it is his reputation which has survived and become part of the common cultural heritage. By contrast the names of Mansūr or Mutawwakil are known only to specialists. This is mostly, of course, because he was the caliph of the *Arabian Nights*. In these stories it is Hārūn, along with his special friend Jaᶜfar the Barmakid and the court jester Abu Nuwās, who roam the streets of Baghdad and meet with bizarre and picaresque adventures. Although the earliest versions of the *Nights* which have survived date from the fourteenth century, we can see the beginning of this mythologizing of the reign of Hārūn much earlier. Within a couple of generations of his death, writers such as Ibn Abi Tahir, the Grub Street hack of ninth-century Baghdad, were elaborating the stories of poets, singers, harems, fabulous wealth and wicked intrigues which were to form the basis of the legend.

It is not difficult to see why the era of Hārūn came to be regarded so soon as something of a golden age, the 'Golden Prime' of Hārūn. These were almost the halcyon days, the Edwardian summer of the caliphate. After his death, and at least partly through his fault, the caliphate was rent by a prolonged and very damaging civil war. Though the Abbasid dynasty certainly regained much of its power in the first half of the ninth century, the caliphate soon began to disintegrate, caliphs were beset by recurrent financial crises and Baghdad itself suffered the ravages of two major sieges with all the attendant suffering and destruction. In the ninth and tenth centuries, the era of Hārūn, however imperfect, appeared a time of magnificence, power and prosperity. After all, nobody ever knows they are living in a golden age until it is over and they can look back and realize what has been lost.

Strangely enough for a man who became so famous and whose later life is comparatively well documented, we are unsure of the date of Hārūn's birth.[1] It may have been any time from 763 to 767, but 766 is the most likely date. It is difficult to resist the implication that an air of mystery was deliberately cultivated, perhaps to obscure the fact that older siblings by different mothers were passed over in the succession. We can be sure that Mūsā, later to be the caliph Hādī, and Hārūn were both born in Rayy, in central Iran, where their father was serving as viceroy of the east, and that their mother was Mahdi's favourite concubine, Khayzurān. Nor would contemporaries have been ignorant of the significance of their names. Mūsā was Moses, the leader of his people and the great lawgiver, Hārūn was Aaron, his younger brother and junior partner, but also, of course, his eventual successor.

Of all Mahdi's numerous sons, only Mūsā and Hārūn were groomed for the succession. His father seems to have taken care to give both the brothers a proper political education. In later centuries Abbasid caliphs were thrust on the throne with little experience of life beyond the walls of the palace and no real contact with the politicians and soldiers on whom their success would depend. Mahdi, however, encouraged his boys to be self-sufficient and to build their own followings among the courtiers. Hārūn would certainly have been taught to read and write at an early age, and he would also have learned the basic rules and beliefs of Islam, though in later life he never showed more than a conventional albeit genuine piety.

The young prince's first major public engagement was when his father took him on pilgrimage to Mecca and Medina in the autumn of 777. This was a big occasion. In Mansūr's reign the Holy Cities had been the centre of the uprising of Muhammad the Pure Soul against Abbasid rule and there were wounds to be healed and fences to be mended. As usual, Mahdi did it in style. He demonstrated his piety by restoration works in the great sanctuaries. He was warned that the building of the Kaaba in Mecca was in danger because of the weight of the great cloths that were used to cover it. Successive caliphs had piled one on top of the other until the structure was in danger of being brought down by them. One by one the rich fabrics were stripped off: from late Umayyad times these were fine silk brocades, but the earlier ones were simpler fabrics from the Yemen. It must have been a wonderful collection of dated textiles, a historian's dream. In Medina, Mahdi enlarged the Mosque of the Prophet and sought to restore the original simplicity of the interior. As we have seen, he ordered that the *maqsūra* enclosure be removed. The wooden pulpit from which Muhammad had preached still existed, but Muʿāwiya, the impious Umayyad, had caused it to be heightened to make it more impressive. Now Mahdi determined to reduce it to its primitive simplicity. However, this was not to be: experts warned him that the nails that held Muʿāwiya's additions on had gone deep into the wood of the Prophet's pulpit and if he tried to take them out he might end up by destroying what he had intended to restore. Wisely, he left it alone.

He took measures to address the more mundane needs of the people of the Holy Cities: 300,000 gold *dīnār*s were brought from Egypt and another 200,000 from Yemen and distributed to the inhabitants. Along with the money came vast numbers of robes: as always with the Abbasids, textile diplomacy was an important part of politics. It was all superb public relations, and the young Hārūn must have basked in his father's reflected glory. And it worked: when another member of the Family of the Prophet attempted to raise the people of the Holy Cities against the Abbasids in 785, most of them resolutely refused to join him.

It was shortly after this that Hārūn's education was entrusted to a man who was to have a decisive influence on his life. Yahya ibn Khālid ibn Barmak was by now a senior member of the bureaucracy and an intimate of the royal family. He became Hārūn's tutor and chief political adviser, guiding him in his training in administrative and military affairs. But he was more than that: Hārūn referred to him, after Mahdi's death, as his father, and Yahya certainly provided the emotional support and encouragement that Hārūn so badly needed. But the relationship was a two-way street, for the smooth and cultivated Persian bureaucrat had now attached his fortunes, and those of his family, to the career of his young protégé. It was vital for them that Hārūn should succeed. They invested heavily in his career, so he could not be allowed to retire into obscurity, even if he wanted to. Yahya and his family were playing for high stakes.

Rather as with young members of the British royal family, the next step in Hārūn's education was in the military, with the difference that, given his status, he was immediately appointed to command armies in person.

In the spring of 780 he was commissioned to lead an army against the Byzantines.[2] The war against the Byzantines was no ordinary campaign. The Greeks were the ancient foe and the war against them was the classic *Jihād*, the struggle of Islam against its most persistent enemy. Muhammad himself had sent expeditions against them and the leadership of these campaigns, like the leadership of the Hajj, was one of the signs of sovereignty. Just as his Hajj to Mecca and Medina had shown him as the leader of the Muslims on pilgrimage, so the sending of his son against the Byzantines would show the ruling dynasty to be the leaders of the *Jihād*. It would give the young Hārūn a training in military affairs and, just as important, it would give him the opportunity to build up a body of supporters among the military.

In the early Abbasid period, the campaigns against the Greeks were an almost annual ritual. The Muslim armies were based on the cities of the plains to the south of the Taurus mountains, Tarsus and Massissa in Cilicia, Hadath and Malatya farther to the east. Here in the warm lowlands the Muslim armies would winter, far away from the harsh and snowy winters of the Anatolian plateau. In the spring, when the new grass could fatten their horses, they began to move. According to one Muslim source, they followed the spring up into the mountains. Here they encountered the stubborn defenders of the peaks and steep valley of the Taurus mountains. The Byzantines may have spoken Greek but their lifestyles had little in common with the refined life of ancient Athens or late antique Constantinople. They were hardy mountain folk, who lived more like the *kleftes* of the eighteenth and nineteenth centuries, those tough Greek bandits who defied Ottoman rule from the rugged peaks of the Taygetus. They lived in villages, rocky castles perched on pinnacles of the Taurus mountains, and sometimes in great complexes of caves and tunnels, of the sort that can still be seen at Derinkuyu and Kaymakli in Cappadocia. It was these people who excavated and decorated the numerous small rock-cut churches and monasteries that draw tourists to the area today.

Most Muslim military expeditions in this area were fairly small scale-affairs led by local commanders. The terrain was harsh and unforgiving and they often encountered fierce resistance from the local people. Even when they overwhelmed the enemy garrisons, there was precious little to steal from these poor mountain areas: if they went too far towards the lusher areas around the Aegean coasts and the Sea of Marmara, they risked a confrontation with the imperial Byzantine army. So most years the Muslims contented themselves with a summer-time foray into the uplands and were careful to make sure that they were back in their bases before the onset of winter. But an expedition led by the caliph's son would be a much more serious affair.

When the time came for the expedition to set out in mid-March, Mahdi left the young prince Hādī in charge in Baghdad while he accompanied Hārūn through Syria to the frontier. Before they left Baghdad, he had summoned Yahya ibn Khālid and told him that he had been selected to look after the administration and finances of Hārūn's army. Also with the army was the veteran chamberlain, Rabī, who had served Mansūr so well. Working together on this campaign, Rabī and Yahya built up a close political relationship which was to be very important in the future.[3]

Other senior members of the Abbasid family were also sent, and some of them at least, far from treating the young prince with the respect due to an heir to the throne, regarded him with amused contempt. They observed him prancing around and striking military poses and decided that he was a figure of fun:[4] it was not a good omen for his future standing with the Abbasid establishment. Nonetheless, the expedition was a small-scale success. The army reached the frontier castle of Samalu, siege engines were set up and after thirty-eight days of blockade, and a fair number of Muslim casualties, the garrison made terms. They agreed to surrender the castle on condition that they were granted their lives and were not split up. In the event they were taken as a group to Baghdad, where they founded a small Christian community on the east side around a church that became known as Dayr al-Rūm, the Monastery of the Greeks, and which remained a centre of Christian life in Baghdad down to the Mongol conquest of 1258. The conquest was a modest one, and the fortress soon reverted to Byzantine control, but it could be claimed as a victory, and as for the young prince, well, it was all experience.

The caliph must have been convinced that his plan had been a good one for two years later, in 782, Hārūn was again appointed to lead an expedition.[5] This time it was on altogether a grander and more ambitious scale. No expense was spared to ensure the success of the venture. Almost 200,000 gold *dīnār*s and 21 million silver *dirham*s were taken to pay wages and for supplies. This was to be a massive expedition – there are said to have been more than 100,000 soldiers involved – which went much farther and deeper into Byzantine territory than the usual annual raid.

According to the Arab sources, the campaign was a triumph. One of the court poets produced some verses which claimed, with some licence, that Hārūn had besieged the Greeks in Constantinople 'with piercing spears, until her walls were dressed in shame' and 'her princes came offering their tribute'.[6] The Byzantine army was defeated and Muslim troops reached the Bosphorus. The empress Irene was obliged to sue for peace. A three-year treaty was made and Irene agreed to pay a tribute of between 70,000 and 90,000 *dīnār*s a year, which, of course, would not nearly make up for the money the caliph had invested. She also agreed to make markets available for the Muslims on their way home. This points to the real weakness of the Muslim position: invade with a small army and it could be defeated by the Byzantines; invade with a large one and it would be unable to feed itself on the empty steppes of central Anatolia. Hārūn may have been lucky to extricate himself and his army without major losses. At home this was presented as a victory – the Byzantines were said to have suffered improbably large losses and over five thousand prisoners were taken along with twenty thousand horses. So great was the booty that animals, coats of mail and swords were sold in the camp for ridiculously low prices. On the other hand, it seems that no major strongholds were taken and no lands had been ceded to the territory of the caliphate. Our Arab accounts probably reflect efforts to put a positive spin on an expedition whose success was rather more questionable.

It seems to have been after this campaign that Mahdi had oaths of allegiance sworn to Hārūn as heir apparent after his brother Hādī. It was at this time too that he was given the title of Rashīd.[7] By the end of his father's reign, Hārūn had been appointed viceroy of all the west, from Anbar just west of Baghdad as far as Tunisia, over which the Abbasid caliphs still maintained some control. He was responsible for the administration of this vast area, though in reality it was his mentor, Yahya the Barmakid, who did the real work.[8] Inevitably there was gossip at court to the effect that Mahdi intended to replace Hādī with his younger brother,[9] but no public decision was made.

The two brothers seem to have developed very different characters. Hādī was tall, fair skinned and good looking, except that he suffered from a harelip, which meant that his mouth was often gaping: when he was young, he was sometimes called 'Mūsā Shut-your-Mouth',[10] and the humiliation must have rankled. He was by all account a strong, energetic, physical man: when he heard about his father's death, he made the journey from Jurjān at the south-eastern corner of the Caspian Sea, where he was leading an army, to Baghdad in just twenty days.[11] He seems to have been popular among the military but had little time for intellectual pursuits. He also had a ferocious temper and his unpredictable outbursts were a source of great alarm to his courtiers. His attitude to his younger brother swung between open affection and respect at times and violent hostility at others.

If there is one thing about Hārūn we can be certain about, it is that he was his mother's darling. We do not know why this came to be: perhaps it was his good looks and his quiet and retiring nature in contrast with his brother's boorishness. The report that he wanted to retire into private life with his wife Zubayda, rather than coping with the stress and anxiety of being heir to Hādī, is consistent with other indications we have of his character. The image of the childish prince being laughed at as he pretended to be a soldier is an abiding one. The court physician, Jibrīl ibn Bukhtīshu, once observed that Hārūn was the shyest of the caliphs he had known and was reluctant to look men in the eye, perhaps suggesting a certain lack of self-confidence.[12] His reign as caliph is marked by the growing seclusion of court life. There are no reports that he preached in public in the mosque in Baghdad and the stories of his piety show a man at his private devotions in a palace oratory in the dark hour before dawn. It may be too that this deep-seated insecurity accounts for his reliance on the Barmakids followed by his abrupt and brutal destruction of them.

It was these two very different personalities who were the main protagonists in the dramatic events which unfolded in Baghdad between the death of Mahdi in August 785 and Hādī's death in September 786. It was thirteen months of intrigue and drama in the hothouse world of Abbasid court politics.

The circumstances of Mahdi's death were dramatic enough. He was struck down while still a young man in rude good health. Typically we are given two completely different versions of what happened. According to one story,[13] the caliph was on a hunting trip at Masabadhān, a small town that lay on the edge of the Iraqi plains in the lowest foothills of the Zagros mountains. It was August, and he may have gone to escape the fierce summer heat of Baghdad. His steward Wādih recounted how he had been with the caliph until evening prayer when he had gone to his own quarters. The next morning he got up early to ride across the desert to where Mahdi was staying. As he did so he became separated from his slaves and travelling companions and met 'a naked black man' who greeted him with the traditional words of condolence, 'May God give you great reward in your master, the Commander of the Faithful'. Wādih sought to strike him, for prophesying the death of the ruler was tantamount to treason, but the apparition vanished. When he reached Mahdi's camp he was greeted by the black eunuch Masrūr with exactly the same words as the spectre had uttered. Shocked, he went in to see a shrouded corpse.

'But when I left you after the afternoon prayer he was as happy and sound of body as he could be! What on earth happened?'

'The dogs startled a gazelle,' Masrūr explained, 'and he kept on after them. Then the gazelle ran into the doorway of a ruined building. The dogs pursued it and his horse pursued the dogs. He hit his back on the doorway and died on the spot.'

According to Muslim custom, corpses must be buried on the day they die. In this remote location there was no bier on which to carry him so they put him on a door and buried him under a walnut tree where he used to sit. His son Hārūn said the funeral prayers over him. Such were the accidental death and modest obsequies of the third sovereign of the Abbasid dynasty. When the great Arab geographer Yāqūt was writing his dictionary of place names in the early thirteenth century, over four centuries later, the tomb of the caliph was still known in the little village where he had been laid to rest.

The other version of the story belongs to the 'harem intrigue' school of historical explanation and should be treated with the scepticism such explanations usually deserve. Once again we are at Masabadhān, but this time we are in a palace and the caliph is sitting in an upper room, looking out of the window. Now Mahdi's slave girl Hasana had conceived a jealous hatred of a rival who she suspected of luring away her master's affections. To dispose of her she had a couple of delicious-looking pears set on a dish. She put poison in one of these and replaced the top so it looked quite normal. The girl who was ordered to take the pears to the intended victim, predictably, passed under the window where the caliph was sitting. He called her over and reached out to take the poisoned pear from the dish. As soon as he ate it, he experienced violent stomach ache and was dead within the day. 'I wanted you to myself,' said the miserable Hasana, 'but now, my lord, I have killed you.' The two stories are, of course, completely contradictory, but they show two completely different ways of looking at the political events of the period: it is the contrast between the cock-up theory of accidental and random events pitted against the conspiracy theory that everything must have a hidden meaning and purpose, that the obvious explanation for events can never be the true one.

The unexpected death of the caliph caused an immediate crisis. There was no dispute about the identity of the new caliph; that was Hādī, but he was in distant Jurjān. At the court at Masabadhān and in Baghdad, there was an air of panic. When news of the caliph's death became public, there was likely to be trouble as the troops rioted to demand special payments. Like the praetorian guard of the Roman emperors, they regarded the accession of a new ruler as an opportunity to enrich themselves and they would not let it pass. The problem was exacerbated because Hādī was the favourite of the military, while Hārūn and his advisers were looked on with some suspicion. But the new ruler was a thousand miles away and officials at court were scared to make decisions that the irascible Hādī might object to when he returned.

The immediate response of Mahdi's entourage was to be anxious about Hārūn's security: they warned him that he would not be safe when the soldiers in Masabadhān heard that Mahdi was dead and advised him that they should keep the death secret and return to Baghdad, taking the body with them for burial. When they reached Baghdad, and the necessary arrangements had been made, they could make the news public. Hārūn, of course, turned to Yahya the Barmakid for advice. Yahya argued that the death could not be kept secret and that when the troops found out that they were escorting the body of the caliph, they would demand three years' pay, or even more, before they would allow the body to be buried. It is interesting to see the Abbasid establishment so frightened of the army, which was supposed to support and defend them, a fear that has so many echoes in later military regimes. Yahya went on to argue that they should bury him ('God have mercy on him') there secretly so no disrespect should take place. They should placate Hādī by sending the chief of intelligence straight to Jurjān, with the caliph's signet ring and the Prophet's staff. Then the soldiers should be paid 200 *dirham*s each and told they could go on leave. 'Once they have their *dirham*s,' he argued, 'they will only think of their families and homes and will only want to go to Baghdad.' And so it proved: the soldiers, no doubt delighted with this unexpected good fortune, left the camp and streamed back to the capital.[14]

The problem was only postponed. When the troops found out that they had been duped, there was a riot. The house of Rabī, who had been left in charge in Baghdad, was attacked and part of it burned. It was at this juncture that Khayzurān, mother to the new caliph Hādī and of Hārūn, now next in line to the throne, took charge, summoning Yahya the Barmakid and Rabī to advise her. Money was found, the troops given two years' pay and the crisis averted.

When the new caliph arrived, the city was peaceful but the political atmosphere remained tense. After he had spent twenty-four hours relaxing with a favourite slave girl whom he had not seen while he had been away on campaign, Hādī set about appointing a new government. Yahya the Barmakid was allowed to continue as manager of Hārūn's affairs while the new head of the army office, and commander of the guard, was a young man who was to play a key role in the tragedy that unfolded a quarter of a century after Hārūn's death, Alī ibn Īsā ibn Māhān. Hādī was deeply suspicious of Rabī's role in the succession, accusing him of taking matters into his own hands. Rabī was in fear of his life; he made a will and entrusted it to his old friend Yahya the Barmakid. In the end they were reconciled but Rabī, who had served both Mansūr and Mahdi so long and so faithfully, soon died of natural causes.[15] Much of his status was inherited by his son Fadl, who, like Alī ibn Īsā ibn Māhān, was to be one of the key players in the politics of Hārūn's reign and the tragedies that followed.

Hādī established himself in the palace his father had built at

Isabadh, on the east side of Baghdad, while his brother Hārūn and his household occupied the Palace of Eternity, which Mansūr had built between the Round City and the river.[16] What happened over the next thirteen months was the subject of rumour and speculation, at the time and long afterwards. The facts, as far as we know, were that Hādī dithered between being determined to respect his father's will and keeping Hārūn as heir apparent and removing him from the succession. He was faced with a clear dilemma. On one hand he had a son, Jaᶜfar, who he would certainly have wanted to be caliph after him. This was not just because of parental affection and pride. Many in the military wanted to secure the succession for Jaᶜfar because they distrusted Hārūn and his coterie. It was important for them that Hādī remain caliph, but if he died, and strong young men often died in their prime, that he was succeeded by someone who would continue his policies. What made this idea even more tempting was that his brother did not seem to be ambitious for the crown and gave hints that he would be content to retire into private life with his new bride, the princess Zubayda.[17] All these siren voices, his own heart and the promptings of his supporters pushed Hādī in the direction of deposing his brother and making his son his heir.

But it was not as easy as that. His brother had powerful supporters, notably the Barmakids. Hārūn might be content to retire into private life but the Barmakids had invested heavily in the young prince's future: they were not prepared to see him ousted from his position without putting up a fight. Besides, as the Barmakids and others pointed out, tearing up an oath of allegiance was not something to be undertaken lightly for, if the oath to Hārūn were declared null and void, then what was the value of oaths to Jaᶜfar?[18] To add to that Jaᶜfar was only a young boy and there were strong feelings against giving the oath of allegiance to a mere child.

But the biggest obstacle to any plans Hādī may have had came from his own mother. Quite why relations between the caliph and his mother became so bad is impossible to tell. Hādī certainly resented the fact that his officers continued to visit his mother to ask for favours: 'What business have women discussing men's affairs?' he exclaimed to his leading officers, and went on to ask them how they would feel if their mothers were consulted in the same way.[19] After a barrage of such none-too-subtle hints, courtiers stopped going to Khayzurān and she was left lonely, isolated and powerless.

As the spring of 786 turned into summer and Baghdad sweltered in the hot sun, the political temperature must have become almost unbearable, the city awash with rumours about the relationship between the two brothers. To escape from the suffocating pressure, Hārūn left town to go hunting in the desert at a place called Qasr Muqatil, and stayed there out of harm's way for forty days, but Hādī used his absence to stir up opinion against him at court, and he returned. Finally, in mid September, the storm broke: the young caliph was dead and his short reign ended. Some said that he died from natural causes and that he had been ailing for some time. But there was also a story that his death was much more sinister. His own mother, they whispered, had ordered one of her slave girls, with intimate access to the caliph, to place a pillow over his face and sit on it until he suffocated.[20]

Whatever the cause of the caliph's death, Khayzurān was in a position to know of it before most, and she summoned Yahya the Barmakid and other allies, who moved fast. On the very night he died, men arrested the young Jaᶜfar. Hārūn was fast asleep, naked under his quilt, when Yahya the Barmakid came to find him. He woke him up and greeted the startled prince as caliph. Hārūn's immediate reaction was panic; he feared a trick that would put him at his brother's mercy, but he was slowly convinced.[21] By the time the next day dawned, it was all over: Hārūn rose early, dressed and went over to Isabadh, where his brother had lived, and led the prayers over his dead body, as he had led them over his father's corpse just over a year before.

Hārūn was now generally acknowledged as caliph. The swift night-time coup had surprised his opponents and they had no time to react. The new caliph was probably twenty-one at the time of his accession. He had been well trained in war and administration, but this does not seem to have given him the self-confidence and judgement that any ruler needs.

From his dramatic accession to the throne in September 786 until the fall of the Barmakids in early 803, the young caliph enjoyed comparative peace and prosperity. One indication of the uneventful nature of these years is that Tabari's great chronicle, which is the main source for the period, is often very brief: some years are covered in only a few lines[22] whereas the author might devote over a hundred pages to years of crisis.

This was also the golden age of the Barmakids. Yahya, old and experienced, had of course played a major part in Hārūn's accession. The young caliph now relied on him to help him through the challenges of exercising power. Tabari describes the caliph appointing Yahya as vizier [23] and saying, 'I have invested you with the rule of my flock. Removing the burden from my shoulders to yours. Govern them as you think right; appoint to office whom you will and remove whom you will. Conduct all affairs as you see fit,' and he gave him his signet ring. Ibrāhīm al-Mosuli, the aspiring court poet, saw fit to commemorate this verse:

> *See you not how the sun grew faint*
> *And when Hārūn ruled, gave again his light?*
> *O joy that God's trustee is now Hārūn*
> *He of the generous dew, and Yahya his vizier.*

It may not have been great poetry, but it made the point. Until her death three years later, Khayzurān remained influential: Yahya deferred to her and acted on her advice. There are some indications that Yahya wished to give up the burdens of government, and early in 798 he requested permission to retire to Mecca. This he duly did, but he was back in Baghdad the next year, perhaps because he felt that he was indispensable.[24]

Increasingly important was the younger generation of Barmakids, Yahya's sons Fadl and Jaᶜfar. Fadl is said to have been almost exactly the same age as the caliph and to have been his milk brother, but it was with his younger sibling Jaᶜfar that Hārūn made his closest personal bond. Fadl emerges as the solid, competent brother, the safe pair of hands. In 794 he was appointed to the all-important governorship of Khurasan. Here he built mosques and frontier fortresses and persuaded the prince of the remote mountain country of Ushrusana to accept Abbasid suzerainty. And he made money too: when he returned from the province the next year, he brought with him sacks of *dirhams*, each carefully sealed up.[25]

Jaᶜfar seems to have been the more glamorous of the two brothers. It is Jaᶜfar who figures as Hārūn's companion in adventure in the Hārūn stories in the *Arabian Nights*, and other sources make it clear that the caliph enjoyed a very close, almost erotic friendship with him. Jaᶜfar too enjoyed his moment of success in the provinces in 796, when he was sent to suppress unrest in Syria.[26]

Despite these forays into distant parts, the Barmakid brothers and their father spent most of the time at the royal court. They were given a number of formal posts in the administration, and these were shuffled round among them: in 796, for example, the custody of the royal seal was transferred from Jaᶜfar to his father Yahya. It was not the formal offices they held, however, but their intimate and easy access to the caliph which made them so powerful. The long evenings Hārūn and Jaᶜfar spent together, listening to singers, discussing poetry, enjoying the best food and wine, meant that they could influence policy and arrange for favours like no one else.

The Barmakids too had a genius for publicity and selling their own achievements. There were many governors of Khurasan in Hārūn's reign but most of them are little more than names: only Fadl the Barmakid had his exploits recorded in the chronicles and only Fadl was praised in a long and sonorous poem by the leading panegyrist of the moment, Marwān ibn Abi Hafsa:

> *Gentle he was to all who gave the Caliph obedience*
> *But he poured the blood of rebels for Indian swords to drink*
> *His blades brought hypocrites and unbelievers low*
> *An ever lasting glory for the people of the Faith.*[27]

And much more in the same vein.

Our account of Jaᶜfar in Syria is comprised of a few lines about his pacification of the rebels, a long poem extolling his prowess and expatiating on the good fortune of the Syrians in having him visit, and two versions of a studied and rhetorical oration he has said to have made to the caliph on his return. In words so unctuous and flattering that they may even have made contemporaries cringe, he goes on about his gratitude to the caliph, who had been more generous to him than any of his peers, had made him 'one of the men of my time', and whose renewed favour ' eclipses all that has gone before'.[28]

Extravagant compliments certainly attracted royal favour. And, of course, the money helped too. When Fadl returned from Khurasan, he no doubt told the caliph in great detail about his achievements; he was also careful to give the members of the Abbasid family, leading military men and bureaucrats generous gifts, a million *dirham*s here, half a million there.[29] The reputation for generosity was continuously cultivated.

The extravagance and hype with which they surrounded themselves should not obscure the real achievements of the Barmakid family. There can be no doubt that they developed and streamlined the administration of the state: after their fall the mail piled up unopened in sacks. They provided leadership and inspiration for generations of secretaries who contributed so much to Abbasid culture in the next century. Their salons were a forum in which ideas could be discussed with a freedom not possible in the more circumscribed surroundings of the caliph's own audience.

While the Barmakids effectively took care of the administration, Hārūn attended to the formal and ceremonial functions of his office. The summer after his accession, at the first opportunity, he went on pilgrimage to Mecca, distributing huge sums to the people of the two Holy Cities, just as his father had before him. He was to go on the pilgrimage seven more times, in 790,[30] 791,[31] 794,[32] 796,[33] 798,[34] 802[35] and 804.[36] No other caliph of the Umayyad or Abbasid dynasties came near to equalling this record of eight pilgrimages (or nine if you include the one he had made with his father in 777) and it shows the importance he attached to this role, especially when we remember that each expedition would have taken around two months and, even for the caliph, it would have been attended by all the discomforts of the long desert journey from Iraq. His wife Zubayda also went on pilgrimage and was to spend a considerable part of her enormous wealth in charitable bequests to reduce the hardship endured by poorer pilgrims.

The pursuit of the holy war, the other sign of leadership of the Muslim community, was pursued with vigour. Hārūn had, after all, considerable experience of campaigning against the Byzantines from the expeditions he had led in his father's day. One of the first things he did after his accession was to reform the administrative system of the frontier provinces to provide more resources for the *Jihād*.[37] In 797 he led an expedition into the Taurus mountains and captured a small fortress: for the first and only time a caliph personally led both the *Jihād* and the Hajj in a single Muslim year (181).[38] Virtually every year, expeditions set off for Byzantine territory, often led by members of the Abbasid family, and from 806[39] Hārūn led a series of massive strikes into the heart of the ancient enemy.

Much of Hārūn's ample leisure was spent in the search for new places to live. It is ironic that the caliph whose name is most closely associated with Baghdad, and whose legendary exploits are set in the city, does not really seem to have enjoyed it very much. He called it the steam room (*bukhār*),[40] and seems to have disliked it for its heat and climate. He may also have been looking for a site with more hunting opportunities in the vicinity. Besides, it was the city of his father and grandfather, and he may have wanted a new place on which he could stamp his own identity.

He looked first in the higher, fresher lands in the lower foothills of the Zagros. In 788/9 he chose a site called 'The Meadow of the Castle' (*Marj al-Qal'a*) and decided to build there, but fell ill and abandoned the project;[41] two years later he decided on a site by the Tigris at Bazabda and Baqirda, where he built a palace. An anonymous poet produced a piece of doggerel to commemorate the moment, which is interesting in the insight it offers into the caliph's motives:

> *Baqirda and Bazabda for summer or for spring*
> *At Baqirda and Bazabda the sweet, cool fountains sing.*
> *And Baghdad, what is Baghdad? Its dust*
> *Is shit, and its heat is appalling.*[42]

Despite the 'sweet, cool fountains' the caliph seems to have abandoned the site and, as far as we can tell, never went there again.

In 796 he made a more determined attempt to find a new residence. On his return from pilgrimage he went first to Basra to inspect a big new irrigation canal which Yahya the Barmakid had constructed. After that he went to Hira, just south of Kūfa, which had been the capital of the Lakhmids, an Arab dynasty that flourished in the era before the coming of Islam. The site was celebrated in Arab history and legend and the mythical castle of Khwaranaq was a byword for opulence and luxury. Hārūn began building and gave plots of land to his entourage so that they could build houses for themselves. The project did not last long. Hārūn found that the allure of ancient greatness was spoiled by its proximity to the tiresome people of neighbouring Kūfa. Once more he moved on.[43]

He finally settled on the city of Raqqa on the middle Euphrates in what is now Syria. Raqqa had been a Roman site with the name of Callinicum. Hārūn's grandfather, Mansūr, had established a new settlement outside the ancient city walls which he called Rafiqa or the

Partner. By Hārūn's time, the two settlements had merged, and Rafiqa had become the centre of the city, now generally known by the old name of Raqqa.

Visiting Raqqa today, it is hard to see why Hārūn preferred it over all the other possible residences. The partly restored walls of Mansūr's city enclose many of the dusty and unremarkable buildings of the modern town. New quarters of concrete houses have spread out in all directions. There is scarcely a green thing to be seen, and the hot winds of the Syrian steppes seem to blow continually. To the south of the old city, the Euphrates, swift and turbid, glides by. In modern times it is hardly used for navigation, there are too many shoals and sandbanks, but in Abbasid times people, caliphs included, did go by barge from Raqqa to Baghdad, so communications were good. Perhaps surprisingly, Hārūn chose to build, not by the river where water would have been easily available and there was the chance of a cool breeze off the river, but north of the old city. Here the flat lands of the Jazira stretched uninterrupted to the horizon, briefly verdant when the grass appeared in the spring but hot and arid in the summer. There was plenty of space here, and Hārūn built his palaces scattered across the landscape. In recent years, aerial photography and excavations have revealed the plans of many of these buildings but little of the structure survives, and even the foundations are being overwhelmed by new development.[44]

Hārūn may have liked the site partly because it was a useful staging post on the route to the Byzantine frontier. There was hunting too in the plains beyond the palaces. It was here in 798 that he had the oath of allegiance taken to his son Ma'mūn.[45] Two years later, in 800, we find him coming down the Euphrates from Raqqa to Baghdad by ship.[46] When he set out on his fateful pilgrimage in the late autumn of 802, he left his household (*huram*) and the treasury in charge of a senior member of his guard at Raqqa:[47] the city had really become his home.

When Hārūn left Raqqa to go on the 802 Hajj, he had more on his mind than leading the Muslims in this important rite. Now probably aged 35 or 36, he had decided that it was time to make arrangements for the succession. He was a comparatively young man, still in good health, but this was a time when death frequently came suddenly and without warning. If the caliph died without leaving a generally accepted heir, the whole future of the dynasty would be in peril. The idea of primogeniture, which had become the normal way of regulating succession to the rule in western Europe by the twelfth century, was never widely accepted ,in the Islamic world. Primogeniture had many disadvantages – it could result in the accession of very young or completely inadequate monarchs and it left younger brothers excluded, unprovided for and potentially disaffected – but it did go some way to preventing the jostling and fierce factional rivalries that were characteristic of many Islamic monarchies. In a polygynous society, elite males might father numerous sons by different women, any of whom might be eligible for the succession to the throne. In practice, only a few, mostly older, sons or sons of favourite women were selected. Each of these would attract a constituency of supporters, just as Hārūn's own candidature had attracted the support of the Barmakids. Each faction would be determined that their man should inherit, and rivalries over the succession became the main forum for political debate in the caliphate.

In 791/2, five years after his accession, Hārūn had made the Muslims swear allegiance to his five-year-old son Muhammad, who was given the title of Amīn. We are told that a number of members of the Abbasid family were 'stretching out their necks for the succession to Hārūn because no heir had been named'. Muhammad was not just the son of Hārūn: his mother was the Abbasid princess Zubayda, and there were powerful voices within the ruling family urging that he should be appointed. According to the fullest account we have,[48] it was Zubayda's uncle who persuaded Fadl the Barmakid to take the initiative because Muhammad 'was almost like your own son and his succession would be in your interest'. Fadl understood that only the succession of one of Hārūn's sons could secure the Barmakids' position in the long term, and when he was appointed to the governorate of Khurasan, he took matters into his own hands. He distributed large sums of money to the army and so induced them to take the oath of allegiance to the young prince. What began in the provinces was taken up in the capital and then in the rest of the empire. Not everyone was pleased, and senior members of the Abbasid family resented being obliged to take the oath to a young boy, especially as he was clearly the Barmakids' protégé.

In 798 Hārūn arranged that the oath of allegiance should be taken to another son, Abd Allah, called Ma'mūn, as heir to Amīn. The oath was first taken at Raqqa and then the young prince was sent down to Baghdad with senior members of the Abbasid family so that the oath could be sworn to him in the capital. He was placed in the tutelage of Jaᶜfar the Barmakid and was given formal authority for Khurasan from Hamadhan to the eastern frontiers of the empire.[49]

Bearing in mind Hārūn's own miserable experience as heir apparent to the heir apparent, it seems foolish of him to have replicated this position for his own children, but he may have had good reasons. Amīn was young, but there could be no guarantee that he would reach adulthood; the caliph may well have wanted 'an heir and a spare'. Ma'mūn's mother, about whom we know very little, was probably the daughter of a Persian nobleman from Khurasan who had rebelled against the Abbasids and been killed as a result. What is clear is that her family had powerful friends among the Khurasani aristocracy and they may have urged the Barmakids, who were also, of course, Persian nobles, to arrange this.

The caliph must have been only too aware of the problems these sorts of arrangements could cause, and it was to circumvent these that he decided to make a formal compact between the two brothers that would clarify the issues and prevent any misunderstandings in the future.

The 802 pilgrimage took place in December and the air in the Holy Cities must have been comparatively bearable, certainly better than the stifling heat when the pilgrimage fell in high summer during the 780s. Hārūn set out from Raqqa with his two sons, passed to the west of Baghdad without entering the city, and then travelled along the desert route to Medina. One of his objectives was to show off his sons in the Holy Cities, just as he had been shown off by his own father. When they arrived in Medina the inhabitants were summoned: they first came to the caliph, who gave them donations, and then to each of his sons, who gave them further donations. Then they moved on to Mecca, where the ceremony was repeated. It was said that a million and a half gold *dīnār*s were distributed in this way.[50]

Then came the real business of the expedition. Hārūn had two long, solemn agreements written out, one for each son, setting out in immense detail the obligations each had to the other. The texts of the two agreements have been preserved in full in Tabari's *History*, and we can see exactly how Hārūn was trying to obviate possible causes of conflict. Amīn was to be caliph first, and the most onerous obligations were put on him. Not only was Ma'mūn to succeed him, even if he had grown-up sons of his own, but his brother was also to have almost complete autonomy in his great governorate of Khurasan and the east. Ma'mūn was to be in charge of all the apparatus of government and taxation, including the postal service and the state textile factories, and of all the military forces. Amīn was to allow him access to all his estates and goods in any part of the empire, was not to entice his officials away from him, and if any of them deserted Ma'mūn for Amīn they were to be returned. Finally Amīn had to acknowledge that if he broke any of his promises, then the caliphate would pass to Ma'mūn immediately and he would have to resign.

The document signed by Ma'mūn was much shorter. He promised to accept his brother as caliph, not to give aid to any of his brother's enemies and to send troops to help him if he was attacked. And there was a sting in the tail, for he was obliged to promise that Amīn could nominate anyone he wished as heir to Ma'mūn.

The documents were then signed and witnessed by the judges present. The texts were read in front of the leading men of the state and all the pilgrims, and they were then deposited in the sanctuary at Mecca for safe-keeping.

There was a third document, couched in the same formal and grandiloquent prose, which was sent to all the provinces to explain what had been done, stressing that it was God's will, and part of His grace to the Muslims that Amīn and Ma'mūn had been appointed heirs: 'God has willed this and none shall reject it. He has concluded the matter and none of His servants can detract from it or stop it, or turn away from what He wills of what has gone before with His knowledge...The command of God cannot be altered, His decree cannot be rejected and His judgment cannot be delayed.'[51] Hārūn stressed throughout that God had decided on these arrangements and that his sons had made the agreements willingly and in good faith. Finally he ordered that the governors should read out the terms of the agreement to all the Muslims in their area.

Hārūn may have hoped that he had solved the thorny problem of succession. The documents seemed to have anticipated all potential causes of dispute. The authority of God, His caliph and the whole weight of Muslim public opinion had been marshalled to support the agreement. All the grandeur of high-flown Arabic rhetoric had been employed to make the agreements solemn and binding. No caliph had ever made such a public and comprehensive attempt to regulate the succession.

But many had their doubts: 'some of the common people', the chronicler notes, 'said, "he has settled the empire's affairs very well" while others said, "No, he has cast dissension among his sons and the consequences of his action are to be feared by his subjects."'[52] We also have the text of an anonymous poem (critical poems are usually anonymous, for obvious reasons) in which the poet expresses his dismay at what the caliph has done:

> *He tried to prevent quarrels among his sons*
> *And to produce love between them*
> *Yet he has planted hostility without fail*
> *And occasioned battle for their company*
> *And caused violent conflict between them*
> *And strung to their avoidance chains.*
> *Woe to the subjects in a little while*
> *For he has presented them with terrible grief.*

The poem as it has come down to us was no doubt written later with the benefit of hindsight, but it did not need a prophet of genius to see that, despite all Hārūn's efforts, trouble was brewing.

Hārūn and his court returned to Iraq at the beginning of 803. It was at this point that he made a move which astonished almost everyone at the time and has remained a subject of continuing speculation ever since. He ordered the destruction of the Barmakids: Yahya and his son Fadl were placed under arrest and his favourite Jaʿfar was summarily executed in the middle of the night, his body being cut in pieces and displayed on the bridges of Baghdad for every passer-by to see. Their possessions were confiscated and their officials arrested.

A number of participants in the drama have left what purport to be first-hand accounts of the drama. Masrūr the eunuch, whom Hārūn used on many confidential missions, tells how he was sent to find Jaʿfar in the middle of the night and bring his head to the caliph.[53] He found him sitting with Jibrīl ibn Bukhtīshu, the chief physician to the court, and a blind singer called Abu Zakkār. According to Masrūr's account, the poet had just finished singing a song which went:

No young man can escape it, come what may
Death comes at last by night or day.

Masrūr told Jaᶜfar bluntly that he must now answer to the caliph.
Jaᶜfar seems to have been in no doubt what this meant, and asked for
permission to make his will and free his slaves. Masrūr, who knew
Jaᶜfar well and had probably shared many convivial evenings with
him, could hardly refuse, but messengers kept coming from the
caliph urging him to hurry. Meanwhile Jaᶜfar tried to reason with
Masrūr or at least to buy time: 'He only ordered you to do this while
he was drunk. Don't do anything until the morning or at least discuss
it with him again.' So Masrūr returned to the caliph, who was in bed
at the time, but Hārūn's response was coarse and direct: 'Bring me
Jaᶜfar's head, motherfucker!' Masrūr returned to his victim and once
more Jaᶜfar persuaded him to return with a last plea. The caliph was
now furious, and shouted at Masrūr that he would find someone else
who would bring first Masrūr's head and then Jaᶜfar's. Finally Masrūr
went and fulfilled his grisly orders.

A more sinister story comes from a Turkish attendant at court.
According to him, Hārūn had gone out hunting alone with Jaᶜfar and
showed him every sign of affection, even putting his arm around
him, which he had never done before. When they reached the place
where they were staying, Hārūn said that if he had not been spending
the night with his women, he would not have been parted from him.
He should go to his residence and drink and make merry with music
so that at least they would be doing the same thing. Jaᶜfar insisted
that he only enjoyed these things if he was doing them with the
caliph, but Hārūn was insistent. Even after they had said good night
and each had gone to his own place, Hārūn sent a string of servants
with delicacies, incense and sweet-smelling herbs until finally he
dispatched Masrūr to demand his head.[54]

Meanwhile Hārūn was giving orders to ensure that there were no
disturbances and that none of the intended victims could escape.
Sindi ibn Shāhik was a freedman and one of Hārūn's military
entourage. He reports that one day he was sitting down when he saw
a servant coming with the post. He handed Sindi a small letter and
when he broke the seal he found it was from Hārūn in his own hand-
writing: 'Sindi, if you are sitting when you read my letter, then get up
and if you are standing then do not sit down before you come to me.'

He went immediately and found that Hārūn was on a boat on the Euphrates near Anbar, west of Baghdad, accompanied only by the son of his chamberlain, Abbās, son of Fadl ibn Rabī, and some servants. When Sindi came before him, he told the servants to go and ordered Abbās to go around the boat and tidy up the cushions that had been scattered around. Now there were just the two of them, and Hārūn ordered Sindi to come close. 'I have sent for you in a matter so secret that if the button of my shirt knew it, I would throw it into the Euphrates!' Then Sindi was ordered to go immediately to Baghdad, gather reliable companions and put guards at the doors of all the residences of the Barmakids so that no one could come in or out. 'The Barmakids', the caliph assured him, 'won't be moving at that time.' Sindi went to Baghdad as fast as he could and did as he had been ordered. It was not long before Jaᶜfar's head was brought to him with a letter from Hārūn telling him to carve up the body and display it on the three bridges in the capital.[55]

The outlines of the events are fairly clear. Although many of the details and dramatic devices in these accounts may be the product of later reworking, there can be no doubt that Hārūn acted swiftly and secretly to destroy the power of the family that had done so much to ensure his accession to the caliphate and the success of his first seventeen years as ruler. Yahya and his son Fadl were under arrest and were never to regain their freedom, Jaᶜfar was cruelly executed and his corpse subjected to the most public humiliation.

What we cannot be sure of is the reason why he acted as he did. A number of contemporaries have left accounts of what they believed had happened. Jibrīl ibn Bukhtīshu, the physician, who certainly knew all the participants in the drama well, points to a gradual estrangement between Hārūn and Yahya as Hārūn began to grow out of and then resent the dependence he had had on his old mentor. Perhaps Yahya just presumed too long that nothing had changed. Jibrīl recalled how one day Yahya had come into the caliph's presence without asking formal permission. Hārūn showed his irritation: turning to Jibrīl, Hārūn asked him whether people came into his home without asking. When Jibrīl said they did not, the caliph continued petulantly, 'What is wrong with us, then, that people come in without asking?' Yahya was horrified at this change of attitude and tried to make amends. He pointed out that he had long been accustomed to going to see the caliph, in the most informal circumstances, when he was naked on his bed or just in his waist-wrapper. He had not realized, he continued, that this intimacy, which the caliph had once liked, now irked him so much. In future he would always ask permission and was quite content to be like the more junior courtiers. This time Hārūn was embarrassed at his outburst and apologized, saying he was concerned only that people were gossiping about it. But Jibrīl, and presumably Yahya too, could tell that the atmosphere had changed.[56]

Minor humiliations began to be inflicted on Yahya at court. Hārūn gave orders to Masrūr, who was in charge of the pages, that they should no longer rise when Yahya came in. When he realized this, 'Yahya's face turned ashen grey'. There were more minor humiliations: the pages and chamberlains no longer looked him in the eye, and if he wanted a drink of water he had to ask several times.[57] Jaᶜfar's intimacy with the caliph is said to have worried Yahya, who feared that this closeness might be a source of danger if things went wrong.[58]

There are two strands of explanation which go farther than the idea of a growing personal antipathy and resentment. One of them concerns relations with the family of Alī. In general, relations between Abbasids and Alids in the early part of Hārūn's reign were fairly cordial, a trend that seems to have been partly the work of the Barmakids, who encouraged a conciliatory policy. There was, however, one Alid, Yahya ibn Abd Allah, who posed a potential security risk. He had fled from Medina to the wild mountainous area at the south-west corner of the Caspian Sea where he had been sheltered by the local Daylamite people, who lived beyond the reach of the Abbasid government. He clearly posed a threat to Abbasid rule, particularly as the Daylamites were a warlike people who might cut the great Khurasan highway where it ran along the southern edge of the Elburz mountains. And of course any member of the House of Alī might attract support much more widely across the Muslim world.

When Hārūn appointed Fadl ibn Yahya the Barmakid as governor of Khurasan in 792, part of his brief was to deal with Yahya. The Barmakids were generally disposed to take a conciliatory line with the Alids and Fadl began a correspondence with Yahya, trying to persuade him to give himself up. He also sent a million *dirhams* to the local ruler of Daylam, who was protecting Yahya, 'to make things easier'. Finally Yahya agreed to give himself up in exchange for a guarantee of security of life and limb, written in Hārūn's own hand and witnessed by legal scholars and the most senior members of the Abbasid family.[59] Yahya duly came to court, but he seems to have been confined, either under house arrest or in prison. Shortly afterwards the unfortunate man died in custody in mysterious circumstances.[60]

All this had occurred a decade before the fall of the Barmakids, but at least one contemporary authority maintained that relations with Yahya were the main cause of the family's disgrace.[61] The story goes like this:

When Yahya was under arrest he was put in the charge of Ja'far the Barmakid. In conversation with Ja'far, Yahya played on Ja'far's conscience, warning him that he might be incurring the hostility of the Prophet of God himself if he did not help his prisoner. Finally Ja'far relented and allowed him to go. According to one account, Hārūn asked Ja'far about the imprisoned Alid during a convivial evening. Ja'far began by saying that he was in prison, shackled in close confinement, but he soon suspected, 'for he was a man of the finest mind, and very shrewd', that Hārūn knew what he had done. He was reduced to saying that Yahya was very ill and did not have much longer to live so he had let him go. Hārūn appeared to accept his explanation and even added that he himself would have done the same, but as soon as Ja'far left the room, he muttered that he would kill him for his disloyalty.[62]

A more circumstantial version of the same story[63] is set in Hārūn's court. In it an unknown man appeared and said he had a confidential message for the caliph. Hārūn asked that he wait until the hottest part of the day when the courtiers had retired for their siestas. He dismissed his sons and told his servants to withdraw out of earshot. The man then said that he had been in an inn in Hulwan, on the Khurasan road, just where it left the plain before entering the Zagros passes. There he had seen Yahya ibn Abd Allah in a rough woollen cloak. There was a group of people with him but they kept a discreet distance.

All this came as news to Hārūn, who had imagined that Yahya was safely in custody with Ja'far the Barmakid. He first needed to make certain that the man was telling the truth. The man explained that he had known Yahya before, and when the caliph asked him to describe the Alid, he was able to reply: 'he is of medium height, light brown colour, bald over both temples, has fine eyes and a pot-belly'. In response to further questions, the man said that he had not heard Yahya say anything but that he had prayed the afternoon prayer. When asked what his own background was, he explained that his family had been supporters of the Abbasid revolution in Merv but he himself had been born in Baghdad. In this version, Hārūn does not confront Ja°far about the treachery he has discovered, but it is an important factor in turning the caliph against his old friend in the long term.

There is also a 'harem intrigue' explanation of the sudden fall of the Barmakids.[64] Tabari recounts it from an otherwise unknown source, but the story enjoyed a long afterlife, being recounted with further elaborations and details by later writers. According to this version, Hārūn was very fond of his sister Abbāsa, and wanted her to be able to join him and Ja°far in their drinking parties. It was quite out of the question for a princess of the ruling family to join with a non-relative (Ja°far) on such intimate and informal occasions. Hārūn decided on a stratagem to get round this difficulty. 'I am marrying her to you,' he told Ja°far, 'so that you will be allowed to look at her when I bring her to parties, but only on condition that you do not touch her.' They were married on these conditions and Abbāsa duly attended the parties, but one evening, when Hārūn had left them and they were both a bit drunk, they had sex. According to later versions, Abbāsa really fancied Ja°far and, aided by her mother, tricked him into having intercourse with her in the dark when he thought she was one of his slave girls.[65] Abbāsa became pregnant and, scared that her brother would find out, sent the child to Mecca to be brought up with a nurse. In Tabari's version, there is a falling out between Abbāsa and one of her slave girls and the girl tells the whole story to Hārūn, filling in the details about who was looking after the infant and what jewels her mother had given her. In another, later, version, it is Zubayda, Hārūn's wife, who gives the game away because she is jealous of the Barmakids and wants to undermine them. When he went on pilgrimage, Hārūn found the child and confirmed the details. It was then that he determined to kill Ja°far.

As an explanation for these tragic events, the story is very improbable. The great fourteenth-century Arab historian Ibn Khaldūn tried to dismiss it, but vivid and memorable stories acquire a life of their own. The 'harem intrigue' became a classic form of popular historical discourse and the story of Abbāsa is one of its most typical examples.

The fall of the Barmakids puzzled contemporaries and it is impossible to suggest reasons with any certainty. It may be simply that Hārūn had outgrown and resented their tutelage. Certainly the other theories, the Alid conspiracy and the harem intrigue, hardly seem enough to explain these momentous events. But the explanations in themselves are an interesting reflection of the framework in which people at the time tried to explain and make sense of political events.

And of course the fall of the Barmakids provided a wonderfully vivid example of the fickleness of fortune and the transitory nature of worldly power and riches. The poets of the day were unrestrained in their laments for the past glory of the family, not least because they had been such generous patrons. One harks back to that most typical of classical Arabic tropes, the desert journey and the deserted campsite, and uses it to produce a lament for lost glory:

> *Now we rest, and rest our steeds;*
> *Stopped is the traveller and he whom he travelled for.*
> *Tell your mounts, 'You're saved a night journey*
> *Crossing the desert one after another.'*
> *Tell the fates, 'You got Jaʿfar;*
> *After him, you'll never get anyone better.'*
> *Tell the gifts, 'After Fadl you must cease'.*
> *Tell the afflictions, 'Every day you'll be renewed.'*

Another poet laments the drying up of generosity:

> *Fallen the stars of giving: withered the hand of the dew*
> *Dry are the seas of generosity after the Barmakids*
> *Fallen the star of the sons of Barmak*
> *By which the guide knew his way through the desert.*

The poets might grieve over the loss of their benefactors, but there seems to have been very little political reaction to the fall of the Barmakids, and certainly no open protest. Their supporters and clients no doubt felt it better to keep a low profile.

There is one exception, and that is the poignant story of Ibrāhīm ibn Uthmān ibn Nahīk.[66] Ibrāhīm came from one of the military families of Khurasani origin who had been the backbone of the army of the early Abbasids. He himself had been left in charge of the *huram* and the treasury in Raqqa when Hārūn had left to go on his 802 pilgrimage. No one could seriously have doubted his loyalty to the caliph or his dynasty. Ibrāhīm was greatly distressed by the fall of the Barmakids. In the privacy of his own home, when he had had some drinks with his slave girls, he would boast about how he would revenge Jaᶜfar, calling for his sword, called the Doomdealer, which he would unsheathe, saying how he would slay Jaᶜfar's killer. There is no indication that this was anything more than drunken boasting, and it was certainly not for public consumption. No one would have known about this except that his son thought it necessary to tell Fadl ibn Rabī about it, and Fadl told the caliph. The caliph interrogated the son, and Ibrāhīm's secretary, who corroborated the story. Even then the caliph was reluctant to act, saying, 'It is not right for me to kill one of my old friends on the word of a youth and a eunuch. They may have plotted this together, the son hoping to inherit his father's rank, the servant to settle a score.'

Hārūn decided to put Ibrāhīm to the test. One night, when dinner had been removed, he invited Ibrāhīm to come and drink with him. They sat down together and Hārūn sent away the slave boys so that there were just the two of them. Then he asked Ibrāhīm if he could keep a secret, for there was something that was weighing heavily on his mind and keeping him awake at night. Ibrāhīm, no doubt flattered by this confidence, said that he could. Then the caliph continued, 'I have regretted the death of Jaᶜfar the Barmakid more than I can say. I would happily give up all my power if only it would bring him back. Since his death I have not slept properly nor have I enjoyed life at all since I killed him.' It was blatant entrapment and Ibrāhīm, no doubt well gone in wine by this time, fell for it. He burst into tears and told Hārūn he had acted in haste: Jaᶜfar had been an outstanding man and there was no one like him.

Suddenly the atmosphere changed. 'The curse of God fall upon you, you son of an uncircumcised woman,' shouted the caliph. Ibrāhīm instantly knew that he was doomed. He rose up, 'scarcely knowing where he was going', and went home to his mother. 'Mother,' he said, 'I am a dead man!'

'Please God, no!' she said. 'What is the matter, my son?'

'The matter is that Hārūn has caught me out so that if I had a thousand lives, I could not save a single one of them.'

Hārūn did nothing, but only a short time after this Ibrāhīm's son, the one who had first betrayed him, came upon him and killed him with his sword. The son may have hoped to inherit his father's position, but his infamous behaviour does not seem to have done him any good and the historical record is silent about his fate.

Hārūn was to rule for another six years, and it is easy to see these as something of an anti-climax. Certainly in intellectual and cultural terms, the court was seriously diminished by the loss of these generous and broad-minded patrons. But Hārūn was still a comparatively young man who might easily rule for another twenty years, and he certainly had plans for the future.

No one could take the place of the Barmakids at court. Fadl ibn Rabī now consolidated his position as the caliph's chief administrator and adviser. He was the son of that Rabī who had served Mansūr and Mahdi so long and faithfully. After his father's death in 786, the young Fadl inherited much of his wealth and status. Like his father, he attracted the support of the freedmen and other servants who worked in the palace and who formed a powerful pressure group. He was both competent and loyal to the caliph but perhaps rather dour and shifty, without any of the flamboyance and spectacular generosity of the Barmakids. But we must always remember that the sources give a glowing picture of his rivals while Fadl himself inspired no such literary adulation. Rabī seems to have had good relations with Yahya the Barmakid, but these did not continue into the next generation. Fadl appears repeatedly in anecdotes as the rival of the Barmakids and the channel by which those who opposed them could get the ear of the caliph.

Hārūn's last years were dominated by two main issues, the war against Byzantium and problems in the province of Khurasan.

Hārūn had never lost interest in the *Jihād* against the Byzantines, and in the years after the fall of the Barmakids he very consciously developed his role as leader of the Muslims against the ancient enemy. He had a special *qalansūwa* made for himself with an inscription saying *Ghāzī wa Ḥājj* (Warrior for the Faith and Pilgrim) written on it,[67] and he devoted time and energy to leading the Muslims in person. And of course the poets celebrated him in these two roles:

He who seeks you or wants to find you
Must look in the Holy Cities or the remotest frontiers
In the land of the enemy, on a fiery horse
Or the land of wellbeing (?) on a camel's saddle.[68]

The immediate reason for the renewed offensive against the Byzantines was the fact that the empress Irene, who had made the previous agreement with Hārūn, had been deposed, and Nikephorus appointed in her place. He renounced the treaty and is said to have written to Hārūn with a chess metaphor: 'the Queen who was my predecessor put you in the knight's square and herself in the square of the pawn and sent you the sort of wealth that you should really have been sending to her, but that was because of the weakness of women and their foolishness'. He went on to say that if the money was not returned there would be war between them. Hārūn put on a public display of indignation, calling for pen and ink and writing on the back of the letter: 'In the name of God, the Compassionate, the Merciful. From Hārūn, Commander of the Faithful, to Nikephorus the dog of the Byzantines: I have read your letter, son of an infidel woman. You shall see my answer, and it will not be in words.'[69]

With this exchange of unpleasantries, war was effectively declared. In the autumn of 803 Hārūn led his army to the small Anatolian city of Heraclea and ravaged the area around it, after which the Byzantines sued for peace.[70] The truce did not last long. In the summer of 806 the Byzantines raided into Muslim frontier territory, taking a number of prisoners. In response Hārūn led a major expedition, said, probably with considerable exaggeration, to have numbered 135,000 men. The caliph took with him many of the most senior and experienced soldiers in the Abbasid army, and there was a large contingent of volunteers who saw this as an opportunity to show their zeal for the Faith and practise the *Jihād*. The city of Heraclea was once more the objective, and this time it was taken in August 806 after a thirty-day siege. The inhabitants were deported and settled in a new Heraclea, just up the Euphrates from Raqqa. There were also naval campaigns in which Cyprus was ravaged and numerous prisoners taken.

Once more Nikephorus sued for peace, promising to pay a general tribute but also a personal poll tax for himself and his son, a particular and individual humiliation.[71] We also have a story from this campaign which puts relations between the two sovereigns in rather a different light. According to this, Nikephorus wrote to Hārūn about a slave girl from Heraclea whom he had betrothed to his son. She had been captured and he was writing to ask whether she could be returned. For good measure, he also asked for some perfumes and one of the caliph's tents. Hārūn had the girl found and seated on a couch in his own tent. He then gave the girl, the tent and all its furnishings, along with the perfumes, to the Byzantine envoys and added some dates and sweetmeats as an extra. In return Nikephorus sent a donkey-load of money, a hundred robes of silk brocade, two hundred robes of linen brocade, twelve falcons, four hunting dogs and three horses, all suitably princely gifts. We need not believe the story as it stands, though it is contemporary or near contemporary: it is wholly unbelievable that the emperor would betroth a slave girl from an obscure provincial town to his son. It does, however, portray relations between the two monarchs in a more chivalrous, even romantic, vein, a world of luxury goods and beautiful women and presents an interesting contrast with the more rigorist views of *Jihād*.

The other focus of Hārūn's activity was the great province of Khurasan in the north-east of the empire. This area had been the original centre of the Abbasid movement, but many of the people were now becoming disaffected. The root cause of the discontent seems to have been tensions between two groups. One was the descendants of the members of the original Abbasid armies, now mostly living in Baghdad and the west and often called *Abnā*, or the Sons. They had mostly come from fairly modest social backgrounds in the area, and even if their leaders had become rich in the service of the Abbasids, they still wanted to control their ancestral homeland and benefit from the taxation raised there. Opposed to them were groups of local aristocrats and landowners, sometimes rather grandly called 'kings', who saw no reason why they should continue to be taxed and oppressed by members of the *Abnā*. With the sole exception of Fadl the Barmakid, who came from an aristocratic family that had supported the Abbasids from the beginning, the governors of the province were members of the *Abnā*.

Since 796 the governor had been Alī ibn Īsā ibn Māhān, an important figure among the *Abnā* and a military man who had been one of the short-lived caliph Hādī's chief supporters. Alī ibn Īsā has had a bad press from the historians, but not all the accounts of his oppression and injustice should be taken at face value. Nonetheless, it is clear that he practised extortion on a large scale and that he exploited the local landowners for the benefit of the *Abnā*. One of his victims told how he was forced to feign paralysis to escape the attention of Alī's heavies, and the father of Tāhir, later to be the leader of Ma'mūn's forces, felt it wise to leave the province until things improved and take himself off to Mecca.[72]

As long as Alī retained the support of the caliph, he was untouchable. In 805, in response to complaints from the province, Hārūn decided to go to Khurasan in person to sort matters out. It was a bold and unprecedented step. Although Khurasan was the cradle of the dynasty, no reigning caliph had ever been there before. When he reached Rayy, on the western frontier of the province, he paused for about four months until Alī came to him with vast loads of presents, money, rare furnishings, musk, jewels, vessels of gold and silver, weapons and horses. He was also careful to give generous gifts to the caliph's sons, secretaries and all the members of his court.[73] The extravagant bribery had its effect and Alī was allowed to retain control of the province.

Soon after this, however, real trouble broke out in the area in the shape of a rebellion in Samarqand, led by one Rāfi ibn Layth. Rāfi was the grandson of Nasr ibn Sayyār, the last Umayyad governor of Khurasan, a man who had opposed the Abbasid movement at every stage until he had been killed in battle. His family seem to have continued to be important members of the local aristocracy, however. The story of the revolt begins with a lonely woman, whose name we do not know, married to a rich Arab in the city. He had pushed off to Baghdad and left her in Samarqand. She soon heard that he had taken concubines and had children by them. She was very fed up and tried to find ways of freeing herself. Her plight came to the attention of Rāfi. He was attracted by the woman and also by her enormous wealth. He devised a really dodgy scheme whereby she would declare that God had a 'partner' (i.e. she was not a monotheist: saying that God had a 'partner' was an accusation frequently levelled at Christians) and thereby cease to be a Muslim. This would automatically mean that she was divorced. But the penalty for apostasy was death, so Rāfi suggested that she should immediately repent. She would then be free to do as she wished. By anyone's reckoning this was a pretty dubious procedure, but Rāfi reckoned he could get away with it and duly married the divorcee.

Meanwhile her ex-husband in Baghdad had complained to the caliph, who wrote to Alī in Khurasan demanding that he force the couple to divorce and that he punish Rāfi by flogging him and parading him round Samarqand in chains on a donkey. Rāfi reluctantly agreed to the divorce but was still put in prison. Eventually, after a good deal of confusion, Rāfi escaped with the help of a local official and took his revenge by killing Alī's governor of Samarqand. Rāfi may have been a rogue but he clearly had lots of friends, and he was soon acknowledged as governor of his home city in open defiance of the authorities. He attracted widespread support in Transoxania among those dissatisfied with Alī's government, and when Alī's son was sent with an army to deal with him, he was driven away. Gradually the rebellion attracted more support; the local ruler of Shash (Tashkent) joined his forces and Alī's son was killed.[74]

As long as Alī had kept the province under control, and continued to send the presents, Hārūn was content to keep him in office. Now that he seemed to be losing the plot, he determined to dismiss him. He knew, however, that he had a difficult task on his hands, for Alī was a powerful and unscrupulous man who could call on many supporters, especially among the *Abnā* in Baghdad. Tabari gives a long and detailed account of how he was able to do this which reveals the limitations of the powers of the caliphs. He had to catch Alī unawares and give him no opportunity to raise his supporters.

Hārūn called upon the services of Harthama ibn Ayan. We know nothing of the origins of Harthama – he seems to have been something of an outsider among the Baghdad military – but he was devotedly loyal to the caliph and could be relied upon to act in his interests alone. The caliph wrote to Alī in Khurasan saying that he was sending Harthama to help him against his enemies. Meanwhile Harthama was ordered to gain Alī's confidence before presenting him with the caliph's letter announcing his dismissal.

Harthama moved with elaborate caution. When he reached Nishapur, he assigned each of his followers a district to take over and made them promise to keep the matter secret. A day's journey from the capital at Merv, he distributed lists of members of Alī's family and staff who were to be arrested. He also wrote to Alī asking him to send servants to collect the money he was bringing, but when they arrived his men made excuses and held Alī's agents back, saying that they needed to make special arrangements for the horses to transport the money. When Harthama finally arrived in Merv, Alī was unsuspecting and came out to greet him. As they entered the city they embraced on horseback and exchanged courtesies: 'You go first!' 'No, you!' They ate together, and Alī said that he had cleared a palace for Harthama in the fashionable Majan canal area of the city.

It was only at this point that Harthama said, 'Actually, I have some matters to discuss which cannot be put off,' and it was then that he produced Hārūn's letter. As soon as he had read the first line, Alī knew what had happened. The opening words, 'You son of an adulteress', can have left him in little doubt, and the letter went on to reproach him for abusing his power. 'I have appointed Harthama ... to grind his heel upon you, your sons, your secretaries and your agent.' He was to be arrested and all his wealth confiscated.[75]

Alī, totally taken by surprise, allowed himself to be put in chains while Harthama went to the great mosque and addressed the people, stressing that Alī had been deposed and a new era of justice would begin.[76] However, it was not so easy to restore peace in the province, and Rāfi and his allies among the local aristocracy refused to be reconciled. Faced with this open rebellion in so crucial an area, Hārūn decided to go in person to assert the authority of the caliph. It was a bold and determined move to establish his personal authority.

The caliph left Raqqa by boat in February 808 for Baghdad, where he remained for some time. On the afternoon of 5 June he left the capital for what proved to be the last time, with a large army and his son Ma'mūn, who was to be viceroy of Khurasan. By the end of the year he had reached the ancient city of Tūs. The omens were good: he was met on the road by 1,500 camels laden with Alī ibn Īsā's treasure, and received news from Harthama that he had captured Bukhara. He sent Ma'mūn ahead to take control, while he remained, sick, at Tūs. It was here, on 24 March 809, that he died and was buried in the country house in which he was staying. He was probably 47 years old.[77]

IV

The War between the Brothers

At the moment of Hārūn's death, the caliphate had never looked more prosperous and secure. True, there were problems in Khurasan, problems the caliph was travelling to redress, North Africa remained as difficult to control as ever, and the Caucasus frontier might prove vulnerable to the attacks of Khazars and other Turkic nomads, but these were all problems which could be dealt with. The ancient enemy, the Byzantines, were in no position to pose a serious threat and recent campaigns against them had been more of a military promenade than a fight to the death, and great for the prestige of the caliph, who could advertise himself as the champion of Islam. The fall of the Barmakids in 803 had certainly left a gap at the heart of the administration – officials spoke of bags of letters piled up unopened in offices, but tax revenues continued to flow in, poets were still paid and the royal court moved with all its accustomed splendour. Nothing, in short, gave any warning of the horrors to come.

At first all seemed to go with impeccable efficiency. News of the caliph's death was brought by one of the royal servants, using the network of post horses, the *barīd*, which held the empire together and provided its information superhighway. The servant, a eunuch called Rajā, covered the 1,900 kilometres between Tūs and the capital in an extraordinary eleven or twelve days, which meant an average speed of about 150 kilometres a day. Speeds like that were not bettered before the coming of motor transport in the twentieth century. He brought with him the insignia of royalty, the mantle of the Prophet, the sceptre and the caliph's seal.[1] When he heard the news the heir apparent, Amīn, moved from the riverside Palace of Eternity into the old palace by the great mosque in the heart of the Round City, built by his great-grandfather. Caliphs seldom stayed there any more but it remained the setting for solemn and formal events. The next Friday (6 April 809), the new caliph ordered people to assemble in the mosque. He led the prayers in the usual way and then mounted the pulpit, where, after praising God, he announced his father's death. He promised a reign of peace and security for all. Then the leading figures in the state came to pledge their allegiance in person, no doubt taking his hand in the traditional way. After the elite had taken their oaths, the caliph himself retired, leaving one of his uncles to take the oath from less important people while a senior court officer, Sindi ibn Shāhik, was entrusted with the task of securing the loyalty of the military commanders and of paying the troops a bonus of twenty-four months' salary, just to make sure that the succession passed smoothly. The ample resources Hārūn had left in the treasury meant that there was no problem in doing this.

Meanwhile, in Merv, the capital of Khurasan, similar ceremony was being played out on a smaller scale. Prince Ma'mūn went to the Government House and addressed the people from the pulpit, announcing his father's death and tearing his clothes as a sign of his grief. Like the mosque in Baghdad, Government House in Merv was a place redolent of Abbasid tradition. It was here that Abū Muslim had first established himself and openly called the people to obey the Abbasids. The great dome he had constructed with open arches on either side was still the greatest monument in the city. The oath was taken to Amīn as caliph and, once again, the troops were paid.

Power seemed to have passed with smooth efficiency from one generation to another, just as the old caliph had stipulated, but under the surface all was not well. The divided-inheritance scheme designed with such care by Hārūn had polarized the ruling class between the two princes, Amīn and Ma'mūn. Almost without exception the Abbasid establishment, the members of the royal family, senior administrators like Fadl ibn Rabī and the leading military men supported Amīn and believed that the old caliph had given Ma'mūn far too much autonomy and power: eventually he would have to be removed from the succession and replaced by one of Amīn's own sons. Ma'mūn had no such solid base of support, but many of the rich Khurasani aristocrats who had opposed Alī ibn Īsā and supported Rāfi ibn Layth began to see that by supporting Ma'mūn they could take control of their own province and not have to put up with governors sent from distant Baghdad. Furthermore Ma'mūn's mother, though long dead, was one of them, and her memory could be invoked to whip up support.

Hārūn's death was unexpected and many important people found themselves wrong-footed by it. Fadl ibn Rabī was with Hārūn in Tūs when his master died, but he really needed to be in Baghdad to manage the affairs of the new caliph and Amīn certainly needed him. When he had heard that his father was ill, Amīn had sent an agent to the court. He had with him letters written in Amīn's own hand for his brother Sālih, who was in the royal party, other members of the court and for Ma'mūn. The letters were secreted in the hollow legs of wooden chests covered with leather. When this man appeared in the royal party, Hārūn was deeply suspicious and ordered his arrest, but the agent refused to confess to his real mission. Now the caliph was dead he came to Fadl and the letters were handed out: Sālih was ordered to make sure that the army was under the control of officers Amīn could rely on. Fadl himself was ordered to return as quickly as possible to Baghdad, carrying with him the caliph's treasury. The letter to Ma'mūn was not unfriendly and simply exhorted him to obey all the terms of the agreements that they had made.

Despite these cordial greetings, the rest of 809 and the whole of 810 saw a growing estrangement between the two brothers which developed into outright hostility. There were many different pressures and cross-currents. The two princes themselves do not seem to have held any personal animosity. Many advisers on both sides urged a peaceful solution to any differences. A lot of anonymous voices called for compromise: 'People say that if a matter is dangerous, it is better to give your rival part of what he wants than to come into open conflict with him by refusing'[2] and 'If you are worried that yielding voluntarily will have consequences, the breach that will be caused if we do not avoid a split will be even more serious' were among the sentiments expressed. The dread of disorder and violence within the Muslim community was palpable.

But there were other, more strident voices, who were determined that they would have their way, even if the young princes were reluctant and the vast majority of the people wanted peace. On Amīn's side, Fadl ibn Rabī, Hārūn's veteran chamberlain, pressed Amīn to have his own son Mūsā adopted as heir apparent in place of Ma'mūn. Even a young and healthy man like Amīn might die suddenly: Fadl could not risk Ma'mūn taking over in these circumstances. With him stood Alī ibn Īsā ibn Māhān, the ex-governor of Khurasan whose exactions had caused the problems Hārūn had been trying to solve when he died. Alī was now released from prison and assumed a leading position in the war camp. He led the *Abnā* – those soldiers in Baghdad of Khurasani origin who believed that they should control the government and live off the taxation of their ancestral homeland. For them, direct rule of the province from Baghdad was a principle on which they could not compromise.

Faced by the might of the Abbasid establishment and the military, Ma'mūn might well have been prepared to accept his brother's demands but he too had a Svengali-like character urging him to resist. This was another Fadl, Fadl ibn Sahl. He came from one of those prosperous Persian landowning families of rural Iraq whose fortunes had survived both the Muslim conquest and the Abbasid revolution. None of his kinsmen until now had played a part in politics and Fadl and his brother Sahl were the first members of the family to be converted to Islam. Although they adopted the new religion, and certainly spoke and wrote fluent Arabic, the brothers were very conscious of their Persian heritage.

Fadl ibn Sahl had found himself in the entourage of the young prince Ma'mūn in Merv. He saw his opportunity and started to build up a coalition of support for his master in Khurasan. He would appeal to all sections of opinion in the huge province that could be united in their detestation of rule from Baghdad. He played on the memory of Ma'mūn's Persian mother, saying that he would be among his maternal uncles and that the Persian aristocracy of the province would support one of their own. Others could be won over by tax concessions. Gradually Fadl succeeded in gathering support for resistance to Amīn's demands. Many in Khurasan remained reluctant, not wanting to open the gates of civil war or fearing that the project would fail. Ma'mūn himself needed constant encouragement not to lose his nerve.

Meanwhile the diplomatic prelude to war was being played out. We have the text of a number of letters the two princes, or their advisers, wrote to each other. The tone is polite but increasingly icy. The purpose was not so much to avoid war as to show that, when it did start, it would be the fault of the other party. Amīn demanded the handing over of certain frontier districts and revenues that he claimed his brother did not need. Ma'mūn replied by saying that there had been a misunderstanding: the frontiers of Khurasan were threatened by powerful enemies (the Turks) and he needed these resources. 'Son of my father,' he went on, 'do not make me come into conflict with you when I willingly grant you obedience, nor to become estranged from you when I want to be on friendly terms.'[3] Amīn's advisers were unimpressed and wrote back in his name, 'I have received your letter in which you show ingratitude for God's favour towards you…your refusal to obey me was more tolerable than your ingratitude to God. I only made the requests for your benefit and the well-being of the majority of your subjects. It would also establish you in a position of security and peace.'[4]

Fadl ibn Sahl then moved on to the offensive. He wrote asking that Amīn send Ma'mūn's wife and two sons, who were still in Iraq, to Khurasan to be with him. To refuse to send his family to him would certainly demonstrate Amīn's lack of goodwill. Again the language was polite: 'Although my family are adequately provided for by the Commander of the Faithful [Amīn], who has become a father to them, they cannot help desiring and longing for my protection.'[5] He also requested that Ma'mūn's private wealth should be sent: the money was necessary for the defence of the frontiers. The reply was polite but firm: Amīn would take responsibility for Ma'mūn's family: after all, the journey from Iraq to Khurasan was long and might be hazardous. As for the money, the caliph could make better use of it for the benefit of the Muslims.

At the same time the drift to war continued. Fadl ibn Sahl ordered roadblocks to be set up near Rayy, on the western frontier of Ma'mūn's domains, so that Amīn could not send agents to spy out the land. He had also dispatched an agent to Baghdad. This man sent back his reports with a woman, putting the letters in the hollowed-out board of a packsaddle: 'the "woman" passed through the border posts unmolested and unsearched, as if she was just going from one village to another'.[6] The news that came from his agent confirmed Ma'mūn's worst fears. Fadl ibn Rabī was determined to remove him from the succession and was casting around for any excuse to do so. He was also hoping to encourage people in Khurasan to reject Mamūn's rule.[7]

In the autumn of 810, the breach was almost complete. In November Amīn crossed this Rubicon when he ordered that Ma'mūn should no longer be acknowledged as heir in the Friday prayers and should be replaced by his own son Mūsā. At the same time he sent messengers to Mecca to take down the great signed documents with which Hārūn had attempted to regulate the succession beyond doubt. The texts were taken to Amīn in Baghdad, where he personally tore them up and destroyed them.[8] After this there could be no turning back. By the end of 810, just eighteen months after Hārūn's death, the phoney war was over.

Both sides now began to make their military preparations. In Baghdad Fadl ibn Rabī set about assembling a large army to invade Khurasan and depose Ma'mūn. The army was said to have been 50,000 strong, and people in Baghdad claimed it was the largest and best-equipped army they had ever seen.[9] There were ample funds to raise the salaries of the troops.[10] There was also new equipment, two thousand ornamented swords and six thousand robes of honour and, so we are told, silver chains with which to bind Ma'mūn when he was captured.[11] The command of this formidable force was entrusted to Alī ibn Īsā ibn Māhān. In many ways it was a sensible choice. He and his family enjoyed unrivalled prestige among the Baghdad military, the *Abnā*, and he knew Khurasan well. On the other hand, his tenure as governor of the province had caused enormous resentment among the local people. Alī's appointment may have helped to unite the Baghdadis behind Amīn but it certainly united the Khurasanis behind Ma'mūn. There were those who said that Ma'mūn's political guru, Fadl ibn Sahl, had asked his agents in Baghdad to encourage his appointment, knowing that it would unite opinion in Khurasan behind Ma'mūn.[12]

The army set off full of confidence. Alī left Baghdad in the late afternoon of 14 March 811, proceeding by slow stages through the canals and palm groves of the Iraqi countryside. The young caliph came with him as far as the canal-side city of Nahrawan, where he turned for home while Alī led his men towards the passes of the Zagros mountains.[13] As he marched along the road through the gorges and meadows of the Zagros mountains, heading for the upland plains of central Iran, he met caravans of merchants coming from Khurasan. On being questioned they told him that Ma'mūn had sent a small force to Rayy to guard the frontier of his domains.[14]

When the news that Amīn had removed Ma'mūn from his position as heir reached Merv, Fadl ibn Sahl, who had now become Ma'mūn's chief minister, sent troops to the frontier city of Rayy, being careful to organize supplies for them in this barren area. Compared with Alī ibn Īsā's large army, Ma'mūn's force was minute, only three or four thousand men. They would be facing odds of ten to one. As commander of the force, Fadl ibn Sahl chose a young Khurasani aristocrat, Tāhir ibn Husayn. Tāhir's family were hereditary rulers of a small principality called Bushang, which lay just to the west of Herat, on the modern Iranian–Afghan frontier. The family may have been of Arab origin and had been Muslim for several generations but they had never played a major role in the politics of the area. Tāhir, whose father Husayn was still alive, must already have acquired something of a reputation as a leader, but Fadl ibn Sahl was clearly taking something of a risk by appointing him rather than one of the more experienced military commanders to this key role. He may have felt that this was a sort of suicide mission which would be bound to fail. In the event, the appointment proved to be of immense significance and Tāhir's family were to become the most important in the caliphate after the ruling Abbasid family themselves.

Alī's large force marched along the old Khurasan road which led through the Zagros passes to Saveh and around the northern edge of the Great Desert of central Iran. By May he was approaching Rayy, where Tāhir's small force awaited him. Rayy lay a few kilometres south of Tehran, then no more than a tiny village. The city was in an important strategic position, commanding the narrow corridor of fertile and watered land between the Great Desert to the south and the steeply rising Elburz mountains to the north. As Alī's army approached, they would have seen the snow glistening on the distant peaks to the north and the wheat and barley ripening in the fields. The city itself was an ancient one, known to Alexander the Great and his army a thousand years before. Like many Iranian cities, it had expanded enormously during the early Islamic period. The young prince Mahdi had based himself there when he was governor of Khurasan in the 760s. He had built a large fortified extension to the city, which was officially known as Muhammadiya (Mahdi's name was Muhammad), but as usual the old name had stuck. Tāhir could have stayed in the city and confronted the enemy from behind these walls but he is said to have been worried that the people might rise against him if they thought that the city was in danger of being sacked by Alī's men, so he decided to go out and face them in the open field.[15]

We shall never know exactly what happened on that May day in 811 when the two armies met. Our best source is an eyewitness account by one Ahmad ibn Hishām, another young Khurasani aristocrat who was Tāhir's chief of security.

> We encamped at Qustana which is the first stage from Rayy towards Iraq while Alī and his army were some 7 farsakhs [40 kilometres] away in the desert. Alī thought that when Tāhir saw him, he would hand over Rayy to him. When he saw that Tāhir was prepared to fight, he turned off the main road to find a suitable camping place. We camped by a river and he camped nearby, separated by some sand flats and low hills. Shortly before dawn a man came and told me that Alī had sent messengers to the people of Rayy and they had responded favourably to him but we went out to the road with the man and said 'This is the route they would have taken but there are no hoof-prints and no sign that anyone has been along.'
>
> I went to Tāhir and woke him up. 'Are you going to pray?' I asked. 'Yes,' he replied and he called for water to wash himself and got ready. I told him about the report and we prayed together. Then we went out on reconnaissance and saw Alī's army but decided not to attack across the sand flats. Tāhir ordered me to draw up our forces. Alī approached with his army. The desert was filled with white and yellow from the swords and the gold. They charged and almost reached our camp before we drove them back with great difficulty.

Ahmad then suggested an attempt at negotiation, more to show Alī that he was in the wrong and undermine the morale of his men than to seek a peaceful solution.

> We attached the texts of the agreements he had sworn to Ma'mūn to two spears and I stood between the lines and shouted 'Truce! Do not shoot at us and we will not shoot at you' and Alī said, 'You have it'. I then said, 'Alī, do you not fear God? Isn't this the text of the oath of allegiance [to Ma'mūn] that you yourself had people swear? Fear God for you have reached the door of your grave!' 'Who are you?' he asked and when I told him my name he said to his troops, 'There will be a thousand dirham reward for anyone who brings him to me.'

Then the fighting resumed in earnest.

There were people from Bukhara with us and they fired volleys of arrows at Alī, saying that they would kill him and take his money. Then a man came out from Alī's army and Tāhir attacked him, grasping the hilt of his sword with two hands, struck him and felled him. Then Dāwud Siyāh [Black David] attacked Alī himself and felled him. Alī was mounted on a black and white destrier which Amīn had given him as a mount. Such a horse is thought unlucky in battle.

Ahmad also heard another, different account of Alī's death.

A young man also called Tāhir said 'Are you Alī ibn Īsā?' to which Alī replied 'Yes', imagining that his opponent would be frightened but this Tāhir attacked him and killed him with his sword. Muhammad ibn Muqātil attempted to cut off his head but only succeeded in pulling out some tufts of his beard which he sent to Tāhir announcing victory. I did not know about Alī's death until someone told me that the enemy commander had been killed.

Alī's companions continued to shoot arrows but, without their leader, they faltered and were slowly driven back.
'I went back to the scene of the encounter,' Ahmad continued,

and found a leather bag which had belonged to Alī. It contained a tunic, a coat and an undershirt. I put them on and prayed two prostrations of prayer in thanksgiving to God who is exalted and blessed. In his camp we found 700 bags with 1,000 dirhams in each one. The men of Bukhara who had taunted him saying that they would take his money, had taken possession of a number of mules carrying chests. They thought it was money but when they opened the chests they found they contained wine from the Sawad of Iraq. They divided up the bottles, saying, 'We have certainly worked hard for our drink!'
Then I went to Tāhir's tent and found that he was worried because I had been away for so long. One of my pages was carrying Alī's head in a horse's nosebag.[16] 'Good news!' he said. 'This is a tuft from Alī's beard.' 'Good news indeed', I replied to him, 'this is

Alī's head'. In thanksgiving to God, Tāhir freed all of the slaves who were with him. They brought the body of Alī; the aides had tied his hands to his feet, carried on a beam as a dead donkey would be carried. Tāhir ordered the corpse to be wrapped in a felt cloth and thrown into a well.

According to other briefer and less personal accounts there was a fierce and fairly conventional battle whose outcome was decided when Alī ibn Īsā ibn Māhān was hit by arrows from Tāhir's forces.[17]

The victory at Rayy had transformed the situation entirely. Good news travels fast. The letter that Tāhir wrote to Ma'mūn and Fadl ibn Sahl was taken by couriers who travelled all day and all night. The messengers rode on Thursday night, Friday night and Saturday night, arriving in Merv on the Sunday. The distance is about 1,150 kilometres, so the letter must have travelled about 400 kilometres a day. It shows just how efficient the Abbasid system could be.[18] The news reached Ma'mūn's court just in time. It was generally believed, even by the most optimistic of his supporters, that Tāhir would be defeated and Alī's army would come to conquer and pillage. There were many who thought that the deposition of Ma'mūn would be a price worth paying to avoid that fate.

Fadl ibn Sahl, the mastermind behind Ma'mūn's policy, was exhausted: he had not slept for three days and nights as he tried to prepare a relief force to support Tāhir. A servant announced that the mail courier had been spotted in the distance. When the messenger came in there was a moment of terrible suspense as the man stood silent, probably breathless from his exertions. Fadl feared the worst and asked him what he was hiding, but the man finally gasped 'Victory!' and handed over Tāhir's letter, in which he said, 'I am sitting here with Alī's head before me and his ring on my finger.' Fadl rushed to Ma'mūn's residence and went in to announce the good news. There could be no turning back now. On Tuesday, Alī's head arrived and orders were given that it should be paraded round Khurasan, just to convince everyone that he was really dead.[19] Tāhir was quick to take advantage of his victory. Without waiting for instructions he pushed on to the west. Alī ibn Īsā's son Yahya attempted to regroup but to no avail.

Tāhir's astonishing victory had saved Ma'mūn from disaster and vindicated Fadl ibn Sahl's policy. It had also changed the whole nature of the conflict. Up to this point the issues had been whether Ma'mūn would retain his privileged position in Khurasan and, more importantly, whether he should continue to be accepted as Amīn's heir. Now there were two caliphs, Amīn in Baghdad and Ma'mūn in Merv, each supported by backers who were determined to see their man triumph. There was no talk of dividing the empire. There would be a winner and a loser. The winner's supporters would form the new ruling elite, the power and the palaces would be theirs. The losers could look forward to a life of destitution and obscurity, if they were lucky, death if they were not.

Even after the battle of Rayy, the odds were stacked in Amīn's favour. He still controlled the richest province of the empire, Iraq, and the bulk of its armed forces, especially the *Abnā* of Baghdad, who had sustained the dynasty for so long. The Abbasid family were firmly behind him and the treasury which Hārūn had left still contained sufficient resources to fund a major campaign. Ma'mūn, on the other hand, was confined to the north-east of the empire and supported only by a group of Khurasani aristocrats and their followers. Even his own wife and sons were effectively prisoners in Baghdad. He did, however, have one major advantage. When Amīn had ordered that the documents regulating the succession should be removed from Mecca, when he had destroyed them with his own hands and removed Ma'mūn from the succession, he had clearly broken the solemn agreement he had made. His most fervent supporters might feel uneasy about this, and for many people in the Muslim community the flagrant breach of a sworn oath had tarnished his caliphate irrevocably.

In the aftermath of his victory, Tāhir knew that he had two choices. He could fortify and garrison the frontier at Rayy, keeping Khurasan safe for his master and in effect making it a separate state. On the other hand, he could take the war forward and pursue the enemy to western Iran and Iraq. The changing seasons added another imperative: the passes in the Zagros mountains might well be closed by snow from November onward and it would be much easier to winter his army in the mild lowlands of Iraq rather than the windswept bleakness of the Iranian plateau. He did not wait for orders, nor did he hesitate. Almost immediately he began to lead his army to the west, across the uplands of the lands of ancient Media and through the Zagros to Iraq. A relief force sent from Baghdad was defeated at Hamadhān and Tāhir secured his lines of communication by expelling Amīn's governor from Qazvin and garrisoning the town with his own troops.[20] By early autumn he had reached the plains of Iraq at Hulwan. Here, where the climate was mild and fodder plentiful, he made his camp and waited.

It had taken two months for the news of the defeat at Rayy to reach Baghdad. The news was as unexpected as it was unwelcome. Apart from sending the inadequate relief force to Hamadhān, the response was confused and divided. Amīn seems to have been unable to provide firm and effective leadership. It is from this period that we have a series of stories that may well be contemporary and which were certainly circulated to discredit his leadership. It was alleged that he was a homosexual, more interested in his slave boys and eunuchs than in anything else. He is said to have been fishing in the river with his favourite companion of the moment, the eunuch Kawthar, when news arrived of the defeat at Rayy. 'Go away,' he is reputed to have told the messenger, 'Kawthar has already caught two fish and I have nothing yet.'[21] A savage satirical poem was circulated which seems to have reflected a widespread mood in Baghdad:

> *The caliphate has been ruined by the vizier's [Fadl ibn Rabī's] malice*
> *The Imam's [Amīn's] dissoluteness and the counsellor's ignorance*
> *Fadl is a vizier and Bakr a counsellor*
> *Who desire what will be the death of the Caliph*
> *This is nothing but a path of delusion*
> *The worst of roads are the paths of delusion*
> *The Caliph's sodomy is amazing*
> *While the vizier's passive homosexuality is even more so.*
> *One of them buggers, the other gets buggered*
> *That is the only real difference between them.*
> *If the two only made use of each other*
> *They could manage to keep it quiet*
> *But one of them [Amīn] plunged into the eunuch Kawthar*
> *While being fucked by donkeys did not satisfy the other [Fadl ibn Rabī]*
> *Lord, take them quickly to Thyself*
> *Bring them to the punishment of hellfire*
> *Make an example of Fadl and his party*
> *And crucify them on the bridges over the Tigris!*[22]

These allegations were probably complete fantasy but they were widely circulated and people in Baghdad chose to believe them.

Fadl ibn Rabī set about recruiting more forces to oppose Tāhir, now at Hulwan and dangerously near the capital. It was not easy. Disillusion with the leadership and Tāhir's amazing success meant that those who served wanted to be properly rewarded. The *Abnā* of Baghdad were prepared to fight but they demanded to retain their salaries and near-monopoly of military power. They were not prepared to cooperate with any other groups in a common effort.

A possible alternative to the power of the *Abnā* were the Arab tribesmen who followed tribal shaykhs like the chiefs of Shaybān. The great chiefs of the early Abbasid period, Maᶜn ibn Zā'ida and his nephew Yazīd ibn Mazyad, were now dead, but Yazīd's children still enjoyed great prestige. Fadl now sent for one of them, Asad. He arrived to find the vizier sitting in the courtyard of his house, red-eyed and furious. Before Asad said anything, he launched into a tirade against Amīn, who

> has abandoned himself to fate like a foolish slave girl. He takes counsel with women and pursues dreams. The pleasure seekers and reckless men who are with him have gained his ear. They promise him victory and make him expect a good outcome, while destruction is coming towards him faster than a torrent towards a sandy plain. I fear by God that we shall perish when he perishes and we shall be destroyed when he is.

Then he turned to the matter in hand. He had summoned Asad because he was the 'Knight of the Arabs and the son of their knights'. The compliment was rich with echoes of the heroic warriors of the pre-Islamic period, and the virtues of the brave and hardy Arabs of the desert. He could rely on his determination and he urged him to move fast against the enemy. Asad was not so easily convinced; his men would need money: after all, the *Abnā* of Baghdad were always being given gifts and benefits and he wanted the same for his men. He also demanded to be given a free hand to use the cities and districts he conquered as he saw fit, but what was worse was that he wanted the two sons of Ma'mūn to be handed over to him to be used as hostages. Fadl excused himself by saying that the decision would be left to the caliph. Amīn was furious, saying that he had already offered promotion to high command and control over all the tax revenues of Khurasan. 'Now you want me to kill my children and spill the blood of my own family.' He concluded, 'You are nothing but a mad Bedouin,' and ordered Asad's arrest.

Of course, this did not solve the problem of recruiting Bedouin volunteers for the army. Amīn and Rabī searched around for another man who could command the same sort of prestige and decided to approach Ahmad ibn Mazyad, Asad's uncle, who seemed to have the necessary qualities. Ahmad was in the country, going by boat with his family, his freedmen and his entourage to visit a country estate of his in southern Iraq where the Tigris flowed into the Great Swamp. It was dark and he was only a mile from his property when he heard the voice of a messenger of the postal service. As he wondered out loud what a courier was doing at this time in this place, the messenger shouted to the boatman, 'Is Ahmad b. Mazyad with you?' When he was told that he was, the rider dismounted and gave him the caliph's letter. After he had read it, he said to the messenger that he was very close to his estate and asked permission to visit it and give the necessary instructions and he would come the next day. The messenger was adamant: he had to come immediately. So Ahmad returned there and then, pausing for a day in Kūfa to collect equipment and supplies, and then went on to Amīn.[23]

When he reached the capital, he went first to Fadl ibn Rabī. He found him with one of the leaders of the *Abnā*, Abd Allah ibn Humayd, who Fadl was also trying to persuade to lead his men against the enemy. Fadl was gracious and complimentary, saying that the caliph was going to offer Ahmad a rank above anything his family had attained before. Then he ordered horses to be made ready and the three of them went to the caliph. They found him in the courtyard of his residence, and he bade Ahmad come closer until he was almost touching him. He explained how he had been unable to work with his nephew Asad but had been told that he, Ahmad, was a fine man and a great warrior. Ahmad agreed to lead the force and Amīn ordered Fadl to give Ahmad the registers containing the names of Asad's men as well as men from the Jazira and the Bedouin who were around the camp. Ahmad went through the registers and selected some twenty thousand men. He and Abd Allah ibn Humayd then set out to confront Tāhir at Hulwan, Ahmad with his twenty thousand and Abd Allah with twenty thousand *Abnā*. The caliph

urged them to cooperate against the common enemy. They should
have been able to overwhelm Tāhir with ease.

In the event, they never had the chance to prove themselves in
battle. They camped at Khaniqin, nowadays the border post between
Iraq and Iran on the main road. Tāhir stayed in his fortifications a
few miles away at Hulwan. From here he sent agents to the enemy
camp. They played on the fears and jealousies between Ahmad's men
and Abd Allah's, saying that the others had obtained special favours
and higher rates of pay. The camp was soon in complete disorder,
Abnā and Bedouin fighting each other. They abandoned Khaniqin
and straggled back to Baghdad in complete disarray.[24] The same
sorry story was repeated elsewhere. When Amīn sent his cousin, the
veteran Abd al-Malik ibn Salih, to Syria to raise soldiers, he initially
met with an enthusiastic response. Many Syrians who had been
excluded from the military after the Abbasid revolution saw this as a
way to recover their status. But once again the jealousy of the *Abnā*,
fearful of losing their salaries, made cooperation impossible.[25] Faced
with the threat from outside and the inability of the caliph to provide
effective leadership, even the *Abnā* began to quarrel among themselves, one faction kidnapping and deposing the caliph before a rival
group released and reinstated him.[26] In the midst of this disorder,
Fadl ibn Rabī, who had done so much to foment discord and encourage Amīn to attack his brother, went into hiding. He did not reap-
pear in public until eight years later, when Ma'mūn finally entered
Baghdad in triumph.

From his base at Hulwan, Tāhir could observe all this with quiet
satisfaction. He was not strong enough to risk an all-out assault on
Baghdad, but every day that passed saw his enemies plunged into
further disorder. At some time in the autumn, Ma'mūn and Fadl ibn
Sahl sent a new commander, Harthama ibn Ayan, with reinforcements to take over from Tāhir. Harthama had served Hārūn for
many years and, as part of the Abbasid establishment, had a loyalty
to the dynasty which Tāhir, for one, lacked. Tāhir had probably
never met Amīn; Harthama had known him well since childhood.
Nonetheless, unlike other members of the establishment, he had
supported Ma'mūn. He worked for his master faithfully but tried to
arrange compromises when he could. Harthama took over at Hulwan
while Tāhir, by now something of an expert in fast-moving warfare,
set out in a broad sweep to conquer southern Iraq.

Some of the local governors held out against him. Muhammad ibn Yazid al-Muhallabi was Amīn's governor at Ahwāz. Lying in the fertile lands of Khuzistān, watered by the rivers from the Zagros mountains and famous for its linen industry, Ahwāz was a prosperous and thriving centre. Muhammad was the scion of one of the oldest and most respected families in the caliphate. His great-great-grandfather, Muhallab, had led his Azdi tribesmen from Oman to Iraq in the years immediately after the Arab conquests of the 630s. He had been one of the great heroes of early Islam: in poetry and legend his memory lingered on. His descendants had been advisers to caliphs and governors of Khurasan. They had also fallen out with the Umayyads and transferred their allegiance without difficulty to the incoming Abbasids. Muhallabis were appointed as governors of parts of Iraq, Sind, Egypt and Tunisia. Along with their political power, they had built up a network of commercial contacts, and it seems that they grew rich from the trade that flowed through the great port of Basra at the head of the Gulf. Muhammad ibn Yazid had an impressive heritage to maintain.

When he heard of Tāhir's advance, he assembled his forces and went out to meet the enemy on the edge of the settled lands, with the fields and villages behind him. He then began to lose his nerve and, consulting his followers, decided to fortify himself in his capital at Ahwāz while he summoned reinforcements and members of his tribe from Basra to support him. So he retreated with Tāhir's men hard on his heels, determined not to let him regroup. When he reached the city, he turned to fight but the enemy were already upon him, pelting his men with stones as a prelude to battle. Slowly his forces were driven back and his men began to flee. Muhammad then addressed his freedmen, saying that his army was breaking up but that he would not flee: 'I shall dismount and fight by myself until God decrees what he wants. Any of you who want to go, go now! By God, I would rather that you survived than that you perish and are destroyed.' They replied, 'Then we would be betraying you, by God! You freed us from slavery, raised us up from humiliation and enriched us when we were poor. How could we abandon you at this stage? No, we will advance with you and die beside the stirrup of your horse. May God curse this world and give you life after your death!' Then they dismounted, hamstrung their horses (so that they could not flee) and advanced, killing many of the enemy before

Muhammad was struck with a spear and fell. The poets lamented him:

> *A just and generous man has passed away.*
> *I have lost in him my heart and my hearing*
> *And my eyes are overwhelmed with tears*
> *He was succour in times of drought*
> *But now the rain clouds of spring have disappeared.*[27]

There were few others who shared Muhammad's sense of duty and honour or who were prepared to sacrifice themselves for the discredited Amīn. As Tāhir's forces moved on from Ahwāz, the local governors hastened to surrender. The governor of Basra, the biggest city in the area, surrendered by post. When Tāhir's men approached Wasit, the local commander summoned his master of horse as if to prepare for war:

> the man brought him a horse but [the commander] kept shifting his eyes from one horse to another for there were a number before him. The Master of the Horses saw the panic in his eyes and said 'If you are going to flee, this is the one for you. She gallops further and faster than any other!' So the commander laughed and replied, 'Bring the escape horse here! It is Tāhir so we need not be ashamed to flee from him'. So both of them left Wasit and fled.[28]

Meanwhile, in the Holy Cities of Mecca and Medina, a different drama was being played out. The governor here, Dāwud ibn Īsā, was a member of a cadet branch of the Abbasid family. He had been appointed by Amīn and had led the pilgrimage in his name twice. However, when Amīn sent his men to remove the sworn covenants from the Kaᶜaba, Dāwud was shocked. He assembled the doorkeepers of the Kaᶜaba and all the prominent Muslims who, like himself, had witnessed the signing of the documents. He reminded them how they had all sworn to support the wronged against the wrongdoer. 'Now', he continued, 'he [Amīn] has deposed his brothers and has had allegiance sworn to his infant son, a babe not yet weaned. He has wrongly had the two documents removed from the Kaᶜaba and had them burned. I have decided to renounce my allegiance to him and to swear allegiance to Ma'mūn as caliph.' The assembled notables said that they agreed with him. Dāwud then sent criers all round the city, urging people to come to the mosque to midday prayer. He had the pulpit placed near the Black Stone itself (in the corner of the Kaᶜaba which is the focus of Muslim devotion), and encouraged the people to come close.

He then began to speak. He was a powerful orator and the people listened. He reminded them of their special responsibilities as upholders of the covenant that had been lodged in their own city. Amīn had 'violated the conditions he had voluntarily agreed to in the Sacred House' and he should be deposed. 'I have cast off Amīn,' he concluded, 'just as I have cast off this *qalansūwa*' (the tall formal headdress). He took off his *qalansūwa*, which was made of striped Yemeni cloth, and threw it to one of the servants at his feet. Then he put on a formal black *qalansūwa* instead, came down from the pulpit, sat at one end of the mosque and invited the people to swear allegiance to Ma'mūn. They came in groups and for several days he sat there. When each group came, he read them the oath of allegiance to Ma'mūn and they took his hand. The breaking of the oath had fatally damaged Amīn's caliphate in the Holy Cities and the next time the pilgrimage was made pilgrims from all over the Muslim world acknowledged Ma'mūn as their caliph.[29]

By August Ma'mūn was acknowledged as legitimate ruler in most of the caliphate. Baghdad, however, remained in the control of Amīn and his diminishing band of supporters. The city was now half a century old. It had developed enormously from the official government complex that Mansūr had founded. In the intervening fifty years it had attracted a vast number of immigrants from all over the Muslim world. While some of these were soldiers and bureaucrats and other categories of government employees, many more were landless or unemployed, drawn to the city in the hope of making a living in the *sūq*s or selling bits and pieces on the streets. As in any Third World capital today, a vast area of shanty towns had sprung up. The lives of these people were a world away from those of the pampered courtiers who surrounded Amīn or the well-paid soldiers on the official registers. If they were to resist Tāhir's forces, the fight would be long and hard.

On 25 August 812 Tāhir established a camp by the Anbar Gate, which was to be his headquarters for the next year. To the north-east of the city, Harthama ibn Ayan, who had brought his troops from

Hulwan, took up his position. To the south-east a third army led by Musayyab ibn Zuhayr established itself in a position to control the river access from Basra and the south. By this time most of the regular army, including the bulk of the *Abnā*, had deserted Amīn, and it must have seemed, as summer drew to an end, that the conflict would soon be over. Tāhir and his men were denied victory by the populace of Baghdad, especially the urban proletariat, who began a fierce and determined resistance to the attackers.

The chroniclers refer to these people by a variety of derogatory names, roughly translatable as mob, scum and terms to that effect. They are also referred to as 'naked ones', not because they did not wear any clothes but because they had no armour with which to defend themselves. The sort of conflict that ensued can be gleaned from the story of one encounter between a regular soldier of Tāhir's army and a group of irregular defenders. Tāhir's man went out one day to join the fight and, seeing a group of 'unclothed' men without any weapons, said to his companions, his voice full of scorn and contempt, 'Is it only these people who are fighting us?' His more experienced colleagues confirmed this and said that they were like a plague. Confident of his training and his equipment, iron helmet, chain mail and sword, the soldier roundly abused his fellows for not taking advantage of their opponents' lack of weapons and armour. He strung his bow and advanced to deal with them. One of the enemy came to meet him with a pitch-covered reed mat on one arm and a horse's nosebag full of stones under the other. Whenever the soldier shot an arrow, his irregular opponent covered himself, using the mat as a shield. Then he would pick up the arrows and put them into a makeshift quiver he had constructed with part of the mat. Whenever an arrow fell he would pick it up and shout, 'A *dāniq*!', a *dāniq* being the small copper coin he could get for selling the arrow. When the soldier had used up all his arrows he decided to attack the man with his sword, but his opponent took a stone from his bag and hurled it in the soldier's face with a sling, following it up quickly with another one. Finally the soldier wheeled round and retreated, exclaiming that his enemies were devils, not human beings at all.[30]

Most strikingly, these irregulars gave vent to their defiance in a number of poems which have come down to us. After one bruising encounter, when Harthama's forces had been driven back by the irregulars and he himself had been captured and had had to be rescued by one of his officers, a local poet described what he saw:

> *A naked man without a shirt*
> *Goes out in the morning to look for one*
> *He attacks a man in a coat of mail*
> *That blinds the eye with its brightness*
> *A man in armour exposed to his murderous assault*
> *Has no place of refuge*
> *How many a brave horseman*
> *He has sold cheaply*
> *Calling out, 'Who will buy*
> *The head of an armoured warrior for a handful of dates?'*[31]

The siege that developed in and around the city was a vicious and brutal conflict. Women and children, who usually escaped the effects of more regular warfare, were frequently the victims. The effective breakdown of law and order gave opportunities to criminals. In the western suburbs, 'thieves and criminals of the area despoiled anyone they could lay their hands on – men, women and the sick, both Muslim and non-Muslim. They did things the like of which we have heard of in other countries at war.'[32]

While some of the poetry glorifies the naked warriors, much more of it laments the ruin of the city. This is a very different sort of poetry from the courtly verses so much appreciated by caliphs and literary critics. It is rather a form of protest poetry, lamenting the destruction of the city and the hardships caused to innocent people. One anonymous poem captures something of the sadness of war:

> *I wept tears of blood over Baghdad when*
> *I lost the ease of a pleasant life*
> *We have been given sorrow for joy,*
> *A dearth instead of plenty*
> *The eye of the envious has afflicted Baghdad*
> *And made its people die by the mangonel**

---

* The mangonel (Ar. *manjaniq*; both the English mangonel and the Arabic derive from the Greek) was the swing-beam siege engine of the sort that was called trebuchets in the later medieval West. They seem to have been used for the first time in the late sixth century. They were the usual artillery of Muslim armies and could be used for bombarding fortifications or as anti-personnel weapons.

Here are people who have been overcome and burned by flames
There a woman mourns a drowned man
Here a beautiful, dark-eyed woman
In a perfumed shift
Flees from the fire into the looting
While her father flees from the looting to the fire.
Call on someone to take pity, but there is none to take pity
Here are people who have been driven from their shelter
And their property is being sold in every market
Here lies a stranger far from home
Headless in the middle of the road
He was caught in the middle of the fighting
And no one knows which side he was on
The child does not stay to care for his father
And the friend deserts his friend.[33]

Another poem, attributed to an otherwise unknown bard called Khuraymi, laments Baghdad's fall from grace, with a powerful denunciation of the war and violence that had brought such misery to ordinary, blameless people:[34]

They said, when Time had not yet made sport with Baghdad
When her misfortunes had not yet caused her to fall
When she was like a bride, whose hidden part
Was as enticing to the young man as what he could see.
A paradise on earth! The abode of happiness
Her people were in a delightful garden
Where the flowers shone brightly after the raindrops.

Then Amīn and Ma'mūn began their conflict.

Have you seen the kings, what they did
When nobody restrained them with good advice?
How would it have harmed them if they kept to their pact
And if their zeal for justice had been strong
If they had not competed to shed the blood of their supporters
And sent out warriors to fight against each other
And if the goods of this world gathered for them had satisfied them?

All the prosperity brought by earlier caliphs had been destroyed.

> *Have you seen the palaces rising into view*
> *Their chambers concealing women like statues?*
> *Have you seen the villages the kings have planted*
> *When their fields are green*
> *Surrounded by vineyards, palm trees*
> *And fragrant herbs from which the birds take their seeds?*
> *Now they are empty of people*
> *Their gardens have been defiled with blood*
> *Desolate and empty! Dogs howl in them,*
> *The visitor can no longer recognise them*
> *Now misery is their constant companion*
> *And joy has forsaken them.*
> *Behold Baghdad! There bewildered sparrows*
> *Build no nest in its houses*
> *Behold it surrounded by destruction, encircled*
> *With humiliation, its proud men besieged.*
> *From the banks of the Euphrates*
> *To the Tigris where the ferries have stopped*
> *Fire, like the neck of a red-maned horse, stampedes*
> *With its ruddy ones around it.*
> *One man burns the city while another pulls it down*
> *And the scoundrel sates himself with plunder.*
> *The markets of Karkh are deserted*
> *And the vagrant and the wayward prance around.*

The poet then goes on to describe the mangonels that did so much damage to the mud-brick and wooden houses and their inhabitants. At one point he compares the flight of missiles, the size of human heads, to a flock of birds.

> *In every gated street and on every side*
> *There is a siege engine whose moving beam raises its voice*
> *With stone missiles like human heads*
> *The evil man loads the sling.*
> *It is as if over their heads there were flocks*
> *Of sand grouse taking flight in commotion*
> *The shouts of the men come from beneath them,*

While the swinging beams hurl their missiles.
Have you seen the unsheathed swords
That men are brandishing in the markets?
Horses are prancing in the lanes
Carrying Turks with pointed daggers
Naphtha* and fire are in the roads
And the inhabitants are fleeing because of the smoke.

The poet then returns to the images of the women exposed to shame and abuse, the young men killed in the streets as they tried to defend their homes and families. Finally the poem changes tone abruptly as the poet calls on Ma'mūn's vizier, Fadl ibn Sahl, to put an end to this misery. It looks very much as if this last section was added to convert the denunciation of the warmongers into a panegyric.

As the siege wore on, conditions in the city worsened. Tāhir, furious at seeing his forces defeated by the 'naked ones', began a systematic blockade, preventing ships coming up from Basra and the south with supplies from going to Baghdad, diverting them to the Euphrates and to his own forces. On other areas of the front, the besieging forces allowed supplies to enter the city in exchange for enormous bribes.[35] Tāhir also began the systematic demolition of houses in the areas where resistance was fiercest and dug trenches to fortify the areas he had taken. What he did not destroy was ruined by the defenders. The city became a sort of medieval Stalingrad, and a vast swathe of the town to the north and west of the Round City was laid waste.[36] Amīn began to raise money by selling off the materials of his palaces; the gilded ceilings and wooden roofs were all destroyed by him or burned by Tāhir.[37]

As the year wore on and the spring of 813 turned into summer, Amīn's position deteriorated. Many of his prominent supporters among the Abbasid establishment slipped away as Tāhir threatened to confiscate their estates. The richer merchants of the Karkh area considered writing to Tāhir to distance themselves from the common people who were leading the resistance. 'The streets are choked with them. They do not own houses or property in Karkh. They are pickpockets and sellers of cheap sweets or people from the prisons. Their

---

* Naphtha (Ar. *naft*) was crude oil, which springs naturally from the earth in parts of central Iraq and around Baku in Azerbayjān. Rags soaked in naphtha were attached to arrows or other projectiles and set alight.

only shelters are the mosques and baths. The merchants among them are mere street vendors who deal in trifles.' Women are forced to support themselves by prostitution and old men collapse in the street. They, the respectable merchants of the area are powerless against them. In the end they did not dare send the message, but the debate shows up the social tensions that had emerged during the siege.

Amīn himself was coming under increasing pressure. On 23 September he was forced to abandon the Eternity Palace where he had been living because of the stones from the mangonels. He ordered that the audience hall and the carpets be burned, and retreated into the fortified Round City. The Eternity Palace, little more than fifty years old, was never used again and seems to have fallen into ruin.[38]

Supplies were running dangerously short; a servant girl describes how she managed to find a chicken and a loaf for the caliph but 'the drinks store was empty'.[39] The poet prince, Ibrāhīm ibn Mahdi, described a last, melancholy party with the doomed caliph as he sat overlooking the river, and how the girl called upon to sing could only come up with sad and ominous songs.[40] Deserted by most of his followers, Amīn attempted to save his life by surrendering to an old friend of his father's, Harthama ibn Ayan, who was leading the armies besieging the east bank. He had reason to hope that he might be treated mercifully. Tāhir was determined that this cosy arrangement would not work out. Amīn tried to escape to join Harthama at night by boat along the Tigris but the craft was overturned by Tāhir's men and the whole party was pitched into the water. What followed is described to us by one of the defeated caliph's companions, Ahmad ibn Sallām. His account (see below) is full of closely observed detail, such as the cushion and the pile of mats, and reflects with great vividness the fear and confusion of the night: we never learn for certain, for example, the identity of the sinister man in the iron chair, though it may have been Tāhir himself. But it is also revealing of the emotions Ahmad felt. However difficult and stupid Amīn had been in his glory days, he was now a fellow human being in acute distress, and Ahmad's compassion as well as his undiminished reverence for the victim as part of the ruling family come across clearly.

As the boat sank in the swiftly flowing waters of the Tigris, Ahmad saw the caliph rip off his clothes and throw himself into the river. Ahmad himself struggled ashore and was grabbed by one of

Tāhir's men and led to a man sitting on an iron chair by the river, illuminated by the fire that had been lit in front of him. The man who had captured him explained in Persian (local people spoke Arabic) that he was one of the survivors of the wrecked boat.

'"Who are you?" said the man in the chair. I replied that I was Ahmad b. Sallām, chief of police to Harthama. "You're lying!" he replied but I insisted I was telling the truth. Then he went on to ask me where Amīn was.' Ahmad told him what he had seen and was then led off by a mounted man with a rope around his neck. When he complained that he could not keep up with the horses, the commander roughly ordered his captor to dismount and cut off Ahmad's head. Now Ahmad had to think quickly. He explained that he was a rich man and that in the morning he could send to his steward in his house in east Baghdad who would send 10,000 *dirham*s as a ransom. So for the moment he was allowed to live, but it was made clear that if the money did not arrive in the morning, he was a dead man.

He was taken to a large house near by which had belonged to one of the government secretaries and was interrogated again about the whereabouts of the caliph. Afterwards he was shut in a bare room, furnished with two or three cushions and some mats rolled up in the corner. He settled down to wait.

After about an hour there was a sudden sound of horses outside, the door was opened and a group of men came in shouting 'Zubayda's brat!' [Zubayda was Amīn's mother.] They pushed in a bedraggled man who was naked apart from some loose fitting trousers and a turban which covered his face. Then they left him with a few men on guard. When the noise had subsided, he unwrapped the turban and I saw that it was Amīn. My eyes filled with tears and I asked God's blessing on him. Then he noticed me for the first time and asked 'Who are you?'

'One of your servants,' I replied.

'Yes, but which one?'

'Ahmad b. Sallām, a judge.'

'Yes, I remember, we met once at Raqqa and had a very pleasant time. Now you are not my servant but my brother and my friend.'

After a pause he said, 'Ahmad.'

'Yes, my lord.'

'Come closer and hold me tight in your arms.' So I embraced

him and felt his heart beating so wildly that it felt as if it would break out of his chest and I held him until he calmed down. Then he asked, 'Ahmad, what will my brother do? Do you think they will kill me or give me a safe conduct?'

'Of course he will forgive you!'

Then he began to clutch the ragged cloth which was around his shoulders, shivering, so I took off the blanket I had around me and told him to wrap it round himself. 'May God bless you', he said, 'for bringing me something good in this place'.

While we were standing there, there was a knock on the door and a fully armed man came in and looked at Amīn closely, to make sure who he was, and then strode off, locking the door behind him. At that moment I knew the Caliph was a dead man. Then he begged me to stay close to him and I could feel that he was terrified. About midnight there was the noise of horses and another knock on the door. In came a group of Persians with drawn swords in their hands. Amīn stood up to his full height and said 'We are from God and to Him we return'.

The soldiers hesitated, crowding around the door, pushing each other forward and urging each other on. I slipped away and hid behind the mats in the corner while Amīn grabbed one of the cushions and began to curse them, saying that he was the cousin of the Prophet, the son of Hārūn and brother of Ma'mūn. Then one of them came forward and struck him on his forehead with a sword but Amīn thrust the cushion into his face and tried to grab the man's weapon. He cried out that he was being killed and instantly they all rushed at him. One of them stabbed him in the chest. They wrestled him to the ground and cut his throat from the back of his neck. Then they took his head to Tāhir, leaving the corpse behind. At first light they came and rolled the body up in its clothes and took it away.

When it was morning I sent for my steward who brought the ten thousand dirhams and I was allowed to go.

Sadly for the people of Baghdad, the death of Amīn did not mean the end of civil war. Nearly six years were to pass between his death in September 813 and the arrival of Ma'mūn as caliph in August 819. The main cause of the problem lay in the policies of the vizier, Fadl ibn Sahl, the architect of Ma'mūn's successful defiance of his brother.

He was determined to keep his master at Merv in Khurasan and to rule the entire caliphate from there. He probably wanted to make sure that it remained in the control of himself and his friends among the Khurasanian aristocracy. The policy provoked great resentment among all groups in Baghdad – the Abbasid family, the soldiers of Amīn's disbanded army and the ordinary people all saw it as a threat to their status and livelihoods. Iraq became ungovernable, while areas farther west, such as Syria and Egypt, slipped away from the caliph's rule.

Fadl tried a variety of stratagems to try to attract support in Iraq. In March 817 Ma'mūn proclaimed that his heir would not be a member of the Abbasid family but a descendant of Alī and Fatima, Alī, called Ridā, the Chosen One. The intention was to attract support among those in Iraq who wanted to see the caliphate ruled by the Family of the Prophet. In the event the plan backfired. The Alids supporters were unimpressed by this half-hearted measure; after all, Ma'mūn was a young man who might rule for years and change his mind at any moment. The Abbasid family were enraged and most people in Baghdad seem to have shared their hostility to the plan. They then chose an Abbasid caliph of their own, Ibrāhīm, son of the caliph Mahdi, the poet prince. He himself admitted that he was wise in other men's affairs but foolish in his own, and he was always a political lightweight, but he attracted enough support to make it clear that Fadl's policy of rule from Khurasan was simply not going to work. If Ma'mūn were to be an effective caliph, he would have to make radical changes.

V

Poetry and Power at the
Early Abbasid Court

From the foundation of Baghdad in 762 until the collapse of their power in the early tenth century, the court of the Abbasid caliphs was the main focus of cultural activity in the Muslim world. It was here that artistic and intellectual fashions were set. Aspiring artists and writers from all the lands of Islam flocked to the doors of the caliphs in the hope of attracting patronage and, just as important, of establishing their reputations. Of course, there were those who felt that this court culture was both corrupt and frivolous. In pious circles in the cities of Iraq and the provinces there were serious scholars who collected the traditions of the Prophet and theorized about Islamic law, and regarded the goings-on at court with indifference or disgust. In the long term their contribution to the development of Islamic civilization was immense, but they seldom engaged with the salons and debates of Abbasid ruling circles.

Courts develop cultures for all sorts of reasons, but perhaps principally to assert the common identity and interests of the court elite. In Abbasid circles, the distinction between the elite (*khāssa*) and common people (*āmma*) is a recurrent feature of literary discourse. The elite were distinguished, among other things, by their greater knowledge and understanding. To participate in the court culture was to assert your membership of the elite, to show that you had the education, taste and resources to participate in the high culture of the time. This is not to deny that members of the court had genuine interests in poetry and song or enthusiasm for science and philosophy, but rather to say that the study and patronage of these cultural forms had an essential social role as well, defining the connoisseur as a member of the elite.

Abbasid court culture was not a static and unchanging set of values but evolved as new generations and new groups within the elite sought to establish their cultural credentials. In very broad terms, the early Abbasid caliphate, up to the death of Amīn, was the age of poetry, when poetry and song were the most sought after and valued forms of cultural expression. In the ninth century a more general courtly culture developed which extended to literary criticism, philosophy, the exact sciences and areas like cookery and the possession of fine books. In contrast to the courts of, say, Renaissance Italy or eighteenth-century Versailles, visual arts, especially painting, played a very small part in the formation of these elite cultures.

Instead, early Abbasid court culture was dominated by poetry and song. The dynasty inherited a poetic tradition whose origins lay far back in the *jāhiliya*, the time of ignorance before the coming of Islam. In those days the poets were essential figures in Bedouin tribal society, cementing tribal identities, praising bold and generous champions, the beauty of women and the excellence of camels. Some poets also concentrated on extolling the loner and the outcast. Throughout history Arabs have admired these early poets, seeing them as exemplars of ancient values and the fine use of language.

But the poetry of the *jāhiliya* was firmly rooted in its time and place. After the Muslim conquests of the settled areas of the Middle East, there emerged a whole population of Arabic speakers, many of them highly educated, for whom the desert was a strange and even hostile environment. They lived in a courtly or urban milieu in which the values of tribal society were little more than a historical curiosity. A new age required a new poetry, yet the language and tropes of the antique still weighed heavily on the artists of the Abbasid period.

The public poetry of the Abbasid court was largely praise poetry, recited in the great assemblies when both courtiers and a wider public would appear before the caliph. Rulers and other great men desired eulogies in which the poet waxed lyrical on their virtues and achievements and commented, none too subtly in many cases, on their generosity. Praise poetry was the bread and butter of literary life. A successful but not outstanding poet like Ibn al-Rumi (d. 896) could make a respectable living through praise of important figures in the caliph's circle, ministers and viziers. Ninety per cent of his considerable output was eulogy of his patrons.[1]

Appreciating poetry from different ages written in different languages is always problematic, but to modern Western ears the praise poetry of this tradition is especially hard to empathize with. The poetry of lost love, of nostalgia for better days, of the pleasures of feasting and drinking wine can set up resonances across the ages; long and apparently absurdly exaggerated accounts of the prowess, courage and generosity of some forgotten minor potentate can hardly encourage the same reaction.

What, then, did the patrons expect to gain in exchange for the money they showered on their panegyrists? At the most basic level, of course, everyone likes to be told how wonderful they are, particularly in a public recitation or meeting: they may even come to believe it themselves. Yet even the least cynical observer must have been aware that the compliments were being elaborated largely so that the poet would be generously rewarded rather than being the result of an outpouring of unsolicited enthusiasm. Successful and popular praise poetry would be circulated way beyond the occasion for which it was originally produced. Panegyrics by masters like Abu Tammām would be reproduced in anthologies and commented on by learned critics, and the poetry would spread and immortalize the memory of the patron. Perhaps we can see a parallel in the court portraiture of *ancien régime* monarchies in western Europe. When we admire a heroic portrait, an image of Philip IV of Spain by Velázquez, for example, we know that Philip was a monarch with his share of imperfections and that the painter has made him look bolder and more impressive than he ever was in real life. But this apparent 'dishonesty' does not prevent us from appreciating the painting as a work of art. So it must have been for much of the audience for this praise poetry; of course it was exaggerated, but that did not detract from the skill of the poet or the imagination and originality of his compliments and comparisons. Just as the European monarch would assert his prowess and legitimacy in a heroic portrait that would be widely discussed, and of which prints and reproductions could be made and circulated, so the Abbasid potentate tried to use the dominant art form of his day, poetry, to spread and enhance his reputation.

Poetry was also a discourse for spreading ideas of legitimacy. The poets would set forth how the achievements of the patron's ancestors and his own virtues and talents were sure signs of God's approval and entitled him to the respect of his fellow men. Perhaps most of all, the patron was asserting his position as one of the elite, in a great tradition of patronizing praise poetry that stretched back to the pre-Islamic past: patronizing praise poets was what members of the elite did; other people outside the charmed circles could not do this. To have poets eulogize you, however suspect and mercenary their motives might be, was to assert your right to be considered a member of the *khāssa* (elite).

Poetry was recited in public, often by the poet himself, who would strive to make an impression and win rewards. Boldness, daring and a quick wit were required to secure attention; the Abbasid court was no place for blushing violets. The great public audiences could be terrifying. Something of the opportunity and anxiety that attended these public performances can be glimpsed in an account of one such occasion in Mahdi's time by a participant, the poet Ashjā al-Sulami. The caliph had given permission for the public to enter his presence, so they all went in and he told them to sit down. So they did, presumably cross-legged on carpets, while he sat on his throne. It so happened that Bashshār ibn Burd (a fellow poet) sat down beside Ashjā. The caliph sat in silence and so did the public: everyone waited for someone to break the ice. Then Bashshār heard a voice and he said to Ashjā, 'Who is that?' Ashjā replied that it was Abu'l-Atāhiya.

'Do you think he will dare recite in this assembly?' Bashshār asked. 'I think he will.'

Mahdi ordered him to recite and he began:

> *What is the matter with my mistress?*
> *What is the matter with her?*
> *She is disdainful*
> *And I put up with it.*

At this point Bashshār jabbed Ashjā with his elbow and whispered, 'Did you ever see a bolder fellow, to dare to pronounce such a verse in such a place?' This was the occasion for formal praise poetry, not some sentimental lament about unhappy love. Soon, however, Abu'l-Atāhiya had turned it around.

> *The caliphate came to him, submitting to his will*
> *Sweeping its train along*
> *It was fit for no one but him*

And he alone was fit for it.
If anyone one else had aspired to it
There would have been an earthquake.
If the daughters of our hearts [innermost thoughts] do not obey him
God will not accept our [good] deeds.

The poem had been neatly brought round to offer a clever compliment to the ruler and so, as Ashjā remarked rather ruefully, 'That day Abu'l-Atāhiya was the only man who left the audience with any reward.'[2]

From the time of Mahdi there developed a more intimate forum for poetry and song where a wider variety of topics could be broached. This was in the smaller-scale meetings, often held at night, with wine available, when the caliph could relax with his *nadīms*, intimate courtiers, and varied, even scandalous, verse could be produced and set to music. And of course the most memorable of these poems were published and circulated among the wider literate public.

Love has always been a suitable subject for poetry, and love poetry, often entangled with praise poetry, was an important aspect of courtly literature. Attitudes to love as reflected in literature, which is of course not the same as attitudes to love in real life, changed gradually. In the world of the pre-Islamic poets love is usually mentioned in the context of loss, of nostalgia and memory for what had been in the past. It was also very physical; the male protagonist desired, and sometimes obtained, straightforward sexual relations with the women he thought about. There was no indication that the suffering caused by loss of love could be beneficial or improving: it was simply bad news. After the coming of Islam, attitudes seem to have developed in two different directions. On the one hand there was a whole genre of frivolous, even scandalous, verse characterized by the poet Umar ibn Abi Rabīᶜa, who is chiefly remembered for his descriptions of picking up girls during the Hajj, even as they walked around the Kaᶜaba itself. There are no signs in this poetry of restraint and little space for unfulfilled desire.

The other strand is attributed to poets of the Banū Udhr tribe and is sometimes known as Udhri poetry. These verses, or verse cycles, describe a world of passionate but unfulfillable love. Yearning and suffering are the main subject matter; it is not just that sexual

consummation does not happen, but that it is known to be impossible from the beginning. The most famous product of this literary
movement was the poetic tragedy of Majnūn and Layla, whose tragic
love affair has something in common with Romeo and Juliet.
Majnūn (the name means Mad) is driven out of his mind by impossible love for Layla and retreats into the desert, only to find on his
return that his beloved is dead, whereupon he in turn dies of a broken
heart. In the world of the Udhri poets, love is both noble and
unimaginably sad. The story of Majnūn and Layla lived on to inspire
later generations of Arab and Persian poets and painters of
illuminated manuscripts.

In the court poetry of the Abbasids, love is once more brought
under control and made suitable for polite society. Being in love with
unattainable women, or boys, was entirely suitable for members of
the *khāssa*; even caliphs fell in love and wrote poetry about their
yearnings, however brief or imaginary these may have been. Some,
like the poet Abu Nuwās, developed an outré and transgressive attitude to physical enjoyment, but most authors kept the temperature
down: unhappy love was fashionable, it established the lover as a man
of sensibility and feeling, who could appreciate fine literature and
seek for himself the most elegant way of describing the pain he felt.
This refined and slightly etiolated attitude to love identified the lover
as a member of court society, participating in the polite discourse of
the circle he felt he belonged to.

The poet occupied a marginal and sometimes dangerous position
in the Abbasid court. Like a rock star of the twentieth century he was
permitted, and in some ways expected, to transgress the normal
bounds of social behaviour. Abu Nuwās could boast of his delight in
wine drinking and his predilection for attractive boys in ways that
would have been quite unacceptable from others and might well have
resulted in dire punishment. At the same time, the poet remained the
servant of his patron, poets were expected to wait on the caliph at any
time, and failure to respond could result in chastisement and the
threat of death, though these threats were probably exaggerated for
dramatic effect. As we shall see, poets who allowed themselves a
moment of quick-witted fun at the expense of the powers that be
could pay a heavy price.

The career of court poet was genuinely open to talented people
from all social backgrounds. There were poets like Ibrāhīm, son of

the caliph Mahdi, who came from the highest ranks of the ruling family, but there were others whose origins were very modest indeed. Of course, a poet needed patronage, and a good deal of luck, if he were to make it to the royal audience, and many excellent poets must have languished in obscurity. Even allowing for this, the degree of social mobility is impressive and the biographies of poets give us a rare insight into the way in which outsiders from disadvantaged backgrounds could establish themselves in the court elite.

The caliph Mansūr was eloquent and a master of impromptu repartee. He certainly knew his classical Arabic poetry and could produce a telling quote to make a political point, but he was not a great patron of poets. His son and heir Mahdi was a genuine lover of poetry and song. Already, when he was crown prince, writers and musicians gravitated to his circle. When he became caliph he could give free rein to his impulses and the Abbasid court began to be the scene of literary life.

Literary life was dominated by three great poets whose reputation long outlasted the dynasty that had brought them to fame; Bashshār ibn Burd, Abu'l-Atāhiya and Abū Nuwās are still considered among the great masters of classical Arabic poetry, and their story is as memorable for their different and contrasting personalities as for their different styles of poetry.

Bashshār ibn Burd's history was a product of the great displacements of people that characterised the early Islamic period. His grandfather came from Tukharistān on the upper Oxus valley in what is now northern Afghanistan. He was taken prisoner of war during one of the Arab campaigns in the area and brought to Basra as a slave. His son was freed by the rich Arab woman who gave him his liberty and the family became freedmen of the Arab tribe of Aqīl.

Bashshār grew up a large, ungainly man, famously ugly, his face pockmarked by smallpox. He was also blind from birth, but he was clearly born with a fine feeling for language and a prodigious memory. When asked how he managed to use striking visual images in his poetry when he had never been able to see anything at all, he replied that 'lack of sight strengthens the acuteness of the heart and cuts out interference from things which are visible. It intensifies a man's language and stimulates his genius.'[3]

Bashshār was a product of the meeting of Arabic and Persian cultures typical of the Abbasid period. He himself was brought up in an

Arabic-speaking environment and wrote in Arabic, but he remained very conscious of his Persian ancestry. A long genealogy was concocted which connected him with the nobility of the old Sasanian empire and he used his (Arabic) poetry to pour scorn on the traditional Bedouin stereotypes. In one long celebration of his own heritage, he boasts how he is descended from the Persian royal family and goes on to extol the Persian supporters of the Abbasids who had brought the dynasty to power and conquered Syria, Egypt and, with a certain amount of poetic licence, distant Tangier. His father, he boasts,

Never sang a camel song, trailing along behind a scabby camel
Nor approach the colocynth to pierce it for very hunger
Nor the mimosa to knock down its fruits with a stick
Nor did we roast a skink with its quivering tail
Nor did I dig and eat the lizard out of the stony ground.[4]

All the stereoptyical images of the crude and uncultured Bedouin are contrasted with the elegance and refinement of the old Persian nobility.

Neither his appearance and uncouth manners, nor his denigration of the traditional Arab image, could disguise his genius with language. Bashshār celebrated the achievements of the caliph Mahdi at the Abbasid court with as much eloquence and gusto as he had previously shown when praising the Umayyads. He always prepared for his recitations by clapping his hands, clearing his throat and spitting, first on one hand and then the other. Then he would launch into performances of his praise poetry that outshone anything produced by his rivals and critics. His love poetry was full of a refined longing for his unattainable (and possibly imaginary) Abda.

You pages, pour me out a potion
Pour me to drink her soft, sweet kisses
I suffer drought; its healing draught
Is drinking from her moist fresh lips.
The smiling corners of her mouth are brilliant as camomile;
Her speech is like embroidery, a mantle with embroidery
Lodged in the core and kernel of
My heart, she is insatiable.

She said to me: 'I'll meet with you a few nights hence.'
But day and night will wear away, and nothing new will come my way.
She is content without me; my
Portion is sighs to gnaw a heart of steel.[5]

The sentiments are no doubt conventional and even artificial, but the images are startling and fresh. It was these innovations which led later critics to see Bashshār as the inaugurator of the 'modern' style which was to distinguish Abbasid court poetry from the literature of the *jāhiliya* and the Umayyads.

Being a court poet was not always plain sailing, especially for a man like Bashshār, who was well known for the pungent expression of his views. His pessimism and lack of obvious piety meant that his enemies could accuse him of being a *zindīq*, a Manichaean heretic, and the penalty for that was death. He could turn his eloquence to the poetry of insult and abuse and was not always as careful as he might have been. In the end his outspokenness and ready wit were his undoing. On one occasion he was rash enough to attack the caliph Mahdi himself, criticizing him for abandoning his duties to his minister Ya꜄qūb ibn Dawud and devoting himself to pleasure:

Wake up Umayyads! Your sleep has gone on too long!
Your caliphate has been ruined, O people! Search
For the caliph of God among the tambourines and lutes![6]

There are a number of different stories about the events that finally caused his destruction. According to one,[7] he insulted the brother of Ya꜄qūb ibn Dawud, who had been appointed governor of his native Basra. Ya꜄qūb was incensed and told the caliph that Bashshār had insulted the caliph himself. When pressed, the vizier, with apparent reluctance, produced a scabrous couplet, in which the caliph was accused, amongst other things, of fornicating with his maternal aunts and which crudely suggested that he be deposed and that his son Mūsā 'be shoved back up Khayzurān's [his mother's] cunt'. Unsurprisingly, the caliph was angry and ordered that Bashshār be brought to him. Ya꜄qūb, afraid that the truth would come out and that Bashshār would produce another golden panegyric and get himself off the hook, had him ambushed and murdered by his agents in the marshes between Basra and Baghdad.

Abu'l-Atāhiya (748–825) was born to a very modest family in Kūfa, and the young poet at one stage scraped a living selling pots. He had no chance of a formal education and his poor background seems to have left him with something of a chip on his shoulder. Like Bashshār, he showed a natural gift for language and joined the circle of a man called Wāliba ibn Hubāb, a figure as famous for his bohemian and openly gay lifestyle as he was for his poetry. Like many ambitious young men, he gravitated to Baghdad, and his big break came with a panegyric of the caliph Mahdi. As we have seen, he attracted attention at court and began to produce poetry on other subjects, including some rather half-hearted love poetry dedicated to a woman called Utba, a slave girl belonging to the caliph's wife Rīta. One year, as a gift for Nawruz, the Persian new year, he presented the caliph with a large jar (remember, he was a pottery seller) in which there was a perfumed garment, with the request that the caliph present him with Utba. At first the caliph was minded to do so but she was incandescent: 'I am a member of your household!' she cried. 'Will you give me up to a nasty man who sells jars and scrapes a living writing verses?' He relented and instead ordered that the poet's jar be filled with coins. When Abu'l-Atāhiya went to the finance office he demanded that they fill it with gold *dīnār*s but the accountants refused; he could have a jar of silver *dirham*s or nothing – the choice was his. He agonized but eventually accepted the money offered. As Utba tartly remarked, the fact that he was so concerned about the money did not suggest that his love was ever very serious.

Abu'l-Atāhiya continued to serve Hādī and Hārūn as a fairly conventional court poet, but in about 795 he had a major change of heart. He abandoned both love poetry and panegyric and concentrated on writing ascetic verse. The themes he chose were the transitoriness of life and the short-lived nature of earthly pleasures. These sentiments were expressed in a simple, natural language which gave them widespread appeal.

> *Hereafter thou shalt see, shalt see*
> *Things hidden now from thee, from thee*
> *In fullness of time thou shalt see*
> *What makes the rest from the sleeper flee;*
> *The rich and happy thou shalt see*
> *Depart from hence to dust and dearth*

In all that happens, thou shalt see
The course of things eternally.[8]

The third member of the trio, Abu Nuwās (d. *c.*814), seems to have been untroubled by such intimations of mortality. His father had been a soldier in the army of the last Umayyad caliph and his early life was spent in Kūfa, where he became the pupil, and probably the lover, of the poet Wāliba ibn al-Hubāb, who had also, as we have seen, taught Abu'l-Atāhiya. He then moved to Baghdad, but at first his panegyrics found little favour at the caliphal court and he attached himself to the circle of the Barmakids. After their fall in 803 he became a close companion of the heir apparent, later caliph, Amīn, and the decade 803 to 813 represented his glory days, when membership of an affluent and free-living court circle allowed him to develop all aspects of his verse. He died shortly after his patron Amīn was killed.

Abu Nuwās is well known as the jester and rogue of the *Arabian Nights* accounts of Hārūn's court, but in reality he was a brilliant and intermittently serious poet whose work was immediately recognized as classic. It was collected and commented on by literary critics over the next century and a half. His style was fresh and original and his attitudes unrestrained by the dictates of conventional morality.

In addition to the obligatory panegyrics, Abu Nuwās celebrated the princely lifestyle. He was one of the greatest exponents of hunting poetry and wine poetry.

> *Behold an ostleress in whom remained a trace of youthful bloom*
> *towards the hostelry of whom*
> *we three set out one eve*
> *the night upon us and around did hang, as though it were a gown*
> *and neither man nor jinn*
> *rode with us, but in the sky*
> *the stars were pendant upon high*
> *to guide us to our goal*
> *At last we beat upon her door*
> *(first taking pause to have a snore)*
> *'Who knocks?' she cried, 'Us', we replied*
> *'A group of youths who met by chance*
> *before your door, by happenstance benighted wandered hither.*
> *Refuse us and our band must scatter*

Unite us and we're friends for ever'.
'Come in', she said, 'a welcome visit.
You're fine young blades and brainy with it!'
'Pour by the book,' said we to her
'Full bottles bring, no less, no more'
She brought fine wine like the sun with rays
Like stars, fair wine in glass ablaze.
'You name your price,' said I, 'pray let
us know the price and you will get
our custom here for ever'
'Hanun's the name,' she said, 'the price
nine dirhams, three times three, a glass
and that's my going rate.'
When night was nearly on the turn,
she came with scales to test our coin:
I said, 'We didn't bring a lot of money with us: could you not
Take one of us in pawn?'
'You be the pawn,' she said to me,
'and if with cash you're not set free
I'll keep you prisoner with me
Forever.' [9]

So wine poetry twists and melts into the erotic, and nowhere more so than in the person of the boy who is serving the wine.

A boy of beckoning glances and chaste tongue.
Neck bowed enticingly, who scorns the rein.
Proffers me wine of hope mixed with despair,
Distant in word and deed, yet ever-near. [10]

Abu Nuwās dwells on the idea of his lover as a cruel tyrant; pain and pleasure are closely bound up together:

His face a goblet next his lip
looks like a moon lit with a lamp;
Armed with love's weaponry, he rides
On beauty's steed, squares up eye's steel –
Which is his smiles, the bow his brow
The shafts his eyes, his lashes lances.

And the poet is powerless to resist:

> *On every path love waits to ambush me*
> *A sword of passion and a spear in hand:*
> *I cannot flee it and am sore afraid of it*
> *For every lover is a coward,*
> *My hearth affords no amnesty and I*
> *Have no safe-conduct if I stir outside.*[11]

On other occasions the poem is both humorous and erotic, the boy lover both a vulnerable youth and a clever and manipulative young person.

> *I caught sight of someone who*
> *no longer seemed to care for me,*
> *sitting on a prayer mat*
> *with a group of school-boy slaves:*
> *he darted a glance at me –*
> *that's the way he hunts his prey*
> *(All this was at Hafs's academy*
> *lucky old Hafs!)*
> *Hafs exclaimed, 'Away with him!*
> *The boy is nothing but a dunce;*
> *ever since he's been at school*
> *He hasn't paid attention once'*
> *One by one and layer by layer*
> *They stripped his clothes and laid him bare,*
> *Threatening to fetch a strap*
> *(limp and flaccid) to his back;*
> *whereat my beloved yelled,*
> *'Teacher, teacher, I'll behave!'*
> *'Please, Hafs, let him off,' said I*
> *'he'll be a good little boy,*
> *learn his book off pat and do*
> *anything you want him to.'*[12]

Music, along with poetry, was central to court culture, and the two arts often came together in song. There can be no doubt that the courts of Mahdi, Hārūn, Amīn and to some extent Ma'mūn were the high point of ancient Arab musical culture. The number of singers, the originality of the songs and the reputation and rewards of composers and performers were never equalled.

The setting for these performances was the intimate gatherings in the caliphs' residences, far from the public court and censorious eyes of critics and moralists, for then, as today, many pious Muslims deeply disapproved of music. In these sessions the musicians would be separated from the caliph by a curtain, so that he, and any intimates and women he might have with him, could hear the performance but remain unseen. Sometimes it was impossible for the performers actually to know who was listening. Frequently, however, as the wine was passed round and the evening wore on, the barriers came down and the caliph would relax. Musicians such as Ibrāhīm al-Mosuli and Ibn Jāmi probably enjoyed a more relaxed intimacy with the ruler than any of the senior politicians or military men.

The ensembles were usually small, five or six musicians at most. The most common instrument was the lute (*al-ʿūd*, in Arabic: the English word lute is derived from the Arabic term, as are French *luth*, Italian *liuti*, Spanish *laud* and German *Lauth*). The origins of the instrument are lost in antiquity but a new and more developed form was perfected in Iraq in the late eighth century by a musician called Zalzal. This was called the Shabbūt lute because its body resembled the fish of that name. This was the four-stringed instrument with the hollow ovoid or pear shaped sound chest which has remained a favourite instrument among Arab musicians down to the present day. It was usually played with a wooden plectrum. Lutes of this sort can still be seen for sale in the *sūq*s of Damascus and Aleppo, and among any group of traditional Arab musicians.

Another stringed instrument was the *tunbūr* (English pandore), which was distinguished from the lute by its longer neck and smaller sound-box. The sound-box was often drum shaped and covered with a skin that gave it a noisy tone, suitable for solo performance.[13] It was usually mounted with two or three strings, and in early Abbasid times was known in two types, a Baghdadi one and a Khurasani one. In an anecdote about Mansūr's puritanical ways, he is shown not knowing what a *tunbūr* was – it had to be explained by a servant, who had seen one in Khurasan. This may suggest that the instrument was newly imported from the east in early Abbasid times.

The main wind instrument was the *mizmār*, sometimes known by its Persian name *nay*. This was a single reed tube with eight holes, to allow the playing of a complete octave. We also hear of the metal trumpet (*būq*), though this seems to have been used more in military music than in performances at court. Percussion was provided by the drum (*tabl*) and the *duff*, a tambourine that could be either square or round: tambourines with bells or jingling plates are not attested before the twelfth century but may have been used at this time.

The leading singers and musicians at the Abbasid court had immense reputations. Men such as Ibrāhīm al-Mosuli and his son Ishāq and the Abbasid prince Ibrāhīm ibn al-Mahdi were celebrated in history and legend. Female singers and composers such as 'Arīb were celebrated for their intelligence and beauty as well as their talents. Singers often had a doubtful reputation and were thought to be a bad influence on the young. The caliph Mahdi, who loved music himself, gave strict instructions that singers should be kept away from his impressionable young sons, Hādī and Hārūn: needless to say, ways were found around this prohibition, but it was the singers, not the princes, who were punished when this was discovered. In Hārūn's reign, the young princes of the Abbasid house greeted the arrival of new famous singers with all the enthusiasm of besotted fans.

Singers often came from impoverished backgrounds and perhaps provided a breath of fresh air in the claustrophobic world of the Abbasid court. Ibrāhīm al-Mosuli (743–804) (the man from Mosul) is an example.[14] His family had belonged to the Persian nobility of the province of Fars in south-west Iran, but his grandfather Maymūn had been forced to flee the oppression of an Umayyad official and had gone to the new Arab city of Kūfa in Iraq. They lodged with an Arab family, and Ibrāhīm's father, Māhān, married a woman from a small landowning family in Fars who had also sought asylum in Kūfa at the same time. Ibrāhīm was born in the city shortly before the Abbasid revolution, but his father died of plague when he was only two or three years old and he lived with his mother and her brothers.

When he went to elementary school, he was lucky enough to be in the same class as one of the children of Khuzayma ibn Khāzim. Khuzayma was one of the leading figures in the Abbasid army. His family came from north-east Iran and spoke Persian, which may have created a bond with the young Ibrāhīm, and he soon became attached to the family and their tribe, the Tamīm. Later, when the caliph Hārūn quizzed him about his connection with the Tamīmīs, he explained, 'they brought me up and were very good to me. I grew up among them and we had ties of milk-brotherhood.'

He was not a natural schoolboy. As his son said later, 'My father was entrusted to the elementary school where he learned nothing; he was always getting beaten and kept in detention and derived no benefit from it at all.' When he was older, he started to become interested in singing and hung around with young men who wanted to make music. His mother's brothers strongly disapproved of this behaviour and he was forced to go on the road.

It was after this that he acquired the surname al-Mosuli, and a number of stories were told to explain how this happened. According to one, he went to Mosul in northern Iraq, where he stayed for a year. When he returned to Kūfa, one of his old singer friends greeted him with the words 'Welcome to the young man of Mosul!' and he became known as al-Mosuli from then on, despite the fact that his connection with the city was marginal. According to another story from that time, he fell in with a group of highway robbers. After a successful exploit they would get together to enjoy themselves, drinking and singing. Here the young Ibrāhīm picked up the basics of music-making and proved to be the best of band. He then decided he wanted to be a singer and left his accomplices to seek his fortune.

His next stop was the Iranian city of Rayy. We do not know why he decided to settle there but it was an important staging post on the road that led from Iraq to Khurasan and he may have felt that such a busy transit point would provide opportunities. Here he stayed, learning Persian and Arabic singing, and married a Persian woman called Dūshār, to whom he addressed his first surviving poem, and another wife called Shāhak, who was to be the mother of his famous son Ishāq.

He still felt himself to be very much an apprentice and was living off the money he had brought from Mosul and singing with groups of friends in Rayy. One day a eunuch, who had been sent by the caliph Mansūr with a message to a government official in Khurasan, passed through. He heard the young singer performing in a house in Rayy and was very taken with him. Before he left, he gave him a valuable sable coat. The official in Khurasan was clearly pleased with the message, for when the eunuch passed through Rayy on his return journey he had been given 7,000 *dirham*s and many fine clothes. He came to Ibrāhīm's house and stayed for three days. As he left to return to Baghdad, he gave him half the clothes and 2,000 *dirham*s in cash. It was the first money he had ever earned from singing, and he told his benefactor that he would spend it only on things that would improve his skills.

It was time to move on again. Ibrāhīm had heard of a singing teacher called Juvānbuya. Juvānbuya was a Persian who kept his old Zoroastrian religion and now taught singing in the port city of Ubulla, at the northern tip of the Gulf. Ibrāhīm set off, presumably with his wives, though we are not told this, for Ubulla. When he arrived he found that Juvānbuya was not at home so he waited for him to return. He explained what his position was and what he wanted to learn and he was welcomed into the teacher's home. Here he was given one of the wings of the house for his own use, and the teacher appointed his sister to look after him and she brought him all he needed. That evening he returned home with a group of Persian singers and Ibrāhīm joined them as they sat in the *majlis*. We can imagine them, the simple mud-brick and wood house, carpets on the floor, teacher and pupils sitting cross-legged in a circle. There was wine, fruit and aromatic herbs. Oil lamps would be lit and a lute passed round. They began to play and sing, but Ibrāhīm felt that none of them could teach him anything. When his turn came, at least as Ibrāhīm tells the story, he played and sang and they all stood up and kissed his head and said that he had put them to shame and that they had much more to learn from him than he did from them.

His reputation obviously spread and his talents soon came to the attention of Muhammad ibn Sulaymān, the fabulously wealthy Abbasid prince who had made Basra his base. Ibrāhīm was soon part of his circle. The prince was generous but possessive and forbade Ibrāhīm to return to Kūfa when he wanted to go. One day one of the caliph Mahdi's eunuchs was visiting. These people always seemed to have worked as part-time talent scouts and when the eunuch saw Ibrāhīm he abruptly told Muhammad that 'the caliph needs him more than you do'. This time Muhammad rebuffed him but the messenger returned to Baghdad and told Mahdi about the young singer. The eunuch was sent back with orders that could not be disobeyed. Ibrāhīm was taken into the caliph's presence: he had arrived, and his fortune was made. It was not all plain sailing from there. Mahdi disapproved of his bohemian and unruly behaviour, and especially his wine drinking, for Mahdi never touched alcohol. But his talent and ready wit always saw Ibrāhīm through.

By the time of his death, the penniless vagabond and impoverished student had become vastly wealthy. His son reckoned that 24 million *dirhams* had passed through his hands, excluding his regular salary of 10,000 *dirhams* per month and the revenues from his landed estates. As befitted a man of great wealth, he was extravagantly generous. Food was always available: he claimed that he always had three sheep on the go, one in the pot, another skinned and hung up and a third still alive. As soon as the one in the pot was finished, the next ones were cooked and slaughtered. He was equally generous with presents of clothing and money for slave girls. Like a great chief of old, his capital lay in his reputation for generosity, not in hoarded wealth. When he died he had only 3,000 *dīnārs* in the world, and 700 of these were needed to pay his debts.

There are many interesting points about this picaresque narrative. One is obviously the importance of the Persian as well as the Arab tradition in the making of music. It seems that Ibrāhīm's style, which was to be so influential in the development of Abbasid court culture, was a fusion of these two traditions. What is also striking is the role of the Abbasid government: it was a government agent passing through Rayy who gave Ibrāhīm his first break, and it was another government agent who saw him and brought him to Baghdad. Without these contacts, he might have been little more than a small-time musician in a dull provincial town.

The role of poetry, music and song was central to the cultural and social life of the Abbasid court. We have a mass of information about the lives of the artists and we have the texts of the poems they wrote. Yet in the end there is so much we cannot recover. The Arabs of this period never developed a system of musical notation. The melodies that delighted the caliphs and brought fame and fortune to singers such as Ibn Jāmi and Arīb are forever lost to us. Even when Abu'l-Faraj al-Isfahāni was writing his great *Book of Songs* in the tenth century, some of the famous melodies of the classic period were being lost.[15] He tried to collect all he could, perhaps from some old woman in the harem who had sung the songs many years before in her youth. But when the chain was broken it could never be mended: when the last singer died, a song was lost for ever. All we have of this great musical tradition are the lyrics and the stories of the singers and their patrons.

VI

Landscape with Palaces

Whether they were based in Baghdad or Sāmarrā, the Abbasid caliphs held court in Iraq. The modern borders of Iraq enclose two very different areas. To the north of Baghdad, the land is a semi-arid steppe through which the two great rivers of the Tigris and Euphrates run. Their banks are high and stony and only in a few areas can water be drawn from them for irrigation. Permanent settlement has always been confined to a few riverside locations, such as the point on the Tigris where ancient Nineveh stood on the east bank and, much later, where the Muslim city of Mosul developed in the seventh and eighth centuries.

South of Baghdad is a different world. Here the two great rivers flow through a wide alluvial plain whose black earth, silt deposited through the millennia by the rivers, was enormously fertile. It was this earth which gave the land its Arabic name, the Sawād, literally the Black Land. Here the gravelly windswept plains of northern Iraq gave way to a landscape of canals, palm trees and rich grain fields. It is as flat as the reclaimed lands of the Netherlands. Two harvests of wheat and barley a year were common, fish abounded in the rivers and connoisseurs said that the Iraqi dates were the best in the world. Sugar cane was widely grown and so was the flax that provided the raw material for the thriving textile industries of urban centres such as Ahwāz. It is not surprising that the Garden of Eden was traditionally located in this luxuriant landscape.

The intensity of the farming of these rich acres had supplied the resources for some of the earliest great cities of human civilization, Ur in the third millennium BC, Babylon in the second and first. It was here that writing and record-keeping were first developed to a high standard. Along with ancient Egypt, it was one of the birthplaces of bureaucracy and written culture. Unlike in Egypt, time has not dealt kindly with the remains of the ancient civilization of Iraq. There are no great temples such as Karnak, no tombs like the Valley of the Kings, and no tourist boats cruise the waters of the great rivers. The remains of Ur and Babylon are little more than piles of mud, comprehensible only to the specialists. The alluvial plain has no good building stone: instead cities, palaces and temples were constructed in brick. The mud and clay that produced the agricultural wealth also produced building materials. The bricks were either fired bricks, baked hard in kilns, or the mud bricks, simply dried in the scorching Mesopotamian sun. Mud brick, sometimes called adobe, from the Arabic word *tūb*, is a very efficient building material. Cheap and versatile, it also has very good insulating properties. It does not, however, make elegant ruins. Over centuries fired brick was usually looted and reused, while the mud brick simply dissolved back into the landscapes from which it had originally been crafted.

Unlike Egypt, the agricultural civilization of Mesopotamia was very artificial, the product of human ingenuity, care and investment. The flooding of the Nile was, until the building of the Aswan high dam in the 1960s, an entirely natural phenomenon. The river rose and spread not just the water but the life-giving silt over the land. There were good years and bad, but nature's bounty was repeated whether humans took advantage of it or not. In the Sawād the rivers needed to be harnessed and managed. In much of the area around Baghdad and Babylon, where the two rivers come closest together, the Euphrates flows some metres higher than the Tigris. With ingenuity, water can be led from one through the agricultural lands to flow into the other. The irrigation canals lay on top of levees so that the water could be led off them to the fields. Such canals needed constant maintenance: if they were breached, or simply developed holes in the banks, the water would rush out and collect in pools which soon became marshy and saline. The agricultural lands of Mesopotamia were potentially the richest in the world, but it needed stability, care and foresight to develop this potential. Early rulers such as the Sumerians and Babylonians had provided this. The tradition was maintained by the Sasanian shahs of Iran, for whom the plains were both a winter residence and a major source of income. The early Abbasids were the last of the great dynasties to keep up this resource base and use it to sustain a major empire. By the beginning of the tenth century, a combination of mismanagement and warfare had reduced much of the canal system to ruins and the alluvial lands suffered a devastation from which they have never recovered.

While the system was maintained, the rewards were enormous. In the late eighth century, a bureaucrat working for the Abbasid administration in Baghdad made a checklist of the revenue that could be expected from each of the provinces of the empire.[1] Iraq from Baghdad to the Gulf was estimated to yield four times as much as the next richest province, Egypt, and five times as much as Syria and Palestine. According to this account, Iraq paid or should have paid (as often in financial records of this period, it is impossible to know what relationship the figures given have with what was really paid) 160 million silver *dirham*s to the treasury. The *dirham*, the thin silver coin that the Muslims inherited from the Sasanian shahs of Iran, weighed around 3 grams, so each year the people of this area paid half a million kilograms, or 500 metric tons, of silver coinage to the treasury of the caliphs. It was on this vast cushion of wealth that the Abbasid court supported itself. Without this money, the palaces could not have been built, the army could not have been paid, the poets would have starved and the women woven and patched their own garments.

After the success of the revolution that brought them to power in 750, the Abbasids naturally gravitated to Iraq. They were attracted by the great wealth of the area but also by the well-established tradition of support for the Family of the Prophet to be found among its inhabitants. Their most important military support came from distant Khurasan, 1,600 kilometres away to the north-east. Geography alone made it unsuitable as a dynastic centre, but Iraq had good communications with the province and the old Khurasan road that led from the plains of Iraq through the defiles of the Zagros mountains and the passes known as the Gates of Asia to the Iranian plateau was one of the great highways of the ancient world.

Iraq was an ideal base for the new regime, but neither of the established Muslim cities of the country recommended themselves. Kūfa, near the site of ancient Babylon, had a long tradition of political disturbances and faction fighting. The port city of Basra, gateway to the Gulf and the Indian Ocean, was too remote and also dominated by established interests.

There were other good reasons to look for a new site. Away from the constraints of an established urban centre, the caliph had the freedom to plan his city as he wished without trampling on the properties of his subjects. Not only could he plan architecture on a grand scale, he could also reward his chosen followers. The court of the caliphs was an economic magnet which would draw people from all over the Middle East. The richest men in the world lived there, and it was a centre of conspicuous consumption. There were large numbers of soldiers, not so rich, it is true, but still with good salaries to spend. There were petitioners, poets and fortune hunters of all sorts who would want to be near the court. Real estate would be at a premium. The caliph could distribute land which he had bought cheaply to his followers, who could develop it and make their fortunes.

At first the Abbasids lived in small towns or simply in tents, as Mansūr had when he ordered the execution of Abu Muslim. In 762 he decided to develop a new capital at Baghdad, then a small village of no real importance. It was a shrewd choice. As the caliph himself pointed out, supplies could come by river from all directions; grain down the Tigris and Euphrates from the north, dates and rice from the south and luxury goods from as far away as China. 'If I settle in a place where things cannot be imported by land and sea, prices will be high, goods will be in short supply and food supplies will be difficult.'[2] Only good water transport could make possible the provisioning of a great city. This careful economic planning was one of the factors which ensured that Baghdad would not suffer the fate of other ephemeral capital cities, which were abandoned as soon as the founder and his dynasty disappeared, but remained a thriving metropolis right down to the present day.

The city Mansūr built has entirely disappeared. Even its outlines cannot be traced on the map from surviving remains. A generation ago, it may have been possible to recover some traces of the original walls and foundations and answered some of the queries that have teased historians, but the opportunity was lost and the pace of recent development makes it unlikely that anything substantial can be retrieved. What we do have, however, are two very full descriptions of Mansūr's work[3] and anecdotes and details in numerous other sources. There are also some surviving fortifications from the period at the city of Raqqa and the desert palace of Ukhaydir, which can be used to give some idea of what the city looked like. In a tantalizing way, we can reconstruct a virtual Baghdad: we can see in the mind's eye where the canals ran, we can follow roads from the ceremonial city, through the *sūq*s and the booksellers' market. We can go through the winding unpaved streets, past the fast-food stalls to the textile and jewellery quarters, to the poorer quarters where the new-comers squatted and the roads petered out in the dusty desert margins. We can pass the blank walls of the mud-brick, single-storey houses with the flat roofs so useful for sleeping on in the hot summer nights, and know, though of course we cannot see, that each house surrounded a courtyard, which, whether grand or mean, would be the real centre of family life. We know where the great men of the regime built their palaces and where their gardens ran down to the banks of the Tigris. We know the names and positions of the mosques they worshipped in and the cemeteries in which they were buried.

The caliph planned his new city on a large scale, and for a man who was notoriously mean with his money he was prepared to invest huge sums in the project. He conceived his city at the time in 762 when his rule was threatened by the rising of Muhammad the Pure Soul and his brother, and he wanted security and barracks for his army. At the same time, he also wanted a mosque and palace complex that would impress visitors and be a real imperial capital, not just a luxury fortress. The centrepiece of his project was a perfect-ly round city, with four gates, facing north-east, south-east, south-west and north-west, with roads leading to Khurasan, Basra, Kūfa and Syria. At the centre of this city lay the mosque, and alongside it the palace, known as the Golden Gate. What happened in the rest of the interior of the Round City is not entirely clear: it seems that it was originally intended as space for markets, but these were soon moved outside the walls and the whole area became a sort of official compound for soldiers and bureaucrats.

Historians have been much interested in the origins of this grandiose idea. The Sasanian shahs had built round cities, traces of which can still be seen in places such as Firuzabad in Fars. None of them, however, seems to have been as logically planned or as power-fully defended as Baghdad. The Umayyad caliphs had built cities and palaces but none of them was circular in form. It is likely in fact that the overall conception owed much to the caliph himself. Looking at traditional Middle Eastern cities today, Damascus, Aleppo, Fez,

Marrakesh or Sana'a, it is easy to imagine that Muslim cities were unplanned and simply developed organically and naturally. The narrow *sūq*s and winding streets, often leading to dead-end alleys, suggest an informality and lack of government control. The plan of Baghdad, and later of Sāmarrā, shows that this was only part of the story and that the caliphs could plan on the same magnificent scale as their Roman and Sasanian predecessors.

The Arabic writers who describe the building of the Round City delight in giving us statistics: the architect Rabāh, who was in charge of the building of the main wall, said that between each gate (that is each quadrant of the circle) every course was made of 162,000 bricks. As the workmen moved higher, the wall became slightly thinner and only 150,000 and then 140,000 bricks were used.[4] Most of these would have been mud bricks held together with wet clay, but where fired bricks were used they were cemented with lime mortar.[5] The bricks themselves were carefully made to specification. According to one source[6] each one was about half a metre square (a cubit) and weighed about 80 kilos (200 *ratl*s), though there were variations. Many years later, when a section of the wall was being demolished, the labourers found a brick with a note written on it in red saying that it weighed 117 *ratl*s (about 46 kilos). They weighed it and found that it was just that.[7] As with all figures from this period, we have to be cautious in taking them as accurate measures, but the impression is given that this was an enterprise tightly controlled by the bureaucrats and quantity surveyors.

This vast engineering project, involving the laying of millions of huge bricks, to say nothing of the more skilled work of building domes and arches, was not the product of slave labour, or even, as far as we can tell, of any sort of conscripted workers. There were said to have been 100,000 workmen engaged on the project, although this is probably an exaggeration, and they were all paid at a daily rate calculated in small copper coins that were a fraction of a silver *dirham*. An ordinary labourer might get one twelfth of a *dirham* a day, the foreman twice that. This does not sound very much until we read that a sheep cost a *dirham*, a lamb a quarter of a *dirham*. A *dirham* would buy 30 kilos of dates or 8 litres of oil. It looks as if even the humblest labourer could keep himself and his family in basic foods and have meat on occasion. No wonder men were attracted from all over the Middle East to work on this project.

At the centre of the Round City lay the mosque and the palace, the two theatres of royal display. They shared a common wall and a door led directly from the palace to the royal enclosure in the mosque.[8]

The mosque built by Mansūr was a simple design. It was a roughly square building with a large central courtyard. Around the court was a portico supported by wooden columns and at one end a prayer hall, also supported by wooden columns. There is no mention of impressive gateways or of fine decoration in the interior. It was a place for Muslims to gather, rather than a work of high religious art. In the late Roman period, governors of cities had used the theatres to address the people on their appointment or in times of crisis or danger. Mansūr used the mosque for the same purpose. He frequently preached before the congregation at Friday prayer,[9] and much of his authority and reputation must have been based on this public performance of monarchy in the mosque at the heart of his Round City.

His son Mahdi is known to have preached in public on several occasions,[10] but thereafter caliphs seem to have abandoned the practice, or at least the Arabic authors no longer describe them as giving sermons in the mosque. Perhaps they were not so confident of their ability to handle the crowd. It was part of a more general seclusion of the monarchs behind the gates of their palaces.

We have fuller descriptions of the palace.[11] It seems to have been roughly 200 metres square. At its heart was a great *iwān* about 15 metres by 10. At the back of the *iwān*, a door led into an audience room 10 metres square covered by a vaulted ceiling. Above this there was another square chamber covered with a dome, 10 metres high to the springing of the cupola. The exterior of the dome was green and was some 40 metres above ground level. At the top of the dome there is said to have been the statue of a horseman, and the dome could be seen from the outskirts of the city. The palace of the Golden Gate with its green dome did not remain the residence of the caliph for long; Mansūr himself usually resided in the Eternity Palace, which he constructed by the river outside the walls of the Round City. However, it did retain a symbolic importance for the Abbasids: according to an early-tenth-century author, 'it was the crown of Baghdad, a guidepost for the region and one of the great achievements of the Abbasids'. When it collapsed on 10 March 941, 'during a night of torrential rain, awesome thunder and terrible lightning', its fall was held to presage the collapse of the dynasty itself.[12]

The caliph was searching for a monumental architectural setting for his authority. For his models Mansūr looked to the great palaces of the Sasanian shahs, whose style provided much of the inspiration for Abbasid royal display. Only a few kilometres from Baghdad stood the mighty bulk of the palace of the shahs at Cteisphon. Its huge brick arch, which still stands to this day, was the largest pre-modern brick span anywhere in the world.[13] This great arch, though ruined and battered, provided the classic setting for the exercise of great power. It was a source of inspiration and competition. According to a story that may not be true but which is still suggestive of the awe in which this building was held, Mansūr tried to have it demolished to reuse the bricks but, like those sultans of Egypt who tried to demolish the pyramids, he found that the monuments of antiquity were able to defy all his efforts.

There were other Persian royal buildings to provide an example of how monarchs ought to display their power. By the great Khurasan road, where the route from Iraq begins to ascend through the Zagros mountains, stood the Sasanian palace of Qasr-i Shirin (Shirin's Palace). It must have been familiar to Mansūr and his courtiers. Qasr-i Shirin was on altogether a more modest scale than Cteisphon but its remains suggest that it combined the two architectural elements that formed the core of Mansūr's palace and its successors, the *iwān* and the dome chamber.

While nothing survives of Mansūr's work, a more or less contemporary Abbasid palace still exists in large part at Ukhaydir, some 80 kilometres into the desert south-west of Kūfa.* Ukhaydir is a vast structure, huge and lonely in the flat, stony wastes. Gertrude Bell, the great archaeologist and traveller, visited Ukhaydir in 1909 and wrote, 'Of all the wonderful experiences which have fallen my way, the first sight of Ukhaydir is the most memorable. It reared its mighty walls out of the sand, almost untouched by time, breaking the long lines of the waste with its huge towers, steadfast and massive, as though it were, as I had first thought it, the work of nature, not of man.'[14] Even Archibald Creswell, the learned but very dry historian of early Muslim architecture, was moved to write that 'Ukhaydir in

---

* Ukhaydir was almost certainly built by Īsā ibn Mūsā, an Abbasid prince who led the armies that defeated the rebellion of Muhammad the Pure Soul in 762. He was at one time heir apparent to Mansūr before being replaced by the future caliph Mahdi in 764. He retired from public life with the vast payment he had received in compensation and it may have been at this stage that he built this remote palace. He died in Kūfa in July 784.

its loneliness is one of the most impressive buildings I have ever seen'.[15] The palace stands within a large, fortified rectangular enclosure 175 metres by 169 metres, slightly smaller, if we are to believe the sources, than Mansūr's residence. The walls are about 17 metres high (almost the same height as those of the Round City of Baghdad) and, again like those of Baghdad, are defended by numerous round towers. The visitor would arrive through the main gate and under the portcullis. Portcullises were known to the Romans and were used in early Muslim military architecture. However, unlike the classic iron grid of the Western medieval portcullis, Muslim ones seem to have been solid wood or iron doors which could be raised and lowered from above. The visitor proceeded along a dark passage, through a hall covered by a brick vault with chambers for attendants on either side, into the blazing light of a large courtyard, surrounded by blind arcades of pointed arches supported by pillars. Directly across the court there was an open *iwān* topped by a square portal.

The *iwān* was smaller than Mansūr's in Baghdad, 10 metres deep by 6 across and covered by a barrel vault. The door at the far end led into a square chamber which may have been where the prince waited for his visitors. The *iwān* and audience hall were both flanked by smaller rooms, some finely decorated.

The fabric at Ukhaydir is mostly rubble masonry with baked brick used only for the vaults. There are no stone columns and the pillars are brick and rubble. In its ruined state, it looks crude and inelegant, with none of the fine surfaces and delicate carving of classical stone architecture. But this is not what the eighth-century visitor would have seen. The walls, which look so jagged and bare today, were all intended to be covered in stucco plaster. Like three-dimensional wallpaper, this was carved in repeated patterns of stylized plants and vines. The stucco may have been painted and the floors covered with rugs. Away from the grander rooms, the interior surfaces would have been covered by a simple plain plaster, fragments of which can still be seen. The effect would have been one of sombre opulence, especially when contrasted with the bright, harsh light of the courtyard and the surrounding desert. The palace was provided with a small mosque and that most important of amenities in the desert, a bath house where the weary and dusty traveller could refresh himself and change his travel-stained clothes.

The palace was not designed to impress by the sheer scale of the architectural forms, but by drawing the visitor through a series of spaces leading up to the audience hall. Like the enfilade of rooms in a seventeenth-century European palace, this ensured that guests were screened and graded. Humble or unwanted visitors would hardly be allowed beyond the main court, honoured guests would be received in the *iwān* or the audience chamber, intimates would be allowed into the smaller rooms that flanked the ceremonial spaces. It would have been in one such space that Īsā ibn Mūsā was waiting with his son to be admitted to the caliph Mansūr's presence when he noticed that the beams of the wooden roof were being shaken and he was getting covered in dust. When he was finally summoned, he came into the royal presence in filthy clothes. It was then that it became clear that the caliph, who wished to humiliate him in public, had arranged for this to be done.[16]

We have numerous accounts of what was said in audiences held by the caliph in his palace, but few give us any indication of the architectural environment. Delegations from the provinces were received in the *iwān*.[17] In one story[18] we are told that seven hundred courtiers would attend Mansūr's audience every day. When the audience began, the curtain over the entrance to the hall was opened[19] and they were admitted. In Mansūr's time this was done in strict order of rank by the chamberlain, Rabi, and no special pleading would persuade him to change the ritual, though caliphs could and did force people to enter last if they wished to insult or humiliate them.[20] Different classes of people entered in their appointed order. The poet Ishāq al-Mosuli was famed for his knowledge of literature and law as well as his abilities as a singer. One day he requested that he should be allowed to enter Ma'mūn's audience with the writers and intellectuals rather than with the singers and this was granted. After this he decided that he would like to be promoted further and join the religious scholars (*fuqaha*), and this was done too. His final social triumph was witnessed by two of his scandalized colleagues, observing from the side of the audience hall: Ishāq was led by the hand by none other than the chief judge, and when he reached the caliph he asked permission to appear in Abbasid court black on Fridays and join the caliph in his private enclosure in the mosque.[21] Ishāq had used the formal setting of the audience to show that he was a cut above his fellow singers.

In a story from the time of Mansūr we hear how the caliph sat

cross-legged on a raised platform covered with *farsh* (quilts and cushions), though at other times we hear of caliphs sitting on chairs that
seem to have been portable thrones. To Mansūr's left and right sat
the immediate members of his family, including his son and heir
Mahdi, if he was in Baghdad.[22] The hero of the story in which this is
described, Maᶜn ibn Zā'ida, wanted to attract the caliph's attention,
so one day he dressed in a wildly eccentric manner with a large coat
of mail, a long loose turban and a curved sword which dragged along
the ground. It had the desired effect. When the audience was over
and people were leaving, Maᶜn was just about to leave through the
curtain when the caliph summoned him to come back: Rabi was
ordered to clear everyone else from the palace. There followed an
acerbic exchange in which the caliph took an iron mace from under
the *farsh* and threatened Maᶜn with it. However, he was placated and
assured of Maᶜn's loyalty, and offered him a difficult assignment as
governor of Yemen. He then took out, again from the *farsh*, a
diploma of appointment, clearly a standard form which had been
prepared in advance, and wrote Maᶜn's name on it. The next day
Maᶜn set out.

Maᶜn's eccentric costume was all the more noticeable because
court dress was usually required at the audience. From the time of
the revolution that brought them to power, black had been the colour
of Abbasid banners and uniforms. This usually included the high
conical caps known as a *qalansūwa*, usually made of silk, which may
have resembled a tall tarbush or fez.[23]. These strange hats were supported by an internal framework of wood or reeds and were compared to tall tapering wine jars. Hārūn disliked this headgear, which
had perhaps come to seem old fashioned by his time, but it was
brought back into fashion by the caliph Muᶜtasim in the early ninth
century. Away from court, the turban was the usual headgear for
Muslims of all classes, though royal turbans were naturally more
splendid: the gold embroidery on the turban of the ill-fated caliph
Amīn was said to have been absolutely dazzling.[24] There was also a
long *taylasān*, perhaps resembling the hood on an academic gown.[25]
Coming away from court, it would have been a relief to reach one's
own house and get out of the heavy formal attire.[26]

The audience was the occasion for the appointment of governors
and the reading of proclamations. When the caliph Mahdi wanted to
persuade one of the leaders of the House of Alī to come out of hiding

and surrender himself, he made a public statement in his audience that the Alid would be safe and would be well treated. Encouraged by this guarantee, the fugitive did surrender, and both public and legal opinion ensured his safety.[27] Caliphs also used the audience as a safety valve for complaints against the administration. This institution, known as the *mazālim*, was an audience in which, at least in theory, members of the public, whatever their status, could appear before the caliph or his deputy to seek redress, usually against the oppression of officials. Caliphs were urged to do this as part of good Islamic government. Hādī urged his chamberlain not to prevent anyone from coming to see him, 'because that would deprive me of God's blessing'.[28] When the caliph had not held such a session for three days his vizier reproached him for neglect of duty and the caliph duly held an open session when he redressed grievances all day.[29] The sources are full of improving anecdotes about how just rulers responded to the complaints of the poor and dispossessed against the petty tyrants of the administration. How far this was wishful thinking and how much it reflected reality is difficult to say, but the political philosophy is clear: the caliph should be available in public to redress the wrongs endured by his subjects.

Beyond the public areas lay the domestic sphere. In Ukhaydir this took the form of a series of smaller courts, rigidly rectangular in pattern with rooms opening off them. Each of these units was separate from the others, and they were connected by long vaulted corridors. It is impossible to know how they were used; some may have been available for guests and their entourages, others reserved for the wives and family of the ruler.

One of the features that made Muslim palaces of this period different from the western European great houses with which we are more familiar was that few of the rooms had specific, identifiable functions. The *iwān* and audience hall were clearly differentiated and their architectural forms reflected their function. The same was true of the palace mosque, distinguished by its covered hall, open court and most clearly by the *mihrāb* or niche showing the direction of Mecca, and the bath house with its series of small domed chambers. Apart from these, the domestic quarters seem to have been used for all sorts of general purposes as the need arose. Architecturally they were usually simple and unimpressive: effect and luxury were achieved by furnishings and, above all, by fabrics. The *farsh* could be moved from one room to another without difficulty. Unlike in medieval Western palaces, or indeed the Topkapi in Istanbul, there were no purpose-built kitchens that can be distinguished. Even the grandest people usually sat on carpets on the floor or on *farsh*. Large carpets, known as *bassāt*, were common, but the prayer rug or *musalla* was the high-status seat; Mansūr in his palace sat on one.[30] When the chamberlain Rabī was not offered a prayer rug to sit on when he visited a rival in the administration, he knew it was an insult and immediately began plotting his revenge.[31]

The private status of the domestic quarters meant that few outsiders had access to them, but we do have a few descriptions to help us out. As usual, these take the form of anecdotes about people and their doings; references to the setting are only incidental. One man who was allowed behind the scenes was Muhammad ibn Sulaymān. He was a cousin of the caliphs Mansūr, Mahdi and Hārūn from a cadet branch of the Abbasid family. His relationship was obviously considered close enough for him to be accepted as family and allowed where others could not penetrate. He was an interesting character in his own right. His branch of the family had been established in the great port city of Basra, and they became immensely rich. Muhammad himself was a competent politician and soldier with apparently no ambition to become caliph himself. He played an important role, for example, in securing the peaceful succession of Mahdi when his father Mansūr died on pilgrimage. He was also a great hoarder. When he died in the autumn of 789, the caliph Hārūn sent agents to seize his vast wealth. They turned out the attics and storerooms and found vast quantities of furnishings and fabrics, perfumes, jewels and all sorts of utensils, besides slaves, horses and camels. He seems never to have thrown anything away: there were presents from the lands around the Gulf, Fars, Sind, Oman and eastern Arabia. He had even kept the ink-stained clothes he had worn as a schoolboy. They also found great stores of fish, spices and cheeses, almost all of which had gone bad. Displaying a total lack of consideration for others, the agents threw a large quantity of rotten fish into the street outside the palace and the citizens of Basra were obliged to avoid the thoroughfare for days because of the stink.[32]

Muhammad ibn Sulaymān once came to visit Mansūr on a cold winter's day after he had been ill. He was amazed by what he found.

I was let into an inner area of the palace I had never been shown before. I went into a tiny apartment consisting of one room with a portico on one side supported on one teak column separating it from the court. He had hung rush mats up in the portico as they do in mosques (in the winter). I went into the room and there was a felt mat and nothing else apart from his quilt, his pillow and a blanket. I said to him, 'Commander of the Faithful, I wish you were out of this room!' but he replied, 'This is the place where I sleep, uncle'. 'And this is all there is?' I asked. 'It is just what you see', he replied.[33]

No state beds, canopies or decorated ceilings here: the most powerful man in the world slept on his quilt on the floor of a small bare room. Salām al-Abrash, who as a eunuch member of the domestic staff also had access to the private quarters, remembered that the caliph had an apartment with a courtyard and a tent with quilts and cushions. His son Mahdi slept in an alcove with a portico outside, where his attendants also slept so that they could hear him if he needed anything.[34]

The idea of living in a tent within a built palace may seem strange at first but it was not uncommon. We have seen how Mansūr held court in tents, even when conducting momentous business such as the murder of Abū Muslim before the building of Baghdad. Mahdi too held court in a tent pitched in a courtyard of the palace when he received Īsā ibn Mūsā's renunciation of his rights to the caliphate.[35] Architectural evidence for similar practices can be found elsewhere in the Muslim world; the khans of Khiva in Khorezm in the nineteenth century used to pitch their yurts in the palace courtyard on specially made platforms. They preferred to live in the tents in the winter because they were warmer, and in the airy chambers of the palace in the summer.

Not everybody lived in such austere conditions. One day in 782/3 the vizier Yaʿqūb ibn Dāwud was summoned by the caliph Mahdi to a chamber in the interior of the palace. He found the caliph in a room furnished with rose coloured cushions and fabrics, looking out over a garden full of roses and peaches and apples in blossom. In the room sat a slave girl of astonishing beauty, also dressed in a rose-coloured gown. 'Do you like it?' asked the caliph, to which Yaʿqūb replied that it was indeed very beautiful and he hoped the caliph would enjoy it. 'Take it all,' the caliph said, and added for good measure, 'and the girl too so that your pleasure in it may be complete'. The grateful vizier left to enjoy the caliph's largesse. So delighted was he with the girl that he could not bear to be parted from her, even when guests arrived. In fact, he had fallen into a classic honey trap. The caliph suspected Yaᶜqūb of treasonous connections with members of the Alid family and the girl was a spy. From her position behind the curtain, she could hear everything and reported back to her real master.³⁶ Yaᶜqūb soon found himself transported from his rose-filled bower to a black and noisome dungeon from which he emerged only many years later, an old and broken man who wanted nothing more than to retire to Mecca and live out his days in simple obscurity.

The caliphs took measures to get away from the stifling heat of the Iraqi summer. Again it is Muhammad ibn Sulaymān who describes these domestic details.³⁷ The Sasanian kings, he explained, used to have the roof of a room covered with fresh wet clay every day. They would also have reeds and willow shoots set up around the room and ice put in between them. The monarch would take advantage of this simple air conditioning to enjoy his siesta. The Abbasids improved on this simple system when wet fabrics were stretched across the windows. Mansūr is also said to have been the first to use a *khaysh*, what was known in British India as a punkah, that is a piece of cloth or sacking stretched on a rectangular wooden frame and hung from the ceiling which could be moved to and fro (by a punkah wallah) to provide a cooling fan.³⁸ They soon discovered that the heavier and wetter the cloth was, the more effectively it cooled. We also hear of caliphs sitting in summer houses, portable structures of wood and fabric open on one side, overlooking the river.³⁹

Palaces were mostly of one storey but some did have some upper-floor rooms. Mahdi was sitting at an upper floor window when he saw the girl passing with the bowl of pears, one of which had been poisoned, as we have seen, causing his death.⁴⁰ Hādī had a fine belvedere in a palace in which he lived in Iran before becoming caliph.

Muhammad ibn Sulaymān gives a description of Hārūn's siesta arrangements in the noon-time heat. He found the young caliph wearing just a thin tunic and a waist wrapper with a wide border decorated in red. The room was bare with no carpets and the door open to allow in a cool breeze. Hārūn disliked having a *khaysh* in the room because it irritated him (or perhaps because he wanted privacy), but there was one outside to create a breeze in the chamber.

On very hot days a silver bowl would be placed in the room and filled with perfumes, saffron and rosewater. Each day seven slave girls were brought in. They undressed and put on specially provided linen tunics which had been dipped in the perfume. Then they would sit on a pierced chair with incense burning slowly under it until the garments were completely dry and the girls fragrant with perfume. Only then were they ready for their master's pleasure.[41]

THE PALACES OF SĀMARRĀ

The palaces of the caliphs in Baghdad, the Golden Gate, the Eternity Palace down by the river, Mahdi's palace at Rusafa on the east bank and all the others, have disappeared entirely and left no traces on the landscape of modern Baghdad. By contrast, there are extensive remains of the palaces constructed by the caliphs at Sāmarrā in the short period from 836 to 892 when the city was the capital of the empire.[42] The structures of the buildings have mostly crumbled but the outlines of the plans can be seen clearly from the air, and there has been some excavation. None of the buildings has yielded any inscriptions to confirm who ordered their construction and when, but, by using the extensive literary descriptions of the site in its heyday, we can identify many of the royal dwellings.

The principal palace and seat of government was known as the Dār al-Khilāfa or Palace of the caliphate. It stood in a prominent position on a low bluff about 10 metres above the floodplain of the Tigris river. The whole complex is about 125 hectares in area and occupies a vast rectangle, about 1,346 metres from west to east and 1,150 from north to south, more than six times the size of Mansūr's Golden Gate in Baghdad. The main axis runs from west to east, and it was here that the most important public buildings were to be found. Overlooking the gardens that used to lead down to the Tigris was the great public gate (Bāb al-Āmma). This is the only part of the complex which still survives to its full height and, even though it is much restored and has lost its surface decoration, it remains a powerful symbol of authority. It was up through this gate that visitors would arrive, whether voluntarily or not. It was here that the rebel

Bābak was brought by elephant before his execution in 838, and it was here that the body of the disgraced general Afshīn was crucified for all to see before being burnt and the ashes thrown into the Tigris.

The public gate led into the Dār al-Āmma or Public Palace. Here a vaulted hall, no doubt lined with guards on state occasions, led to a small courtyard, then to another range of buildings and through another court to the audience hall itself. Just to the south of this there was a bath, perhaps so that visitors could make themselves smart before meeting the caliph. The audience hall consisted of a central domed chamber with four *iwāns* leading off on either side. At the south end of the south *iwān* there was yet another court at the end of which stood another domed chamber, richly decorated with wall paintings. It is likely that the cruciform audience hall was the setting for public audiences, but more favoured and intimate companions of the caliph might be entertained in the south dome. Continuing on the west–east axis, the visitor would pass through more courts until he reached a grandstand overlooking the racecourse which marked the eastern end of the palace complex. To the north and south of the main ceremonial axis, there were numerous smaller chambers. In one of them was the state treasury, *bayt al-māl*, and the Dome of Complaints (*qubbat al-mazālim*), where the ill-fated caliph Muhtadi attempted to revive the old traditions of public access to the ruler in 870.

To the north of the main axis, and slightly to the east of the audience hall, lay the Great Sirdāb (from Persian *sard* meaning cold and *āb* meaning water). This was a round, sunken, shady pool surrounded by small rooms and courts and a bath house. The court poet Ibrāhīm al-Mosuli had a *sirdāb* with a pool of water that was fed by a running stream and which discharged into a garden. He liked to spend the hot part of the day sleeping there, and it is likely that the caliphs used theirs in the same way. When the poet slept in his, he was taught a beautiful new song by two cats, one white and one black, which lived under the steps. They warned him that anyone he passed it on to would be turned into a jinn. And that is exactly what happened: he taught it to a singing girl of his and she was turned into a jinn. What the caliphs dreamed of in their *sirdābs* is lost to posterity.[43]

To the north of the *sirdāb* lay a rectangular enclosure within the larger palace. This can be identified with a building known in the sources as the Jawsaq al-Khaqani. The word *jawsaq*, probably to be pronounced *gawsaq*, derives from the Persian *kūshk*, meaning small palace or pavilion. After its use at Sāmarrā, the word was used to describe later palace buildings including the pavilions in the Topkapi Palace in Istanbul. From there it enters French as *kiosque* and English as kiosk. It is interesting to reflect, as you buy a newspaper from a small shop on a British train station, that its name derives from the palace of the Abbasid caliphs on the banks of the Tigris in Iraq. The Jawsaq enclosure was probably the more private and domestic part of the palace, secluded from the main public reception areas. Here too was the pavilion, known as the Perfect, which Qabīha, mother of the caliph Muᶜtazz, designed for her son.⁴⁴ It also served as the burial place of four of the Sāmarrā caliphs, including Muᶜtasim, the founder of the city. None of their tombs has been identified.

The plan of the palace is reasonably clear but it is more difficult to visualize the appearance of the buildings. The outside walls were constructed in fired bricks. Long blank surfaces with semicircular towers at regular intervals gave them a grim and fortress-like appearance. They were almost all of one storey with flat roofs; the caliph Muhtadi in 870 attempted in vain to escape from his pursuers by running from palace to palace over the flat roofs of Sāmarrā. The rooms inside were constructed of fired or mud brick and the ceilings were either vaulted or roofed with wooden timbers. The walls of the reception rooms would have been covered with patterned stucco and fresco painting and, of course, all the interiors would have been rich in carpets and hangings. A century and a half later, the writer Shābushti describes a throne room at Sāmarrā as it was remembered.

The caliph Mutawwakil had it decorated with great images of gold and silver and made a great pool whose surfacing inside and out was in plates of silver. He put on it a tree made of gold in which birds twittered and whistled [perhaps the earliest example of the use of these automata]. He had a great throne made of gold on which there were two images of huge lions and the steps to it had images of lions and eagles and other things, just as the throne of Soloman son of David is described. The walls of the palace were covered inside and outside with mosaic and gilded marble. 1,700,000 dinars were spent on this palace. He sat in the palace on his golden throne, dressed in a robe of rich brocade and he ordered

that all those who entered his presence should be dressed in finely
woven brocades.

He then goes on to say how the caliph suffered from insomnia
there and developed a fever. When he recovered, he ordered that the
throne room be demolished and the gold decoration be melted down
and minted as coin.[45]

The Palace of the Caliphate remained the seat of government and
private residence for most of the Sāmarrā period, but many other
palaces were built. Muᶜtasim's successor Wāthiq lived in a palace
called the Hārūni (his own given name was Hārūn), which lay on the
floodplain of the Tigris to the north-west. Mutawwakil too lived
there for much of his reign. The site of the Hārūni is known, but
because of its low-lying situation it has been badly damaged by
flooding. It was obviously quite a building: there is a brief description
of the caliph sitting in the palace in a portico dominated by a high
dome which was 'as white as an egg, except for what looks like a half
metre thick belt around the middle which was made of teak plated
with lapis lazuli and gold. It was called the Dome of the Girdle.'[46]

Mutawwakil (847–61) was a prodigious builder of palaces. Arabic
sources list some twenty-two of these and put the total cost at well
over 200 million *dirham*s, and later generations of historians mar-
velled at his extravagance and the resources available to him.[47]
Mutawwakil was the last caliph to be free of major financial constraints. Some of these palaces were no doubt quite small but the
largest covered enormous areas.

To the south of the city centre he constructed the Bulkuwara
Palace for his son and second heir, Muᶜtazz. The plan, which can be
clearly distinguished from the surface remains, was based on the
Palace of the Caliphate with a central axis leading from the river
bank, through a cruciform audience hall to courts and gardens
beyond. South of the main axis lay a number of smaller courts
arranged in regular patterns and surrounded by small rooms. It was
in the great *iwān* of this palace that Mutawwakil held the magnificent party with which he marked the circumcision of his son
Muᶜtazz.[48]

Mutawwakil's greatest project was his new city, modestly called
Mutawwakiliya, which he began building in October 858 immediately to the north of the inhabited area of Sāmarrā. He clearly regarded

this new city as an important aspect of his royal dignity: 'Now I know that I am a king,' he is said to have remarked, 'for I have built myself a city to live in.' The new city had a new mosque, of which substantial fragments remain, and, of course, a new palace.[49] This is said to have cost an astonishing 50 million *dirham*s, or between a quarter and a fifth of the total sum he spent on palace building. The palace was built at the northern end of the site and seems to have been deliberately constructed so that the caliph could keep his distance from the soldiers and the people of the city to the south. To the west it was bordered by the Tigris, to the north and east by a large canal. Like the Palace of the Caliphate and the Bulkuwara it extends from the river eastwards, and the actual palace is more than a kilometre from west to east. There were audience halls, with vaults of fired brick at the east end away from the river, but the most conspicuous feature was a gate and audience hall overlooking the river. It was probably here that the caliph sat drinking and talking one night in December 861 as his Turkish assassins crept in through the river gate.

The palaces of Sāmarrā were a prodigious example of caliphal grandeur and extravagance. Space was no object, and on the open gravel plains of Sāmarrā they could lay out their buttressed curtain walls and apparently endless chambers and courts as far as they wished. There was ample space for horse-racing tracks, polo grounds and enclosures for hunting. All the major palaces were characterized by domed and vaulted audience halls on the main axis and residential courts to the north and south. In none of them is there an area that can be identified as the harem. Materials were cheap and building was usually completed very fast. Mutawwakil was established in his new palace within two years of beginning the project. Apart from the Palace of the caliphate, which was used and modified throughout the Sāmarrā period, they were very short lived. The two large palaces of Shah and Arus on which Mutawwakil had spent a total of 50 million *dirham*s were demolished by the caliph Mustaʿīn (862–6) and the materials given to his vizier.[50] Mutawwakil's palace was abandoned and pulled down as soon as he was dead, having been occupied for a few months at most.

THE NEW PALACE IN BAGHDAD

When the caliph Mu^{c}tadid re-established Baghdad as the capital in 892, he began work on the construction of a new palace which was to be the home of the caliphs until the Mongols took the city in 1258. It was rebuilt continuously but it remained on the same site, on the east bank of the Tigris, downriver from the older-established quarters of Rusafa and Shammasiya. The palace of the Round City was occasionally used as a prison, but the Eternity Palace by the river on the west bank is heard of no more, and we must assume that both of them were ruinous and deserted.

As well as the new palace, the royal family also used the palaces on the Tahirids on the upper west side as a home for the princes of the blood who were not members of the reigning caliph's immediate family. The old palace built by Mahdi at Rusafa on the east bank was used as a sort of dower house for unmarried princesses of the royal family and members of the harem who were not serving the current caliph. We have no descriptions of either of these palaces to give us any idea of what they may have looked like.

The other centre of power in Baghdad was the Dār al-Wizāra, or House of the Vizierate. This had belonged to Sulaymān ibn Wahb, who had been vizier briefly in 877. After his disgrace, his palace became the official residence of the viziers, a sort of Abbasid 10 Downing Street, and it was no doubt extended and embellished. It is said to have covered an area of about 150,000 square metres (300,000 square cubits).[51] It was in Mukharrim, on the east bank, a short way upriver from the caliph's palace, with which it enjoyed the advantage of easy communication by water. The House of the Vizierate was seen at its grandest in 917 during Ibn al-Furāt's second term of office when two Byzantine envoys came to the capital.[52] They stayed in a palace on the east bank which had belonged to a vizier of the caliph Mu^{c}tadid but which now seems to have been a sort of official guest house. Ibn al-Furāt ordered that soldiers, dressed in brocade tunics with pointed caps, also in brocade, should line the way from the guest palace to the House of the Vizierate. Inside the palace, he arrayed his own *ghulāms* along the route that led from the gate to the audience hall where the envoys were to be received.

The two Byzantines entered through the public area of the palace (*Dār al-āmma*), where members of the public could come on business. They found the court there full of soldiers and the vizier's chamberlain told them to sit down under the colonnade that ran around the edge. Then he took them down a long corridor to the court of the Garden House and directed them towards the hall where the vizier sat. It was all a most impressive spectacle. Ibn al-Furāt himself awaited them in the magnificent hall with its gilded ceiling. The walls were hung with curtains that looked like carpets, presumably being of the same pattern – 30,000 *dīnārs* had been spent on furnishings, carpets and fabrics for the occasion. The vizier was seated on a splendid prayer rug with a high throne-back behind him. There were eunuchs in front of him and to his left and right while the court was filled with military commanders and prominent figures. The envoys were suitably overawed by all these troops.

They stood in front of the vizier and made their requests through their interpreter, an Arab military commander who had served for a long time on the Byzantine frontier and knew Greek well. They requested an exchange of prisoners and asked the vizier for an audience with the caliph himself. Ibn al-Furāt replied that he would see what he could do. Then they were led out by the same routes by which they had come in, back to the guest palace.

The architectural setting for this interview is not entirely clear. Miskawayh, who gives the description, uses the word *majlis* to describe the area where the vizier sat. It seems that it was covered, but it certainly looked out on to the court where the soldiers and others were gathered and where the envoys stood. The implication is that it was an arched *iwān* which opened on to a courtyard, though Miskawayh never uses the word. Whether the gilded ceilings were brick vaults, as in surviving examples at Ukhaydir and Sāmarrā, or flat wooden constructions is not clear.

As the financial problems of the state became more severe and assets were sold off to pay for current expenditure, the House of the Vizierate was threatened and in 933 it was divided into lots and sold off.

The real seat of power was, of course, the Palace of the Caliphate, also known as the Palace of the Sultan or the Palace of the Kingdom (Mamlaka). A palace on this site had originally been built by Ma'mūn before the civil war. He then passed it on to his agent in Iraq, Hasan ibn Sahl, and it became known as the Hasani Palace. He in turn gave it to his daughter Burān, who lived in it for years while the caliphs resided in Sāmarrā. When Mu‘tadid returned the caliphate to Baghdad in 892 he took possession of it from the old lady and it became the permanent residence of the caliphs.

Under Mu‘tadid and Muktafi, the original Hasani Palace was greatly expanded and a whole new area called the Crown Palace (Qasr al-Tāj) was added, the caliph Muktafi taking fired brick from the old Sasanian palaces at Cteisphon for the purpose. The palace now became a virtual city within a city, a vast complex of courts, corridors, halls and gardens surrounded by a fortified wall with gates that could be closed in time of emergency. It was a sort of Islamic equivalent of the Forbidden City in Beijing. The palace was divided up into numerous smaller groups of buildings, a reception room, the women's area (*dār al-huram*), apartments for princes, and the apartment of the chamberlain, who was responsible for security and order in the complex as well as controlling access to the ruler. A visitor wandering through the semi-derelict complex in the late tenth century said it reminded him of the whole city of Shiraz but whether this referred to its size or the general shape is not clear.

Nothing of this palace complex has survived. We have a number of descriptions which give us some idea of the building the complex contained but they do not give a clear idea of the overall plan. Many of the most important rooms overlooked the river, and there were gates that led to stairs down to the river bank where the barges of visitors could moor.

As with the Palace of the Vizierate, accounts of the arrival of the Byzantine ambassadors in 917 give us the clearest picture of the palace in its prime. The whole occasion was a major public relations exercise on the part of the caliph, and even more his vizier, Ibn al-Furāt. In reality, the ambassadors were not very important and the issue they came to discuss, the exchange of prisoners, had been accomplished many times before without any fanfare; the ambassadors may well have been surprised and somewhat overwhelmed at the scale and style of their reception. But in Baghdad the financial problems that were to bring down first the vizier and later the caliph were already apparent. Ibn al-Furāt was resorting to one of the oldest tricks in the political book, a foreign policy triumph to distract attention from domestic failings. Presumably the envoys took home to Constantinople an account of the wealth and culture of the Abbasid government, but the real audience were the people of Baghdad and the wider caliphate. From a public relations point of view, the visit was clearly a success; we have three or four different accounts of it and they dwell in loving detail on the splendour of the arrangements and the impression that they made on the representatives of the ancient enemy. It is from this publicity that we can try to reconstruct the function and appearance of the Abbasid palace.

The visit of the envoys to the caliph was an occasion of great public interest. According to a tradition passed down in the royal family from one of the caliph's concubines, the envoys were kept waiting for two months in Tikrit on the Tigris, so that the palaces and the display could be prepared for them.[53] When they arrived the whole city turned out to see them. The markets, streets, roofs and alleys of the east bank were full of people anxious to catch a glimpse of the envoys, and every shop and room that faced the street was rented out for a large sum. On the river, all the different types of boats were decorated and displayed in order. As they came from the guest palace, the two Byzantines passed by ranks of mounted troops, in uniform with saddles of gold and silver, fully armed.

The fullest account of the reception of the ambassadors was pre-served by Hilal al-Sabi (d. 1056), a historian of the Abbasid adminis-tration and court who claims that he based his version on a description written by one of Muqtadir's grandsons.[54]

He begins with a description of the 38,000 curtains that were hung in the palace. These were made of gold brocade with images of goblets, elephants, horses and camels, lions and birds. They came from Wasit in Iraq, Armenia and Bahnasā in Egypt. In addition there were 22,000 carpets and runners from Dawraq in Khuzistan and Jahrum and Dastagird in Fars which were placed in all the corri-dors where the ambassadors walked. Yet more carpets from Dabīq in Armenia and Tabaristān were hung in the halls and alcoves where they could be seen but not walked on.

The ambassadors entered by the great public gate and were taken first to a palace called the Inn of the Horses (*khān al-khayl*), which was a large court surrounded by arcades with marble columns. To right and left of the court were horses with gold and silver saddles, attended by their grooms. Then they were taken down corridors and passages to the wild animal enclosures (*hayr al-wahsh*). Here beasts were brought in from the garden and came right up close to the people, sniffing them and eating from their hands. They came next to a court where there were four elephants, adorned with brocade and satin. On each elephant there were eight men from Sind and fire-hurlers (for shooting incendiary weapons). The ambassadors were said to have been awe-struck by the sight. Finally they were taken to the lion house, where there were fifty lions to the left and fifty to the right, muzzled with chains, each held by its keeper.

Having finished with the zoo, the envoys then went to the New Kiosk, which stood among gardens. In the centre was an artificial pond, about 15 metres by 10, made of burnished tin, surrounded by a river, also made of tin, which shone more brightly than silver. In the 'pond' were four fine boats with brocade and gold and silver work from Dabīq. Surrounding it was a garden containing, it was said, four hundred palm trees 2.5 metres tall, each dressed in carved teak from top to bottom with brass rings around them. From each branch hung fine dates, not yet quite ripe. Along the walls of the garden were various different types of citrus fruit, probably at this time sour oranges, lemons and limes: sweet oranges do not seem to have been found in the Middle East or Europe until the late fifteenth century, when they were imported from India by the Portuguese.[55]

The next place to be visited was the celebrated House of the Tree. In the centre of the court there was an artificial tree in the middle of a large, apparently natural pool. The branches of the tree were mostly made of silver, though some were of gold, and there were gold and silver birds of many species perched on the twigs. At certain times the trees swayed, the leaves rustled and the birds would sing. The tree was crowned with jewels in the shape of fruits. The House of the Tree was said to have been built by the caliph Muqtadir. Similar trees are recorded in Byzantine palaces and in palaces in later medieval Europe. The Spanish traveller Clavijo saw one in Tamerlane's palace in Samarqand during his visit in 1405. It was as tall as a man and contained rubies, emeralds, turquoises, sapphires and pearls shaped like fruits. The golden birds sat on the branches as if to eat the fruit.[56] As with other aspects of royal display, it seems that the Abbasid court style set the pattern that many other courts sought to emulate long after the Abbasid royal palace had been looted and ruined.

From the House of the Tree, the envoys were taken to the Palace of Paradise, which contained rugs and ornaments beyond number. In the vestibule of this palace there was an armoury with ten thousand gilded breast-plates hung on the walls. Then they went down a corridor 150 metres long, on either side of which were hung ten thousand suits of armour, consisting of leather shields, helmets, coats of mail and ornamented quivers and bows. Standing on both sides there were two thousand white and black eunuchs.

Finally, after having toured twenty-three palaces, they arrived at the Ninetieth Court (there seems to be no explanation for the name). Here there were guards fully armed with swords, axes and maces. They passed lines of chamberlains, sons of court officers and troops all dressed in the official Abbasid colour of black. Everywhere, attendants provided iced water, drinks and fruit juice.

The caliph awaited them in the Palace of the Crown, which stood by the Tigris. Muqtadir sat on an ebony throne covered with brocade from Dabīq. He was also dressed in Dabīq brocade embroidered with gold with a high cap on his head. On his right were nine strings of precious stones with another seven on his left, made up of the most amazing jewels which eclipsed the daylight with their brightness. Five of the caliph's sons sat before him, three to the right and two to the left.

The ambassadors came forward and bowed, explaining that they would have kissed the carpet, as Abbasid protocol demanded, if they had not been concerned that Abbasid envoys would be made to do the same in their country. We are not given many details of the interview itself: the caliph seems to have been spoken for by court officials, but he personally handed them a long written reply to the Byzantine emperor. Then they were led out through the private gate to the Tigris, where their boats took them back to the guest palace.

Thus was Muqtadir's court remembered a hundred years later when the glories of the Abbasids had long since vanished. How far it represents the reality of his reign is almost impossible to say, and certainly the numbers are likely to be exaggerated. However, the account tells us a lot about court style, about what palaces ought to have been like. The palace complex was a maze of courtyards, corridors and halls. There were enclosed gardens, both natural and artificial, and a zoo. We know from other sources that there were baths and mosques. None of the individual buildings seems to have been very grand, and there is no evidence that they were more than one storey high. The palace sought to impress with the richness of ornament and above all with the sumptuous fabrics on wall and floor. The guides who brought the envoys to the caliph were clearly intent on showing them the best Abbasid court culture had to offer, and to take them through the vast numbers of courts and chambers. It must have seemed to them that they had walked miles before they saw the ruler. But we must remember that we are told that it had taken two months to prepare the festivities: perhaps the day-to-day life of the palace was much less grand.

We get a very different view of the palace from the story of the deposition of the caliph Qāhir twelve years later in the spring of 929.[57] Misgovernment and financial crisis had led to the deposition of Muqtadir, who had presided over the reception of the Byzantine ambassadors. To replace him, the military commanders who led the coup had gone to the Palace of Tāhir on the upper west side, where the Abbasid princes usually lodged, and selected a young man of no experience or proven ability, and installed him with the title of Qāhir, 'the Victorious'. The coup had been supported by the infantry in the caliphal army, who now demanded the traditional donatives that the military were given to celebrate the accession of a new caliph. The chief of police, Nāzūk, ordered that the gates of the palace complex be shut, but he did not want to risk a confrontation with the disaffected troops so he ordered his own men not to use violence against them.

The palace was virtually under siege, and soon the infantry began to enter the building by the windows overlooking the river. The new caliph, Qāhir, was receiving congratulations in the portico of the Ninetieth Court near by and could clearly hear the noise the troops were making. Nāzūk was apparently much the worse for wear, having spent the night drinking heavily. When he appeared at a window to try to calm the soldiers, they rushed at him and he panicked and fled. Trying to escape, he came up against a door that he himself had ordered to be bricked up the previous day; he was trapped and killed. The soldiers took his body down to the Tigris and impaled it on a wooden screen that ran along the river bank.

The infantry now began to call openly for the restoration of the old caliph, Muqtadir, and the vizier and the chamberlains wasted no time in making themselves scarce, leaving the unfortunate Qāhir virtually alone. Meanwhile, the palace servants, all of whom were still eunuchs or favourites of Muqtadir's, locked the gates.

The miserable Qāhir turned to the only one of his supporters who remained with him, Abu'l-Ḥayja the Hamdanid. Unlike most of the courtiers and military men, Abu'l-Hayja was a Bedouin Arab, from the ancient and famous tribe of Taghlib. As he was on the point of joining the general exodus, Qāhir clung to him and pleaded, 'Abu'l-Hayja, are you going to desert me?' and, says the chronicler, Abu'l-Hayja's pride was aroused; a Bedouin chief does not abandon the man who has sought his protection. 'No, by Allah, I will never desert you!' he said, and turned back.

Abu'l-Hayja and Qāhir had to escape from the palace, now full of danger and hostile or treacherous servants. Once they had made it into the city they could go into hiding or flee to join Abu'l-Hayja's tribesmen in the free and open plains of the Jazira. They tried the door of the chamber, and found it locked. Then there was the sound of shouting. The senior servant still with them was one Fā'iq, nicknamed 'Bowl-face'. He now sent one of the messengers to find out what the noise was. The man returned to say that Abu'l-Hayja had been killed. Bowl-face told him to think carefully what he was saying and he repeated it three times before Bowl-face said to him, 'Abu'l-Hayja is right here, you fool!' Then the messenger said that he had made a mistake and it was Nāzūk, the chief of police, who had been killed.

The death of Nāzūk meant that there was no hope of rescue from within the palace. Their lives now depended on escaping. Abu'l-Hayja demanded that Bowl-face open the door which led to the river banks but Bowl-face, whose loyalties were very doubtful, said that there were many doors behind that one and it would not do them any good. Still, he agreed to open the door. When the two went out they found themselves on the steps of the water wheels that raised water from the river to the palaces. Hand in hand they climbed the steps. What they saw must have confirmed their worst fears; as far as the eye could see, up and down the banks and in front of the gates of the palace, hostile soldiers were gathered.

Qāhir went down and Abu'l-Hayja tried to encourage him. 'Go on, my lord,' he said, 'by the grave of [my ancestor] Hamdān, I will never desert you as long as I live!' So they hurried on through the now deserted Palace of Paradise, where the Byzantine envoys had been dazzled by the display of carpets and armour twelve years before, and on into an open square. Here they met a mounted slave and Abu'l-Hayja asked him where he had come from, to which the man replied that he had come from the Nubian Gate. Abu'l-Hayja realized that this was a possible escape route. He took the slave's horse and, stripping off his black court robes, disguised himself in the slave's coarse woollen *jubba*. He told Qāhir to wait for him and set off. He was soon back. The news was not good. He told Qāhir that he had reached the Nubian Gate and asked the gatekeeper, Jaᶜfar, to open it. Jaᶜfar said that he could not: the head of the unfortunate Nāzūk had just been brought there and there were crowds of troops who had come to see it. They would have to look for another way out.

The palace that had seemed so impressive and opulent to the Byzantine envoys had become for Abu'l-Hayja a deadly labyrinth of narrow corridors, blocked doors and treacherous servants. They now went back through the Palace of Paradise and other courtyards until they came to the Citron House. Here Bowl-face showed his true colours: he hung back a little and said to the few servants who were still with them, 'Go in and finish off your master's [Muqtadir's] enemy.' There were about ten of them armed with bows and clubs. When Abu'l-Hayja saw them, he drew his sword, wrapped the woollen *jubba* around his arm as a shield and charged. The servants fled in terror and some of them fell in the pool. Then he retreated to the Teak Room in the garden of the Citron House. The slaves in the pool now clambered out, but he charged them again and they fled to a door at one corner of the court. When they opened it, they found one of the infantry officers carrying a bow and arrows and with two black slaves armed with swords and shields.

'Friends, where is he?' the officer asked.

'In the Teak Room,' they replied.

'Go and provoke him so that he comes out!'

So they abused him and he reacted as they had hoped. He charged out, 'like a furious camel', shouting the traditional defiance of a Bedouin against his enemies. 'O tribe of Taghlib, shall I be slain between walls?' (like a city dweller, rather than in the open desert like a true Bedouin). The officer shot him with an arrow that entered just below his breast and another that penetrated his throat, and then released a third. By this time his hand was unsteady and the third arrow hit his thigh. Abu'l-Hayja seized this arrow and broke it. He pulled out the arrow from his breast and tried to run but soon collapsed. One of the black servants came and cut off his right hand, which held his sword, while another cut off his head. Then one of the eunuchs snatched the head and made off with it, presumably to collect his reward.

Muqtadir, meanwhile, had been carried on the shoulders of his supporters from his barge to the steps of the Ninetieth Court, where Qāhir had held court so recently. When he arrived his first concern was with what had happened to Abu'l-Hayja. He sent to the stewardess Zaydān, whose apartments, as usual, seem to have been an oasis of tranquillity during all this mayhem. She replied that he was in the Citron House. Immediately Muqtadir called for ink and paper and wrote with his own hand an amnesty for Abu'l-Hayja. He gave this to one of the eunuchs, telling him to be quick or it would be too late. It already was. When the eunuch who had grabbed his head appeared, Muqtadir demanded to know who had killed him. One of the officers signalled to the eunuch to keep quiet and said that he had been attacked by a mixed band. The eunuch, who had hoped for a generous reward, was lucky to escape with his life. Muqtadir remembered Abu'l-Hayja's kindness to him in the recent past and all the support he had received from his family. There was no doubting the genuineness of his grief – Muqtadir must often have lamented the loss of so faithful a servant of the caliphs during the difficult few years before his own head was cut off on the field of battle and paraded before his enemies. Qāhir lived to reign another day. Brought before Muqtadir, he threw himself on the ground and was pardoned and sent back to the house of Tāhir where the princes lived.

The palaces of the caliphs had evolved out of all recognition since the days when Mansūr had held court in a tent. The Golden Gate palace he built was tiny compared with the vast structures laid out at Sāmarrā or the world within a world which was the palace of the later caliphs in Baghdad. Early Abbasid caliphs still travelled, conducting their administration in a camp or hunting lodge. By the reign of Muqtadir, the caliph's palace had become his kingdom, at once a fortress, a scene for the public performance of monarchy, a luxurious dwelling and a death trap.

VII

The Harem

The Abbasid caliphs all maintained a female household which in many ways was distinct from the male world of army, administration and the public court, although the two different spheres interacted in many different ways. Conventionally this household is described as the *harīm* (harem) and seen as a secluded world of luxury, idleness and intermittent danger. As early as the tenth century commentators were condemning the extravagance and political influence of the harem as a major cause of the failing powers of the caliphs.[1]

The term *harīm* means the protected or inviolable part of the house where only males closely related to the owner are allowed to visit. In fact the term is seldom used in the sources of the period. More commonly the caliph would refer to his *huram*, a plural word of the same root, meaning his women and, more generally, those under his protection. The *huram* was a group of people rather than a particular building or physical location.

Under the first Abbasid caliphs, the women of the ruling family seem to have maintained their own households and palaces, very much like their brothers and male cousins. By the early tenth century, if not before, there are indications that the women were more enclosed in the vast and sprawling royal palace and the harem had become a separate, purpose-built, enclosed structure, like the famous harem of the Topkapi Palace in Istanbul. In 974, when the caliphs had lost virtually all their political power, Adud al-Dawla the Buyid, now the effective ruler of Baghdad, visited the caliphal palace. He was shown round the vast complex of buildings and courtyards, much of it deserted and falling into ruin, by the chamberlain Mu'nis al-Fadl. When they came to the harem, however, Mu'nis stopped and explained that no man except an Abbasid caliph had ever been inside it, but of course, if the amir wished to see it, he could. Tactfully Adud al-Dawla declined the offer and continued the tour of the rest of the complex.² Clearly by this time the harem was a separate, clearly defined area of the palace. It is not clear when this had come to pass. In an anecdote told to explain the fall of the Barmakids in 803, Mas⁽ūdi, writing in the mid tenth century, tells of Yahya the Barmakid supervising the *huram* of Hārūn al-Rashid, and apparently locking up the gates of the *huram* at night and taking the keys home with him. He also forbade the women to be served by their eunuchs. This provoked the wrath of Hārūn's formidable wife Zubayda, who then determined to undermine the power of the Barmakid family.³ However, this looks like the back projection of later norms to the early Abbasid period, and probably tells us more about the position in the mid tenth century than in the late eighth. It is impossible from the archaeological evidence to identify any specific areas of the palaces at Sāmarrā as the harems, although by this time (mid ninth century) there probably were separate, enclosed women's quarters.

By the late ninth century, the harem of the caliphs had already acquired a fantastic image as a world apart, a closed environment of luxury and sexual excitement tinged with a frisson of cruelty and danger. Consider this story from the *Book of Songs*, one of many anecdotes dealing with the celebrated poet and singer Ibrāhīm al-Mosuli.⁴

One day the caliph Hārūn told the poet he intended to spend the morning with his harem and the evening drinking with the men. The poet was to keep himself in readiness, not seeing anyone or drinking any wine until the summons came; if he did not, he would be punished by death. He kept himself to himself all day and after the evening prayer he was summoned to the palace. As he approached he saw a large basket suspended by ropes from the walls of a palace and a slave girl standing beside it who invited him to sit in it. The poet suspected this was a trick to make him late and put him in the wrong with the caliph, but after some argument she persuaded him. As soon as he sat in the basket, it was pulled up to the roof of the palace. There he saw more slave girls, who were laughing and enjoying themselves. When they first caught sight of him they said, 'By God, the one we wanted has arrived!', but when they looked more closely they realized that they had made a mistake and hastened to put on their *hijāb*, exclaiming, 'O enemy of God, what has brought you to us?', to which he replied in the same spirit, 'O enemies of God, who were you expecting and what has he got that I don't?' They did not seem put out by this and went on laughing, with the poet joining in.

Then one of them said, 'The one we wanted has disappeared but this is an elegant fellow [*zarīf*], let's party with him.' Food was brought and he was invited to eat, which he did somewhat reluctantly. Then wine was produced and they began to drink. After a while, three of the girls came out and began to sing, while the others modestly stayed behind a curtain. An argument developed as to who had composed the songs they were singing, and it was then that Ibrāhīm finally revealed his identity, saying which songs he had composed and which were other people's work.

The girls were thrilled, and they all came out to enjoy themselves. When Ibrāhīm said that he had to leave they demanded to know why, so he told them what the caliph had said to him. They replied simply that he was in a delightful confinement and promised to let him go after a week. He feared it would be the death of him but stayed all the same. When they said goodbye to him, they made him promise that if he survived he would return. Then he got into the basket and was lowered to the street again.

When he reached the caliph's palace, he found that people had been searching for him all over Baghdad, his property had been ransacked and his income cut off. The eunuchs hurried him into the caliph's presence. Hārūn abused him, accused him of treating his orders with contempt, wasting his time with the lower classes and ended by calling for the sword and the execution mat.

Like Scheherazade in the *Arabian Nights*, the poet knew that storytelling alone could save his life and said that he had the most amazing tale and asked to be allowed to tell it. The caliph, of course, agreed, saying that if the story were truly remarkable, he might spare him. When Ibrāhīm had finished, the caliph was silent for a while and then said, 'This is amazing! Can you bring me to the place?', and when Ibrāhīm promised he could, Hārūn relaxed and invited him to sit down and have a drink.

The next day he went back to the place as arranged and there was the basket and the slave girl. Once more he was pulled up and the girls were delighted to see him and gave thanks to God for his safety. He spent the night there, and when he left he told the girls he had a brother to whom he was very attached: could he bring him along to meet them? They replied that he was welcome. He made an arrangement for the next day and went to Hārūn and told him.

When the time came, Ibrāhīm and Hārūn set off together in disguise. When they came to the place, they went up in the basket, but, as Ibrāhīm said later, 'God sent me a warning' – he had told the girls to keep themselves hidden and not to let his companion hear a word from them until he said so and make sure that the songs and poems they chose were decent. They accepted that and kept themselves completely hidden. Hārūn and Ibrāhīm drank a great deal. The caliph had ordered Ibrāhīm not to address him by his title, but when he was well gone in wine he said by mistake, 'O Commander of the Faithful...' and the girls leapt up behind the curtain and were gone in an instant. Then Hārūn turned to the poet and said, 'You have escaped from a terrible fate. If one of them had shown herself to you, I would have had your head cut off! Let's go!'

It emerged that the girls belonged to him and that he had become angry with them and imprisoned them there. The next day he sent along eunuchs who returned them to his own palace. The poet was given 100,000 *dirham*s and the girls later sent presents and favours.

We do not need to believe this story, which may well be an old folk tale reworked in a contemporary setting, to be true to see it as historically interesting, and it is a vivid illustration of the popular image of the caliph's harem in Baghdad literary circles. The story is traced back to one Ahmad ibn Abi Tāhir, an authority on literary history and anecdotes who died in 893. The story therefore dates from about half a century after the caliph's death and shows how the mythic elements of the image of caliph and harem were already well developed. The mysterious palace, the assertive, sassy girls kept as virtual prisoners, the jealous caliph and the clever, quick-witted poet as transgressor of the social norms of the period are clearly established. It is difficult to tell whether this is based on the realities of Hārūn's reign or the realities of the author's own time, but it makes it clear that by the mid ninth century the caliph's harem was a secluded, separate world in which anything could happen and where pleasure and danger coexisted in time and place.

The women of the ruling family had not always lived in the seclusion of the caliph's palace. In the eighth and early ninth centuries prominent ladies at court had their own palaces in Baghdad.

Khayzurān had a palace in Baghdad that was later owned by a military commander, Ashinās, showing that this was an independent dwelling, not a part of the caliph's palace. Mansūr's daughter Asmā had a palace on the east bank next to the palace of Mahdi's son Ubayd Allah.[5] In the next generation, Mahdi's beloved daughter Banūqa had a palace with grounds, and near by was the palace of her sister, Abbāsa,[6] who was later alleged to have had a scandalous relationship with Jaᶜfar the Barmakid. Zubayda built a palace during the reign of her son Amīn on land on the west bank which had belonged to one of the Barmakids. A cousin, Umm Abd Allah bint Īsā ibn Alī, had a palace in the commercial quarter of Karkh, 'where the honey sellers are'.[7] One of Hārūn's daughters, Umm Habīb, acquired a palace on the east bank in the reign of Ma'mūn which became a sort of dower house for the daughters of caliphs who did not have their own places. By the late ninth century, this function had been taken over by the Mahdi's palace at Rusafa, also on the east bank.[8]

Ma'mūn's wife Burān had inherited a palace on a prime site on the east bank of the Tigris from her father, a senior figure at Ma'mūn's court. When she was an old lady, long after her husband's death, the caliph Muᶜtadid, the man who brought the caliphate back from Sāmarrā to Baghdad in 892, asked that the palace be handed over to him for use as a residence. The caliph's wishes could not be denied and Burān accepted the loss with good grace:

> she asked for a few days respite so that she could move out and hand it over to him. She then repaired the palace, plastered and white-washed it and decorated it with the best and most exquisite furnishings, hanging all sorts of curtains on its portals. She filled the cupboards with everything that might be of use to the Caliph and arranged for men servants and slave girls to answer whatever need should arise. Having done this, she moved and sent word to the Caliph that he could go ahead with the transfer of his residence.

Muᶜtadid was delighted and Burān's palace became the core of the palace of the later Abbasid caliphs.[9] There could be no doubt that Burān was mistress of her own household.

Burān's handing over of her palace to the caliph marked the end of an era. After the return of the caliphate to Baghdad, we hear no more about princesses having separate palaces or town houses. As far as we can tell, the *huram* now lived in apartments in the Palace of the Caliphate, the great sprawling residence that was developed on the site of Burān's establishment on the east bank of the Tigris. It seems as if prominent women had their own apartments within this complex and it is probably from this time that the harem, as a separate women's quarter within the palace, first emerges.

During the ninth century, it seems as if the palace originally built by Mahdi when he founded the part of Baghdad on the eastern side of the town known as Rusafa had become a sort of dower house for female members of the Abbasid family and their attendants. The last of the great ladies of the Abbasid caliphate, Muqtadir's mother, known as Sayyida (the mistress), lived in apartments in the Palace of the Caliphate, but she had built a tomb complex (*turba*) at Rusafa. It was here that she kept an emergency cache of money, said to have been 600,000 *dīnār*s,[10] and it was here that she was laid to rest after her death.

The composition of the *huram* varied, and its numbers certainly increased as the Abbasid caliphate developed a more elaborate palace structure.

There are few indications of the numbers of women who might be found in a harem, or the numbers of their attendants. Hārūn al-Rashīd is said to have had more than two thousand singing and servant girls in his *huram*,[11] and records suggest that there were around twenty-four concubines who bore him children.[12] In another source, it was claimed that the mid-ninth-century caliph al-Mutawwakil had four thousand concubines and had had sexual intercourse with every single one of them.[13]* Given that he was caliph for fourteen years, or slightly over five thousand days (and nights),[14] and his well-established reputation as a heavy drinker, the figures suggest a stamina and determination few of us could hope to emulate. However, as these figures come from that old gossip Mas°ūdī, who was always on the lookout for a sensational story, we should perhaps take them with a pinch of salt.

It might seem obvious that the legal wives of the caliphs would be

---

* This inevitably, but quite irrelevantly, brings to mind Gibbon's famous comment on the household of the Emperor Gordian: 'Twenty-two acknowledged concubines and a library of sixty-two thousand volumes, attested the variety of his inclinations; and from the productions which he left behind him, it appears that the former, as well as the latter, were designed for use rather than for ostentation' (*Decline and Fall*, i, p. 312).

the leaders of the *huram*, but in fact that was rarely the case. Under Muslim law, the caliph, like any other man, would be permitted to take up to four wives, as long as he could look after them all equally. Mansūr's wife was Arwā, better known as Umm Mūsā. She was of aristocratic origin, descended from the pre-Islamic kings of Himyar in Yemen, and was presumably quite a catch for the impoverished Abbasid. He had married her well before the revolution that brought the dynasty to power. She had, apparently, insisted on a pre-nuptial agreement that he would take neither wife nor concubine as long as she lived. The sources say that he made many attempts to have the agreement annulled but in all cases she was able to persuade the judges to maintain the contract. After her death in the tenth year of his reign, he is said to have been presented with a hundred virgins. We should be sceptical about such stories, but we can be certain that his two sons by Arwā, Mahdi and Jaʿfar, are the only two he ever considered for the succession.[15] He also seems to have married one Fātima, who was descended from the great hero of early Islam, Talha, by whom he had three sons; there may have been others. We know that he had at least two concubines, a Kurdish slave girl whose name is not known and a Byzantine girl called the 'Restless Butterfly', but we know of them only because they bore him sons.[16]

His son Mahdi married only once before he became caliph, a very respectable and conventional marriage to his cousin Rīta, daughter of the first Abbasid caliph, Saffāh. This seems to have been a companionate marriage, but neither of the two sons she bore him was considered for the succession. At the same time as he married Rīta, he also acquired the young slave girl Khayzurān, who was to be the dominant figure among his *huram*. Perhaps surprisingly there is no tradition of hostility between Rīta and Khayzurān, and Rīta was a considerable help to her husband during the anxious and uncertain period when he was establishing his position after his father's death.

When he became caliph, Mahdi married Khayzurān, a bold breach with tradition since she did not come from the same aristocratic milieu but was a slave who needed to be formally manumitted before the marriage. At the same time he also made a more conventional marriage to Umm Abd Allah, another of his cousins,[17] and the next year he married Ruqayya, another suitable partner, descended as she was from the caliph Uthmān (644–56).

The next caliph, the short-lived Hādī, is not known to have

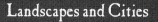

TOP: Humayma. (Jordan) Now ruined and deserted, this was once a flourishing village. Part of the remains of the home of the Abbasid family, a series of rooms around a central courtyard, can be seen in the foreground. (Author)

ABOVE: Humayma. The reconstructed walls of the small mosque by the house of the Abbasids where the men of the family would go to talk, share their meals . . . and plot revolution. (Author)

OPPOSITE ABOVE: The Gates of Asia. The old Khurasan Road at Bisitun (Iran) where it passes through the Zagros Mountains. This road linked Baghdad with the Iranian plateau and it was along here that the Abbasid armies marched in 749 to overthrow the Umayyads and Tahir's troops rode in 812 to overthrow Amin. (Author)

OPPOSITE BELOW: The Ancient Walls of Merv (Turkmenistan). The city, already a thousand years old, was the centre of Muslim rule in Khurasan, and the place where Abu Muslim first proclaimed the Abbasid caliphate. (Author)

ABOVE: Merv. Outside the city walls lay the fortified palaces of the Iranian aristocracy. These may have been built by Tahir and his family in the early ninth century. (Author)

TOP: Baghdad. Virtually nothing remains of the city of the early Abbasid caliphs but this nineteenth-century drawing by Lieutenant J. Fitzjames, RN, captures something of the atmosphere, the domes and palaces by the Tigris and the bridge of boats across the river. (Published illustration from F. R. Chesney, *Narrative of the Euphrates Expedition*, London, Longmans, 1868)

ABOVE: Basra. The great port city of southern Iraq lay among the canals and the palm groves which produced the most delicious dates, seen here in a romantic drawing by Lieutenant Colonel Estcourt of the 43rd Light Infantry (also from Chesney).

Raqqa on the Euphrates was developed by the
Abbasid caliphs as a military base for campaigns on
the Byzantine frontier. It became Hārūn al-Rashīd's
favourite residence. In this aerial photograph from
the 1930s we see the Abbasid city walls and, in the
foreground, the outlines of Hārūn's palace. (French
military, Armée du Levant, 1939)

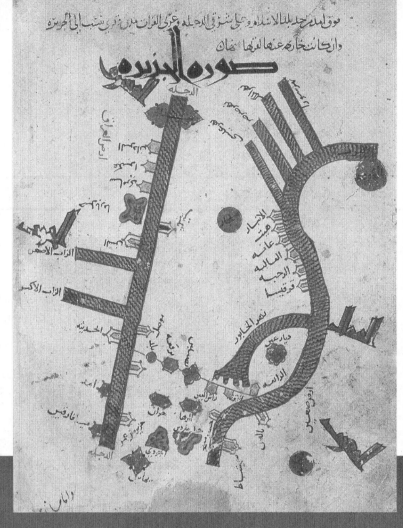

This tenth-century map of northern Iraq shows the Tigris and Euphrates. North is at the bottom of the page and the Tigris ends at Baghdad. The Greater and Lesser Zab rivers flow into the Tigris and the Khabur into the Euphrates. The cartographer has also shown the canals which led from the Euphrates to the Tigris at Baghdad. (Bridgeman/Egyptian National Library, Cairo)

BELOW:
The dried-up bed of the great Nahrawan Canal which irrigated the fertile Sawad of Iraq, the breadbasket of the Abbasid caliphate. The canal was breached by a military adventurer in 935 and never flowed again. (Author)

TOP: Ukhaydir (Iraq). The vast ruined palace was constructed by an Abbasid prince in the late eighth century. It gives an idea of the appearance of the fortifications and palaces of Mansūr's Baghdad, under construction at the same time. (Creswell, Ashmolean Museum, Oxford)

ABOVE: Ukhaydir. The main court of the palace. The arch of the main *iwān* which led to the audience hall

ABOVE: Ukhaydir. Upper gallery. Simple shapes, painted arches and barrel vaults characterize the architecture of the palace. (Creswell, Ashmolean Museum, Oxford)

RIGHT: Ukhaydir. Audience Hall. The bare walls would have been covered with stucco decorated and patterned plaster. Rich hangings and carpets would have added colour. (Creswell, Ashmolean Museum, Oxford))

Sāmarrā (Iraq). The plan of the Abbasid city can be clearly seen from the air. In the foreground is the wide main street lined by the compounds and palaces of the elite soldiers and bureaucrats. In the middle distance the mosque built by Mutawwakil (847–61) in his new quarter of the city. (RAF c. 1930 Crown copyright)

ABOVE: Sāmarrā. The Great Mosque. (848–52) The outer walls of this huge structure have an almost military appearance. (Author)

RIGHT: Sāmarrā the Great Mosque. Nothing remains of the interior of the mosque, just an empty enclosure. On the far side can be seen the great spiral minaret. (Author)

ABOVE: The Malwiya, the great spiral minaret of Mutawwakil's mosque, still dominates the Sāmarrā ruinfield: note the size of the figure at the top. (Author)

LEFT: Sāmarrā. The gate of the palace of the caliphs. This huge triple arched entrance is the only part of the palace to survive to its full height. (Author)

Sāmarrā. Two impressions of the palace of the caliphs by Ernst Herzfeld, who began excavations of the site just before the First World War. In the upper one we see the dome of the main audience hall and the courts surrounding it. Below, the main gate as seen from the river bank across the gardens. (Sāmarrā, Djausaq. Reconstruction of portal and stairs to lake, D-1101. Original drawing. Ernst Herzfeld Papers. Freer Gallery of Art and Arthur M. Sackler Gallery Archives. Smithsonian Institution, Washington, D.C. Gift of Ernst Herzfeld, 1946)

ABOVE: Sāmarrā. Wall decoration from the palace of
Mu'tazz (d. 869), used to give an elegant finish to the
mud-brick walls. (Creswell, Ashmolean Museum,
Oxford)

RIGHT: Sāmarrā. Two dancing girls pouring wine.
Only small fragments of the mural paintings which
decorated the palace have survived. (Istanbul:
Turkish and Islamic Museum)

ABOVE: Cairo. The mosque of Ibn Tulun, constructed by a Turkish general from Sāmarrā in 876–9, is the finest surviving example of an Abbasid imperial mosque. (Author)

RIGHT: The courtyard of the mosque of Ibn Tulun. The heavy piers, pointed arches and stucco decoration are characteristically Abbasid. (Author)

A mounted warrior from Penjikent, near Samarqand. The aristocratic culture of the principalities of Transoxania had a profound effect on Abbasid court style. (Bridgeman/Hermitage, St Petersburg)

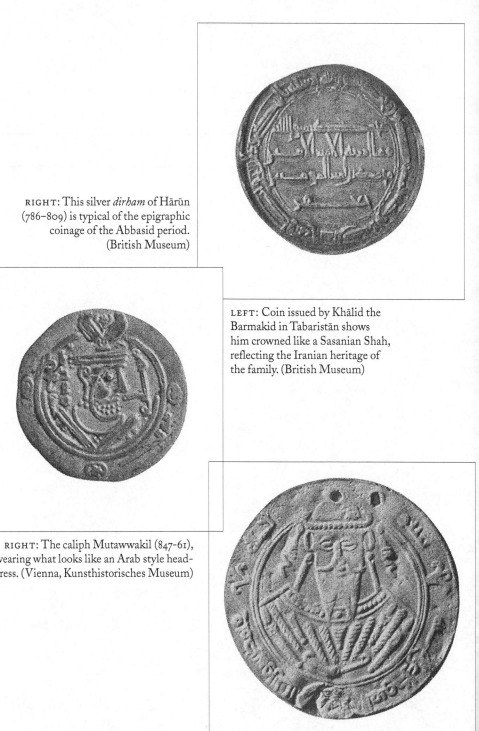

RIGHT: This silver *dirham* of Hārūn (786–809) is typical of the epigraphic coinage of the Abbasid period. (British Museum)

LEFT: Coin issued by Khālid the Barmakid in Tabaristān shows him crowned like a Sasanian Shah, reflecting the Iranian heritage of the family. (British Museum)

RIGHT: The caliph Mutawwakil (847-61), wearing what looks like an Arab style head-dress. (Vienna, Kunsthistorisches Museum)

LEFT: The caliph Muqtadir (908–32), seated on the throne with a beaker of wine in his hand. (Berlin, Staatsmuseum, Munzkabinett)

RIGHT: The caliph Muqtadir mounted and armed with a sword. He rides in the Arab fashion, with a single rein held in one hand. (British Museum)

LEFT: The caliph Radi (934–40), seated on a prayer rug, playing a lute. (British Museum)

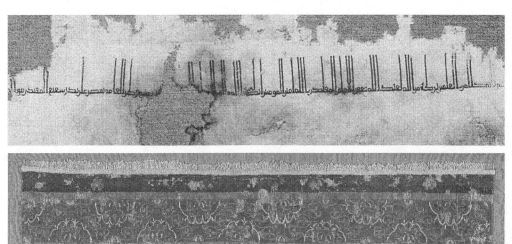

TOP: Fine textiles were an essential part of court culture, almost an alternative currency. This linen fragment with its elegant inscription was made in Egypt and bears the name of the caliph Muqtadir, the vizier who commissioned it and the manager of the state textile factory. (Berlin, Museum of Islamic Culture)

ABOVE: Tapestry panel: an example of the finely woven linen textiles produced by the Abbasid government workshops. (Egypt, al-Bahnasa, Abbasid Period, ninth century AD. Tapestryweave; wool and linen, 80 x 83. cm. © The Cleveland Museum of Art, Purchase from the J. H. Wade Fund, 1959.48)

This silver gilt dish made in Tabaristān in the late eighth century. In this party scene the ruler enjoys food and wine in a garden setting. The dish shows how Sasanian court styles were transmitted to the Abbasids. (British Museum)

Bronze aquamanile in the form of a falcon, made in Iran and dated by the inscription on its neck to 796–7. An early and rare survival of the luxury metalwork of the Abbasid period. (Bridgeman/Hermitage, St Petersburg)

This bronze astrolabe, made by one Ahmad ibn Khalaf at the
end of the ninth century, is said to have belonged to the caliph
Muqtadir (908–32). (Paris, Louvre/Bridgeman)

The Legacy of the Abbasids

Patron, Musicians and Singers, from a 1219 manuscript of Isfahāni's *Book of Songs*. The stories in the *Book of Songs* kept the memory of the culture and luxury of the Abbasid court alive in the Muslim world. (Bridgeman/Egyptian National Library, Cairo)

The caliph Hārūn al-Rashīd visits a bath house in this 1494 miniature by the great Persian painter Bihzad. Note how carefully he has placed his crown on the top of his folded clothes in this meticulously observed scene. (British Library/Bridgeman)

TOP: Abbasid court style influenced many later Islamic rulers. In this audience, held by the Qajar ruler, Nāsir al-Dīn Shāh (1848–96). The civil and military courtiers line up in their ranks before the sovereign. In essence, they were following the practice described in the reign of Mansūr. (Reception at Gulistan Palace (c. 1870s–1930s). Gelatin silver print from glass negative. Myron Bement Smith Papers. Freer Gallery of Art and Arthur M. Sackler Gallery Archives. Smithsonian Institution, Washington, D.C. Gift of Katherine Dennis Smith, 1973–85. Photographer: Antoin Sevruguin, negative number 51.4.)

ABOVE: The great curtain has been opened so that the shah on his throne can be seen by the courtiers and a petitioner makes his request. (As above)

married at all; though he had nine recorded children, seven sons and two daughters, they were all by concubines.[18] Hārūn famously married his cousin Zubayda, who was his lifelong love and mother of his heir apparent, Muhammad Amīn. He also married other women after he had become caliph. One of these was Ghādir (d. 789), who had been his brother Hādī's concubine, to whom Hārūn was very attached. In the latter part of his reign, after 803, Hārūn made four more marriages, all to members of the extended ruling family. Umm Muhammad and Abbāsa were second cousins, Umm Abd Allah a more distant cousin. The other wife, Azīza, was the daughter of Khayzurān's brother. He also married a woman whose first name is not known but who was a descendant both of the third caliph Uthmān and of Hasan ibn Alī ibn Abī Tālib, and so of the Prophet himself. None of these aristocratic marriages produced any children, and it is likely that they were intended to keep the family together by reinforcing links between its various branches. Perhaps surprisingly, two of these women, Umm Abd Allah and Azīza, had previously been married to, and divorced by, other members of the ruling family, while Ghādir had had a well-known relationship with the caliph's brother. In some cases it looks as if taking these women into his *huram* was a question of offering them protection and status. Azīza died young but the rest of these wives survived the caliph.[19]

After the death of Hārūn in 809, with rare exceptions caliphs do not seem to have married. This impression may simply be due to lack of information, but more probably it reflects a real change in dynastic structure. The reasons for the change remain obscure. It was clearly not because they had lost interest in women, or in the fathering of children. It is more likely to have been due to the fact that they no longer felt bound by the conventions of aristocratic Arab society, and above all that they wanted to sever rather than reinforce the ties with their own kin. Their chief supporters were now eastern Iranians and Turks, many of them of servile origin: it was neither appropriate nor seemly that they should make alliances with such people. The change is connected with the emergence of the queen mother, rather than the wife or favourite, as the leading figure in the *huram*. None of the ninth- and tenth-century caliphs had lovers like Khayzurān or Zubayda who emerge as powerful or rounded figures. Instead it is their mothers who dominate court life.

Interestingly, a very similar process can be seen in the Ottoman court seven hundred years later. The documentation is much fuller for this period, and it can be shown without any doubt that Ottoman sultans stopped marrying after the mid fifteenth century,[20] with the exception of Sulaymān the Magnificent (1520–66), whose marriage to Hurrem (the Roxelana of the Western sources) in 1534 caused surprise and considerable outrage among Ottoman traditionalists. The public were especially troubled that the sultan seemed to be confining his attention to a single woman in a way that seemed entirely unnatural: he must have been bewitched.[21] In the sixteenth century, the female favourites, among whom Hurrem was simply the most successful, ruled the harem. By the beginning of the seventeenth century this had changed. The harem was now ruled by the Vālide Sultān, the queen mother: favourites disappeared and the concubines of the sultan were shadowy, transient figures whose names were hardly known. The rise of the queen mother was accompanied by other changes in the way the palace worked. Princes were no longer sent to the provinces to gain experience and acquire following and prestige among the people. Instead they were confined to the imperial palace without courts or properties of their own. The women of the imperial family, many of whom had had their own separate households in the fifteenth and sixteenth centuries, were now confined to the main harem.[22]

The household of the Abbasid caliphate, eight hundred years earlier, had evolved in a very similar way. Not only did caliphs stop marrying but the queen mother became the most important woman in the harem and the caliph's children were confined to the palaces of Baghdad and Sāmarrā, rather than being sent to govern the provinces. The palaces that had been owned by the daughters and cousins of Mansūr and Mahdi reverted to the crown or were distributed to Turkish soldiers.

Ma'mūn did marry once, and it was a most spectacular occasion that was remembered for centuries afterwards for the lavishness that seemed to later generations to sum up the splendour and richness of the Abbasid era. The whole occasion was about the elaborate display of courtesy and wealth, a sign of the return of good times after the long and terrible years of civil war. It is also the only caliphal marriage ceremony about which we have any detailed information.[23]

The bride was Burān, owner of the palace in Baghdad that became the caliphs' residence after 892. Her father was Hasan ibn Sahl.

Hasan had been Ma'mūn's political agent in Iraq during the civil wars that followed Amīn's death, while his brother Fadl had been the caliph's mentor and chief adviser until his fall from grace and execution. The marriage was partly a reconciliation and thank-you offering to a family to whom the caliph owed so much. Hasan himself seems to have had a sort of mental breakdown towards the end of the war, and had lived in retirement for the six years that had followed Ma'mūn's arrival in Baghdad. He had become practically a recluse, a melancholy and anxious man, afraid of the dark and very superstitious.

The wedding was held in a small town called Fam al-Silh on the Tigris, some 200 kilometres south-east of Baghdad. Here among the palm groves and canals of lower Mesopotamia lay some of the richest agricultural estates to be found anywhere in the Middle East, and the town itself boasted a Friday mosque and markets; although, as in many of the towns in this area, it was derelict and ruined by the later Middle Ages, in the ninth century it was at the height of its prosperity.

The bridegroom travelled by boat from Baghdad. Abbās, his son, had gone on ahead, and on his arrival there was an elaborate exchange of courtesies. Hasan and Abbās met outside Hasan's compound on the banks of the Tigris, where a special kiosk had been built for the occasion. When the two men met, first Abbās prepared to dismount as a sign of respect and Hasan besought him not to, then it was Hasan's turn to attempt to show his respect by getting down, but Abbās restrained him. Finally they embraced while still mounted and proceeded to Hasan's house, Abbās in the lead.

Ma'mūn himself left Baghdad on 23 December 826. It was Ramadan, and when he arrived at Fam al-Silh it was the time of evening prayer. He, his son Abbas and his father-in-law to be, Hasan, were able to break their fast immediately. After they had eaten and washed their hands, the caliph called for wine. A golden goblet was brought and the drink was poured into it. Ma'mūn drank and handed it to Hasan. There was an awkward pause: Hasan, a good Muslim had never drunk wine, yet to refuse could be seen as an insult to the caliph. The attendant winked at him to show that he should accept, so he gracefully found a way out: 'Commander of the Faithful,' he said, 'I will drink it with your permission and following your order,' for if the caliph himself had commanded him to do it, how could it conflict with Islam? The caliph replied that if it had not been his order, he would not have held out the goblet to him. So the tension was relaxed and they drank together.

The next night there was a parallel marriage when Hasan's son Muhammad was married to his first cousin. On the third night the wedding itself took place. Burān was attended by two senior ladies of the Abbasid family who had helped her prepare for the great day, including Hārūn al-Rashīd's favourite wife Zubayda, by now a formidable grande dame who had survived the disasters of the death of her cherished son Amīn and the civil war in Baghdad. A real survivor, she was now reconciled with Ma'mūn, the man responsible for her son's overthrow, and living the life of an immensely wealthy dowager.

As they sat together, Zubayda brought a golden plate on which were piled a thousand pearls, which she scattered over the bride. After an unseemly exchange when it was revealed that one of the servants had taken ten of the pearls, they were collected again, put back on the plate and placed in the bride's lap. Then Ma'mūn said, 'This is your wedding present and now ask me any favour you like.' Burān uttered not a word and her grandmother had to encourage her. 'Speak to your lord,' she said, 'for he has ordered you to do that.' So, no doubt prompted by Zubayda, she made two requests. The first was that the caliph should become reconciled with his uncle, the poet Ibrāhīm ibn Mahdi, who had attempted to establish himself as caliph in Baghdad in the latter stages of the civil war, and the second was that Zubayda herself should be allowed to go on pilgrimage. Both these were granted. Then Zubayda presented her with the *badana* of the Umayyads. This was a precious garment, a sleeveless jacket with a row of large rubies down the front and back which had originally belonged to Atika, wife of the Umayyad caliph Abd al-Malik (685–705). It had been passed down through the Umayyad royal family, and after the revolution Umm Salama, wife of the first Abbasid caliph Saffāh, had made sure that she got hold of it.[24] Now more than a hundred years old, it had become a venerable relic, and when Zubayda passed it to Burān, it was a sign that she was to be the leading figure in the *huram*.

That night Ma'mūn and Burān slept together for the first time. A candle (or candles) made of ambergris, weighing more than 3 kilos, was lit to perfume the bedroom. Ambergris is a waxy substance secreted by sperm whales which formed the basis of the rarest and most expensive perfumes made at the time. It seems that it was usually found floating in the sea or washed up on the beach. Like many very expensive luxuries it was not always appreciated by its recipients, and Ma'mūn complained that the smoke was irritating them and had the servants take the candle away and replace it with ordinary ones. According to one later story, this was not the only problem on the wedding night. When Ma'mūn went into his bride he found that she was having her period and withdrew: the next day, when the chief judge Abu Yūsuf offered his congratulations, Ma'mūn replied with that openness which can take modern readers by surprise with a little poem to the effect that the stallion had gone in with its spear outstretched to draw blood but was prevented by blood from another direction.[25]

The next morning Ma'mūn fulfilled one of the promises he had made to Burān. Ibrāhīm ibn Mahdi, who had presumably arrived by boat from wherever he had been hiding, walked up from the river bank to the house where the caliph was staying. He was admitted. When the curtain was lowered and he came face to face with Ma'mūn, he threw himself on the ground, but the caliph said, 'Uncle, do not worry any more!' and Ibrāhīm stood up and kissed his hand. Then he was given robes of honour. The caliph sent for a horse and girded him with a sword before they appeared in public to show that he had been forgiven and restored to favour.

The celebrations continued for a fortnight as the leading figures showed off their wealth and generosity. At one banquet, remembered long after in history and legend, Hasan wrote out slips of paper with names of estates on them and scattered them among his guests. Whoever picked one up could go to the estate and claim it as his own. According to another version of the story, balls of musk were distributed to the guests. Inside each was written the name of an estate, a slave girl or the description of a horse, and the men who received them took them to officers who then ensured that they received their prizes.[26]

The largesse was not confined to the select few. The soldiers in Ma'mūn's army, who normally had to pay for their keep out of their salaries, were delighted to find that everything was paid for, including their own food and the forage for their animals. Even the camel drivers, those who hired the camels out and the boatmen benefited from his generosity. Among the women, there is said to have been some competitive spending, and when one claimed to have spent 25 million *dirham*s, Zubayda dismissively replied that that was nothing and that she herself had spent between 35 and 37 million. The generosity did not go unrewarded; Hasan was given the rich estate at Silh and the tax revenues of the province of Fars in south-west Iran for a whole year. After enjoying his hospitality for a fortnight, Ma'mūn, his entourage and presumably his new bride took leave of their host and left for Baghdad, arriving home on 1 February.

Burān and Ma'mūn enjoyed only eight years of marriage before his death. They do not seem to have had any children but she travelled with him on campaign against the Byzantines and was with him on his deathbed. She survived, living, as we have seen, in her own palace in Baghdad, and died full of years and honour at the age of eighty.[27]

The story of Burān's wedding is one of extravagance and generosity. The marriage was used as a set-piece occasion to show to all the world the splendours of the new court and to banish the memories of civil war, hardship and disruption. It was also a forum for healing wounds within the royal family, a time of reconciliation and the return of favours. It did not, however, set a trend. None of the Abbasid caliphs who followed were born from marriage and none of the queen mothers who ruled the *huram* were married to the fathers of their children.

The girls who formed the Abbasid harem came from many different lands and cultures, but because Islamic law forbids the enslavement of Muslims, they were almost always procured from outside the empire. Some girls were acquired as part of the booty after the defeat of opponents of the caliphs. In the mountains of northern Iran, at the southern end of the Caspian Sea, local principalities survived. Although they professed obedience to the caliphs, they were still in many ways independent. Islam spread slowly in these inaccessible regions and old customs still survived long after they had disappeared from flatter and more urbanized parts of Iran. They were ruled by dynasties who traced their origins to the pre-Islamic Sasanian past, and in some cases claimed that they were in fact cadet branches of the old Persian royal family. When Abbasid forces raided these areas, or local rulers openly rejected Muslim overlordship, princesses of these dynasties were sometimes captured and brought back for the harems of Abbasid notables. Among others, Mahdi acquired a concubine known as Bahtariya, who became mother to his son Mansūr,[28] and the caliph Ma'mūn's mother was the daughter of a noble from Badhghis in what is now western Afghanistan who was brought for Hārūn's harem after her father's suicide. The family of the caliph Muʿtasim's mother, Mārida, came originally from distant Soghdia in central Asia, though she was brought up in Kūfa in Iraq.[29] It is perhaps no accident that it was from the same part of central Asia that her son was to recruit the Turkish guard who formed the new military aristocracy of the ninth century. None of these women was married to the caliphs or other notables to whom they belonged, but their aristocratic origins were certainly part of their appeal, and their political contacts in their countries of origin may have been much more important than the Arab writers suggest, giving the Abbasid friends and relatives in areas renowned for producing tough fighting men.

Berber slaves from North Africa were highly valued as sexual partners and the great caliph Mansūr himself was the son of one such. In the ninth and tenth centuries, however, it was above all Greek girls from the Byzantine empire who formed the aristocracy of the harem, and it was their sons who became caliphs. Wāthiq's mother Qarātīs,[30] Muntasir's mother Hubshiya,[31] Muhtadi's mother Qurb[32] and Muʿtadid's mother Dirār[33] were all of Byzantine origin. The mothers of other caliphs came from Iraq, although Mustaʿīn's mother Mukhāriq is described as a Slav (*siqlabi*), probably suggesting an eastern European origin.[34]

Women also entered the harem because of their talents as musicians or singers. The eighth and ninth centuries were the heyday of the singing girl. In a social environment in which free women from respectable families were increasingly restricted and concealed, the singing girl, always a slave,* could entertain her master and his friends (or, in some cases, his customers). Like the hetaerae of classical Greece or the geishas of traditional Japan, many of them were highly trained, skilled and witty. Along with the male *nadīms* (boon companions) they were the main bearers of the court culture of the

---

* The question of whether a girl was free or a slave was not always clear cut. According to Jāhiz, Ma'mūn asked a girl in the entourage of Zubayda whether she was free or a slave, to which she replied that she did not know: 'When my mistress is angry with me she says I am a slave, when she is pleased with me she says I am free.' At the caliph's bidding she wrote Zubayda a letter to ask what her status was and sent it off by pigeon post. It must have been a good day, for the reply came back that she was free (Jāhiz, *Qiyān*, p. 24).

period. The image of the singing girl in literature, such as the *Book of Songs*, is a lively and attractive one. They are beautiful, of course, and have wonderful voices, but they are also clever, accomplished and assertive, fully capable of putting down a boorish or unattractive man. A good singing girl could have a repertoire of ten thousand lines 'in which there is not one mention of God, or of reward or punishment in the Hereafter'.[35] They were also sexually available, at least to their owners and patrons. Jāhiz, who wrote an essay on singing girls, describes how men fell in love with them and how a talented girl would string several men along at the same time to make the most of them. He also describes how some singing girls lost their professional detachment to the extent of falling in love with their suitors.* At one end of the spectrum, some of them were great artists and at the other they were effectively prostitutes whose musical talents were a front for more basic charms. The pious certainly disapproved of them but, as Jāhiz was at pains to argue, the use of slaves in this way was not against Islamic law.

In the early Abbasid period, the Holy City of Medina was, perhaps somewhat surprisingly, the most famous centre for the education and training of singing girls. The girls, who are usually described as slaves but may in many cases simply have been girls from poor backgrounds who were offered a chance by teachers, or were entrusted to a teacher by their parents, were taught music. They were then sold on. In some cases the caliph himself, we are told, chanced to hear them singing. In others, courtiers would make it their business to send out talent scouts. Large sums of money were involved. Like modern footballers and their transfer fees, girls could be traded up, gaining in value at each transaction. If they reached the highest level, the sums of money involved were enormous. Maknūna, mother of the princess Ulayya, was bought by the caliph Mahdi for 100,000 silver *dirham*s. Another, Basbas, cost the royal treasury 17,000 gold

---

* Jāhiz (who else?) has a discussion about women's enjoyment of sex and whether it is suitable for women to cry out during intercourse in an anecdote which must reflect the attitudes of his own time. He tells the story of an aristocratic woman of Medina in the early Islamic period who was asked this very question by a group of young girls. She replied with a story: 'My daughters, I went on pilgrimage with the Commander of the Faithful Uthmān [caliph 644–56]. When we reached al-Arj on the way back, my husband looked at me and I looked at him. He fancied me and I fancied him and he leaped on me, just as Uthmān's camels were passing. I cried out loud as there came to me what comes to the daughters of Adam and the camels, all five hundred of them, scattered. It was hours before any two of them met up again' (Jāhiz, *Rasā'il*, ii, pp. 129–30).

*dīnār*s. A whole genre of anecdotes emerges about prudent viziers determined to restrain caliphs such as Mahdi and Hārūn from squandering vast sums of money on buying attractive girls.

There were other tensions as well. One story tells how Ibrāhīm al-Mosuli sold a girl called 'the girl with the mole' to Hārūn for the vast sum of 70,000 *dirham*s. One day he made her swear to tell the truth and then asked whether there had ever been anything between her and her former master. She admitted that there had been, just once, and the caliph's love turned to hate and he gave her away to one of the servants called Hammawayh. But he missed her singing and one day reproached Hammawayh for keeping her to himself and arranged to come and hear her the next day. The servant was anxious to do his best to impress his master and hired a mass of jewels to make her look her best. The caliph was surprised to see this great display of wealth from one of his menials. He soon found out what had happened and, as is the way with these stories, paid for the jewels and asked what else she wanted. She asked that Hammawayh, who had presumably looked after her well, be given a government appointment. What is perhaps the most remarkable feature of this otherwise fanciful story is that we know that a man called Hammawayh was indeed governor of Fars in the last years of Hārūn's reign.[36]

Even Hārūn could not always afford to get his own way. Inān was a slave girl from Yamāma in eastern Arabia.[37] She was brought up and educated there and was bought by a man called Nātifi. She was a lively and flirtatious girl and very quick witted when it came to impromptu poetry; she could compete in verse repartee with Abu Nuwās, the most famous poet of the time. Nātifi seems to have been very controlling, and it was said that he beat her and frequently reduced her to tears. At the same time, he refused to part with her. Hārūn became infatuated with her to the extent that Khayzurān became worried that she was usurping her own place in the caliph's heart. She asked the advice of the distinguished scholar Asmaᶜi, who said that he would have a word with the caliph. One day Hārūn was abusing Nātifi for his refusal to sell him the girl, saying that he himself was interested in her only because of her skills as a poet. Asmaᶜi interjected that if poetry was indeed all she had to offer, would he have wanted to have sex with Farazdaq (a famous male poet of the Umayyad age)? The caliph laughed, perhaps seeing the absurdity of his position.

According to one version of the story, Hārūn attempted to buy her but Nātifi said that he would accept no less than 100,000 gold *dīnār*s. Even by Hārūn's standards this was an outrageous price so he tried to bargain; he offered to pay 100,000 *dīnār*s in silver *dirham*s at an exchange rate of 7:1 (the normal going rate was about 20:1). Nātifi still refused and Hārūn was forced to explain to the girl that he could not pay enough to satisfy her master, to whom he had to return her, although she remained in his heart. Some time after this, Nātifi died and Hārūn saw an opportunity. Nātifi left debts which had to be paid from his estate and the lawyers decided that Inān was a fresh young girl who should be sold. So she was taken to the slave market by the Karkh Gate to be sold at auction. She sat on the bench, concealing herself as well as she could, pouring scorn and curses on those who had reduced her to this pass. Now Hārūn had sent Masrūr, his chief eunuch and general factotum, to the auction to buy her. Hearing her abuse of those who had let her down, Masrūr assumed she was referring to the caliph, who had refused to stump up the cash to buy her, and slapped her hard across the face. When the auction began, Masrūr bid 200,000 *dirham*s but a man offered 25,000 more. Masrūr then beat him and shouted, 'How dare you outbid the Commander of the Faithful!' In the end the unknown man bought her for 250,000 *dirham*s and took her away with him to Khurasan, where she died long after Hārūn.

The story may be entirely fictitious but it does paint an interesting picture of the vicissitudes of a 'talented girl's life. It also shows the limits of the caliph's power. He felt unable to punish Nātifi without good legal cause, nor could he simply acquire the girl after his death when the lawyers had decided that she should be publicly sold.

A more improving story is told of two girls whose learning attracted the attention of the caliph and led to them being taken into his household.[38] Hārūn sent for Asma'i, who plays the role of resident intellectual adviser in many of these stories. He came from Baghdad to Raqqa, where the court was established at that time. The first girl was asked what she knew and replied that the most important thing was what Allah had commanded in His Book and then what interested people in poetry, language and literature and history. Asma'i then subjected her to a detailed examination, including topics such as the variant readings of the Koran, to which she responded as if she were reading the answers from a book. He then went on to grammar, poetic metres and historical anecdotes, and found that she excelled in them all. Her companion, though not quite so impressive, would soon learn. When Asmaʿi had made his report and was on his way back to Baghdad, he was overtaken by a man and a slave girl who brought him a rich purse of 1,000 *dīnār*s with the message that his 'daughter' wished to share her prosperity with him: the caliph had rewarded her with money and a wardrobe of clothes and this was his share. Furthermore, she promised to continue her favours and did so until he lost contact with her in the chaos of the civil war of Amīn's reign, when so much of the old court was dispersed.

In this, and in other stories, the slave girl is far from being a passive victim. Rather, membership of the caliph's *huram* was a desirable and profitable move, a career choice for girls who had few other options. No doubt sex-appeal was important, but so was a broad general education and a ready wit.

The social and emotional lives of the women of the harem are almost impossible to recover. There are stories of bitter jealousies and others of friendship and cooperation. One anecdote, however, remains in the memory because of the insight it gives into lesbian relationships within the harem and the dangers with which they were fraught. The story is set at the court of the short-lived caliph Hādī. It is in the evening, and the caliph is sitting talking informally with a small group of intimates. One of these, Alī ibn Yaqtin, is our informant for what occurred. Let him tell it in his own words:

A servant came in and whispered something in his [the caliph's] ear. He rose hurriedly, saying 'Don't move' and then left the room for some time. Then he came in breathing heavily and threw himself back on his cushions, panting for some time until he calmed down. With him was a eunuch carrying a tray covered with a cloth who stood before him trembling. We all wondered what was going on. Then Hādī sat up and said to the servant, 'Put it down' and he set the tray down. Then he said, 'Lift the cover!' and there on the tray were the heads of two slave girls. And, by God, I have never seen more beautiful faces or lovelier hair in the whole of my life. Jewels were entwined in their hair and the air was fragrant with their perfumes. We were amazed. Then he said, 'Do you know what they had done?' 'No', we replied. 'It was reported to us that they had fallen in love with each other and were meeting for immoral purposes. I sent this eunuch to watch them and keep me informed about them. He came and told me that they were together and I caught them under one quilt making love, and killed them'. Then he said, 'Take the heads away, boy!' and carried on the conversation as if nothing had happened.[39]

The story seems to be told to illustrate the caliph's jealous and irascible character, rather than to condemn what the girls were doing, but it is impossible to know how far they, or he, were typical of their time and situation.

There was another side to the harem, far away from the glamorous world of the fashionable singing girl. One of the mysteries of Abbasid family life is the fate of the daughters of the caliphs. Up until Hārūn's reign, it would seem that they were married off to members of the ruling family, including the caliphs themselves. The last such marriages to be recorded were the first-cousin unions of Hārūn's daughters, Fātima and Hamdūna, with the sons of his brother and predecessor Hādī, Ismāᶜīl and Jaᶜfar. At about the same time, the young Ma'mūn was wedded to Umm Isā, a wedding that must have taken place before Hārūn's death in 809. Ma'mūn's marriage at least was consummated and the couple had two children, Muhammad and Ubayd Allah.[40] Ma'mūn used his daughters to forge dynastic links with the Family of Alī, with whom he was very close, with Umm Habīb marrying Alī Ridā and her sister Umm Fadl another member of the family. Alī Ridā died in mysterious circumstances soon after, but Umm Fadl's marriage was certainly consummated.[41]

What happened to caliphs' daughters in the ninth century is entirely unclear. Were they married to members of their family in the traditional way but these nuptials were no longer considered important enough to be recorded by the historians? Or did they live shadowy and secluded lives in the palaces of Baghdad, prevented by their status from marrying at all? It seems impossible to know for sure.

Abbasid princesses lived lives that were both privileged and seriously constrained by the demands of etiquette and social custom. In most cases we know little about these women apart from their names, but one of them, Ulayya bint Mahdi (777–825), became a poet of some renown with the result that some biographical information appears in the *Book of Songs*.

Ulayya's mother, Maknūna, was one of the most attractive slave girls in Medina; she had a beautiful face and, though some critics said her bum was too small, she had fine breasts and a great figure, which she showed off to best advantage. Mahdi was very taken with her and Khayzurān said that there was no other woman who had caused her so much anxiety. Ulayya seems to have been her only child and she grew up to be one of the best poets and singers. She had some sort of birthmark on her forehead and designed a special headband, covered with jewels, to disguise it.

Ulayya spent her life caught in the contradictions of her position. She is said to have been pious and much preoccupied with prayer and study of the Koran. Poetry and song were her only pleasures, but she would, we are told, not drink wine or sing except during her periods, when she was banned from prayer. As she remarked, 'God does not forbid anything without giving some way of making it permissible in exchange', and she said that God did not have to forgive her sins since her poetry was only a game.[42]

Her creative attitude to the constraints of Islamic law did not solve the more fundamental ambiguities of her position. Of her skills as a poet there was no doubt: she could hold her own with the great masters of the time, Ishaq al-Mosuli and Ibrāhīm ibn Mahdi, but unlike them, she could never perform for a public audience. Her relations with her half-brother Hārūn were dominated on the one hand by his affection for her and genuine admiration for her poetry and on the other by his jealous guarding of the honour of the women of his family and the deeply held feeling that it was not suitable for one of them to compose poetry that passed into the public domain, even if she never appeared in public herself. Despite the tensions they seem to have been genuinely devoted to each other. On his final journey to Khurasan in 809, he invited her to accompany him, but she became very homesick for Iraq and he allowed her to return. When he died, she was overcome with grief.[43]

It was only in private family singing parties that she could find an audience. The singing girl Arīb, who, being a female, was allowed to be present, described a day she spent once with Ibrāhīm ibn Mahdi, Ulayya and their brother Yaᶜqūb, who was an excellent player of the *zamar* (a wind instrument a bit like an oboe). Ulayya began by singing one of her own compositions while Yaᶜqūb accompanied her, then Ibrāhīm sang his, again with Yaᶜqūb on the *zamar*, and Arīb said, 'I have never heard anything like their singing before and I know that I never will again.'⁴⁴ Another such occasion was witnessed by one of Hārūn's sons, Abu Ahmad. One day he was with his brother, the caliph Ma'mūn, and two of his uncles, Mansūr and Ibrāhīm, sons of Mahdi, were there too. After a while, Ma'mūn said to Ibrāhīm, 'You can get up and go if you want to.' So he did. He looked and saw that the curtain had been raised on the side of the women's quarters. Almost immediately, he heard the most wonderful voices. His brother the caliph turned to him and explained that he was hearing his aunt Ulayya singing with his uncle Ibrāhīm.⁴⁵

The ambiguous feelings about her achievements extended to the next generation. One of the caliph Hādī's grandsons, Muhammad ibn Ismā'īl, recounted⁴⁶ how he had been at a gathering with the caliph Mu'tasim and a number of poets. Some lines of Ulayya's were sung and the caliph asked who the composer was. There was an embarrassed silence until Muhammad blurted out that the lines were Ulayya's. He knew immediately that he had made a mistake and the caliph deliberately ignored him. However, he retrieved the situation somehow by pointing out that he, like the caliph, was also the nephew of the poetess and therefore shared in any shame that might attach to having a female relative whose poetry was in the public domain.

There was a particular problem with the love poems. It was of course important for the poet to have a beloved. For a male, even a member of the ruling family, this was no problem, any singing girl would do, but for a high-status woman it would give rise to all sorts of scandalous possibilities. Even a wholly fictitious beloved would cause speculation that there was a real man behind the image. Ulayya's solution was to direct her affections at a *khādim* called Tall. Exactly what this meant depends on the interpretation of the word *khādim*. Originally it meant simply a male servant, but at around the time when Ulayya was writing the meaning of the word was increasingly restricted to those servants who were also eunuchs. Certainly by the ninth century it looks as if all *khādim*s were eunuchs. By choosing a eunuch as her beloved, Ulayya could compose love poetry and avoid the breath of scandal.

Ulayya's life was full of paradoxes. On the one hand she was a talented woman who lived a rich and pampered existence. She was highly educated. She could afford to 'buy' poems from Ishāq al-

Mosuli for 40,000 *dirham*s and threaten him with death if he ever let on that they were not hers.[47] When she suspected that the manager of her estates was not playing straight with her she had him beaten and disgraced until his neighbours got together and told her how honest and truthful he really was.[48] On the other hand her life was spent in the archetypal gilded cage: Ishāq al-Mosuli could hear her singing, but only from behind a curtain so that he could not see her. Her poems were often misattributed to others because she could not perform them herself. And there is something sadly poignant about the story of this gifted and spirited woman who, bowing to the decree of unbreakable social convention, could only take as her lover a creature who could never perform the most essential functions of that office.

Most of the women who became the sexual partners of the caliphs are no more than names, or indeed completely anonymous, but in the case of the most famous of them we have enough information to get some idea of their personalities and achievements. Four powerful women dominated the *huram* in their day and have left a reputation in the historical literature and popular memory: these were Khayzurān, wife of Mahdi and mother of Hādī and Hārūn, Zubayda, wife of Hārūn and mother of Amīn, Qabīha, mother of Muʿtazz, and Shaghab, mother of Muqtadir.

Khayzurān dominated Mahdi's *huram* and became the first of the dominant women who played such an important role in the life of the Abbasid court. Her spectacular career meant that she attracted a great deal of media attention and, given that she spent much of her life in the secret, segregated world of the *huram*, much of what was written about her is no doubt guesswork and fantasy. But the image itself is an intriguing one, and most of the imaginative details sit well with the known historical facts of her life.

Her origins could hardly have been more humble. She was a slave girl belonging to an Arab living in the Yemen, and it was in the slave market of Mecca that she attracted the attention of the young Prince Mahdi. Her slender beauty inspired him to give her the name of Khayzurān or Reed, and it is by this that she is known to history. She and Mahdi were devoted to each other and anecdotes suggest a friendly and companionate relationship when, for example, they joked together about his father Mansūr's famous meanness.[49] At least from his side, it was clearly a love match, since she brought no benefits apart from her beauty and emotional intelligence. She was fortunate to bear him two healthy sons, later to succeed to the throne as the caliphs Hādī and Hārūn, who took precedence over all his other children, including the sons of his first wife Rīta.

When Mahdi became caliph, freed her and married her, it was a bold break with convention, and there is some evidence that she was disapproved of by Abbasid ladies of the older generation. A story told by Mas'ūdī claims to show something of her role and personality in what was clearly a socially competitive environment. The scene is Khayzurān's palace in Baghdad, where the mothers of the caliph's children and the young women of the royal family were sitting around on Armenian carpets and cushions. Presiding over the group was Zaynab, daughter of Sulaymān ibn 'Alī. Sulaymān was one of Mansūr's uncles and a founding figure of the dynasty. His daughter had been brought up to maintain the dignity and traditions of the imperial house and Mahdi had advised Khayzurān to spend time with her and learn court etiquette and manners from her example.

A visitor was announced, and in came a beautiful, elegant woman clad in a tattered, ragged robe. The women asked who she was and she replied that she was Muzna, wife of the last Umayyad caliph, now destitute and forced to live among the common people at risk of sexual dishonour; she was, in short, in need of protection. Khayzurān is immediately sympathetic and her eyes fill with tears but Zaynab is made of sterner stuff. She had met Muzna before in very different circumstances when the Umayyads were still in power. She had gone to beg for the body of her uncle Ibrāhīm, who had been executed by the Umayyads, but Muzna had briskly rejected her, saying, 'It is not for women to meddle in the affairs of men,' and sent her away. 'Even Marwān [the last Umayyad caliph],' Zaynab went on, 'was more considerate than you. He swore that he was not Ibrāhīm's murderer. He was lying of course but he did offer to give me back the body or arrange for its burial.'

Muzna replied by saying that their change in fortune meant that Zaynab could be more generous than she herself had been in the days of her prosperity, but Zaynab would have none of it and Muzna left in tears. Khayzurān did not want to defy Zaynab openly but sent one of her slave girls to catch up with Muzna, take her to a quiet room and give her new clothes and see that she was looked after.

Mahdi used to come to spend the evenings with his favourite

women. This was a more informal occasion and Zaynab had left by this time. When Khayzurān told Mahdi of the incident, he congratulated her on what she had done, and when Zaynab next appeared, Mahdi was careful to sit Muzna, now beautifully dressed, in a place of honour. She was allotted rooms in the palace and given property and a staff of eunuchs just like the other women. Saved from destitution and disgrace, Muzna survived as a pensioner of the Abbasids until the reign of Hārūn, and when she died all the *huram* mourned her.

The story is told to show the generosity of Khayzurān and Mahdi compared with the rigidity of Zaynab, but it speaks too of aristocratic solidarity: Mahdi addresses Muzna as 'cousin' and perhaps ponders that if she were dishonoured, the disgrace would reflect on the new ruling family as well as the old.

A central theme of the stories told about Khayzurān at this time is her determination to retain the affection of Mahdi. This was no easy matter: he was a man who enjoyed the company of women in every way, and he and his sometime favourite and vizier could be found in the morning recounting their sexual exploits of the night before.[50] New slave girls, many of them talented singers, were always being presented or purchased and the caliph was clearly very taken with a number of them. Khayzurān could not possibly insist on the sort of monogamy that Umm Mūsā is said to have demanded of his father, but she could and did manage the *huram* so that none of his new lovers ever supplanted her. It seems that their relationship was as firm when he died as it had ever been before.[51]

In addition to her two famous sons, Hādī and Hārūn, and a less well-known brother, Īsā, Khayzurān also gave birth to a daughter, known as Banūqa. She was pretty with a brown complexion and an elegant figure. When she was still young, her indulgent father had given her her own palace in Baghdad. He was very fond of the girl and treated her in many ways like a boy. He would let her ride out in his retinue, dressed as a page in a black cloak and turban with a sword on her belt, 'though I could tell', observed one interested spectator who had watched her pass, 'that the curve of her breasts had raised the cloak'. Mahdi was heartbroken when she died young, and poets vied to produce the most moving elegies for the young princess.[52]

Khayzurān also used her position to advance the cause of her relatives. According to one version, she had sworn blind to the wary old caliph Mansūr that she had no relatives and this was one of the reasons why he allowed his son to become attached to her, since there would be no hangers-on to make demands on the treasury. She must have felt secure in her position before she let on that she had been economical with the truth. She had a sister, Asmā, whom gossip alleged had briefly been Mahdi's lover as well,[53] and a brother called Ghitrīf ibn 'Atā', who enjoyed a rather undistinguished political career during the caliphate of his nephew Hārūn.

Khayzurān was certainly a help and support to her husband during his caliphate, but it was as queen mother that she really became politically important. For reasons we will never know, Khayzurān developed a marked preference for her younger son Hārūn over his older brother Hādī. This had become apparent during Mahdi's lifetime, and after his death her personal preference became a major political issue. There are numerous accounts of the events surrounding the accession of Hādī, his death shortly afterwards and the subsequent accession of Hārūn. Most of these accounts purport to be from first-hand witnesses of events. As might be expected, however, the pictures they paint are often very different: events moved fast and much of what occurred was clearly a family drama, played out in private, and outsiders were reduced to guessing what may have happened.

When Mahdi died, probably in a hunting accident, Khayzurān was in Baghdad, Hādī in distant Jurjān to the south-east of the Caspian Sea, and Hārūn with his father. News of his death was followed by disturbances in the capital as troops rioted. In this difficult situation, Khayzurān seems to have taken control and summoned Rabī the chamberlain and Yahya the Barmakid. Rabī answered her summons and succeeded in pacifying the city but Yahya was more cautious, knowing how much Hādī would resent his mother's role. When Hādī did arrive after a hard ride from Jurjān, he and his mother must have patched up their differences, but tensions soon began to emerge again. One reason for this was that Khayzurān tried to maintain a public role in affairs of state, which her son bitterly resented. Bureaucrats and generals alike continued to visit her to ask for help and request that she use her influence. In the end Hādī felt that he had to put an end to this, threatening with dire punishment anyone who frequented his mother's house. The second problem was that Hādī soon sought to remove Hārūn from the succession and replace him with his own son, Jaᶜfar. One strand in the sources suggests that

Hārūn was not unhappy with this arrangement and that Khayzurān's main concern was to ensure the physical safety of her beloved younger son. Another strand suggests, however, that she took a much more active role and was determined to thwart Hādī's schemes.

What is clear from the sources is that relations between Hādī and his mother had deteriorated completely as he strove to remove her from political influence and her favoured son from his role as heir apparent. Hādī also wanted to destroy Hārūn's chief adviser and supporter, Yahya the Barmakid. As in an old-fashioned murder mystery, there were a number of important figures who might well wish Hādī dead. When the caliph did fall ill, Khayzurān, with all her contacts among the *huram*, was in a position to know the details of his sickness as soon as anyone else. Whether he was poisoned, or suffocated by his mother's slave girls, as some alleged, we shall never know. She had the motivation and the opportunity, but there is evidence that Hādī had been ill for some time and the sudden death of healthy young people often gave rise to gossip. What is clear is that she could act very fast when he did die. She secured the release from prison of Yahya the Barmakid and the subsequent proclamation of Hārūn as caliph before any of young Jaᶜfar's supporters could mobilize.

The accession of Hārūn was certainly a triumph for Khayzurān, and she must have been very influential in the new government, but we hear more about her pious benefactions. She went on the Hajj for the third time and used part of her ample fortune to embellish the shrines. She purchased the house in which the Prophet Muhammad himself was believed to have been born and established it as the Mosque of the Nativity: the shrine, though completely rebuilt, survives to the present day. She did the same for the nearby house of Arqam, where the first Muslims met and water fountains were endowed for the pilgrims to drink from.

In the last three years of her life, Khayzurān moved from being the caliph's favourite to being the first of the great queen mothers of the Abbasid dynasty. Secure in the affection and gratitude of the new caliph, she was also extremely wealthy. According to Masᶜūdī her annual income was 160,000,000 *dirham*s, or the equivalent of half the tax revenues of the entire caliphate, and even assuming that this is a wild exaggeration, the impression is one of great wealth. Like many notables of the time, she invested heavily in land reclamation, financing the digging of a new irrigation canal near Anbar, west of Baghdad, and a quarter in Baghdad was named after her. Her long-time private secretary, Umar ibn Mihrān, was renowned for his frugality and financial astuteness: he was subsequently employed by Hārūn to conduct a surreptitious audit of the finances of Egypt.

Khayzurān died in November 789 and her son accompanied her body to its grave on a rainy autumn day, helping to carry the bier barefoot through the mud. Immediately after the burial, however, he went directly against her instructions by offering the custody of the caliphal seal to Fadl ibn Rabī. It may be that he wanted to escape his mother's tutelage just as much as his brother had done, only he was more discreet and patient.

Khayzurān's place as mistress of the *huram* was taken by Zubayda. Khayzurān had begun life as an outsider from a very disadvantaged background. Zubayda, by contrast, was born and brought up in the heart of the royal family and as both wife and dowager showed the manners and pride of her aristocratic origins. Her mother, Salsal, was one of the siblings whose existence Khayzurān is said to have kept quiet until her position was established. When she came to court, she became attached to Mahdi's brother Jaʿfar, and Zubayda was born to the couple, probably in Mosul, where Jaʿfar had been posted as governor in about 765.[54] She was about the same age as Hārūn and his cousin on both his mother's and his father's side. It is said to have been her stern grandfather, the caliph Mansūr, who, delighted with the fresh and plump baby granddaughter of his, called her Zubayda, or Little Butter Ball.

In the circumstances, the marriage between Hārūn and Zubayda, which probably took place in 782, was an entirely conventional and suitable arrangement. In later centuries the wedding was remembered, along with the wedding of Ma'mūn to Burān and the circumcision feast of Muʿtazz, as one of the great parties of all time. The wedding banquet was held in the Eternity Palace in Baghdad. There were all kinds of precious stones and fine scents, basins of gold *dīnār*s were distributed among the guests and the famous sleeveless jacket of the Umayyad queens, which had belonged to Khayzurān and was to pass in turn to Burān, was passed on to the new bride.[55] What seems to have distinguished this relationship from similar ones was the degree of affection between the couple: Hārūn, shy and insecure as he was, seems to have been especially devoted to and perhaps reliant on her. Stories about the early years of their marriage follow a familiar pattern, as Zubayda becomes concerned about Hārūn's infatuation with a new girl in the harem. On one occasion, she distracts him by presenting him with ten new slave girls, three of whom became mothers of his sons.[56] On another she seeks the advice of Hārūn's half-sister, the poetess Ulayya, and they arrange a procession of beautifully clad singing girls to distract him.[57] In other stories Zubayda rejects the caliph, who is obliged to make things up with her: on one occasion he is angry with her and she in turn refuses to forgive him. Disconsolate and unable to sleep, he orders a bed to be made up overlooking the Tigris and, sitting there, he hears floating across the water a haunting song about the river flowing down to the valley of the beloved. Of course, he sends for the poet and the singer, who entertain him until dawn, when he rises to visit his estranged wife and the two are reconciled.[58]

Zubayda became an immensely wealthy woman. Apart from the gifts apparently showered on her by the caliph, she had extensive landed properties, including urban real estate in western Baghdad, where her palaces, gardens and retainers' quarters were,[59] as well as rural properties in the Sawad of Iraq. She also controlled her wealth and spent it as she saw fit. To manage her assets she had her own secretaries, who sometimes came into conflict with Hārūn's, and her own staff of messengers and maids.[60]

Like Khayzurān before her, she spent much of this money on pious works.[61] She went on the Hajj at least five times. When she went in 806 the Hajj was in the autumn and she found that water supplies had practically dried up and the people were suffering terribly from thirst. Even the sacred well of Zamzam produced only a tiny amount of water. Zubayda set about remedying the situation, ordering that Zamzam be dug an extra 4.5 metres deep, and more water was found.[62] This was just the beginning of a much larger campaign of works.[63] She spent three quarters of a million *dīnār*s on improving the water supply of the city and building an aqueduct from the spring at Hunayn. The 'Spring of Zubayda' on the plain of Arafat, where the pilgrims gathered, was remembered for centuries to come. Her pious works were commemorated in inscriptions. Nor did she stop there. The pilgrimage road across the desert from Iraq was fraught with difficulties, and Zubayda paid for the road to be cleared and watering stations to be set up at regular intervals. While much of her life and achievement are the stuff of gossip and legend, the building of Zubayda's pilgrimage road, the Darb Zubayda (Zubayda's Road), is well attested by the archaeological evidence. Her generosity to the pilgrims was remembered long after her death.

Even before Hārūn's death, Zubayda's role was shifting from that of favourite wife to queen mother. She had only one child with Hārūn, the boy Muhammad, later to be the unfortunate caliph Amīn. He was only five in 791/2 when his mother's influence ensured that he was appointed and publicly acknowledged as heir apparent.[64] The appointment of Hārūn's son Abd Allah as heir after Amīn certainly posed a threat to Zubayda's position, and this is reflected in a whole genre of stories in which she is forced to come to the aid of her less talented son to prevent him from being overshadowed by his half-brother.[65] As Hārūn's reign went on and political factions coalesced around the two heirs, Ma'mūn's advocates were concerned about the support Amīn was getting from members of the Abbasid family 'and Zubayda and all her money'.[66]

Zubayda did not accompany Hārūn on his final journey to Khurasan and she was at Raqqa on the Euphrates when news arrived of his death. She immediately secured his treasures and went south to Baghdad. Her son met her at Anbar.[67] Zubayda certainly supported his cause in the struggle with Ma'mūn but there is no indication in the sources that she played a part in the breakdown of relations between Amīn and his brother which was leading to civil war. There are a number of anecdotes that show her trying to restrain the more inappropriate behaviour of her son and his courtiers, but these must be taken with a pinch of salt for they are part of a deliberate attempt in the sources to blacken Amīn's name and make it clear that he was unfit to rule. The scandalous invective of the poets must have given Zubayda cause for concern, and she is said to have taken action to divert him from his more unsuitable friends. She arranged that a group of her slave girls should be dressed in boys' costumes to try to divert him from his enthusiasm for eunuchs.[68] A historian a century later recounted that,

> She had them wear turbans and gave them clothes woven and embroidered in the royal factories and had them fix their hair with fringes and lovelocks and draw it back at the nape of the neck like young men. She dressed them in close fitting, wide-sleeved robes

called *qabā* and wide belts which showed off their waists and their curves. Then she sent them to her son. He was captivated by their looks and appeared with them in public. It was then that the fashion for having young slave girls with short hair, wearing *qabā* and belts, became established at all levels of society. They were called 'page girls' (*ghulāmiyyāt*).[69]

As Amīn's position deteriorated and the armies of his enemies closed in, his mother stayed with him in the palaces in Baghdad. After his death she resisted suggestions that she should lead a movement to avenge his death, opting instead to make overtures to the victorious Ma'mūn. He accepted her gesture and restored her properties to her. When Ma'mūn returned to Baghdad, Zubayda was quick to greet him, saying that she had lost one son who was a caliph but that Ma'mūn was like a new son to her.[70] After this she seems to have lived a life of wealthy and honoured retirement – we have already seen her role in the magnificent wedding of Burān to Ma'mūn. She died in July 831 and was buried in Baghdad, though probably not in the tomb that now bears her name.

If Zubayda's pious works earned her the blessings of later generations, the same cannot be said of the next of the grandes dames of the Abbasid harem about whom we have enough information to get some idea of her personality. This was the beautiful slave girl called Qabīha, 'the ugly one', by her devoted admirer, the caliph Mutawwakil. In the ninth century it became quite common to give girls disagreeable names, perhaps to draw attention to their beauty or, possibly, to ward off jealousy and misfortune. We know little of her origins or early history. She first appears as the coquettish beloved of the caliph. One story has the caliph getting angry with her and throwing a pillow which hurts her face. She bursts into tears and so does her young son, Mu'tazz, who is with her, and the caliph has to go and find a poet to compose verses to pacify her. On another occasion she presents him with a gift for Nawruz, the Persian New Year, some clear liquid in a rock-crystal goblet. On her cheek she has written the caliph's name, Ja'far, in black musk, and he finds the dark inscription on the white cheek wholly irresistible.[71] It was probably the hold that she had over her master which persuaded him to adopt her son Mu'tazz as his second heir. Interestingly, she is also said to have been an amateur architect, building a pavilion called 'The

Perfect' in the Jawsaq Khāqāni of the caliphal palace in Sāmarrā for her son Muʿtazz.

The circumcision party for the young Muʿtazz joined the weddings of Zubayda and Burān as one of the most famous celebrations of the Abbasid caliphs.[72] Qabīha ordered a million new *dirham*s to be minted with the inscription 'God bless the circumcision of Abu Abd Allah al-Muʿtazz bi Allāh' (the young prince's full name), and these were distributed to the barber who performed the operation and the rest of the guests, the military bodyguard and the servants. The list of guests was a roll-call of all the most powerful and fashionable people in the caliphate. It must have been a day of great triumph for Qabīha. Such success naturally bred resentment; it was widely believed that Mutawwakil's growing preference for Muʿtazz over his first heir Muntasir was one of the reasons for the caliph's brutal assassination in 861.

With Mutawwakil's death Qabīha moved from being a favourite to being the mother of the heir apparent and then the mother of the young Muʿtazz, who was proclaimed caliph on 25 January 866. By this time Qabīha was extremely wealthy. She had her own secretaries and her own household. We hear little about her during her son's short caliphate. When, in July 869, he was arrested and deposed by the same Turks, led by Sālih ibn al-Wasīf, who had raised him to the throne three and half years before, she did little to help him. He desperately needed 50,000 *dīnār*s with which to pay the disaffected soldiery and appealed to her, but she replied frostily that she did not have the cash although she had some promissory notes and, if the Turks would wait, they could be redeemed.[73] But the Turks could not or would not wait and her son perished miserably aged just twenty-four.[74]

Qabīha meanwhile had vanished. It appears that she had already taken precautions in case she had to escape. She had had a tunnel dug from her private apartments in the palace to a secret hiding place. After her son had been deposed, the soldiers went to look for her to confiscate her wealth. They searched the palace but were baffled to find that she had completely disappeared. Even when they found the tunnel, they had no idea where she had gone.

Qabīha became increasingly anxious. She had taken refuge with an ex-colleague of hers from Mutawwakil's harem who was now married to a powerful general. However, she heard that the group who had killed her son were torturing anyone who knew her, and she feared that her secret would soon come out.

Finally, in the middle of August, she went to Sālih and gave herself up. She ordered that some of her possessions in Baghdad should be sold and half a million *dinārs* was brought to Sāmarrā to pay the troops. Sālih, still desperate for money, was convinced that she had more still concealed. An informer came to say he knew where she kept her treasure and Sālih sent a henchman of his along with a jeweller to assess any precious stones that might be found. The jeweller's account of what happened has been preserved.[75]

The informer took us to a small neat house which we entered and searched from top to bottom without finding anything... he then fetched an axe and began breaking open the walls with it, looking for a place where money might be hidden. He went on doing this until he hit a spot on the wall which sounded hollow. When he demolished the wall, a door appeared behind it. We opened it and went in. It led into a tunnel and we found ourselves in a cellar underneath the house above and with the same floor plan. There, stored in baskets placed on shelves, we found the money, something in the order of a million dinars. Ahmad took 300,000 dinars. Then we discovered three baskets, one containing about five kilos of emeralds of a sort which I could not imagine Mutawwakil, never mind anyone else, possessing. A smaller basket contained about two and half kilos of large beads and a third smaller basket contained a kilo and a half of rubies, the like of which I had never seen before. I estimated that the market value of them all was about two million dinars. We removed the entire treasure and took it to Sālih. When he heard of its value he could scarcely believe it until he was shown the actual goods. Then he remarked, 'God damn her! She condemned her son to death for 50,000 dinars when she had wealth like this in just one of her treasuries.'

The new caliph, Muhtadi, ordered that she should be taken on the pilgrimage to Mecca and kept there. She seems to have remained there until she died eight years later in 877.[76]

The last of the great women of the Abbasid court also enjoyed wealth and power but ended her life in tragedy and obscurity. Like Qabīha, Shaghab (Trouble) was given a deliberately ugly name, but she was normally referred to as Sayyida or the Mistress. Her origins were extremely humble: according to one version she had begun life as a slave girl belonging to a daughter of Muhammad ibn Abd Allah the Tahirid, but how she had moved to the caliph's *huram* is not recorded. She owed her fortune to the fact that her young son Muqtadir was chosen by the vizier to be caliph in 908 when he was only thirteen and still living in the harem. It was an unscrupulous move by the vizier, who chose him over better-qualified members of the Abbasid family because he hoped to have a compliant monarch firmly under his control. In fact the young caliph's youth and inexperience meant that his mother and her friends could dominate him much more effectively and the vizier's enemies could make contact with her to gain the caliph's ear.

The Mistress ruled a fully developed female court which existed in parallel to the male-dominated world of the viziers and the military. She had her own courtiers. The most important of these were the stewardesses (Ar. *qahramāna*). The first of these we hear about was one Fātima, who was drowned when her boat got caught under the bridge in Baghdad on a windy day. Military commanders and judges attended her funeral, an unusual mark of respect for a woman. In her place, the Mistress appointed an Abbasid princess called Umm Mūsā. Umm Mūsā made herself indispensable as a messenger between the caliph, who seems to have spent quite a lot of his time in the harem, and the viziers, who could not, of course, go there.[77] One day she went to see the vizier Alī ibn Īsā to ask for the gifts that were going to be distributed at the feasts of the sacrifice among the *huram* and their retinue. Unfortunately it was a time when the vizier was not receiving visitors and his chamberlain courteously explained the position and sent her away. When the vizier found out what had happened, he knew there would be trouble and desperately tried to make amends, but she was furious and having none of it. She immediately went to the caliph and his mother and denounced Alī. This inadvertent snub was one of the things that cost him his job.[78] You could not be too careful with these powerful ladies. She also used her position to allow the vizier's rivals to meet the caliph and to secure government posts for her favourites.[79] But those who succeed in intrigue and manipulation can equally be undone by it. Umm Mūsā had married her niece to a young Abbasid prince who was a grandson of the caliph Mutawwakil. Not only was he rich and extravagant, with sumptuous clothes and beautiful horses and boats, he was also a potential candidate for the throne. To celebrate the marriage, Umm Mūsā gave a lavish party to members of the court, both great and small, which lasted for some ten days. The display cost her dear, and her enemies convinced the Mistress and the caliph that she was plotting to put her nephew on the throne. She and her brother were arrested and handed over to the sinister figure of the stewardess Thumāl. Thumāl had a reputation for cruelty. Before joining the Mistress's court she had worked for an Arab chief called Abu Dulaf, who employed her to punish those of his slave girls and slaves who had annoyed him. She now turned her dubious skills on Umm Mūsā, her sister and her brother, and they were forced to disgorge large sums of money and vast amounts of jewellery, garments, furnishings and perfume. A contemporary writer, Thābit ibn Sinān, estimated that the value of the jewels, fabrics, garments and cash taken from them was 1 million *dīnārs*,[80] and it was said that her and her brother's estates brought in an income of 100,000 *dīnārs* a year.

Thumāl was notorious for her cruelty, but we also hear of another stewardess with a more benign reputation. Zaydān had a role as jailer to important political figures when they fell from grace. To be entrusted to Zaydān, and confined to her quarters in the palace, was to be kept in at least comparative comfort. In June 912 the vizier Ibn al-Furāt was dismissed at the end of his first ministry and was at first made to sit in the heat of the sun in a heavy woollen robe and loaded with chains until he almost died. After one of the servants of the *huram* told Muqtadir about this, the ex-vizier was taken to Zaydān's apartments in the private quarters, where he was comforted and looked after.[81] Thereafter, as Ibn al-Furāt and his great rival Alī ibn Īsā moved in and out of high office, Zaydān's apartment became both prison and refuge to those who were out of favour. When Alī ibn Īsā lost his job in May 928 the proceedings were conducted with some decorum. The caliph's agent went to the vizier and handed him a message saying that he had been dismissed and was to be put under house arrest. Then the agent said he would sit down and wait while Alī went and collected his things. He soon reappeared dressed in his outdoor shoes and wearing a turban and a *taylasān*, with a Koran and a penknife in his sleeve. He asked the agent to look after his women and children, which the agent agreed to do. Then he was taken to the Palace of the Caliphate and entrusted to the care of Zaydān.[82]

After her Muqtadir was made caliph in 908, Shaghab became immensely wealthy. 'Her son gave her as a fief, in instalments, agricultural land with ample revenue. She continued to buy more land up to the day her son was dethroned [for the first time] in 929. The combined annual revenue from the lands she had purchased and the fiefs was some 700,000 *dīnārs*.[83] She had shops and storehouses in Baghdad where wheat was hoarded, and on one occasion, in a time of famine, the caliph had to order that they be opened and the contents sold below the market price.[84] She had her own office (*dīwān*) to administer these estates, whose secretary was appointed by her or one of her stewardesses.[85] Her sister too had had a secretary to look after her own *dīwān*.[86]

In addition to their income from landed estates, the women of the harem also enjoyed subsidies from the public purse. According to a budget drawn up by the vizier Alī ibn Īsā in 918, out of a total annual expenditure of 2,560,960 *dīnārs*, 743,196 was spent on the Mistress, the women, the princes and the eunuchs. If these figures are in any way accurate, it suggests that the allowances paid from the treasury to the harem were worth slightly more than the income from property. These sums compare with the personal expenditure of the caliph on rewards and gifts of 271,520 *dīnārs*, 51,000 on buildings and repairs and 1,280 for paying his boatmen. The harem was certainly a significant drain on expenses, though not nearly as much as the military.[87] Not surprisingly this put considerable strain on the state finances in times of crisis. As early in the reign as 917, Alī ibn Īsā was reduced to paying the *huram* only for eight months of the year and the eunuchs for six, a prudent economy measure that cost him his job, yet again, when a rival persuaded the caliph that he could pay in full.[88]

The queen mother's revenues were hers to dispose of as she wished. As the unfortunate caliph Muʿtazz had discovered, the caliph could not automatically call on them or have access to them as required. The Mistress was equally in control of her own assets. When Baghdad was threatened by the Carmathian rebels* in 928, the vizier Alī ibn Īsā was desperate for money to pay an army to oppose them. The city was in a panic; merchants were shutting up shop, loading their goods on boats to take them downriver to Wasit or

---

* The Carmathians (Ar. *Qarāmita*) were a Shiite group who attracted widespread support among the Bedouin of the Syrian desert and north-east Arabia. They sacked Basra and came near to taking Baghdad itself in 928.

overland to Iran. The army was disaffected and the government was bankrupt. Faced with this desperate situation, he asked Muqtadir to approach his mother to see whether she could help. Alī had to make his case persuasively and diplomatically. 'In the old days', he argued,

caliphs hoarded money for the sole purpose of defending our faith against enemies like the Kharijites and protecting Islam and the Muslims. Now since the death of the Prophet, no more serious disaster has befallen the Muslims than this. He [the leader of the Carmathians] is a infidel who attacked the pilgrims in 924 in an unheard of fashion [the Hajj caravan had been attacked and almost all the pilgrims massacred on the desert road from Iraq to the Holy Cities]. He has spread terror among courtiers and commoners alike. Muʿtaḍid and Muktafī [the previous two caliphs] collected money for precisely this sort of emergency. Now there is very little in the treasury. Fear God, O Commander of the Faithful and speak to the Mistress for she is a pious and virtuous woman. If she has any money that she has saved for emergencies that might threaten her or the state, then now is the moment to use it. If she dosen't have any, you and your court had better pack up and leave for furthest parts of Khurasan [i.e. as far away from the Carmathians as he could get].

The caliph visited his mother and she agreed that half a million *dīnār*s could be transferred from her private resources to the state treasury.[89] It was partly because of this money that Alī was able to organize the defence of Baghdad and the city was saved. Amazingly, this does not seem to have exhausted her reserves; when Muqtadir was deposed in February 929, temporarily, as it turned out, an agent was sent to the Mistress's tomb (*turba*) in the Rusafa quarter of Baghdad, where he collected 600,000 *dīnār*s which she had put there.[90] This seems to be one of the first examples in Islam of the building of a tomb complex during the life of its patron, and it is perhaps significant that it belonged not to the caliph or any general or vizier but to the queen mother. By the time of Muqtadir's death in 932, however, it seems that she had no more resources. When her son was attacked by the army under Muʾnis, a loyal general explained to the caliph that 'the soldiers only fight for money; if this is produced fighting will be unnecessary for most of Muʾnis' followers will desert and he will have to flee or go into hiding': 200,000 *dīnār*s were needed for immediate expenses but neither the caliph nor his mother had that sort of money.[91]

After her son's murder at the end of October 932, the Mistress's fortunes declined still further: there was little status in being an ex-queen mother. The new caliph was Muqtadir's uncle, Qāhir. The Mistress had treated him well and had been generous to him in the days of her prosperity, presenting him with a number of slave girls,[92] but this counted for nothing now. She was in a desperate state; already ill, she was distraught that her son had been killed and not properly buried. Qāhir was convinced that she still had vast wealth and came to interrogate her in person. At first he was gentle, giving her some bread, salt and water, but gradually he became more threatening. She swore that she had no money left, only some chests containing ornaments, clothes, *farsh* and perfume. These were all in an apartment next to the one she lived in in the Palace of the Caliphate. She showed him the apartment and the boxes and added sadly, 'If I had had any money, I would not have given my son up to be killed,' a marked contrast, perhaps, with her predecessor Qabīha. The new caliph was reluctant to believe her. He turned nasty, hit her, hung her up by one foot and beat her around what the chronicler discreetly calls 'the soft parts' of her body. Physical torture of women was virtually unknown in Muslim society of the period, though common enough for men, and Qāhir was going well beyond the bounds of respectable and normal behaviour. Even so, she revealed no more than she had told him of her own free will.

It was at this stage that his ministers arrived, saying that they needed money to give the troops as an accession gift. Qāhir told them what he had done and how the Mistress had persisted in saying that she had no cash. Then he took them to the apartment with the chests. They found robes of richly coloured fabric, Byzantine embroideries and also embroidery from Tustar (in Khuzistān), heavily adorned with gold, leather mats, striped silk and woollen fabrics. Some of the chests contained magnificent robes, a few gold and many silver ornaments, and a great deal of perfume, aloes wood from India, ambergris, musk, camphor and camphor dolls. It was all worth about 130,000 *dīnār*s, excluding the camphor dolls, which were valued at 30,000 *dirham*s: most of it was sold to pay the army but Qāhir was allowed to keep some for his personal use.[93]

The Mistress's landed properties were confiscated and a special office was set up to administer them. She had also set up a number of pious foundation or *waqfs*. Under Islamic law these were supposed to be inviolable; the lands and assets that supported them were protected and the revenues devoted to charitable causes. She had established them to help the poor and needy in Mecca and on the frontiers of the empire. When she was hauled out of prison, she refused to cancel these trusts, telling the judge that it was not lawful to do so (which was true). When the judge reported this to the caliph, he was told simply to swear that she had in fact annulled these trusts and that the lands, along with her other possessions, should be sold.[94] Unlike Zubayda, she would never be remembered for her pious deeds.

After the death of her son, and the humiliations inflicted on her, the Mistress was confined to the palace and died under house arrest on 3 June 933.[95] It was the end of an era: the last of the great women of the Abbasid house had perished in poverty and disgrace. There were to be no more like her.

It was hardly surprising that the vast wealth of the Mistress and the sums spent on the harem attracted the criticisms of outsiders, mostly those who felt that they themselves were entitled to a larger share of the revenues of the state. At the beginning of his reign, it was said that Muqtadir 'devoted all his time to his pleasures. He was shy of men and sent away the companions and singers. He socialized with women and the *huram* and the eunuchs came to dominate the state.'[96] In 929 matters came to a head and the chief military commander, Mu'nis, wrote to Muqtadir saying that the army was complaining bitterly about the amount of money and land wasted on the eunuchs and women of the court and their dominance of the administration. He demanded that they be dismissed and removed from the palace and their goods seized. Muqtadir wrote a long letter in reply. In this he expressed his great respect for Mu'nis and said that these complaints were based on misunderstandings and that if Mu'nis and his followers thought about it they would realize that. However, he was prepared to make some concessions. Some of their estates were to be seized, their properties should be assessed and they should pay any dues they owed to the treasury. He agreed to expel those whom it was lawful to expel from his palace. He added that he himself would take a more active role in administration and went on to deal with some other points Mu'nis had raised. In short, he promised some cosmetic changes, but no real action. Not surprisingly, Mu'nis was wholly dissatisfied with the response. He marched on the palace and, while his supporters made themselves scarce, Muqtadir, his mother, her sister and his favourite slave girls were taken into custody.[97]

In the event, Muqtadir was restored to the throne for a short period but the ill feeling over the women clearly remained. When he was finally killed and the leading men met to discuss who should be caliph, Mu'nis suggested that they should appoint the dead caliph's young son. However, there was fierce opposition: 'After all the trouble it has taken us to get rid of one ruler with a mother and an aunt and eunuchs, we do not need another one,' they argued, and the proposal was dropped.[98]

Some contemporaries, and later historians, have blamed extravagance and political interference by the *huram* for the disasters that effectively ended the power of the caliphate in the early tenth century. They would all have agreed with the vociferous complaints of the caliph Hādī against interference by his mother Khayzurān in political affairs. It is true, as we have seen, that the harem did consume a significant proportion of the tax revenue of the state and that the queen mother, her relatives and friends were vastly rich. No doubt too they used their privileged access to the caliph as a way of securing their position. But the problems of the caliphate ran much deeper than that. The military were both more expensive to maintain and more damaging to the fabric of government and society than the women ever were. And the harem in the age of Muqtadir did make a positive contribution. We have seen how the women's quarters offered accommodation that was both prison and sanctuary to viziers who had fallen out of favour. The Mistress's interventions in politics were often intended to save good viziers and others who had fallen out of favour; she was more mediator than vengeful harridan. The financial resources of the queen mother were also a sort of financial reserve for the caliphs in times of greatest need. In a society where government borrowing from banks or individuals was impossible, the wealth of the harem could be a valuable cushion against financial disaster. The extravagances of the harem were textiles and other luxury goods, purchase of which must have stimulated the local economy. The textile weavers of Tustar and the carpet makers of Armenia, among many others, must have suffered grievously when the harem was no longer a major purchasing power.

The fall of the Mistress in 932 meant the end of the Abbasid harem as it had developed since the frugal and informal days of Mansūr, nearly two centuries before. The singing girls were dispersed to unknown fates, the gorgeous fabrics sold or destroyed, the ancient tunes lost beyond recovery, but the memory of the Abbasid harem was preserved by historians such as Tabari and Miskawayh and in literary memoirs such as the *Book of Songs*. It became the model for all subsequent Islamic royal harems, and it was not until well into the twentieth century, with the final break-up of the Ottoman harem in Istanbul, that the tradition established in Baghdad and Sāmarrā finally came to an end.

VIII

Ma'mūn to Mutawwakil

When the distinguished grammarian and literary critic Tha'lab (d. 904) looked back on his early life there was one particular memory that stuck in his mind. It was August in Baghdad and the summer sun was already high in the sky: 'I saw the caliph Ma'mūn on his return from Khurasan. He had just left the Iron Gate and was on his way to Rusafa. The people were drawn up in two lines [to watch the caliph and his entourage go by] and my father held me up in his arms and said "That is Ma'mūn and this is the year [two hundred] and four [AD 819]". I have remembered these words ever since: I was four at the time.'[1]

Tha'lab's father clearly recognized this as a moment of major importance and no doubt hoped that the arrival of the caliph in the city his great-grandfather had founded represented the dawn of a new era. Ma'mūn had probably decided to leave Merv and come west at the beginning of 818, but his progress had been slow and not without drama. By mid-February he had reached Sarakhs. While he was here a group of men attacked his vizier, Fadl ibn Sahl, in the bath and killed him. Fadl had been the architect of Ma'mūn's policy of staying in Merv, and there can be little doubt that his death was very convenient for the caliph. His assassins were soon caught and turned out to have been men from the caliph's own retinue. They claimed to be acting on his orders but it did not save them and he ordered that their heads be cut off.[2]

In early September he reached the city of Tūs, where his father had died and been buried, and he visited his father's tomb. It was here that another accident befell a prominent member of the caliph's entourage. His heir, Alī al-Rida, died mysteriously. It was given out that he had consumed a surfeit of grapes and had perished as a result, but many thought that he had been poisoned to clear the way for

Ma'mūn to be reconciled to the Abbasid family and the people of Baghdad.[3] He was buried beside Hārūn. Alī may have died but his memory lingered on. Among the Shia, the grave of this new martyr became the focus of pilgrimage. Under the Persian form of his name, Alī Reza, he became almost the patron saint of Iran. The memory of Tūs was almost forgotten, and the centre of settlement moved to the site known simply as Meshed (the place of martyrdom). The shrine grew in wealth and status. In the fifteenth century the Timurid queen Gawhar Shad built a mosque that is still one of the great glories of the Islamic architecture of Iran, and today Meshed ranks along with Qum as one of the two Shiite Holy Cities of Iran. Meanwhile Hārūn's tomb, unadorned and unloved, became the object of derision and abuse.

The caliph must have spent the winter in Khurasan, for we find him at Rayy in June 819. From there he travelled along the great Khurasan road through the Zagros passes, pausing for a day or two at each of the staging posts. When he reached Nahrawān, on the banks of the great canal that irrigated so much of the land to the east of the Tigris, he was met by Tāhir and by members of his family and leading figures in Baghdad. From here he planned his triumphal, unopposed entry into the city.

Ma'mūn was finally accepted as caliph, but he had to make compromises to achieve this. The most obvious was in the question of dress. The Abbasids had adopted the colour black from the beginning and the black court dress was compulsory for formal court occasions. In Merv, however, Ma'mūn and his court had taken to wearing green, which became at this time, if not before, the preferred colour of the supporters of the Alids. Even after he reached Baghdad, no one would be admitted to see him unless they wore green and his supporters would pounce on anyone wearing black. The measure remained deeply unpopular and public resentment was quite open: 'Commander of the Faithful,' he was told, 'you have abandoned the dress of your forefathers, the members of your family and the supporters of your dynasty!' According to one version it was Tāhir in person who finally persuaded the caliph that the wearing of green was never going to be acceptable and that he should revert to black. By the end of the week, the hated green was gone and its going symbolized the final abandonment of Ma'mūn's early policies. From now on he was going to rule as a truly Abbasid caliph and in the city of his ancestors.

He may have been accepted in Baghdad and Iran but in most of the western half of the empire power was in the hands of local war-lords who had taken advantage of the disturbances. Baghdad itself had been damaged and impoverished by continuous fighting, and large areas must have been in ruins. Ma'mūn began by living in the palace his grandfather Mahdi had built on the east side, but he later moved down the river and built a new waterside palace.[4] The Golden Gate palace in the Round City was never lived in by a caliph again, though the mosque continued in use, and the Eternity Palace on the west side was abandoned. Most likely they had both been damaged beyond repair in the fighting and, as often in Baghdad, it was easier to build new than to restore the old.

The caliph's chief supporters in this new policy were Tāhir and his family. After the death of Amīn, the Banū Sahl brothers had effec-tively excluded Tāhir from power. He was sent to Raqqa, far from the centre of events in Baghdad, where he is said to have occupied himself reading philosophy. Ma'mūn had invited him to meet him before he entered the city, and Tāhir became his right-hand man. This was the beginning of a partnership between Tāhirids and Abbasids which was to last half a century and bring a degree of sta-bility to administration and politics. The Tāhirids also made a major contribution to the cultural life of the court and the wider Baghdad milieu. Basically the Tāhirids governed their native Khurasan and, after the caliphs moved to Sāmarrā, Baghdad. At least until the death of Mutawwakil in 861 the system worked well: Baghdad was largely peaceful and taxes were brought from Khurasan on a regular basis. Tāhir and his family were, after all, Khurasani aristocrats by origin, and they must have respected the interests of their aristocratic friends. At the same time the presence of the Tāhirids in Baghdad provided a sort of alternative court which must have made the absence of the caliphs in Sāmarrā more bearable. Ma'mūn had pre-sented Tāhir with an old palace on the upper west side which had belonged to one of Mansūr's eunuchs. Here he and his family built a vast complex of palaces which was generally known as the Harim (enclosure) of Tāhir. In the second half of the ninth century, after the Tāhirids had disappeared from the scene, it became a secondary resi-dence of the Abbasids. The caliphs Muʿtadid (d. 902) and Muktafi (d. 908) were buried there. It was the dwelling place, half palace, half prison, of princes of the ruling family who might have had a claim to the throne. When the geographer Yāqūt was writing in the early thirteenth century, the area was still inhabited, as a small walled town, when all around was desolation,[5] though it had long since ceased to be a residence of the Abbasids.

Tāhir was appointed as governor of Khurasan early in 821. As soon as he was appointed he established a camp in some gardens on the outskirts of the city while he gathered his resources. In May he left for the east.[6] His appointment was a source of controversy at the time and later. There was a story to the effect that Ma'mūn could not bear to be with Tāhir, since seeing him reminded him that Tāhir had been personally responsible for the death of his brother Amīn. Sensing that all was not well, Tāhir prevailed on a friend of his, who had the caliph's ear, to arrange for this appointment, which would take him out of harm's way. Tāhir governed only for a year, but his family controlled most of Iran for the next fifty. Furthermore, some people said that just before his death he openly renounced his allegiance to the caliph by omitting his name from the Friday prayers. Tāhir can be seen as the first of the Persian dynasts to break away from the Abbasids and establish independent states in Iran. In reality this was much less of a break than it might seem with hindsight: Tāhir's successors all acknowledged Abbasid overlordship and the family was inextricably woven into the fabric of the Abbasid state.

Tāhir's son Abd Allah remained in the west and was soon appointed to command Abbasid armies in northern Syria, where local lords were defying the authority of the new regime. Abd Allah ibn Tāhir was a man of whom our sources say nothing but good. We are given a glowing picture of a man who was brave and wise, rich, generous and cultured, a faithful servant to the caliph and a guardian of the people. Whether the reality matched up to the image we can never know, but the achievements were real: Syria and Egypt were brought back under Abbasid control with no major battle or bloodshed and he later governed Khurasan in peace and prosperity.

The historians of the period have preserved the text of a long letter said to have been written by Tāhir, giving advice to his son about how to be a good ruler.[7] The fundamental idea underlying this is that Abd Allah has been given power by God and he must use it for the benefit of the people he rules. He is accountable to God for his actions. He should pray regularly and seek the advice of scholars of religious law when making decisions. There is also a great emphasis on 'moderation in all things', on not moving too hastily, on not being too suspicious or critical of officials under his command while at the same time making sure that they do not oppress the people. The ruler should not pile up great stores of treasure: 'Let the treasuries and store-houses which you pile up and accumulate be composed of piety, fear of God, justice, measures for your subjects' welfare and the prosperity of their land, knowledge of their affairs, protection for the mass of them and help for those who sorrow. Know that wealth which is accumulated and stored away in treasuries bears no fruit but when it is spent on the improvement of the conditions of the subjects, on the provision of their just dues and on removing burdens from them, it thrives and multiplies.'

This benevolent attitude will also make tax-collecting easier and more efficient. The army should be paid regularly and pay rolls should be in order so that 'their happy condition will be a source of strength for you'.[8] Judges should be respected. Taxation is a central issue:

> Look carefully into the matter of the land-tax which the subjects have an obligation to pay. God has made this a source of strength and power for Islam and a means of support and protection for his people but he has also made it a source of trouble for his enemies and the enemies of the Muslims and a source of humiliation and subservience for unbelievers in treaty relations with the Muslims. Divide it among the tax payers with justice and fairness with equal treatment for all. Do not remove any part of the obligation to pay the tax from any noble person just because of his nobility or any rich person because of his richness or from any of your secretaries or personal retainers. Do not require from anyone more than he can bear, or exact more than the usual rate.[9]

Under just administration the land will prosper and this economic growth will deliver higher tax yields.

There is also what might be described as a welfare-state aspect to the duties of the ruler, who should devote himself

> to looking after the affairs of the poor and destitute, those who are unable to bring their complaints of ill-treatment to you personally and those of wretched estate who do not know how to set about

claiming their rights … Turn your attention to those who have suffered injuries and their orphans and widows and provide them with allowances from the state treasury, following the example of the Commander of the Faithful, may God exalt him, in showing compassion for them and giving them financial support, so that God may thereby bring some alleviation into their daily lives and by means of it bring you the spiritual food of His blessing and an increase of His favour. Give pensions from the state treasury to the blind, and give higher allowances to those who know of the Qur'an, or most of it by heart. Set up hospices where sick Muslims can find shelter, and appoint custodians for these places who will treat the patients with kindness and physicians who will cure their illnesses.[10]

It is very important for the ruler to allow people to come and see him to present their complaints. 'Allow people access to your person as much as possible and show your face to them as often as possible. Order your guards to treat them politely, be humble with them and show them the face of your approval. When questioning them, be gentle and grant them a share of your beneficence.'[11]

Officials too must have regular access to the ruler:

Keep an eye on the officials at your court and on your secretaries. Give them each a fixed time each day when they can bring you their official correspondence and any documents requiring the ruler's signature. They can let you know about the needs of the various officials and about all the affairs of the provinces you rule over. Then devote all your faculties, ears, eyes, understanding and intellect, to the business they set before you: consider it and think about it repeatedly. Finally take those actions which seem to be in accordance with good judgment and justice.[12]

The document ends with a general exhortation to piety and obedience to God.

We cannot be certain that Tāhir really wrote this himself but contemporaries seem to have believed that he did. We are told that it was widely distributed. Everyone wanted a text and the caliph had it copied and sent to everyone in his provincial government. The earliest record of the document we have comes from the pen of Ibn Abi

Tāhir (no relation) writing in the mid ninth century, so it is certainly contemporary or nearly so, and must reflect ideas of good governance as they existed at that time.

The ruler is shown as a benevolent despot. His authority is absolute and he is responsible, not to his subjects, but to God. There is no sense of any popular limitations to his power, and certainly no mention of any sanctions his subjects can make use of should he abuse it. The ruler should behave in a benign and conscientious way because he is responsible to God and will be held to account by Him if he fails. He should also look after the welfare of his subjects because it makes sense to do so: prosperous subjects pay more taxes and cause fewer problems. To an extent the advice is worldly and even cynical – being a just ruler makes you richer and more powerful – but it is also about the virtuous circle, an idea Muslim political theorists were to return to time and time again: a strong but gentle tyranny brings benefits to ruler and subjects alike.

The emphasis on moderation in all things is also striking. It is possible that this idea comes directly from Greek philosophy, even perhaps from the reading of philosophy with which Tāhir is said to have whiled away the time during his semi-exile in Raqqa in the final years of the great civil war.

There are also noticeable omissions in the document. Apart from a brief mention of the use of taxation to humiliate unbelievers, nothing in Tāhir's work would give any indication that a large proportion, probably the majority, of the people over whom he ruled were Christians. He is only concerned with how a Muslim ruler should relate to his Muslim subjects. There is no mention of the need to convert non-Muslims to Islam. There is also no mention of the *Jihād* or holy war: the Muslim community is imagined as being at peace with itself and its neighbours.

Tāhir's document was essentially aspirational. We are told that Abd Allah ibn Tāhir, the son to whom it was addressed, followed his advice and, if that is true, it would account for Abd Allah's good reputation in the sources. Needless to say, many rulers did not follow the advice and government was often remote, brutal, greedy and tyrannical, but the letter does give a clear model of what contemporaries imagined good government could be like.

A major objective of the first years of Ma'mūn's reign in Baghdad was reconciliation. The fabric of political society had been torn apart by the long years of civil war. Men who had been colleagues at the court of Hārūn had become bitter enemies and set about destroying each other. Much of the countryside was ravaged and impoverished and the new government made substantial tax concessions to allow some fiscal space for the restoration of prosperity.[13]

At court there were reconciliations on a more personal level. Amīn's mother Zubayda had kept a low profile since her son's death but she was now reconciled with the caliph, who restored some of her properties to her. Ma'mūn's own mother had died when he was in his infancy, and in the old days Zubayda had treated him kindly. Relations were now restored, though they may never have been close, and Zubayda played something of the role his own mother may have done when he married Burān in 824/5.[14] Reconciliation with Zubayda was both cause and symbol of a more general reconciliation with the Abbasid family. Now that Ma'mūn was back in Baghdad and wearing black, they had no problem in accepting him as caliph.

No one could have done more to incur Ma'mūn's anger than Fadl ibn Rabī, the evil genius behind Amīn's attempt to remove Ma'mūn from his position. As the caliph himself put it, 'He seized control of my commanders, my troops, my weapons and everything that my father had left me and went off with them to Amīn [in Baghdad], leaving me alone and isolated in Merv. He betrayed me and he turned my brother against me with the results that we all know. For me, that was the worst thing of all!'[15] Rabī emerged from hiding and was now accepted back into favour because of his and his father's long record of service to the Abbasids and his close links with the family.[16] He was also valued for his long experience of politics and the rising political star of these years, the young Abd Allah ibn Tāhir, sought his advice.[17] When he died, peacefully, in the spring of 824, his passing marked the end of an era.

The anti-caliph, Ibrāhīm ibn al-Mahdi, talented poet but failed politician, had gone into hiding when Ma'mūn came to Baghdad.* For six years he lived a clandestine existence in Baghdad, hiding presumably with friends and relatives, until in August 825 he was picked up by the police. He was out at night disguised as a woman and accompanied by two real women when he was challenged by a guard who demanded to know where he/she was going at this late hour.

---

* See pp. 170–71 above for another account of the reconciliation of Ma'mūn with Ibrāhīm in which it is linked to the caliph's marriage to Burān.

Ibrāhīm seems to have panicked and offered the guard a large ruby ring from his finger if he would let them pass and ask no more questions. This immediately made the guard suspicious. He took them to the commander of the local guard post who ordered the 'women' to unveil. Ibrāhīm refused, but the officer ripped away the veil and his beard was revealed for all to see. He was then taken to the Commander of the Bridge, the head of the guard, who recognized him and sent him to the caliph.

The next day he was put on display in Ma'mūn's palace in front of all the members of the Abbasid family. They put his veil around his neck and his women's clothes over his chest so everyone could see the humiliating circumstances in which he had been captured. But Ibrāhīm was no longer a threat to Ma'mūn and Abbasid blood still counted for something. The caliph remembered the story of Joseph and his brothers and, echoing Joseph's words from the Koran said, 'There is no reproach upon you today. God will forgive you, and He is the most merciful of those showing mercy.'[18] He was put under house arrest in the charge of two senior military officers, but he was allowed plenty of living space and he had his mother and family with him. He was also allowed to ride to Ma'mūn's palace, under escort, to visit him. The caliph was rewarded in the only currency Ibrāhīm still had to offer, a fulsome poem of praise and thanks, and he survived to grace the court of Muᶜtasim in Sāmarrā. When he died in Sāmarrā in July 839, the caliph himself read the funeral prayers over him.[19]

Gradually, Ma'mūn was able to re-establish control over provinces that the Abbasids had lost during the years of impotence and civil war. By a mixture of diplomacy and the threat of force, Abd Allah ibn Tāhir had re-established Abbasid government in Syria in 825 and Egypt in 826. It was true that some areas of northern Iran still resisted the authority of Baghdad, but there was nothing new in that. Apart from Tunisia, which effectively became independent during the civil war, Ma'mūn had restored the empire to the boundaries it had possessed in his father's reign.

In the summer of 830 he decided to follow his father's example and devote himself to the holy war against Byzantium. It was a twin-pronged attack, the caliph himself leading his army from Tarsus in the west while farther east his son Abbās led an army from Malatya.[20] A few minor fortresses were conquered but, as often, the main purpose of the expedition was probably to exhibit the caliph as military leader of the Muslims and his son Abbās as a future caliph.

After finishing his military foray, Ma'mūn returned not to Baghdad but to the old Umayyad capital at Damascus. He seems to have wintered there, and it may have been at this time that he caused the inscription of the Dome of the Rock in Jerusalem to be changed. The inscription, one of the oldest extant examples of Arabic epigraphy, proclaims in clear and stately gold mosaic letters that the builder of the dome was the Umayyad caliph Abd al-Malik (685–705). In an attempt to claim the glory for himself and his dynasty, the caliph caused Abd al-Malik's name to be replaced by his own. The attempt has fooled no one and stands today as testimony of his own petulant vanity or the obsequiousness of his advisers.

After wintering in Damascus, Ma'mūn went north once more in the summer of 831 to the Byzantine frontier. He took Heraclea (which had also been taken by his father a quarter of a century before but reoccupied by the Byzantines during the civil war). Again he returned to Damascus for the winter. In the early spring of 832 he visited Egypt, the only reigning Abbasid caliph ever to do so. After a short stay he headed north once more to the frontier. He laid siege to a castle called Lulua. All did not go in his favour. The garrison resisted and after a hundred days the caliph withdrew, leaving one of his commanders, Ujayf, in charge. Ujayf was then captured by the Byzantines. With the emperor Theophilus himself on the attack, Ma'mūn decided that it was time to make peace. Tabari preserves an exchange of letters between caliph and emperor.[21] Whether genuine or not, they give a flavour of Muslim opinion about the dialogue. The emperor suggests peace so that 'you can remove the burdens of war from us. We can be friends.' He also suggests that peace will allow the growth of trade between Muslims and Byzantines and the release of prisoners on both sides, and he ends by threatening to take the war deep into Muslim territory if his offers are rejected. The caliph replies in a more aggressive tone. His response should be to send a military force 'to seek God's favour by spilling your blood'. His soldiers are 'more eager to go forward to the watering places of death than you are to preserve yourselves from the fearful threat of their onslaught upon you', and he goes on to stress that his men have 'the promise of one of the two best things,[22] a speedy victory or a return to God as martyrs'. The emperor can avoid this by immediately accepting Islam for himself and his people. He then returns to the real world, offering a truce in exchange for payment of tribute, and it seems that this was what actually happened. For all the high-flown rhetoric it was essentially business as usual between two great powers, neither strong enough to dominate the other.

The next spring (833) Ma'mūn set out for the frontier again. This time he seems to have been determined to make real territorial advances and to establish a permanent base on the north side of the the Taurus mountains, something the Muslims had never achieved before. He decided to occupy and fortify the city known to the Greeks as Tyana and to the Arabs as Tuwana (modern Kemerhisar, about 20 kilometres south of Nigde). Troops were recruited throughout Syria, a most unusual move for the Abbasids, most of whose soldiers were recruited in Iran and points east. They were paid 100 *dirham*s for a cavalryman, 40 for an infantryman. In addition to four thousand troops from Syria, there were troops from Egypt and two thousand from Baghdad. This was to be a major operation. In charge of the project he appointed his son Abbās. He set out in May and was soon at work on the site, building an enclosure wall said to have been three *farsakhs* (18 kilometres) long, with four gates, each strengthened by a fortress.[23]

Ma'mūn followed his son north to the mountains, but the great advance of the Muslim frontier that had been planned was never to be. On 9 August 833, the caliph died suddenly of a fever at the little village of Budandūn (Greek Podandos, modern Pozanti) on the road north from the Cilician Gates. He was forty-six years old.[24] We have a supposedly eyewitness account of the circumstances in which he died from a Koran reader who was summoned to accompany the caliph:[25] 'I found him sitting on the bank of the river with [his brother] Muʿtasim on his right hand. He invited me to join them and he and his brother were dangling their feet in the river.' We can imagine the scene easily. It was in the heat of summer and the cool streams of the Taurus mountains must have seemed tempting and delightful.

> He said to me, 'Put your feet in the water too and taste it; have you ever seen cooler, sweeter or clearer water than this?' I did as he said and agreed that I had never seen the like of it. Then he asked what food I thought would go best with it and I replied that he would know best. 'Fresh green dates of the Azad variety', he said.

That very moment we heard the clinking noise of the bridles of the mounts of the postal service. He turned to look and saw that some of the mules of the post had panniers over their hindquarters loaded with gifts. He told one of his servants to see if there were any fresh dates among these gifts and if there were, whether they were of the Azad variety. The servants came hurrying back with two baskets of Azad dates, looking as if they had just been gathered from the palm tree. He gave thanks to God and we all had some to eat and some of the water to drink, but by the time we got up we all felt feverish. The illness proved fatal for Ma'mūn, Muʿtasim was sick until he returned to Iraq but I recovered after a short time.

Masʿūdī gives another account[26] related to him in Damascus, though his informant had no claims to be an eyewitness. Here again the caliph is at Budandūn:

Enchanted by the cool water, pure and limpid, and by the beauty of the countryside and its green vegetation, he had long branches cut and laid above the spring over which they built a kind of pavilion of poles and the leaves of trees and he settled down in this rustic shelter. They threw in a newly minted dirham and the water was so clear that he could read the inscription at the bottom of the river, and so cold that no one could bathe in it.

Meanwhile a fish appeared, about half a metre long and bright as a silver ingot. A reward was promised to anyone who could catch it. An attendant hurried down, took the fish and climbed back onto the bank but as he approached the pavilion where Ma'mūn was sitting, the fish wriggled, slipped through his hands and plummeted back into the depths of the spring like a stone. The water splashed all over the caliph's chest, neck and collar-bone and soaked his clothes. The servant hurried back down, caught the fish and placed it, quivering, in a napkin before the caliph.

'Fry it!'

But that very moment he was suddenly overcome by a shivering fit and could not move. It proved useless wrapping him in blankets and quilts: he continued to tremble like a palm-leaf and cry:

'I'm cold, I'm cold!'

They carried him to his tent, covered him and lit a big fire, but he continued to complain of the cold. When the fish was fried, they brought it to him but he did not even want a taste; his suffering was too great for him to touch it.

It is impossible to tell what truth lies behind the two accounts, but the descriptions of this sad event provide a homely insight into the life of the caliph on the road.

Before he died, Ma'mūn had time to make a will in which he specified how he should be buried.[27] After confessing that he is sinful and praying for forgiveness, he continues:

When I die, turn my face towards God, close my eyes and perform the lesser ablution and the rites of purification over me, and see that I am properly shrouded [coffins are not used in traditional Muslim burial practices] ... Then lay me on my side in my litter and hurry along with me. When you set me down for prayers, let the one among you who is closest to me in kinship eldest in years come forward to lead the worship. Let the prayer leader utter the *takbīr* [the formula *Allahu Akbar*, God is Greatest] five times and on the first occasion begin with the formula, 'Praise be to God, and blessing upon our master and the master of all the messengers who have been sent' as the opening words. Then should come a prayer for the men and women believers, those still alive and those now dead, and then a prayer for those who have preceded us in the faith. Then the leader of the prayers should utter the *takbīr* for the fourth time, and then let him praise God, proclaim the confession of faith to Him, magnify Him and ask him to grant peace. Then load my corpse on your shoulders and carry me along to my grave. Render profuse praises to God and mentions of his name. Place me on my right side and turn me in the direction of Mecca. Unwind my shroud from my head and feet and then wall up the niche with mud bricks and sprinkle earth over me. Then go and leave me to my fate. For indeed, none of you will be able to help me, or protect me from any punishment which may be inflicted on me.

Those present should abstain from speaking ill of him and 'Do not allow any weeping women to be near me, for lamentations trouble the deceased.'

A simple funeral, then, and a fittingly modest end for the greatest sovereign of his time. His body was taken to Tarsus and buried in a house belonging to one of his father's eunuchs. His tomb is still shown to the curious.[28]

Ma'mūn seems to have made no clear provision for the succession. He may have been put off by his father's over-elaborate arrangements and the chaos and misery that had resulted from them. However, it is also possible that he had made arrangements but the record of them was subsequently suppressed. Ma'mūn's son Abbās was by this stage an adult with considerable experience of warfare against the Byzantines to his credit. He would have seemed the natural choice, but instead Ma'mūn was succeeded by his brother Muᶜtasim, from whom all subsequent Abbasid caliphs descended. This meant that there was a powerful motivation for portraying Muᶜtasim's accession as natural and unopposed. Reading between the lines, however, it seems that things were not quite so simple.

Abu Ishāq, known by his regnal title as Muᶜtasim, was younger son of Hārūn al-Rashīd by a non-Arab slave girl from Kūfa called Mārida, about whom nothing more is known. He was probably born in 796 in the Eternity Palace in Baghdad, and so was some ten years younger than his brothers Amīn and Ma'mūn.[29] He had been a boy at the time of his father's death and played no part in the succession arrangements Hārūn had made. He probably spent the years of the civil war in Baghdad. The young prince was single-minded and determined. While the other princes of the blood spent their time with poets and singers, he used his resources to recruit soldiers who would be loyal to him alone. Around the year 815, before Ma'mūn had returned to Baghdad, Muᶜtasim began to purchase Turkish slaves from their masters in Baghdad, among them Ashinās, Ītākh, who had been a cook for his previous master, and Wasīf, who had worked as a maker of chain mail. After the re-establishment of the the caliphate in Baghdad, Muᶜtasim began to buy slaves directly from merchants in central Asia. These slave soldiers were all Turks by race. At this time the Turks did not live in modern Turkey but in the traditional Turkish homelands, the great areas of steppe and grass-land that lay beyond the frontiers of settlement in north-east Iran, in the areas that are now Uzbekistan, Kazakhstan and Kyrgyzstan. They were people of clearly eastern Asiatic appearance (like modern Kazakhs and Kyrgyz) and they lived as nomads in tribes. For

Mu^{c}tasim, seeking to build up his 'new model army', these men had many attractions.

For a start they were strangers to the Muslim world. They brought with them no political baggage in the sense of families and contacts that would distract them from their devotion to him. More important was the fact that they were extremely hardy, used to very primitive living conditions in an extremely harsh environment. In addition they brought with them a new style of fighting, for these men were mounted archers able to fire arrows from a fast-moving horse. Brought up with horses from their infancy, even able to ride before they could walk, they had a natural command of their animals. They lived off mare's milk and horse flesh. Uncorrupted by the manners and politics of settled society, they were ideal fighting men.

Individual Turks had been employed by previous caliphs, but what distinguished Mu^{c}tasim's Turks was that they formed an entire military unit, only a few thousand strong but tough, disciplined and devoted to their master. No other member of the Abbasid family had this sort of military clout.

The coming of the Turks brought a new sort of figure to the Abbasid court, the *ghulām*. The term originally meant youth or pageboy, but the Turkish *ghulām*s were much more than that. They were the elite soldiers of the caliphs, their protectors and sometimes their deadliest enemies. These slender young boys, with their deceptively pretty faces and incipient beards, were often an object of sexual desire. The *ghulām* whose eyebrows are like the curve of the bow and whose eyes shoot like arrows is a frequent subject for Arabic and Persian poets of the ninth and tenth centuries. The same boy could be at once slave, guard, muse and bedfellow to his master. The coming of the *ghulām*s was to change the face of the Abbasid court for ever.

We do not know when, if ever, Ma'mūn adopted his brother as his heir. There is certainly no record of any public acclamation such as those Mansūr, Mahdi and Hārūn had given to their heirs. Was Ma'mūn simply careless or reluctant to accept his own mortality? Was Mu^{c}tasim only made heir apparent as they sat chatting by the river at Budandūn and dangling their feet in the water? Or was the whole idea of the nomination something concocted after the caliph's death by Mu^{c}tasim and his supporters? We know that Mu^{c}tasim's power had been increasing and that Ma'mūn had employed him as a governor in Egypt and elsewhere. When Abd Allah ibn Tāhir had moved to Khurasan on the death of his brother in 828/9, Muᶜtasim had taken his place as the caliph's right-hand man in the west. In these circumstances it is possible that Ma'mūn did indeed adopt him as heir. On the other hand, it would have been strange for him to exclude his own son Abbās. By pure luck, probably, Muᶜtasim was with his brother when he died while Abbās was campaigning on another part of the frontier. His absence at this crucial moment may have cost Abbās the caliphate and ultimately his life. We are told that many in the army supported Abbās and urged him to claim the throne, but either because he lost his nerve or because he did not want to cause civil strife, he took the oath of allegiance to his uncle and told his military supporters that there was no point in further agitation.³⁰

The new caliph had a pale complexion and a black beard tinged with red. He was physically fit and very strong,³¹ the sort of man who could jump on the back of a horse without difficulty. A much later source says that he was illiterate, which would have been most improbable for an Abbasid prince, and it may be that he was not interested in reading.³² He was certainly not an intellectual like his dead brother. On the other hand he had a keen interest in military matters and seems to have felt at ease with the commanders and soldiers of his new army: his first vizier, Fadl ibn Marwān, said that he spent more on military expeditions than anything else. When it came to architecture, it is said that he had no interest in making buildings look decorative and attractive; his only concern was that they should be solidly built. Ibn Abi Duwād, one of his chief advisers, recalls going with the caliph on his expedition to besiege Amorion in 833. Normally Ibn Abi Duwād and the caliph would balance each other on a camel litter, one on either side, chatting as they went along, but on this occasion Muᶜtasim chose to ride alone on a mule, looking up to talk to Ibn Abi Duwād, who would lean down to reply to him. They had left the rest of the army behind and came to a river without an obvious crossing point. Immediately the caliph was out ahead on his mule, splashing around to left and right, looking for a shallow way across, until he found one and Ibn Abi Duwād's camel could follow safely.³³ It is hard to imagine the cosseted Hārūn, still less any of the later caliphs, taking such obvious pleasure in outdoor activity.

Muᶜtasim's first concern was to return to the capital and establish

himself as caliph. The campaign against the Byzantines and the for-
tification of Tyana were immediately abandoned. The new caliph
ordered the destruction of what had been built. All the arms and
equipment that could be transported were removed and the rest was
burned. The colonists who had come to settle the new outpost were
sent home.[34]

He seems to have established his authority in Baghdad without
difficulty. The chief men of his regime were the Turkish army commanders, Ashinās and Ītākh, who had risen from their humble
origins to become the great men of the state and leaders of the new
army. To them Muᶜtasim added a newcomer from a very different
background, known to history as Afshīn. Afshīn was not a name but
a title. Far from being a slave, Afshīn was the ruler of the small
mountain principality of Ushrusana in a remote mountain area
south-east of Samarqand. It was on the farthest fringes of the
Muslim world: beyond lay the impenetrable mountains of the Pamirs
and beyond that China. Very few people here were Muslim; indeed,
the rulers actively discouraged missionary activity: most of their subjects continued to regard their rulers as gods. But Ushrusana was
poor and remote and the young Afshīn was tempted to take service
with the caliph. He could call on a following of hardy mountaineers
who would serve him without question. He became Muᶜtasim's most
brilliant military commander, yet he was always an outsider among
the ex-slaves, cooks and oil merchants who surrounded the caliph.
Ever conscious of his aristocratic origins, he was an isolated figure
who found himself without allies in his hour of need.

The civil administration was run at first by Fadl ibn Marwān, who
had been educated in the traditions of the Barmakids. He was efficient and conscientious but very much a bean-counter. If there was
no money in the treasury to make a payment – a present to a poet, for
example – he would say so. Kind friends advised him to be more
diplomatic: rather than saying baldly that there was no money, he
should assure his master that the payment could be made in a day or
two to give him time to find a solution. He never really got the hang
of it.

One day Muᶜtasim was walking in his palace gardens in Baghdad
with a jester and buffoon of his called Hafti, who had been promised
a gift by the caliph, a gift that Fadl ibn Marwān, who held the purse-
strings, had never paid. Muᶜtasim strode through the garden at a

furious pace, examining the various kinds of aromatic herbs and trees growing there, while Hafti, who was short and somewhat over-weight, struggled to keep up with his master. 'Get a move on!' the caliph kept saying, and Hafti complained that he had imagined himself ambling with a caliph, not running after a courier. And so the conversation moved on to Muᶜtasim saying how fortunate he was and how much he had achieved and Hafti, inevitably, telling him he was not really master in his own house. The story of the unpaid gift came out and, so they said, it was this which convinced the caliph that he had to get rid of his tiresome accountant. Fadl was luckier than most administrators of the age. He lost his job but was allowed to withdraw to the little village of Sinn, on the Tigris south of Mosul, where he seems to have lived in obscure retirement until his death.[35]

He was replaced by a rich businessman, Muhammad ibn al-Zayyāt, Muhammad Son of the Oil Merchant. As his name suggests, Muhammad's father had made serious money supplying Baghdad with oil. Muhammad himself had done well out of government con-tracts, for tents, ceremonial parasols and equipment for riding camels.[36] Fadl ibn Marwān had treated him with the disdain of a civil service mandarin for the brash entrepreneur. When Ibn al-Zayyāt came to court wearing formal court dress, the long black cloak but-toned at the front known as a *durrā'a* and a sword, the vizier demanded of him: 'What right have you, a mere trader, got to wear formal court dress and a sword?' Humiliated, Ibn al-Zayyāt was obliged to give up his pretensions.[37] Now he was one of the half-dozen most important men in the state.

In the autumn of 835 Muᶜtasim made another move which was to have a profound effect on the history of the Abbasid caliphate: he moved the centre of government from Baghdad to a new site beside the Tigris about 160 kilometres to the north. Here he began the construction of the city known ever since as Sāmarrā.

Caliphs had often left Baghdad before: Hārūn spent many of his later years at Raqqa, which became a sort of second capital, but despite the extensive palace developments outside the city walls, Raqqa itself was never more than a modest provincial town. Ma'mūn, as we have seen, visited Damascus more than Baghdad during the last three years of his life.

Muᶜtasim's move to Sāmarrā was on a different scale. From the beginning the caliph intended that the city should be the new permanent capital. There were good reasons for making the move. The Arabic sources stress the tensions between Muᶜtasim's newly recruited *ghulām*s and the local people of Baghdad, especially the *Abnā*, who had provided the elite soldiers of the old Abbasid army. *Ghulām*s were repeatedly finding their comrades murdered in their barracks. The locals saw them as brutal barbarians who could not even speak Arabic and who rode through the streets knocking down men and women and trampling children underfoot. In return the Baghdadis would pull them off their horses and beat them up, sometimes even killing them. As often in the old chronicles, the argument is summed up in a single interview, which is said to have brought the issue to a head and made the caliph take hard decisions.[38]

It was one of the greats feasts of the Muslim year, either the Feast of the Sacrifice or the Breaking of the Fast, and Muᶜtasim was returning from the great open-air prayer place (Musalla) when an old man stood in his way. 'O Abu Ishāq,' the ancient began, but before he could get any further the guard were on him: not only had he blocked the way but he had addressed the caliph by his familiar *kunya* rather than his respectful title, Commander of the Faithful. But the caliph motioned them to let him go and asked the old man what he wanted. The reply was forthright and outspoken: 'May God not reward you well for staying here among us! You are living with us and have brought these barbarians and settled them down to live with us. Through them you have made our children orphans, you have made our womenfolk widows and you have killed our men!' Muᶜtasim listened to all this and then returned to his palace. Nothing is said about the fate of the old man, if he ever existed, but the implication is that his outspokenness caused him no harm. The next year, the caliph decided to relocate to Sāmarrā.

The people of Baghdad resented the coming of the Turks. The stationing of a brutal and licentious soldiery among a large civilian population was never going to be easy. The fact that many of them spoke no Arabic and had converted to Islam recently if at all made relations more fraught. For many of the Baghdadis there was the added aggravation that these new men had usurped their role as the crack troops of the caliphate. It was now the Turks who were getting the high salaries and positions at court while the Baghdadis were retired into civilian life or had at best part-time militia duties. It was hardly surprising that resentments flourished and grew and that violent incidents became more and more common.

There were other practical reasons why a new site was attractive. Baghdad was a fully developed urban centre by this time. It was not easy or cheap to find new areas in which to settle new troops. Sāmarrā, by contrast, was a greenfield site, though the phrase may give a rather more verdant impression than was actually the case: Sāmarrā was founded on a gravelly plateau above the river and the site was not exactly a land flowing with milk and honey. The ground was purchased, mostly from Christian monasteries in the area, very cheaply, 500 *dirham*s here, 5,000 *dirham*s there, all carefully accounted for.[39] There were no natural obstacles to limit expansion. The land acquired so cheaply was given to soldiers and their leaders to develop for housing or let out for commercial purposes. The barren plateau and small gardens were soon producing large sums in rents from merchants keen to be close to the court and the well-paid functionaries and generals of the new regime. Certainly large sums were spent on building and decorating royal palaces, but the whole project was, in part, a gigantic property speculation of which the caliph and his court were the chief beneficiaries.

The scale of the building at Sāmarrā was immense. With no space constraints to inhibit them, Muʿtasim and his successors planned on a grand scale. The city eventually stretched some 15 kilometres along the east bank of the Tigris. There were broad, straight main streets and numerous equally straight side streets. The plots formed between them were given to military commanders to develop. Great mosques were established and huge palaces built with acres of courts, rooms, gardens and parks. Racecourses were laid out and ports were set up on the banks of the river. Though the original city was established on the east bank, suburbs with garden palaces and pavilions were soon established on the west.

Unlike Baghdad, which has always been an inhabited city since Mansūr founded it in 762, much of Sāmarrā was abandoned when the court returned to Baghdad in 892. The water supply had always been a problem. Despite massive investment, Sāmarrā never acquired a network of rivers and canals such as Baghdad had, and when government money was no longer available, much of the site reverted to its natural arid state. This means that much of the original plan of the city and its buildings can still be discerned. At ground level the remains are mostly unimpressive. Apart from a few buildings in baked brick, such as the outside walls of the Great Mosque and the spiral minaret attached to it, the walls of the city are little more than shapeless ridges of mud, slowly deliquescing into the Mesopotamian plain. Seen from the air, however, especially in the slanting sunlight of early morning or evening, the whole plan of the city is revealed. It can be mapped with great accuracy. What we see is very unlike the Islamic city of popular imagination. This is not a place of narrow winding alleys and crooked culs-de-sac but of wide-open straight streets and regular orthogonal planning. It speaks eloquently of the power and authority of the caliphs who built it.

The new regime was established in Sāmarrā, and the new army and the bureaucracy were moved there. Muʿtasim was now master in his own capital, surrounded by the troops who owed everything to him. Baghdad, with its turbulent inhabitants and vigorous commercial life, was well out of the way. He could not have realized how this isolation in the middle of his troops would make Sāmarrā a prison and ultimately a death trap for his successors.

This new regime needed to prove itself to the wider Muslim community. There was a caliph whose claim to the throne was shaky to say the least, and an army largely recruited from non-Muslim backgrounds with no roots in the Islamic world. The caliph set out to deploy his new army in the one arena all Muslims could agree on, the war against the infidel. In this way he could assert his moral right to claim the leadership of the Muslims and the right of his army to live off the taxes they paid.

There were to be three main theatres of war. Two were within the boundaries of the Abbasid caliphate. In Azerbayjān one Bābak, a man of obscure origins, led a resistance movement among the mountain people of the area, trying to keep at bay the growing pressure of Muslim settlers from the south. In the Elburz mountains at the south end of the Caspian Sea, the local ruler, Mazyār, who boasted a pedigree that stretched back far into the pre-Islamic past, also tried to keep the old way of life alive. Both these men are described as rebels against the caliphs, though in reality they both came from areas where Muslim rule had never been more than nominal. Muʿtasim sent armies against both of them. We are particularly well informed about the war against Bābak, where Afshīn fought a masterly and systematic campaign.[40] Bābak's mountain capital was taken and he himself captured and brought to Sāmarrā. Here he was the centre of an almost Roman-style triumph.

It was 3 January 838 when Afshīn reached Sāmarrā with the captive Bābak in tow. In order that the captive be displayed to best advantage, he was mounted on an elephant (it seems that there was only one elephant at court at this time, a present from an Indian prince. How it had made the difficult journey to Iraq we have simply no idea). The elephant was richly caparisoned and the captive himself dressed in a short satin coat and a round cap of sable fur. Then he was led through the two rows of troops lining the main street and past the gazes of the curious populace to the public audience hall of the palace, where the caliph was waiting for him. In a bizarre twist the caliph decided that Bābak's own executioner, Nudnud by name, should do the deed. Presumably he had been brought as a captive too. The cry went up, 'Where is Nudnud?', until he eventually appeared and set to work to practise his trade on his old master. First Bābak's hands and feet were cut off and then his belly was cut open. His head was sent to Khurasan and his body displayed at a site always known thereafter as Bābak's Gibbet. His brother was taken to Baghdad to be executed and displayed there.[41] The caliph's triumph could hardly have been better publicized.

The campaigns against Bābak and Māzyār were led by generals. The campaign against the third infidel enemy, the Byzantines, was led by the caliph himself. As with the other campaigns, the caliphal propaganda machine ensured that we are well informed about the heroic achievements of the army and its leader. The Byzantine emperor Theophilus had attacked and taken the small Muslim town of Zibatra in the remote anti-Taurus mountains, and the local people had appealed to the caliph. The Commander of the Faithful felt bound to respond. At the beginning of April 838,[42] he led his army north to the frontier.

Muᶜtasim's campaign against the Byzantines in the summer of 838 is the most fully reported of all the Muslim expeditions against them,[43] no doubt because the caliph was personally in charge and wanted the heroic achievements of himself and his men to be celebrated. The plan was an ambitious one. There was to be a coordinated two-pronged attack. Afshīn was to lead an army through the eastern passes of the Taurus while Muᶜtasim, aided by his two most experienced Turkish commanders, Ashinās and Ītākh, was to attack through the Cilician Gates to the west. The two armies were to meet at Ankara and then move together to the main objective, the city of Amorion. Moving a large army through the desolate plains of central Anatolia in the high summer presented real logistic problems and the caliph 'equipped himself with weapons, military supplies, leather water troughs for the animals, mules for carrying water and goatskins for keeping it in'.[44] As well as the standard weapons, swords and bows, the army brought mangonels and naphtha.

The caliph himself entered Byzantine territory on 21 June. Despite the preparations, the march was not an easy one and the army suffered terribly from lack of water and fodder. The local people had mostly fled, taking their flocks and stores with them, and, though captives showed the Muslims the way to one group hidden in salt mines, there was never enough food available. Meanwhile enemy troops hovered, waiting to seize any opportunity to attack.

Despite these problems, Ankara, deserted by its inhabitants, was taken, though no attempt was made to garrison it. On 1 August, Mu'tasim began the siege of Amorion.[45] Amorion was not a big town but it had a strategic importance on the road to Constantinople and a symbolic importance as the birthplace of the emperor Theophilos. Originally a large classical city, it had, like most Byzantine towns of the interior of Anatolia, shrunk in the early Middle Ages and was now a small, heavily fortified stronghold.

Mu'tasim's army was divided into three sections, Afshīn in command of one, Ashinās of the second and the caliph himself of the third. Each one was assigned a section of walls and its towers. The Byzantine commander, Aetius, and the people of the town prepared to resist. For the caliph and his forces it was something of a military promenade. Even at the height of the fighting, Mu'tasim and his commanders would disperse at midday and go to their own tents for a lunch break.[46]

The town was well defended and the attack did not go entirely according to plan. On his arrival the caliph had observed the strength of the walls and the width of the moat that surrounded the city. He realized that his mangonels would not be able to breach the walls from the other side of the moat so he decided to have it filled in. In a stratagem that may be unique in the history of siege warfare, he ordered that each of the soldiers be given a sheep. The man was to eat the sheep meat and then fill the skin with earth. Acting like large sandbags, the skins would be brought to the moat and thrown in. Meanwhile the artillery was to be mounted on wheeled carts, each mangonel being manned by four soldiers. In addition there were mobile shelters (the Arabic word is *dabbāba*, which means tank in modern Arabic). These probably looked like the 'mouse' of classical siege warfare. Each of these could hold ten men.

With a disarming frankness that contrasts pleasantly with the generally triumphalist tone of the narrative, the anonymous historian goes on to explain just why this ingenious scheme failed. The skins thrown into the ditch did not provide a flat, regular surface because the men who put them there were too frightened of rocks hurled by the Byzantine defenders to take their time and do the job properly. The caliph then ordered more earth to be put on top to create a flat surface. He had a 'mouse' rolled towards the walls but halfway across the trench it got stuck on the skins and sank. The crew were able to escape only with difficulty and the vehicle itself remained, bogged down and useless, until the end of the siege.

In the end it was treachery within which enabled the Muslims to take the city. It appears that a section of the city wall had been washed away in winter rainstorms. The emperor had written to the governor ordering him to repair it, but nothing had been done for some time. When he knew that the emperor was coming to the area, the governor decided to make some hasty repairs. He got workmen to construct the façade of the wall so that it would look good when the emperor passed by, but behind it was just made of rubble. The secret of the weakness was given away by a Muslim who had been captured by the Byzantines and had converted to Christianity, married and settled in Amorion. He now escaped from the city and came and told the caliph where the city was vulnerable. The caliph immediately concentrated his energies there. He pitched his own tent by that section of the wall and concentrated all his mangonels on it. The defenders tried to protect the wall by lowering great timbers over the side but these were shattered by the mangonels. Later they tried to pad the timbers by putting pack saddles over them but all to no avail. The Muslim commanders, Ashinās, Afshīn and Ītākh, competed with each other to be the first to enter. The fighting was fierce but again they were aided by treachery within: the commander of the sector that had been breached felt that he was not being supported by his comrades elsewhere in the city and surrendered to the caliph.

Muslim troops soon began to swarm into the town; a group of defenders took refuge in the great church which was burned over their heads. Aetius himself took refuge in one of the towers but eventually agreed to surrender, handing his sword over to one of the caliph's officers. The siege had probably lasted only about twelve days.

Then came the division of the captives and the spoils. An interpreter was appointed to separate the prisoners of high rank, who could be ransomed. The rest were then auctioned in groups of five or ten. In order to speed up the process, only three bids were allowed for the women and children. According to a Christian source, the caliph decided that children should not be separated from their mothers but, if this is true, it was a rare gesture of humanity in a brutal environment. Meanwhile the goods were auctioned, each of the commanders being allowed to sell what had been taken from their sectors while an accountant kept a record of what had been sold to ensure that the spoils were fairly distributed. There was a good deal of disorder and the caliph himself had to intervene, galloping out with a drawn sword to prevent looting. As the unfortunate prisoners were being marched through the summer heat down the arid road that led to the frontier, their conditions became worse. The caliph had heard that the Byzantine emperor was coming after him and he wanted to move fast. Orders were given that any captives who could not keep up were to be killed. Soon Muslims too were dying of thirst, and some alleged that the prisoners had killed some of their soldiers. Muᶜtasim acted without mercy; after the upper-class prisoners had been segregated, the rest, numbering six thousand men, were driven into a remote valley and killed.

The expedition had been a triumph for Muᶜtasim and his new army, and the infidel had been convincingly humiliated. The victory was well publicized and celebrated in poetry, including the great ode by Abū Tammām, usually held to be one of the masterpieces of the new, very mannered style of Arabic poetry that was then becoming fashionable at court.

Not all the news was good. The siege of Amorion had brought to the surface simmering discontent among members of the armed forces. The root cause seems to have been tensions between the Khurasani aristocrats who had supported Ma'mūn and the Turks promoted by Muᶜtasim, whom they regarded as no better than slaves.

Some of these discontented soldiers are alleged to have said that they would rather go over to the Byzantines than be lorded over by a 'slave, son of a whore' such as Ashinās.[47]

The plotters are said to have been planning a coup to murder Mu'tasim and put Ma'mūn's son Abbās on the throne. According to the accounts we have, the conspirators decided to strike when Mu'tasim was on campaign in Byzantine territory, presumably because they hoped it would be easier to isolate him. Abbās himself was party to the plot. He was urged to strike while the army was moving through the passes in the Taurus mountains, but he hesitated fatally and said he did not want to attack the caliph until they had taken Amorion, perhaps because he did not want to be accused of sabotaging the holy war.[48] The conspiracy had by now become quite widespread and named individuals had been nominated to kill the caliph and all the prominent Turkish commanders. Given the Hamlet-like procrastination of Abbās, it could only be a matter of time before someone let the cat out of the bag. The weak link in the chain was discovered when one officer, Ahmad ibn Khalīl, complained to a second, Amr al-Farghānī, who was in on the plot, about the behaviour of Ashinās, under whose command they were serving. His companion then assured him that he would soon be rid of the obnoxious Turk and directed him to the agent who was coordinating the conspiracy.[49] It seems that Ashinās was already suspicious of the two, who were already grumbling and asking for a transfer.

Ashinās now put both of them under house, or rather tent, arrest; they were confined but given food, drink and bedding. They were also obliged to travel in litters rather than ride their own horses. There was as yet no hard evidence against them but that was soon to change. Amr had warned a youth of whom he was very fond that if he heard a disturbance from the caliph's tent he should make sure that he remained in his own tent, 'because things could get very dangerous if the troops were restless'. The youth now went to the caliph and told him this conversation. Amr was summoned to the royal tent. He tried to bluff his way out of trouble, saying that the youth was drunk and had completely misunderstood the conversation, but he was interrogated further and handed over to Ītākh.[50]

Ahmad meanwhile was in a panic. He sent a slave boy to find out what had happened to Amr and when he knew that he had been interrogated he tried to turn 'Queen's evidence'. He approached

Ashinās, saying that he had information that could only be communicated to the caliph in person, but Ashinās brusquely replied that he would have him flogged to death there and then if he did not tell him immediately. And so the whole story came out and Ashinās ordered two of the blacksmiths in the army to make shackles.

Meanwhile, Abbās's chief agent, Hārith al-Samarqandi, had been interrogated by the caliph himself and had soon spilled the beans. Now Abbās himself was under arrest. Muᶜtasim treated him kindly and led him to believe that he had been forgiven. He had lunch with the caliph and then returned to his tent. In the evening Muᶜtasim invited him again; they sat together and the caliph plied him with wine. Soon Abbās was giving him the names of all those who had pledged support to him.

As the victorious Muslim army made its way back through the Cilician Gates to the plains of northern Syria and Iraq, Muᶜtasim unleashed a purge of almost Stalinesque ruthlessness against the plotters. He pursued the commanders who had been involved in the plot relentlessly; they were all arrested and executed with an ingenuity that amounted to real sadism. Abbās found, quite literally, that his drinking days with the caliph were over. When he and his escort reached Manbij in northern Syria, he was asked what he would like to eat and chose delicious but salty dishes; when he asked for a drink, it was refused. He was wrapped in a felt blanket and was dead very soon.[51]

Amr al-Farghānī was taken as far as Nisibin in northern Iraq. Muᶜtasim had camped in a garden and he called the owner to dig a pit, the depth of a man's height. As the owner began to dig, Muᶜtasim sent for Amr. The caliph was sitting in the garden having had several glasses of wine when the captive was brought in. He said nothing to him directly but ordered some Turkish guards to strip him and whip him. When the owner of the garden came to say that the digging was complete, Muᶜtasim ordered that he be beaten with clubs, dragged to the pit and thrown in. Amr uttered not a sound. Then the earth was filled in on top of him.[52]

Ahmad ibn Khalīl was taken back to Sāmarrā, where he was put in a pit which was covered over, although bread and water were passed down to him. One day Muᶜtasim asked Ashinās, who had custody of Ahmad, how he was. On being told, he simply said, 'This fellow must, I think, have grown fat under these conditions.' He did not need to elaborate. Ashinās ordered the pit to be filled with water so that Ahmad should drown. In the end, the water drained away through the sandy soil and Ahmad was handed over to an executioner.[53]

Over seventy officers were killed by a variety of ingenious methods.[54] The ruthlessness and cruelty would have made a big impression in themselves, but it is also clear that the fate of the captives was well publicized and accounts of their sufferings come down to us in a number of different sources. The intention was clearly to punish the guilty, or those alleged to be guilty, and to spread terror among anyone else who was considering challenging the regime. Perhaps we can see here an insecurity almost amounting to paranoia among a caliph whose claim to office was questionable, to say the least, and a small group of soldiers and bureaucrats who had effectively hijacked the Islamic state.

There remained one man who was very much the odd man out in this tightly knit group – Afshīn, prince of Ushrusana. Whether he was actually involved in plotting against the caliph or was, as seems more likely, simply framed by his enemies we shall never know. It was alleged to the caliph that Afshīn was plotting to poison him, or that he was going to escape to Ushrusana through the Khazar lands to the north of the Caucasus with a great deal of money, or that he had been in treasonous correspondence with Mazyār, the rebel prince of Tabaristān: the number of differing allegations makes one suspicious of them all. What is clear is that the Turks hated him and that he treated them with the disdain of the aristocrat for the slave. What made his position worse was that he had quarrelled with the Tāhirids, who might have been his natural allies since they suspected him, rightly or wrongly, of coveting their governorate of Khurasan.

So despite his outstanding record as a military leader in the service of the caliph, Afshīn found himself on trial. The dramatic events are reported in some detail by Tabari and other sources.[55] His enemies sought to show that he had been treacherous to the caliph but above all that he was an apostate, a man who had abandoned Islam, for the penalty for apostasy was, and still is, death. The trial was held in closed session in Mu'tasim's palace. The chief prosecuter was the new vizier, Muhammad ibn al-Zayyāt, the son of the oil merchant, and he had collected a whole procession of witnesses to prove his point.

The first to take the stand were two men in threadbare garments who uncovered their backs to show that they had been stripped bare by flogging.

'Do you know these men?' Afshīn was asked.

'Yes, one is a muezzin and the other an imam. I gave them each a thousand lashes because I have an agreement with the local princes that I should leave each people to their own religion. These two men came to a pagan temple and threw out the idols and turned it into a mosque. So I punished them with 1,000 lashes.'

Muhammad pursued the accusations of paganism. 'Is it true', he asked, 'that you have a book ornamented with gold and jewels and covered in satin that contains blasphemies against God?' Afshīn explained that it was a book of the wisdom of the Persians which he had inherited from his father. He had accepted the wise sayings and ignored the rest. 'After all,' he concluded, addressing Muhammad, 'you have the Books of Kalīla and Dimna [traditional animal fables translated from Persian] and the Book of Mazdak [more fables] in your house.'

The next witness was a Magian priest or Mobadh. He came forward to accuse Afshīn of eating the meat of strangled animals (that is, animals not slaughtered according to halal rules). He added that Afshīn had expressed contempt for Muslim customs and had never used depilatories on his pubic hair or been circumcised. Afshīn was furious. He knew that the Mobadh was on the point of abandoning his old religion for Islam, and demanded to know whether anyone could take such a man seriously as a witness: 'was there a door or a secret window between your house and mine through which you could see what I was doing in the privacy of my own home?' When the Mobadh admitted there was not, Afshīn rounded on him for betraying confidences and saying that he was untrustworthy in every way.

The next accuser was another Iranian aristocrat, who had presumably been primed well in advance. He started with an apparently innocuous question: 'How do your people address you in correspondence?', but Afshīn knew it was a trap and simply said that he was addressed as his father and grandfather had been before him. When asked to explain, he refused to answer. His accuser went on to say that the formula used in the local language of Ushrusana actually meant 'To the God of Gods' and that Afshīn was making the same claims as a pharaoh. Afshīn's defence that this was simply a harmless tradition he did not want to abandon cut little ice.

The next witness was Mazyār, the prince of Tabaristān who was now a prisoner in Sāmarrā: he may have hoped that his testimony against Afshīn would save his life but, if he did, he was to be sadly disappointed. He accused Afshīn of entering into treasonous correspondence with him and comparing the caliph's troops to dogs and flies. Afshīn simply denied the charge and said that any correspondence he had had with Mazyār was simply to lure him into a trap.

Finally Ibn Abi Duwād, the chief judge, returned to the issue of Afshīn's attitude to Islam. 'Are you circumcised?' he asked. Afshīn replied that he was not, so Ibn Abi Duwād enquired why, since circumcision 'signifies the completion of one's Muslim faith and purification from uncleanliness'. To which Afshīn answered, 'Is there no place for fear in Islam? I was afraid to cut that part of my body in case I died!' His accuser was unimpressed: 'You can be pierced by spears and slashed by swords but that does not prevent you from fighting in battles and yet you say you are anxious about cutting a foreskin?', to which Afshīn replied, quite reasonably, that injury in battle was an accident he might have to endure but circumcision was a self-inflicted injury that might kill him. And besides, he did not believe that not being circumcised amounted to renunciation of Islam. Later, in prison awaiting execution, Afshīn explained more about the circumcision accusation. He said that it was a trap set by Ibn Abi Duwād to humiliate him in public. He was asked whether he was circumcised: if he said no, he was condemned; if he said yes, he would be asked to expose himself to all and sundry to prove it and, as he said, 'I would rather die than expose myself to all those people.'[56]

Afshīn had defended himself with vigour and wit and had made mincemeat of the prosecution case. But this was a show trial and in show trials there is only one verdict. Ibn Abi Duwād announced that the case was now proved and ordered Bughā (the Ox) the Turk to seize him. His cloak was pulled over his head and tied hard around his neck and he was taken away to prison. Some say he was poisoned, others that he was starved to death, but everyone knew that his body was exposed on a gibbet in front of the public gate of the palace before being burned and thrown into the Tigris.[57]

Mu'tasim did not survive Afshīn for long. He seems to have fallen ill in October 841 but survived until January 842, aged 47. In some ways he had achieved great things. He had organized and recruited a new and efficient army which had extended the power of the caliphs to areas in northern Iran that they had never really incorporated before, and had inflicted a startling reverse on the old enemy. He had established a new capital and administrative centre which continued to grow after his death. But the foundations of this new state were very insecure. Most of the Muslim population, to say nothing of the non-Muslim majority, were subjects of a regime with which they had few connections either of personal links or of sentiment. Many must have felt deeply alienated from the clique of generals and bureaucrats who had now taken over the *umma*.

Something of these concerns is voiced in an anecdote that seems to date from the last years of his reign, certainly after the death of Afshīn.[58] Like many anecdotes of this period, it is as memorable for the evocation of the domestic life of the monarch as for the political message it bears. Ishāq ibn Ibrāhīm, the Tāhirid governor of Baghdad, had been invited to play polo with the caliph. When he arrived he found Muᶜtasim dressed elaborately in a silk waistcoat with a gold belt and red boots. The caliph demanded that Ibrāhīm dress the same, which he agreed to reluctantly. After a while Muᶜtasim saw that he was playing without enthusiasm. He dismounted, took Ishāq's hand and they went to the bath house. He then asked Ishāq to take off his clothes so that he was naked and did the same. Both naked, they entered the bath house without any slave boys to help them, so the caliph massaged Ishāq and Ishāq returned the favour. Then they left and got dressed. Again the caliph took Ishāq's hand and they went to his council chamber.

When they arrived Muᶜtasim ordered Ishāq to bring a prayer mat and two cushions. Then he asked him to come and lie down beside him, but Ishāq refused and remained sitting. Ītākh and Ashinās appeared but were told to go away out of earshot, but where they could hear if he shouted out.

The caliph was in a melancholy and introspective mood: 'I have been thinking about my brother Ma'mūn. He promoted four men in his service who turned out excellently while I have promoted four men, none of whom have turned out well.' Ishāq naturally enquired who he was talking about and Muᶜtasim named Tāhir, his son Abd Allah, Ishāq himself and another Tāhirid as his brother's success stories. In contrast he had promoted Afshīn, who had been executed, Ashinās, who was 'a feeble hearted coward', Ītākh, who was totally insignificant, and Wasīf, who was useless. Ishāq asked to be allowed to speak bluntly and said to the caliph that his brother considered the roots and made use of them and the branches flourished whereas he, Muᶜtasim, had used only the branches, 'which have not flourished because they lack roots'. What he meant was that Ma'mūn's Tāhirids had contacts and support in the wider Muslim community; Muᶜtasim's Turks had none. It was a shrewd assessment and the caliph acknowledged it, saying that this answer was the most difficult thing he had to bear.

The succession, in early January 842, was the easiest any Abbasid caliph enjoyed. Muᶜtasim had an adult son, Hārūn, who took the title of Wāthiq. The sources are vague about his exact age at the time of his accession but he is said to have been born in 811/12 , when his father was only 16, on the road to Mecca. He was of medium build, handsome with a pale complexion which he may have inherited from his mother, a Greek slave girl. One eye was paralysed with a conspicuous white fleck in it.[59] It is not clear that he had been publicly acknowledged as heir apparent but this did not really matter because power remained firmly in the hands of Muᶜtasim's cabinet, the Turkish soldiers Ashinās, Ītākh and Wasīf, the vizier Ibn al-Zayyāt and the chief judge, Ibn Abi Duwād. It was they who managed the succession and effectively conducted the government of the young caliph.

Of all the caliphs of the period, Wāthiq is probably the one who has left least impression on the historical record.* He seems never to have left Sāmarrā during his short reign, 841–7; he had expressed the intention of going on the Hajj at one stage but was dissuaded by reports of lack of water on the route. He did not share his father's enthusiasm for the holy war and his reign saw a large-scale exchange of prisoners on the Byzantine frontier in 845, authorized by the caliph himself.[60] His caliphate was marked by a series of disturbances among the Bedouin of Arabia, who threatened the Holy Cities and the safe passage of the pilgrims. Turkish troops were sent to suppress them. There was also an attempted rebellion in Baghdad in April 846.[61] This was essentially a popular protest against the Sāmarrā regime and in particular the policy of making people accept the official Muᶜtazilite doctrine of the createdness of the Koran.[62] People

* His very anonymity presented an opportunity for the use of imagination. The novel *Vathek* (1786) by William Beckford (1760–1844) owes almost nothing to the historical reality of Wāthiq. It is a fantastic tale of cruelty, dissipation and a search for the lost treasure of ancient kings, guarded by by Iblis/Satan himself.

were to be roused to action by the simultaneous beating of drums in different parts of the city. Money was distributed to all the participants. Unfortunately for the conspirators, one group used the money to get drunk and started to beat the drums a day early. The police went to investigate and the whole story came out. The leader, Ahmad ibn Nasr, a pious member of an old Baghdad family, was brought before the caliph. He was ready for martyrdom and refused to accept the createdness of the Koran. The caliph called for the leather mat and the great old sword known as Samsāma, which had belonged to one of the heroes of early Islam. He himself struck the first blow and his Turkish soldiers soon finished the old man off. His body was prominently displayed in Baghdad and a note was placed in his ear, explaining that he was an infidel who had stuck to his erroneous views and refused to repent when the caliph had given him the chance.

Wāthiq died quite suddenly of dropsy in August 847. He had apparently been treated by being sat in an oven, which afforded him some relief until he was overcome by heat, but did nothing to cure his condition. No arrangements seem to have been made for the succession, but the matter was still firmly in the hands of the group who secured Wāthiq's own assumption of the caliphate and had dominated the politics of his reign. Ashinās had died, of natural causes, in December 844,[63] but the rest of them, Ibn al-Zayyāt the vizier, Ibn Abi Duwād the judge and Ītākh and Wasīf the Turkish military leaders, along with a few others, gathered to decide who should be the next caliph. At first they wanted to nominate the dead caliph's young son, Muhammad, who was a beardless youth, but Wasīf objected, saying that he was too young to lead the prayers, still less to become caliph. So Muhammad was passed over, but he was to become caliph later under the name of Muhtadi, for a short and stormy reign.

They then considered various other princes. One of those present remembered walking through the palace and seeing prince Jaᶜfar there, dressed very informally and sitting, talking to some Turks. Jaᶜfar asked what news there was and was told that the cabal was still deliberating. Shortly afterwards Jaᶜfar himself was summoned and told that he was now Commander of the Faithful. Sensible man that he was, he was immediately terrified that this was some sort of trick to test his loyalty and that Wāthiq was still alive. Only after he saw the caliph's body wrapped in a shroud would he accept the proffered homage. Ibn Abi Duwād put a tall *qalansūwa* on his head, wound a turban around it and kissed him between the eyes, saying, 'Peace be upon you, O Commander of the Faithful, and God's mercy and blessing.' Wāthiq's body was washed, the funeral prayers were said and he was buried. Then the party escorted the new caliph to the public audience hall of the palace.

The next step was to choose a title for him. Ibn al-Zayyāt suggested Muntasir, but for some reason this was rejected (though it was to be used in the next generation), but the next day Ibn Abi Duwād proposed Mutawwakil. This was generally accepted and the new caliph agreed. Ibn al-Zayyāt, who was in charge of the chancery, ordered that letters be sent out introducing the new caliph and his full title:

In the name of God, the Merciful, the Compassionate. The Commander of the Faithful, may God give him long life, has ordered, may God preserve you, that his official title to be used from his pulpits [that is, in the sermon in Friday prayers], and in his letters to his judges, secretaries, officials and administrators in the government offices and others with whom he is regularly in correspondence, is, 'Abd Allah Jaᶜfar al-Imām al-Mutawwakil 'alā-llāh, Amir al-mu'minīn' [The slave of God Jaᶜfar the Prayer Leader, the Reliant on God, Commander of the Faithful].[64]

Such was his official title: the term caliph was only an informal shorthand usage. Then payments had to be made to the military to celebrate the accession. The surprisingly informal process of inaugurating the new caliph was now complete. There is no mention of the public swearing of allegiance by the wider Muslim community which had attended the accession of the first Abbasid caliphs, but no one seems to have raised any objections.

The new caliph was said to be twenty-six years old. He is described as being a slender man with a pale brown complexion, attractive eyes and a thin beard.[65] We have a contemporary image of him on a small medallion dated to 855, now in the Kunsthistorisches Museum in Vienna. He is not wearing either a *qalansūwa* or a turban but something that looks very like the modern Arab keffiyeh, a cloth covering secured by a rope around the crown of the head. He has a big moustache and, contrary to the description quoted above, a full, double-pointed beard.[66]

If the cabal had imagined that they had selected a pliant young man who would allow them to run the caliphate as they had done in Wāthiq's reign, they were in for a nasty surprise. Mutawwakil may have had no political experience and his accession seems to have surprised him as much as anyone else, but he soon began to show his determination to assert his control over the caliphate. He moved first against the vizier, Muhammad ibn al-Zayyāt, who had served both his father and his brother. Muhammad had a reputation for pride and cruelty, having devised an instrument of torture called an iron maiden, an iron box with spikes on the inside which he devised to pressure men from whom he wanted to extract money. When he lost the caliph's favour, he found he had no friends to rely on.

The fall of Ibn al-Zayyāt is a sort of morality tale, full of interesting details. The caliph's hostility seems to have dated from Wāthiq's reign. For some reason that we are not told, Mutawwakil, or Jaᶜfar as he then was, had incurred his brother's anger: Wāthiq may have thought he was angling for the succession but there is no evidence for that. Jaᶜfar decided to visit Ibn al-Zayyāt to ask him to intercede with the caliph. He found the vizier working on his correspondence. He stood there waiting for a while but Ibn al-Zayyāt continued working and did not greet him. Eventually he motioned to him to sit down, but he carried on with his correspondence until he had finished. Only then did he turn to Jaᶜfar and ask in a threatening way what he wanted.

The young prince explained, but the vizier simply turned to the others in the room and said, 'Look at this guy! He has infuriated his brother and expects me to do something about it!' Then he turned to Jaᶜfar and said, 'Go away, and if you behave yourself you will be restored to favour.' After this bad experience, Jaᶜfar went to see another civil servant, a man called Umar, originally from Rukhkhaj in Afghanistan but now working in Sāmarrā. He found Umar in a mosque and asked him to put a seal on his cheque (*sikk*)* so that he could claim his allowance from the treasury. Umar rejected his request and tossed the cheque into the courtyard of the mosque. Jaᶜfar was not having a good day.

---

* A *sikk* was a paper authorizing the bearer to draw money from the treasury. It was often used in Abbasid times to allow members of the ruling family or other courtiers to receive payments. It is almost certainly the ultimate origin of the English word cheque.

Fortunately, as he was leaving he fell in with another civil servant and complained to him about how Umar had treated him. This man was much more careful and offered Ja°far 20,000 *dirham*s to tide him over until things improved. The offer was gratefully accepted.

His next stop was the judge Ahmad ibn Abi Duwād. Here his reception was very different. Ahmad came to greet him at the door of his house, kissed him and was generally friendly. When Ja°far explained what he wanted, Ahmad agreed to help, though it was some time before Wāthiq came round.

As he later found out, Ibn al-Zayyāt had been even less helpful than Ja°far had imagined. When he left, the vizier had written to the caliph saying that Ja°far had come dressed like a ladyboy[67] and that his hair was too long at the back. Mutawwakil later described how he had been summoned to see his brother and had arrived in new black court dress, hoping to impress him. Instead his hair was grabbed and sheared off and he was struck in the face with it. 'Nothing', he said later, 'upset me more than having my hair cut on my new black robe. I had dressed like that hoping to please him but he had my hair cut on it.'

Now the position had changed entirely. Just six weeks after his accession, Mutawwakil decided to take his revenge. Ītākh was instructed to summon Ibn al-Zayyāt. Imagining he was being invited to a royal audience, the vizier agreed, but on his way he was diverted into Ītākh's house. He began to be apprehensive and his fears were realized when his sword, belt, *qalansūwa* and vizieral robe were taken from him. His pages were paid and told to leave, which they did, under the impression that their master was staying at Ītākh's to drink wine.

At the same time men were sent to Ibn al-Zayyāt's house to con-fiscate all his possessions. They were surprised by how shabby it was. 'I saw four carpets and some jars full of drink,' one of them reported, 'and the room where his slave girls slept; there were rush mats on the floor and cushions around the edge but they slept without any quilts.' All his furniture, riding animals, slave girls and *ghulām*s were seized and men were sent to Baghdad to confiscate his possessions there. Ibn al-Zayyāt was told to appoint an agent to sell everything he had.

The fallen vizier was very depressed, as well he might be. After a few days he was fettered and bound. He refused to eat and drink and wept continuously, lamenting his fate and saying how happy and prosperous he had been before he aspired to the vizierate. He was also deprived of sleep by being pricked with a large needle when he was on the verge of dropping off. According to a story frequently used as a morality tale by later authors,[68] Ibn al-Zayyāt was forced into his iron maiden. At first he was allowed to sit on a wooden board, which gave him some relief, but when the jailer came and he heard the sound of the door opening he would stand up.

His torturer recounted the story with some glee: 'I fooled him one day, I led him to think that I had locked the door without actually doing so. I just closed it with the bolt and waited for a bit. Then I opened the door suddenly and seeing that he was sitting down said "I can see what you are doing!" Then I tightened his strangling cord and pulled away the board so that he could not sit any more. It was only a few days after that that he died.'[69] His corpse, still in the filthy shirt he had been wearing in prison, was carried out on a door and his sons prudently said how pleased they were to be rid of 'this criminal'. He was buried hastily in a shallow grave, and it is said that the dogs dug him up and ate his flesh.

Umar ibn Faraj, the man who had treated the caliph's request for money with such contempt, was also in trouble. He was dressed in a woollen robe and loaded with fetters and all his money and estates confiscated. He obviously lived in more style than Ibn al-Zayyāt – camel-loads of furniture and quilts were removed from his houses. In the end he was let off with a vast fine and even allowed to keep some of his estates in the Ahwaz area.[70]

Reading the sources, it is easy to conclude that Mutawwakil was motivated entirely by the desire to obtain revenge for insults he had suffered as a prince. We cannot discount personal malice as a motive, but Mutawwakil's actions were part of a broader strategy. He had decided to break with the cabal that had dominated politics in the reigns of his father and brother and with many of their policies too. He may have wanted to reconnect with the wider Muslim community. He rejected the Muᶜtazilite doctrine of the createdness of the Koran, which aroused such opposition in Baghdad and elsewhere. He also seems to have wanted to break the Turks' monopoly in the higher echelons of the army and create a more broadly based military force. But the old guard would not give up easily, and the caliph felt he had to proceed by deception and violence.

The next member of the cabal to fall was Ītākh. The ex-cook had risen to be the main enforcer of the regime: it was he who had taken the younger brothers of Ma'mūn's son Abbās and walled them up in a vault in his palace. He was also in charge of the army and of security, and was chamberlain of the royal palaces. Mutawwakil kept him on at first, employing him to arrest Ibn al-Zayyāt, for example, but he knew that Ītākh would have to go if he was to make the political changes he desired. But Ītākh was a powerful man with considerable support among the military: it would not be easy.

The caliph could not risk arresting him in Sāmarrā, where the Turkish troops would come to his rescue. He had to be lured away to Baghdad, where he would have no friends. In the summer of 849 Ītākh was persuaded to ask for permission to go on pilgrimage. Of course, this was granted, and the caliph showed his goodwill by making him governor of every town along the route. On his return Ītākh had intended to go directly to Sāmarrā, bypassing Baghdad to the west, but he was met by the governor of the city, Ishāq ibn Ibrāhīm the Tāhirid. Ishāq had a message for him from the caliph. He should enter the city and attend a reception for members of the Abbasid and Alid families and other Baghdad notables in the Palace of Khuzayma. He could hardly refuse.

The Palace of Khuzayma had belonged to one of the leading generals of the early Abbasid period, but by this time it clearly belonged to the government. It lay in a key position, on the east bank of the Tigris just at the end of the main bridge of boats over the river. Ītākh's host, Ishāq the Tāhirid, was well known and liked in Baghdad, but relations between the aristocratic Persian Tāhirid and the Turkish ex-slave were probably cool at best.

As he entered the city from the west, Ītākh was splendidly dressed in a white-sleeved robe with sword and sword belt and was accompanied by three hundred *ghulām*s who could be expected to be thoroughly loyal to him. It was essential to separate them from Ītākh. Ishāq crossed the bridge first and welcomed Ītākh into the palace. Meanwhile the guards on the bridge had directed all the *ghulām*s following him to pass on by so that when Ītākh went into the palace he was followed only by three or four of his closest pages. The stairs that led from the palace to the river were destroyed in case it should be attacked from that direction. Then Ishāq ordered that the doors should be shut.

When Ītākh looked around him, he knew instantly that he had

been trapped. He exclaimed, 'They have done it.' This time there was no trial. The prisoner remained for two days in the Palace of Khuzayma, where he was fairly well treated. Then Ishāq sent a boat for him which took him under escort upstream to the Palace of the Tāhirids. His sword was taken from him and when he reached the Tāhirid palace he was bound and fettered, with irons on his neck and feet. Also imprisoned were his two sons and his secretaries, a Muslim who looked after the official government part of Ītākh's interests and a Christian who looked after his private estates. The Christian felt it prudent to convert to Islam.

An officer who guarded Ītākh at this time reports that his main concern was not for himself but for his sons. He had experienced hard times before, but they has been brought up in the lap of luxury and could not tolerate hardship. The message was passed on to Ishāq, who ordered that the youths should be provided with seven loaves and five ladles of water every day. The fallen general remained in confinement until his death on 21 December 849. Quite how he died is unclear: he was weighed down with a vast number of iron chains (weighing 80 *ratl*s or about 40 kilos), and this by itself may have killed him, but others said he died of thirst. In a cynical manoeuvre which was to be repeated many times in the next two decades, Ishāq summoned the judges of Baghdad and the head of the postal service to examine the corpse and witness that he had not been beaten or marked in any way. The two sons survived until Mutawwakil's death, when they were released, one dying after three months, the other living to a ripe but obscure old age.

Ītākh's execution and the insistence that he had no marks on his body show a new trend in capital punishment. In the early Abbasid period, the death penalty had usually been performed by decapitation, sometimes preceded by the amputation of hands and feet. There was no axe and no block on which the victim laid his head. Instead the condemned man (there is no record of a woman being beheaded in this period) was obliged to bend forward, either standing or kneeling, and was struck on the back of his neck with a sword. A common euphemism for execution was to say that 'his neck was struck'. The head was removed and frequently displayed in public. Among Turkic people, however, the shedding of blood was regarded as deeply shameful. High-status executions were effected by strangling, suffocating or breaking the back. When in 1258 the Mongols rolled the last Abbasid caliph up in a carpet and had him trampled to death by horses, it was by way of a compliment to his high status, though how far it was appreciated by the victim is not clear. It was probably because Ītākh was a Turk of high social status that he was killed without his body being marked.

The removal of Ibn al-Zayyāt and Ītākh broke the back of the old guard. Ahmad ibn Abi Duwād, the chief judge, remained in office until September 851. It seems that he had a stroke about this time and was unable to carry out his duties. His son, who had followed his father into a legal career, was removed from office and all the family estates were confiscated.[71] Ibn Abi Duwād survived until 854,[72] when both he and his son died apparently of natural causes.

The change of personnel was accompanied by major changes of policy. Since Ma'mūn's time the government had supported the Muᶜtazilite belief that the Koran had been created. It had also worked for a rapprochement with the Family of Alī, treating them with favour and respect. The downside of this was the disparagement of the memory of the first three caliphs of Islam, Abu Bakr, Umar and Uthmān, because supporters of the Family of Alī believed that they had usurped Alī's right to the succession. This policy was now reversed. Though it is too early to talk of Sunnis and Shiites as separate sects, the caliph can be seen as moving from a proto-Shiite policy to a proto-Sunnite one. This was demonstrated very publicly with the destruction of the tomb of Husayn at Karbala. The tomb of Husayn, the martyred grandson of Muhammad, had become a focus of devotion almost as soon as he had been killed. It remains a focus of the devotion and religious enthusiasm of Shiites down to the present day.

In 851 Mutawwakil ordered that Husayn's tomb and the residences and palaces that surrounded it be demolished. The land on which it stood was to be ploughed and sown and it was announced that anyone found in the area after three days would be sent to prison. The local inhabitants fled and the grave was deserted.[73] The tomb was destroyed but not forgotten. A traveller in the mid tenth century found the tomb marked by a large dome and once more the centre of pilgrimage. Later writers said that the ruin of his building at Sāmarrā was Mutawwakil's punishment for the destruction of the tomb.[74]

Along with the measures against the devotees of the House of Alī were measures against the *dhimmi*s (protected peoples), the

Christians and Jews. These did not amount to active persecution or forced conversion to Islam but rather public shaming. In 850 the caliph issued a decree that aimed to enforce discrimination in dress in a way that is unpleasantly reminiscent of the anti-Jewish legislation of Nazi Germany. All *dhimmi*s were required to wear yellow on their clothes. Upper-class *dhimmi*s had to wear yellow hoods, simple belts and to ride with wooden stirrups with two pommels on the backs of their saddles. Their slaves were to wear yellow patches on their fronts and backs not less than four finger spans (8 centimetres) across. *Dhimmi*s who wore turbans should wear yellow ones and *dhimmi* women should wear yellow as well. He also ordered that all renovated places of worship should be confiscated, turned into mosques if they were big enough or demolished if not.[75] Christians and Jews had certainly suffered discrimination before in an irregular and patchy way − Christians in areas along the Byzantine frontier had been threatened because the Muslim authorities were afraid that they might ally with the Byzantines − but Mutawwakil's decrees were the first time a caliph had adopted these measures against *dhimmi*s wherever they were and whatever their jobs were.

The caliph was appealing to the same constituency as he had with his abandonment of Mu῾tazilite theology and the attack on the tomb of Husayn, the traditionist Muslims, above all in Baghdad. Perhaps he felt that by demonstrating their superiority over the *dhimmi*s, he could compensate them for their exclusion from real political power. He was careful to keep control of the populace and not to let things get out of hand. If the proto-Shiites venerated Husayn, the proto-Sunnis of Baghdad had come to venerate Ahmad ibn Nasr, who had led the unsuccessful rising against Wāthiq and been executed by the caliph in person. His body had been refused burial and displayed in public on a gibbet in Sāmarrā while his head was taken to Baghdad. It was a constant reminder to his followers of their humiliation. Mutawwakil gave permission for the body to be buried but the authorities were alarmed at the degree of popular enthusiasm and had to send the police to disperse the crowd: many were arrested and flogged. The body was handed over to the dead man's nephew, who brought it to Baghdad and reunited it with his head. As his bier was carried through the streets, the crowds flocked to touch the wood and, later, stroke the place where his head had lain. The caliph sent a decree ordering that people should be prevented from assembling at the grave: a Sunni saint was in the making and the government was deeply suspicious of any such mass demonstrations of popular feeling.[76]

At the same time, a property developer in Baghdad who owned a number of caravanserais in the city found himself in trouble. He was accused of defaming the companions of the Prophet and the first three caliphs. Under the Muᶜtazilite regime of Ma'mūn, Muᶜtasim and Wāthiq this would have been tolerated and even encouraged. Now it got him into serious trouble. The caliph, who obviously took a personal interest in these matters, wrote to the Tāhirid governor of Baghdad, Muhammad ibn Abd Allah, saying that the unfortunate man should be flogged to death and that his body should not be handed over to his relatives, but tossed into the Tigris.[77]

Mutawwakil's other big concern was the choice of a place to live. Having broken with Muᶜtasim's ministers and the whole Muᶜtazilite establishment, he may have found Sāmarrā too full of reminders of the old regime to be comfortable. Like Ma'mūn in his later years, he seems to have been attracted by the idea of living in Damascus. In the spring of 858 he travelled to the city and announced his intention of taking up residence there and moving all the government offices.[78] This would have meant a dramatic break with Abbasid tradition: Damascus had, after all, been the capital of the hated Umayyads and the Arabs of Syria had a long tradition of hostility to the Abbasids. As a poet put it succinctly:

> *I think Syria gloats over Iraq*
> *Now that the caliph has decided to depart.*
> *If you abandon Iraq and its people,*
> *Remember that a beauty may fade after divorce.*

More worrying than the regret of the poets was the vociferous opposition of the Turkish troops, who were based in Sāmarrā. They rightly saw this as a scheme to undermine their monopoly of elite military power and were determined to prevent it. In the end they prevailed: after a couple of months, the caliph was obliged to bow to pressure and return to Iraq.

This was not the end of his ambitions to build a new capital. He settled on a site just north of Sāmarrā on the east bank of the Tigris. Here he could have security and space to reward his supporters with

valuable tracts of lands. The villages around were compulsorily purchased and the inhabitants expelled. The next stage was to bring
water to the site, a gravelly plain above the Tigris. A massive canal-
building project was begun and twelve thousand labourers are said to
have been employed. All this cost a huge amount of money. As with
other Abbasid building projects, there is no suggestion of slave
labour: these people had to be recruited and paid enough to make
them stay. Interestingly, in view of the caliph's recent legislation, the
man put in charge of this massive project was a Christian secretary.[79]

Mutawwakil's new project was intended to be more than a simple
suburb of Sāmarrā. Although it was connected to the old city by an
almost continuous ribbon of building, he wanted it as a new and separate capital, with its own mosque and of course its own palace,
called the Jaᶜfariya after the caliph himself. Even for a monarch with
the resources of Mutawwakil, it took some time to make the new seat
of government habitable, and it was not until 25 February 860 that he
moved in.[80] His new seat of government, also called Mutawwakiliya,
never developed into a viable city, and the vast unfinished project was
abandoned on his death. The ruins still litter the stony plateau above
the Tigris, and we can still see the trench of the canal that was
intended to bring water to the new city but which never carried more
than a trickle. What the caliph had planned as his new Baghdad
became his mausoleum, and the frayed mud-brick walls of his palace
remain in the parched Mesopotamian landscape as mute testimony
to his ambition: 'Look on my works, ye mighty, and despair.'

IX

Abbasid Court Culture

When the caliph Ma'mūn returned to Baghdad, the city of his ancestors, after trying, and failing, to rule the caliphate from distant Merv, he was faced with the task of rebuilding the Abbasid court. He needed to find new people and create a new cultural ambience and a new court style to bind it together. The Arabic poetry-based culture of the early Abbasid court could provide one strand in this but no more than that. The new caliph gathered around him a new group of courtiers. Very few of them had had any connection with the courts of Mansūr, Mahdi and Hārūn. Some of them may never have visited Baghdad before. Most of them were not of Arab origin, and they made no attempt to claim kinship with the tribes of old Arabia; on the contrary, they were more likely to boast of their descent from the Persian aristocracy of pre-Islamic times. The culture of Bedouin poetry had little resonance for them. Socially, they were drawn from the gentry of Iraq or from the military and bureaucratic elites of northern and eastern Iran.

Although the changes were in many ways a clean sweep, the members of this new court society had two things in common with their predecessors. First, they were all Muslims: some were more devout than others, to be sure, but none of them attempted to restore the old Persian faith. Second, they all accepted that Arabic was the language of high culture. The earliest New Persian (that is, essentially, the language of modern Iran) literature appears during this period, but it was written in Khurasan, north-east Iran, not at the court in Baghdad. Some courtiers, including the caliph Muʿtadid, knew Greek, but Greek science became part of Abbasid court culture only when it was translated into Arabic.

In many ways this new ruling group must have felt very insecure and that they lacked a legitimizing discourse to sustain their new-found dominance. The original Abbasid regime that came to power in 750 could claim to be restoring the rule of the House of the Prophet and so bind the Muslim community together. The new elite could vilify the memory of the deposed and murdered caliph Amin and his advisers and make sure that history realized that Ma'mūn had only been reacting to the wrongs done to him, but this hardly provided a convincing long-term narrative for their takeover of power.

Instead, whether consciously or not, they set about patronizing and developing a court culture that would establish their identity as the elite, the *khāssa*. This culture would demonstrate their refinement and sophistication: shared cultural values would provide cohesion for the new ruling class. The leading figures in the civil administration of the caliphate at this period, the vizier Ibn al-Zayyāt, the chief judge, Ibn Abi Duwād, Mutawwakil's friend Fath ibn Khāqān, and the Tāhirid governors of Baghdad also appear as the most important patrons of literature and learning: court and culture were intimately bound together. It was an exclusive culture: to participate in it you needed both money and education. There cannot be an exclusive group without excluding people and it seems that this culture was intended to establish the difference and superiority of the court elite by challenging and in some cases rejecting the values of the bourgeois Muslim society that was then emerging in Baghdad and elsewhere.

The caliphs themselves were the most important patrons. The tone was set by Ma'mūn, and it is clear that patronage of science and of the translation movement was his own very distinctive personal contribution to the culture of the period. Without his input, this period of creativity would have had a very different character. His successor Mu'tasim was known as a military man and creator of the city of Sāmarrā, but he does seem to have continued something of his brother's patronage of writers and scientists. His son and successor Wāthiq was more interested in intellectual debate. Mas'ūdī speaks of him as loving research and those who undertook it, and hating those who blindly followed tradition, and he goes on to describe an assembly in which leading philosophers and doctors, including Hunayn ibn Ishāq, discussed theories of medicine and astronomy.[1]

The caliph Mutawwakil did not encourage scientific enquiry in the same way. Like all rulers of his time, he rewarded poets for singing his praises and adding a cultural veneer to his court, but the reaction against the Muᶜtazilite views of his predecessors seems to have precluded any interest in secular sciences or, indeed, of philosophy. Masᶜūdī, writing a century later, was clear about the change: 'When Mutawwakil succeeded to the caliphate, he ordered the abandonment of investigation and discussion and debate and everything which people had enjoyed in the days of Ma'mūn, Muᶜtasim and Wāthiq. He ordered submission and the acceptance of tradition. He ordered the senior scholars to expound traditions of the Prophet and teach the *sunna* and generally accepted opinions.'

None of the short-lived caliphs who succeeded after Mutawwakil's assassination in 861 had much time to develop intellectual interests, though the caliph Mustaᶜīn is said to have been very knowledgeable about history and stories of the past.[2] It was not until the accession of Muᶜtadid in 892 that the Abbasid court again became a focus for scholarship. Among others, the caliph supported the grammarians Ibn Durayd in the final phase of his career, Zajjāj, one of Mubarrad's leading disciples, and the great translator and mathematician Thābit ibn Qurra. Zajjāj's[3] most celebrated achievement was to produce a commentary on a notoriously difficult grammar book. When this was brought to the caliph he was so pleased with it that he ordered that it be copied on especially fine paper and that the library of the caliph should have the master copy so that no errors could creep into the text, demonstrating a real concern for academic standards. For his work Zajjāj was enrolled among the courtiers and given a salary of 300 *dīnārs*. He was also made tutor to the caliph's children.

Muᶜtadid also patronized science and philosophy in the person of Ahmad ibn Abi'l-Tayyib al-Sarakhsī, who had been his tutor and became his confidant and companion. He was also appointed supervisor of the markets of Baghdad and amassed a considerable fortune amounting to 150,000 *dīnārs* in cash and goods. Sarakhsī was an intellectual – Masᶜūdī calls him a philosopher – with wide-ranging interests, and a pupil of the great philosopher Kindī. He is said to have written abridgements of several works of Aristotle, works on mathematics, music, government, geography and the art of being a good courtier. But being a confidant of the caliph was always a dangerous position. Ahmad seems to have incurred his master's wrath for divulging a state secret and was executed in 896 when the vizier Qāsim ibn Ubayd Allāh, the villain of many stories about the court of Muᶜtadid, inserted his name into the middle of a list of rebels to be executed. The list was then signed by the caliph, who realized that his old master had been executed only after the event.[4]

Scholarly life in Baghdad during this period centred around the households of the great patrons. There is little evidence of institutional structures, colleges or research centres of any sort, apart from the *kuttāb* schools, which offered a basic elementary education in the reading and writing of Arabic. The children of the upper classes had private tutors who taught them at home. Considerable attention has been paid to the institution of the *Bayt al-hikma* (House of Wisdom).[5] It has been argued that this was a sort of academy where translation from Greek to Arabic took place and where debates were held, a sort of early university. Historians often like to fill the past with plushy institutions in which they can imagine distinguished scholars living comfortable and honoured lives in congenial surroundings. In fact there is very little hard information about the House of Wisdom. It appears that it was an institution inherited from the Sasanian monarchs and was basically a library. Pahlavi (middle Persian) manuscripts were kept there and some were translated into Arabic in the early Abbasid period. There is some (late) evidence that astronomers were employed there in Ma'mūn's reign. However, it was far from being a real university, and the most important and original scholars of the period seem to have had no connection with it.

Without institutions to offer salaries and status, scholars were largely dependent on patrons to provide them with a livelihood, and it was in the salons of the great Baghdad families that intellectual life developed. We have an interesting picture of the lifestyle a scholar could hope for from the biography of Tha'lab. Tha'lab was retained by Muhammad ibn Abd Allah ibn Tāhir, governor of Baghdad, as a tutor for his son Tāhir, and he describes what his position was:

> He gave me a separate apartment in his palace and gave me a salary. I stayed with the child for up to four hours a day and would leave when he wanted to have lunch. His father was told about this so he had the hall and the arches of the courtyard redecorated and provided the rooms with fans and added to the variety of food. But I still left at the same time. When he heard this, he said to the servant who was assigned to us, 'I was concerned that he did not think there was enough food and that he did not find the place

agreeable so we doubled what was served. Now I am told he still leaves as soon as his work is finished. Now you ask him yourself, "Is your house cooler than ours? Or is your food nicer than ours?" and tell him from me, "Your leaving at mealtimes puts us to shame".' When the servant told me this, I stayed. I remained in this situation for thirteen years. As well as all this, he gave me seven rations of *khushkār* bread every day, one ration of *samīd* bread, three kilos of meat, and fodder for one animal [the equivalent, perhaps, of a company car]. He also gave me a salary of 1,000 dirhams per month. In the year of the civil war [865, between the supporters of Musta°īn and Mu°tazz], flour and meat became difficult to get so the clerk in charge of [Muhammad's] kitchen wrote to him about the large size of the allowances. [Muhammad] ordered that a register be drawn up so that rations could be restricted to what was essential. The secretary sent this and it comprised 3,600 people. Muhammad read it and added some more people in his own writing. Then he dropped it and said that he was not going to deprive anyone of what he is used to, 'especially those who say, "Give me some bread to eat!" Distribute the provisions according to the register and keep up the supplies. We either live together or die together'.[6]

Tha°lab was able to amass a considerable fortune in his career. When he died in 904 he is said to have left his daughter 21,000 *dirhams*, 2,000 *dīnārs* and some shops at the Syria Gate in Baghdad worth 3,000 *dīnārs*.[7] In fact his academic work was well enough paid to make him a substantial property owner in the city.

Tha°lab's account gives us a vivid picture of life in a great aristocratic household of the time and shows what an intellectual of the period could hope for from a patron, though it must be remembered that Tha°lab was a literary critic, which was probably, then as now, a more fashionable and lucrative form of cultural activity than being, say, a mathematician or an astronomer.

Patrons could support men of letters by offering them posts in the government. One example of this was the grammarian and critic Ibn Durayd[8] (837–933), an altogether wilder character than the prudent and scholarly Tha°lab. He was born in Basra but was forced to leave the city after it was sacked by the Zanj rebels. He took refuge in Oman and then moved on to Fars. Here he joined the service of the local governor, Shāh ibn Mikāl, and his sons. The Banū Mikāl were an aristocratic Persian family who were very influential in military and political circles in the late ninth century. He became a sort of chief secretary to them and all government letters were approved and signed by him. At the same time he composed celebrated poems in praise of his patrons and wrote a major book, the *Jamhara*, about the science of language. Apparently he was very well rewarded for this but because of his own generosity he, unlike Tha'lab, never saved very much. When the Banū Mikāl were removed from their position in Fars in 920 he moved to Baghdad, where the caliph Muqtadir came to hear of his talents and gave him a pension of 50 *dīnār*s a month for the rest of his life. It was here that he composed most of his work. He had an astonishing memory, even by the standards of the time, for the old Arab poetry of the desert, and his scholarly work reflected this. His critics, of course, said that he made much of it up, and that when he was asked who had written a particular work simply said the first name that came into his head. He wrote on a wide variety of subjects, including philology, etymology, horses, saddles and bridles, weapons, obscure words in the Koran and 'Arabs noted for visiting their friends'.

Always generous and improvident, he was frequently penniless and was well known for his love of wine. 'When we went to see him,' one of his contemporaries said in scandalized tones, 'we were shocked to see lutes hung up on the wall and wine unmixed with water.' He was once reproached for giving wine as alms to a beggar and was quite unrepentant, saying that he had nothing else to give. His lifestyle was not without its perils: when he was working in Fars, he fell off the roof of his house one night and broke his collar-bone, probably, though he does not say it, because he was drunk. This is not quite as bizarre or reckless as it sounds: many people slept on the flat roofs of their houses during the hot summer nights. As he lay in pain trying to sleep, he had a classic literary critic's nightmare in which he recited two of his verses in praise of wine. When he had done, Satan appeared and asked him whether he was trying to do better than the great Abu Nuwās. When Ibn Durayd admitted he was, Satan told him that his verses were not too bad but he had made one solecism, saying that the wine was narcissus yellow and then anemone red all at the same time; the poet woke up abruptly, mortified by this supernatural criticism. Despite these setbacks he survived to a ripe old age, and even in his nineties and after a major stroke remained a fount of wisdom on all aspects of philology, though lamenting:

Wretch that I am! A life of pleasure was not mine
Neither have I wrought a good deed whereby I might please God.

Some people seem to have managed without a patron at all and survived by teaching. One such was Ibn Abi Tāhir Tayfūr (d. 893), author of a history of Baghdad of which, sadly, only one volume survives.[9] He came from a family of Khurasani supporters of the Abbasids who had settled in Baghdad, where he was born. At first he made a living as a teacher in a public elementary school, but later he took private pupils in the booksellers' market, on the east bank of the Tigris. In his lifetime, he was criticized for inaccuracy and ignorance of grammar, and this may be why he never seems to have attracted the attention of a rich sponsor. He was a storehouse of real and fanciful stories about poets and singers of the day, and of all sorts of court gossip, even though he was not part of court circles himself. In late-twentieth-century Britain, he would have worked for *Hello!* magazine, describing and fantasizing about the lifestyles of the rich and famous. Much of this gossip was used a couple of generations later by Isfahāni in his great *Book of Songs* and has come down to us as a result.

Elite cultural activity continued in the traditional areas of religious knowledge and poetry but the ninth century saw major new developments in medicine, the exact sciences and the translation of texts from Greek into Arabic. It is this broad range of secular sciences which gives the intellectual life of the period its characteristic flavour, and it was the Abbasid court's major contribution to knowledge. Court culture is also apparent in what we might think of as more frivolous areas. The ninth century was the first great age of Arabic cookery writing. Interest in food, and literature about food, was considered an important part of palace life. Prominent courtiers such as Ibrāhīm ibn al-Mahdi, poet and sometime caliph, Alī al-Munajjim, intimate of Ma'mūn, and Sūli, the early-tenth-century courtier and historian, all wrote cookery books.[10] Unlike that of the medieval West, where high-status food tended to be based on large quantities of game and other sorts of meat, the cuisine of the Abbasid court favoured stews that often mixed meat and fruit and vegetables. Many of these were of ancient Persian origin, such as the famous *sikbāj*, a sweet dish of chicken with leeks, carrots, honey and wine vinegar. Sweet dishes were also highly valued. Masʿūdī describes how the short-lived caliph Mustakfi (944–6) held a gathering at which his courtiers were invited to recite poems describing the most famous dishes of the age. Against a background of looming tragedy (the unfortunate caliph was deposed and blinded shortly after), those present waxed lyrical on the excellence of different dishes and the elegance of the occasion, a last echo of the glory days of the caliphate.

In the religious sphere, this culture manifested itself in the adoption of Muʿtazilism as the officially sanctioned version of Islamic belief. The Muʿtazilites held that the Koran had been created at a certain point in time by God. This was opposed to the developing Sunni view that it had existed since the beginning of time, even though it had been revealed only at a certain historical moment, that is in the time of the Prophet Muhammad. As with many Christian theological controversies, the differences may seem trivial or even incomprehensible to outside observers, but for Muslims in the early ninth century they became a matter of heated debate and eventually of violent action. If the Koran was created then it could be interpreted and even, conceivably, modified by new revelation or human investigation to suit changed circumstances. However, if it had existed through all eternity, it clearly had an absolute and universal status that could not be challenged in any way. These were issues that struck at the heart of Muslim beliefs.

Muʿtazilism became the ideology of the new court party. In some ways it allowed the use of human reason to investigate the divine mysteries. For the pious who felt alienated from the court for other reasons, it was a sign of the arrogant contempt of the new, parvenu elite for traditional Islam: clever men, influenced by alien Greek philosophy, were probing and questioning God's authority. The leaders of the opposition were to be found in Baghdad, among members the old *Abnā* who had lost their status, military and fiscal, with the coming of Ma'mūn. The stage was set for an intellectual controversy made passionate and violent by social differences.

The government chose to make belief in the createdness of the Koran a touchstone for loyalty. A form of inquisition, called a *mihna*, was set up to examine government functionaries and all who wished to hold office as to their views on this subject. Most prudently decided to accept it but a small number chose the path of active resistance. There were trials and at least one 'martyrdom' among the opponents of the new official ideology, but for the moment, the supporters of Muᶜtazilism prevailed.

The cultural interests of the new elite spread far beyond these theological questions. As in the first Abbasid period, poetry was highly valued. Panegyric was still considered the apogee of literary achievement, and this found its most refined and recondite expression in the praise poetry of Abu Tammām. His elaborate ode celebrating the conquest of Amorion by the armies of the caliph Muᶜtasim was outstanding for its use of abstruse simile and metaphor. Even at the time it required explanation (and we must wonder whether the rough-and-ready soldier Muᶜtasim himself caught many of the allusions and devices). The subtleties and obscurities of this poem have been a continuing source of fascination for commentators, ancient and modern. Perhaps the most striking aspect of it is the way this panegyric is deliberately not popular in tone: it was most unlikely to be recited and remembered in the markets and houses of the ordinary inhabitants of Sāmarrā and Baghdad. It was rather an expression of the mannered and intellectualized culture of the period.

Altogether more approachable is the mass of secular literature covering almost every conceivable topic. Most of these works are essentially *adab*, that is essays that recount stories, traditions or abstruse facts about the matter under discussion. A certain amount of it was outré and scandalous. The oeuvre of one Ibn al-Shāh al-Tāhiri, member of an aristocratic Persian family in caliphal service, included works on 'The Boasting of the Comb over the Mirror', 'The War of Bread and Olives', 'The War of Meat and Fish', 'The Wonders of the Sea', 'Adultery and its Enjoyment', 'Stories about Slave-boys', 'Stories about Women' and a work simply called 'Masturbation'.[11] Basically, he was concerned with food and sex. Sadly, none of these diverting books has been preserved for posterity.

The most famous of these secular writers of entertaining prose was Jāhiz. Like many of the most gifted authors of the period, Jāhiz came from an obscure background in the great southern port city of Basra. Born in around 777, he educated himself by listening to the masters of Arabic literature teaching in the mosques and salons of the city. When Ma'mūn re-established the caliphate in Baghdad, he seems to have attracted his attention as an eloquent defender of Abbasid claims to the throne and the Mu^{c}tazili beliefs that had become the ideology of the new regime. He was in fact a political hack. Soon, however, he began to graduate beyond that, showing himself a master of rhetoric and anecdotal prose in a society that valued these accomplishments very highly. Prominent men in the regime wanted to throw money at him in exchange for his dedications. When he had completed his book on *The Animals*, a collection of animal lore and reflections on human society in seven volumes, the vizier Ibn al-Zayyāt gave him 500 *dīnārs* and some agricultural land. His book on *Eloquence* was rewarded by 550 *dīnārs* from the chief judge, Ahmad ibn Abi Duwād. After the execution of Ibn al-Zayyāt in 847 he gravitated to the circle of Fath ibn Khāqān, the gay aesthete who was Mutawwakil's closest companion and the greatest bibliophile of his day. A letter from him to Jāhiz survives in which he tells the author how the caliph was pleased to hear about the title of the book he was working on, a refutation of the Christians, and that he, Fath, had been responsible for the caliph's favours to him. He should finish the work but meanwhile Fath was arranging that his allowance should be paid, including any arrears. Faced by the brutal murder of Mutawwakil and Fath in 861, and his own increasing infirmity, Jāhiz retired to his native Basra, where he died at the end of 868: it is said, as it was of Giordano Bruno, the Renaissance humanist, that he perished when a pile of his own books collapsed on him. Whether the story is true or simply *ben trovato*, it was a fitting way to go.

Typical of Jāhiz prose was the use of paradox, the delight in arguing contrary points of view in elegant and striking prose. He wrote an essay on the superiority of speech to silence and another in which he argues the opposite. An essay on the superiority of blacks over white men stands conventional prejudices on their head. He wrote a debate between lovers of girls and lovers of boys in which both straight and gay men put their points of view, producing traditions of the Prophet, quotations from ancient poets and every form of refined argument in an effort to prove the superiority of their preferred form of sexual intercourse. This was exactly the sort of witty *jeu d'esprit* which would arouse the anger of the pious, who held that sodomy was a sin punishable by death.

Paradox was something of a hallmark among the literary figures at court at the time.[12] Sahl ibn Hārūn, the Persian official in charge of the House of Wisdom, wrote an essay in praise of miserliness and condemning generosity. The poet Ibn al-Rumi was famous for his real or pretended dislike of roses and the outrageous line in which he compared a rose with the anus of a defecating mule. In other poems he also praised envy, spite and solitude. Perhaps something of the same spirit of contrariness can be seen in the practice of giving beautiful slave girls ugly names, such as Qabiha (Ugly) and Shaghab (Trouble), both mothers of caliphs. The *khāssa* would understand the humour and cleverness, the *'āmma* would be shocked and uncomprehending.

One of the most astonishing and impressive products of this court society was the movement to translate ancient Greek scientific and philosophical texts into Arabic. Interest in the Greek intellectual heritage and patronage of the translators became one of the most fashionable forms of elite cultural activity, perhaps all the more satisfying because of the suspicions it aroused in the minds of the more hidebound traditionalists. It was also one aspect of the culture of the Abbasid court which was to have a profound influence on the culture of the wider Islamic world and Latin Europe, long after the end of Abbasid power.

Immediately after the great conquests of the seventh century, the Muslims had ruled over many Greek speakers and writers. Until the end of the seventh century, Greek had remained the administrative language of Syria and Egypt, so Greek culture was well known. There were also many Greek works that had been translated into Syriac (a written dialect of Aramaic which was the liturgical and literary language of the Eastern Christian, that is Jacobite and Nestorian, Churches) during the Byzantine period. Many of these works were now translated a second time from Syriac to Arabic. The Muslims were interested in those products of ancient Greek learning which they believed to be useful. These included works on philosophy, especially logic, medicine, mathematics, astronomy and the uses of plants. They were not concerned to translate poetry, history or drama. Aristotle, Hippocrates, Galen, Euclid, Ptolemy and Dioscorides were all popular authors, translated and retranslated to make them accessible to the Arabic reading public. Herodotus, Thucydides, Euripides and Sappho all remained entirely unknown.

Translation of Greek texts into Arabic had begun as early as Umayyad times, and there had been sporadic examples under the early Abbasids; Salām al-Abrash, already encountered among

Hārūn's courtiers, was an early but individual example. It was the personal enthusiasm and example of the caliph Ma'mūn which made the translation movement fashionable in ruling circles.

The chief patrons of the exact sciences were a family known as the Banū Mūsā. There were three brothers, Muhammad, Ahmad and Hasan. The Banū Mūsā seem to have come from eastern Iran and Mūsā ibn Shākir is said to have been a highway robber, but like many eastern Iranian notables he came into contact with the caliph Ma'mūn when he was residing at Merv in Khurasan from 809 to 818, and when he died the caliph became guardian of his children, who were given a good education in Baghdad.

We do not know the source of their wealth but they were clearly very affluent. It is likely that they had made a fortune out of tax farming or other government business, and, on one level, their patronage of culture may have been a sort of money-laundering operation, aimed at finding a respectable outlet for ill-gotten gains. Muhammad certainly used his mathematical abilities to assist the government, and no doubt he was well rewarded for this. He and a colleague worked out the exact date of Nawrūz, the Persian festival at the spring equinox, for the caliph Mutawwakil. This was very important because the caliph wished to introduce a new fiscal system in which the new financial year would commence at Nawrūz, so it was essential that there was an exact and generally accepted date.[13]

Muhammad also had something of a political career. He was one of the leading supporters of the caliph Musta'īn and one of those who persuaded the Turks to elect him, in 862. Musta'īn put him in charge of the treasury, where, presumably, he made use of his mathematical abilities.[14] He was in Baghdad when the troops of Mu'tazz besieged the city, and at one stage was sent out to estimate the size of the opposing army (two thousand men and a thousand animals), again putting his mathematical training to good practical use.[15] He also played an important role in persuading the unfortunate Musta'īn to abdicate, a move that led to the caliph's death shortly afterwards.[16]

The Banū Mūsā combined their political role with a keen interest in practical science. According to the thirteenth-century biographer Ibn Khallikān, who says he had read one of their books on engineering and found it excellent, 'Their noble ambition was to master the ancient sciences and the books of the classical scholars and they devoted themselves to this project. They sent agents to the Byzantine

Empire to bring them books. They attracted translators from distant lands and far off places by offering generous rewards. They made known the wonders of science.'

The production of translations that were both reliable and elegant required considerable expertise, and men who proved that they could deliver were well rewarded. The Banū Mūsā, leading and discerning patrons of translations of scientific texts, were prepared to pay 500 *dīnār*s salary a month to top-quality workers (though it is not clear whether this was to each individual or to the group of translators who lived in their houses).[17] This was equivalent to the salaries of senior members of the bureaucracy and vastly more than those of an ordinary craftsman or soldier. As a result, clever and ambitious people flocked to Baghdad to offer their services. Hunayn ibn Ishāq (d. 873) was a Christian from the ancient Christian Arab city of Hira in southern Iraq who worked as a translator for the Banū Mūsā. He is said to have been a master of style in Greek, Syriac and Arabic, and to have visited the Byzantine empire in search of manuscripts. Most of his translations were of medical works, notably Galen and Hippocrates, and, like many translators, he also produced original work in his own right. A biographer gives us an idea of the lifestyle of this gentleman academic:

He went to the bath every day after his ride and had water poured on him. He would then come out wrapped in a dressing gown and, after taking a cup of wine with a biscuit, lie down until he had stopped perspiring. Sometimes he would fall asleep. Then he would get up, burn perfumes to fumigate his body and have dinner brought in. This consisted of a large fattened pullet stewed in gravy with a half kilo loaf of bread. After drinking some of the gravy and eating the chicken and the bread he would fall asleep. On waking up he drank 4 *ratl*s [perhaps 2 litres] of old wine. If he felt like fresh fruit, he would have some Syrian apples and quinces. This was his habit until the end of his life.[18]

When he managed to find time for work amidst this agreeable regime is not entirely clear, but he obviously did for his output was enormous and his academic standards very high.

Hunayn founded what was effectively a family business in translation. His son Ishāq (d. 910) enjoyed a great reputation as a translator and was patronized by the leading vizier of his day, Qāsim ibn Ubayd Allah. As well as translations, he produced a *History of Physicians* which attempted to put the Greek masters in context.[19] Meanwhile his nephew Hubaysh helped him with translation and commentary.

Qusta ibn Luqa (Constantine, son of Luke) (d. 922) was a native Greek speaker from Baalabak (ancient Heliopolis) in Lebanon, a town where the mighty classical temples still dominate the scene today. He came to Baghdad bringing with him Greek manuscripts he hoped would interest patrons in the capital. He wrote a number of original treatises, including works on medicine, nutrition, sexual intercourse, astronomy and problems in Euclid's geometry:[20] nobody could have accused him of being narrow minded.

The third of the great translators, Thābit ibn Qurra the Sabian, came from a more unusual and exotic background. He was probably born in 826 in Harran, now a small, dusty and partly deserted place in southern Turkey, hard by the Syrian border. This otherwise undistinguished provincial town was famous because of the endurance here of the last pagan community to survive from antiquity. At least until the tenth century, the Sabians still practised the worship of the moon-goddess Sin, though they had by this time disguised their beliefs sufficiently to be accorded the status of 'People of the Book', and hence tolerated by the Muslim government. In addition to the old religion, the Sabians had preserved a Hellenic literary culture, and educated Sabians seem to have been at home in Greek, Syriac and Arabic. The young Thābit began life as a money-changer in Harran but was 'talent-spotted' by Muhammad, one of the Banū Mūsā brothers, when he was returning from an expedition to the Byzantine empire to search for books, probably in the mid 850s. When he returned to Baghdad, he took Thābit, then still a young man, with him. As far as we know Thābit lived in Baghdad for the rest of his life and, along with Hunayn ibn Ishāq, he was one of the salaried translators who lived and worked in the house of the Banū Mūsā.[21] In later life he was presented at court to the caliph Muᶜtadid, who was himself a Greek speaker and keenly interested in natural sciences. When Thābit had established himself, a number of other Sabians came to court, and they became a respected group, both as scientists and as historians in the culture of Abbasid Baghdad.[22]

Thābit's forte lay in the translation of mathematical and astronomical works from Greek, but he was also a distinguished mathematician in his own right and produced work of lasting value on subjects such as conics which went well beyond the classical authors.

Perhaps the greatest of the intellectuals who benefited from the translation movement was Yaʿqūb ibn Ishāq al-Kindi. Unlike most of the intellectuals who gathered around the Abbasid court, Kindi was an Arab by descent, from a very distinguished South Arabian family who had settled in Kūfa after the Muslim conquest of Iraq. They were important property owners in the area and Kindi's father had served as governor. He was probably born in Kūfa in the late eighth century but subsequently moved to Baghdad, where he enjoyed the company and patronage of the caliphs Ma'mūn, Muʿtasim and Wāthiq, right at the heart of court culture. With the accession of Mutawwakil in 847, the intellectual climate became less receptive to philosophy and speculative thought. Kindi also suffered from the jealous hostility of the Banū Mūsā family, who, at one stage, secured the confsication of his vast personal library, though it was restored to him in the end. He probably died in 866.

As a person, Kindi was quite difficult. Despite his affluent aristocratic background, he was famous for his meanness and miserliness. Jāhiz, who must have known him well, lampoons him mercilessly in his *Book of Misers*. He used to have lodgers in his house and one of them wrote to ask Kindi whether it would be acceptable for his cousin and his son to come to stay for a month. He already paid 30 *dirham*s a month for a household of six, but his landlord then demanded an extra 10 *dirham*s per month for the extra people. His tenant queried this politely and Kindi replied, at least according to Jāhiz, with an immense and furious diatribe about the problems facing landlords and the tricks that tenants got up to.[23] The poor man must have wished he had never asked.

Kindi is famous as the 'Philosopher of the Arabs'. Though not a translator himself, he was the first man to use Aristotle's work to create an Islamic, Arabic-language philosophical discourse. He was also the first to confront the problems of reconciling faith and reason and, though a pious Muslim, he was regarded with great suspicion by more conservative elements. He is said to have written well over two hundred works, though many of them were no doubt just short pamphlets.[24] As well as philosophy, he wrote on mathematics, astronomy, music and medicine; the main hospital in modern

Baghdad is named after him. His work on swords and their manufacture is the fullest surviving description we have of early Islamic weapons. He was probably the only person who appears in this book whose name would have been widely known in medieval Europe. From the twelfth century many of his works were translated into Latin, usually in Spain, and circulated widely in European universities: some of his writings, in fact, survive only in Latin versions.

The ninth century was the great age of the study of sciences, with Thābit ibn Qurra (d. 901) in mathematics and Hunayn ibn Ishāq (d. 873) in medicine being the leading lights. The clearest example of their intellectual curiosity and practical application can be seen in their project to measure the circumference of the earth. This is described in some detail by Ibn Khallikān.[25] It is perhaps worth recounting this in detail because the account seems to encapsulate the spirit of scientific enquiry typical of the age and, especially, of the circle of the Banū Mūsā.

A thing which they, the first in Islamic time, brought from theory into practice was the measurement of the circumference of the earth. Although astronomers in ancient times, before the coming of Islam, had done this, there is no evidence that any Muslim apart from them had tried it. The caliph Ma'mūn took a deep interest in the sciences of the ancients and was keen to test their accuracy. Having read in their works that the circumference of the globe is twenty four thousand miles or eight thousand farsakhs [three miles make a farsakh]*; that is to say that if one end of a cord were placed at any point on the surface of the earth, and the cord passed round the earth until the two ends met, that cord would be twenty four thousand miles long. He wished to test the truth of this assertion and asked the Banū Mūsā what they thought. They replied that this was certainly the case and the caliph then said, 'I wish you to use the methods described by the ancients so that we can see whether it is accurate or not'. They enquired where a level plain could be found and were told that the desert of Sinjār [in northwestern Iraq] was completely flat, as was the country around Kūfa. They took with them a number of people whose opinion Ma'mūn trusted and whose knowledge in this area he relied on. They set

* In fact the equatorial circumference of the earth is 40,076 kilometres (24,902 miles).

out for Sinjār and came to the desert. They halted at a spot where they took the altitude of the Pole Star with certain instruments. They drove a peg into the ground and attached a long cord to it. They walked due north, avoiding, as much as possible, going off to left or right. When the cord ran out, they stuck another peg into the ground and fastened a cord to it and carried on walking to the north as they had done before until they reached a spot where the elevation of the pole star had risen by one degree. Then they measured the distance they had travelled on the ground by means of the rope. The distance was 66⅔ miles. Then they knew that every degree of the heavens was 66⅔ miles on earth. Then they returned to the place where they had stuck in the first peg, tied a rope to it, and continued to the south, just as they had previously to the north, sticking in pegs and fastening ropes. When they had finished all the rope they had used when going north, they took the elevation of the Pole Star and found it was one degree lower than the first observation. This proved that their calculations were correct and that they had achieved what they had set out to do. Anyone who knows about astronomy will see that this is true. It is well known that the number of degrees in the heavens is 360 for the heavens are divided into twelve constellations and that each constellation is thirty degrees. This makes 360 degrees in all. They then multiplied the number of degrees of the heavens by 66⅔, that is the length of each degree, and the total was twenty four thousand miles or eighth thousand farsakhs. This is certain and there is no doubt about it.

Then the Banū Mūsā returned to al-Ma'mūn and told him what they had done and that this agreed with what he had seen in ancient books. He wished to confirm this in another location so he sent them to the Kūfa area where they repeated the experiment they had conducted in Sinjār. They found that the two calculations agreed and Ma'mūn acknowledged the truth of what the ancients had written on the subject.

The account is revealing of many aspects of the intellectual environment of the time. The first is the respect shown for ancient science. People of this era were well aware that they had much to learn from the achievements of the classical era (much more aware, of course, than their contemporaries in Byzantium or western

Europe). But the story also shows that this respect for the ancients was not an uncritical acceptance of everything they said: Ma'mūn and the Banū Mūsā wished to test the figures for the circumference of the earth for themselves. Finally, we must be struck by the commitment to practical scientific experiment, the establishment of a hypothesis, the use of experimental evidence to prove it and, perhaps most impressive, the care shown to make sure that the experiment could be replicated, in the same area and then in an entirely different one. All this demonstrates a truly scientific approach that has few parallels in the post-classical pre-modern age.

For patronage of intellectuals was one of the ways in which the rich and powerful in court circles established their social prestige. The patronage of scholars was part of the exercise of elite power and the caliphs led the way. There were hierarchies of knowledge. In the non-religious sciences, it is clear that knowledge of literature, of poetry and its background, carried the most prestige and the highest rewards. But there were also patrons who were genuinely interested in science and who were prepared to support it with their fortunes. Like the Italy of the Italian Renaissance, the intellectual world of ninth-century Baghdad was a world where private patrons funded intellectual life and, to an extent, competed against each other for intellectual prestige. This may account for something of the variety and originality of the scholarly life that was one of the great achievements of the Abbasid period. Much of this freshness and vitality was lost with the development of the more formal structures of the *madrasa* (theological school) from the eleventh century onwards.

X

High Noon in Sāmarrā

Come, let us sit upon the ground and tell sad stories of the death of kings.' Mutawwakil was a powerful caliph with a clear vision of how he wanted to rule. The volume of the translation of Tabari's *History of the Prophets and Kings* that deals with his reign is called 'Incipient Decline', but in reality there were few signs that the caliphate was heading for trouble. The caliph still appointed governors from the eastern borders of Iran to the western frontiers of Egypt. Despite occasional unrest, Armenia in the north and Yemen in the south accepted his sovereignty. When he moved his capital to Jaᶜfariya in 860, the caliph was still a young man, probably 38 and he might easily have ruled for another twenty years.

In spite of his youth, the succession was, as always, a key issue and the focus around which factions and intrigues developed. As part of his strategy of undermining the authority of the Turkish generals he decided that his own sons would take over the political responsibilities that had been held by men like Ashinās and Ītākh. In this way the overall power of the dynasty would be re-established.

In the summer of 850 Mutawwakil decided to give three of his sons positions in the succession,[1] Muhammad, who was given the title of Muntasir, Abu Abd Allah, called Muᶜtazz, and Ibrāhīm, called Mu'ayyad. Just like his grandfather Hārūn, Mutawwakil tried to ensure harmony and cooperation between his sons by spelling out in great detail what their obligations to each other were to be. Like Hārūn as well, he decreed that the different sons were to have power in different areas of the empire during their father's life and, in the case of Muᶜtazz and Mu'ayyad, during the reign of their elder brother. Muntasir received Egypt with its immense wealth, the Arabian peninsula, Iraq and western Iran, making his share by far the largest, both in area and in terms of the taxes that could be raised.

Muʿtazz was to get Khurasan, Armenia and Azerbayjān and Fars, while Mu'ayyad was granted Syria and Palestine. None of this meant that the young princes actually lived in these areas – they were all based firmly in Sāmarrā – but it meant that the local governors acted in their names and they may have had some say in the spending of the revenues that came from their provinces. We know that a few years later, around 855, Muʿtazz was put in charge of all the treasuries in his area and that coins were minted in his name.

Needless to say, Mutawwakil's apparently watertight arrangements for the succession gave rise to terrible tensions within the royal family and the court, tensions that were not eased by the caliph's own somewhat erratic behaviour. For reasons that are not clear, Mutawwakil seems to have become disenchanted with Muntasir, treating him with open contempt in court, ordering his courtiers to slap his head and dropping hints that he was to be removed from his position as heir apparent. Muntasir was angry and humiliated. The situation was exacerbated by the fact that his brother Muʿtazz was supported by an ambitious mother, Qabīha, who had won the caliph's heart, and who gave him lavish presents. It was Muʿtazz's circumcision party, not Muntasir's, which was remembered for its lavish display and generosity. Qabīha was working hard behind the scenes to secure her son's succession. Very little is known about Muntasir's mother, a Byzantine slave called Habashiya, except that she came to visit him during his final illness.[2]

As the examples of Amīn and Ma'mūn had shown, tensions between brothers who were potential heirs to the throne polarized the ruling elite into different factions. Muntasir was not the only person at court to feel that his position was under threat. Wasīf was the last survivor of the small group of Turks whom Muʿtasim had originally recruited before he became caliph. His more famous companions were now dead, Ashinās from natural causes and Ītākh because Mutawwakil had ordered his death. Wasīf had survived, perhaps by keeping a low profile, and he still had large estates in Isfahān and the Jibāl area. He also had a number of adult sons who hoped to inherit his position and wealth. One of them, Sālih, was to be a major player in the dramas to come. Given Mutawwakil's longstanding policy of removing the old elite from power, it cannot have been a great surprise to Wasīf when he learned, in October 861, that the caliph was intending to confiscate his lands and give them instead to his new favourite, Fath ibn Khāqān.³ Wasīf and his sons might well have felt they had little to lose by supporting a coup.

Other second-rank Turkish officers also felt that their position was threatened. They had thwarted the caliph's attempt to move the capital to Damascus but he was still working to undermine their monopoly on military power, recruiting troops from North Africa and Armenia. They may have been in danger of losing their position but, fatally for the caliph, they still formed the palace guard that was supposed to protect him.

The tensions came to a head on the last Friday of Ramadan, 5 December 861. This was one of the great public occasions of the Muslim year. Mutawwakil still kept up the tradition of leading the people in public prayers in the Great Mosque of Sāmarrā. People had known about this from the beginning of the holy month of fasting, and visitors, including many important members of the Abbasid family, had made the journey from Baghdad to Sāmarrā for the occasion. It was a time when people could present petitions to the caliph and ask him to redress their grievances. When the great day approached the caliph complained that he was feeling unwell, but despite this he would lead the prayers in person. His chief advisers, Fath ibn Khāqān and Ubayd Allāh ibn Yahya ibn Khāqān, pretending, at least, to be solicitous for his welfare, suggested that it might be a good opportunity for one of his heirs to undertake this very public engagement and so establish his public image. It was agreed that Muntasir should be asked to do it, but on the very morning of the procession the two advisers disingenuously suggested to the caliph that it might be a good idea if the honour was given to Muʿtazz, on the clearly specious grounds that the young prince had had a son the previous day. The caliph gave his permission and Muʿtazz led the prayers: one of the more sycophantic courtiers, hoping no doubt to catch the caliph in his current mood, said that he had known the previous four caliphs from Amīn on but that he had never, 'never seen anyone occupy the pulpit who was superior to Muʿtazz in imposing stature, spontaneous speech, sonorous voice, mellifluous tone and eloquence'. Meanwhile, as his young brother was distinguishing himself in public, the humiliated Muntasir was obliged to remain in his quarters in the palace.⁴

The next Sunday marked the end of the fast with the appearance of the new moon. This was another major public occasion; again the caliph said he was unwell and suggested that on this occasion Muntasir should lead the prayers. This time his advisers were adamant: he had not appeared on the Friday and if he failed to appear on the Sunday too, rumours about his health would start to spread. He must lead the prayers in person. In this, his last public appearance, he processed through lines of subjects stretching for 8 kilometres between his palace and the mosque. As he returned to the palace he is said to have taken a handful of earth and sprinkled it on his head: when asked why he had done this he replied, 'I saw this huge crowd and, realizing they were under my power, I wished to humble myself before God.'[5] Once again, Muntasir was excluded from the state occasion.

Two days later the caliph felt that he was sufficiently recovered to summon his boon companions in the usual way for an evening of drinking and talking. It was Tuesday, 10 December 861. Our knowledge of the events of that terrible night is based on three first-hand accounts. One of the eyewitnesses was a professional singer, Ibn al-Hafsi, who had been summoned along with a few others to join the entertainment. He described the caliph's party but seems to have left before the assassination. A black slave called Ashᶜath was one of the few people with the caliph when the fatal blows were struck and he is the source for the actual assassination. Meanwhile a page called Bunān was with Muntasir and describes his movements and reactions. None of the conspirators left a first-hand account. Not surprisingly, there is some contradiction and confusion in the accounts, the sort of misremembering that you usually find in eyewitness accounts of dramatic happenings, but the outline of events is fairly clear.

Early in the evening Mutawwakil was sitting alone with Fath ibn Khāqān, his closest companion. The boon companions were still in their rooms, waiting to be summoned. He ordered the attendants, including Ibn al-Hafsi and Ashᶜath, to eat. When the dishes were empty, they 'let their hands drop', showing that they were still hungry (as opposed to raising their hands as a sign of satisfaction).[6] When the caliph enquired what was wrong, they complained that one of their number, a man called Nasr, was exceptionally greedy and had eaten much more than his share. Mutawwakil ordered more food to be provided from his own table.

The court assembled later in the evening, probably in one of the rooms in the block of the new palace which overlooked the Tigris. In attendance were a number of pages and singers, the heir apparent Muntasir and one of the caliph's brothers, Abū Ahmad, later known as Muwaffaq, who was to play an ambiguous, even suspicious, role in the evening's events. Behind the curtain, unseen but able to hear everything, were the women of the household. Mutawwakil no doubt intended to join them when the revels were over. A Turkish guard called Bughā (the Ox) the Younger was also in attendance. Ibn al-Hafsi said that he had never seen the caliph more cheerful but, as often in accounts of caliphs' deaths, those present 'remembered' later that he had had premonitions of his end.[7] In this case he is said to have been sent a beautiful green silk embroidered gown by his beloved Qabīha. He was delighted but ordered that it be ripped in half and returned to her. He explained to his companions, 'My heart tells me that I shall not wear it, and I don't want anyone after me to do so.' The courtiers hastened to reassure him: 'This is a happy day, Commander of the Faithful. God forbid that you should say this,' but even as he began to drink and make merry, he kept repeating, 'By God I am leaving you soon.' A story also circulated later to the effect that some Turkish women had sent a note to Fath ibn Khāqān via his secretary giving details of the plot, but Fath did not take it seriously and was, in any case, reluctant to tell the caliph for fear of spoiling his good mood.[8]

Muntasir was once more the butt of his father's ridicule. As the caliph got drunker, his behaviour became more outrageous. A member of the Abbasid family later said that he had been told by the women behind the curtain that he had ordered Fath ibn Khāqān to beat his son around the head with his hand and he began to mock him as 'the Impatient One' (a play on Muntasir's name which effectively accused him of wanting his father's death). Muntasir was mortified by this disgrace and replied, with some dignity, that execution would have been easier for him to bear than this sort of insult.

Finally, at about midnight, supper was served and Mutawwakil set about eating heartily. It was apparently at this time that Prince Muntasir left, accompanied by some pages, including Bunān. When one of them protested that they could not leave before the caliph had risen, Muntasir said that the caliph was too drunk to notice and that the boon companions would soon be leaving. Bughā set about clearing the hall, ordering the boon companions to go to their rooms: he did not want anyone to interfere in his plans. Fath ibn Khāqān protested that it was too early to break up the party but Bughā told him briskly that the caliph had ordered him to send everyone away when he had had seven measures of wine and he had now had fourteen, and besides, the women were waiting behind the curtain. It seems that everyone now left except Fath ibn Khāqān and a few pages, including Ashᶜath, our informant.

Meanwhile, in other parts of the palace, men were moving with sober intent. The guard that night was made up of a group of Turks, led by Mūsā, son of Bughā the Elder, and Bughā the Younger. At some stage during the course of the evening they were joined by four of the sons of Wasīf, the veteran Turkish leader whose estates the caliph was about to confiscate, including the eldest, Sālih. They had locked all the doors of the palace except the one leading to the river bank which was left open for the assassins. The plot was almost uncovered when Prince Abū Ahmad left the party to go to the lavatory and met them. He shouted at them, asking them what they thought they were doing, but they must have ignored him and pushed on with drawn swords. Abū Ahmad retired to his room. Whether he was part of the conspiracy or simply making himself scarce we cannot tell, but he later developed close friendships with some of the Turks who were involved, especially Mūsā ibn Bughā the Elder.

Mutawwakil had heard the shout, but Bughā explained that it was just the guard making a noise. The conspirators nearly panicked at this stage and thought they had been discovered, but Bughā, who must have slipped out, rallied them by saying that they were as good as dead and they might as well strike now and die with honour. They rushed in on the caliph, one of them slashing him with his sword, cutting off his ear and shoulder. The caliph put up a brave fight, throwing himself at his assailant. Fath cursed them for attacking the caliph but Bughā simply said, 'Shut up, you idiot!' Fath tried to shield his master but they were both soon cut open by the swords of the Turks. One of the young pages escaped by slipping under the curtain into the women's quarters and the rest, including Ashᶜath, ran away. The caliph and his favourite lay alone in a pool of blood.

It is not clear what Muntasir had been doing during this time. The page Bunān provided an alibi for his movements at the time when his father was being done to death. According to the page, the young prince was discussing the arrangements for the marriage of one of his attendants, and the first he knew of his father's murder was when Bughā came to him and greeted him as caliph. However, it is hard to believe that he had no inkling of the plot, and he certainly moved fast to provide a cover story for public consumption. According to one version of this, Mutawwakil had been murdered by Fath ibn Khāqān and Muntasir himself had slain Fath in righteous anger.[9] But shortly after this, Muntasir was giving out that the caliph had choked on his wine.[10]

Whether he was involved in the plot or not, Muntasir knew that he had to move quickly the next morning if he was to establish his control. Ubayd Allah ibn Yahya ibn Khāqān, the vizier, had not been at the fatal party because he was working late in his office in another part of the palace. When he heard pandemonium breaking out, he sent a man to ascertain what had happened. As soon as he found out about the assassination, he tried to leave the building and find the young prince Muᶜtazz, well aware that he might be in danger from his jealous brother. He left with his servants and entourage but they found all the doors of the palace locked. They were forced to break down the doors that gave on to the river bank. Then they took boats and went downriver to Muᶜtazz's residence. They were too late, the place was deserted, and Yahya feared for the worst.[11]

In fact things were not as bad as Yahya had feared. The story is now taken up by a man called Saᶜīd the Younger, who was an assistant to Muntasir's secretary, Ahmad ibn al-Khasīb. Ahmad had immediately set about drafting an oath of allegiance, though, having never done this before, he had to ask the advice of his own private secretary to work out an appropriate formula. Meanwhile the narrator was sent off to find Muᶜtazz and bring him to swear allegiance. He left very reluctantly: he knew it was a dangerous mission and he would rather have stayed with the new caliph and helped with the administration of the oath. The city was in chaos – groups of armed men were everywhere and there was a widespread feeling that Ubayd Allah ibn Yahya ibn Khāqān and Muᶜtazz might rally the non-Turkish troops to dispute the succession. Saᶜīd made his way through the streets, being careful not to give straight answers when people asked who he was and what he was doing. When he reached Muᶜtazz's palace, it seemed deserted; there were none of the usual guards, gatekeepers or beggars waiting around outside.[12] He knocked loudly, and after a long wait the door opened. He explained who he was and that he was the messenger of the caliph Muntasir. Again he was kept waiting, but in the end he was invited in and the gate locked behind him. He was terrified: if Muᶜtazz really was going to contest the succession, then Muntasir's messenger would certainly be for the chop.

Baydūn, a trusty servant of Muᶜtazz and his mother, came to speak with him. Saᶜīd told the official story about how Mutawwakil had choked to death. Then Saᶜīd was ushered in to meet the young prince. He repeated the story about the caliph's death and offered the young prince his condolences. Then he urged him to come and take the oath of allegiance to his brother to establish himself in the new caliph's good books. Muᶜtazz wanted to wait until morning but Saᶜīd, helped by Baydūn, persuaded him that he should go immediately. He called for his clothes, and when he was dressed they set out, Saᶜīd being careful to go by back roads where they were unlikely to meet people who might try to change Muᶜtazz's mind. Saᶜīd made small talk, trying to reassure him about his brother's good intentions. When they passed Ubayd Allah ibn Yahya ibn Khāqān's palace, Muᶜtazz asked what Ubayd was going to do. Saᶜīd had to resort to blatant dishonesty, saying that Yahya would certainly pledge allegiance and that Fath ibn Khāqān, who was of course dead, had already done so. It was a scary journey. A horseman kept approaching Baydūn, probably trying to persuade him not to take Muᶜtazz to the palace. Eventually they reached the new caliph. He was friendly and affable, embracing his younger brother, consoling him for the death of their father. The other heir, Mu'ayyad, soon arrived with another palace official, and both the young princes took the oath of allegiance. By the time the people of Sāmarrā awoke on Wednesday morning, Muntasir had firmly established himself as caliph.

The tragic and violent events of the night of Tuesday, 10 December 861 were catastrophic for the long-term future of the Abbasid caliphate. It was not of course the first time a caliph had been killed: Amīn had paid with his life for the folly and ambition of his chief supporters, but this was murder, cold and calculated. Now it had been done once, it was only too easy to imagine it being done again. The Turkish guard had demonstrated their power and made it clear that any caliph who would not, or could not, respond to their demands would not last long.

Muntasir seems to have been a generous and well-meaning ruler but his short reign was dogged by rumours and allegations about his father's death. Though they may have been no more than moralistic fantasy, stories were told of his melancholy and anxiety about his own death, the product of a guilty conscience.

He began resolutely by organizing a major campaign against the Byzantines: a victory here might clear the air and establish his reputation. He could not afford to leave the capital so soon after establishing his authority, so he put Wasīf, the last of the old Turkish leaders, in charge. The new caliph took care that the expedition was well publicized. He sent a letter, dated 13 March 862, to the Tāhirid governor of Baghdad, Muhammad ibn Abd Allah ibn Tāhir, which was intended to be read out in public and to make the case for *Jihād*.[13] It is the most complete justification for the holy war surviving from this period. He begins by stressing the excellence of Islam and then gives the main Koranic texts which encourage participation in the *Jihād* and promises those who fight in it all the joys of paradise. He then stresses his own commitment: 'The Commander of the Faithful desires to come close to God by waging Holy War against his enemy, by carrying out His obligations in the religion that He entrusted him with and seeking closeness to Him by strengthening His friends and permitting injury and revenge against those who deviate from His religion, deny His messengers and disobey Him.'[14]

He then goes on to say that he has dispatched Wasīf to the frontier. He will arrive at the frontier city of Malatya on 15 June and begin his invasion of Byzantine territory on 1 July. This letter is to be read to the Muslims, presumably in the mosque at Friday prayer, so that volunteers will be encouraged to go and help in the campaign. We cannot tell how successful the appeal was; the campaign was aborted on the caliph's death.

The new ruler's second act was to remove his brothers, Muᶜtazz and Mu'ayyad, from their position as heirs. It was true that he had given solemn promises to his father to respect their rights, but political pressure from his supporters in the Turkish military, especially Wasīf and Bughā, meant that it was impossible for him to keep them. If he should die suddenly, as indeed he did, then they would be faced with the accession of their enemy Muᶜtazz and his supporters. Muᶜtazz and Mu'ayyad had to go.

Mu'ayyad, the younger and less assertive of the brothers, has left an account of how this was done.[15] The two princes were summoned and installed in apartments in the caliph's residence. Mu͑tazz asked his brother why he thought they had been brought there and Mu'ayyad replied with brutal honesty: 'To depose us, you miserable fellow!' Mu͑tazz said that he did not believe that this would happen, but just then messengers arrived with the deposition documents. Mu'ayyad was in no doubt that he could not refuse and immediately agreed to sign, but Mu͑tazz replied that he could not agree and that they could kill him if they wanted to. He was roughly manhandled into a room and the door was locked. Mu'ayyad, at least by his own account, now tried to sort the matter out. He roundly abused the guards for their lack of respect to a member of the ruling house and said that he would go to the cell to reason with his brother.

When he arrived, he found Mu͑tazz in tears. He lost no time in telling him that he had to abdicate, especially in view of what they had done to their father (Muntasir's rather feeble stories about Mutawwakil's death had obviously not convinced them at all). Still Mu͑tazz hesitated. 'Shall I give up a right I have already exercised in the provinces under my authority?' 'This "right" killed your father,' his brother replied, 'don't let it kill you!' Finally Mu͑tazz agreed.

Mu'ayyad then told the messengers that he had agreed to abdicate and that he would write whatever they dictated. A secretary had come with an inkwell and some paper so Mu'ayyad sat down to write that he was incapable of ruling and wished to abdicate. Again Mu͑tazz refused despite his brother's brisk command, 'Write, damn you!' Finally, in their own hands, they wrote the humiliating document:

In the name of God, the Merciful, the Compassionate.

The Commander of the Faithful Mutawwakil, may God be pleased with him, assigned the succession to me and had the oath of allegiance taken to me without my consent and when I was a minor. When I reached the age of understanding, I realized that I could not do what he asked of me and that I would not be a suitable caliph for the Muslims. Whosoever has taken the oath of allegiance to me can now rescind it. I free you from it and release you from your oath. I have no binding covenant or compact with you. You are released from it. '

After they had finished writing, they were summoned to meet the caliph. Mu'ayyad asked whether they should obtain new clothes or

come as they were and was told that they should change: this was
going to be a formal and solemn occasion. Fresh clothes were called
for and they went in. They found Muntasir in his audience hall with
the courtiers lined up in ranks to witness the proceedings. There
were members of the Abbasid family, Muhammad ibn Abd Allah
the Tāhirid from Baghdad, army commanders, government officials
and secretaries. The young princes must also have been uncomfort-
ably aware of the presence in the ranks of their father's murderers,
including Bughā the Younger, who had commanded the guard on
that fatal night. Muntasir asked whether they had written their abdication documents: Mu'ayyad hastened to agree and Mu°tazz
mumbled his assent.

Then the caliph made a remarkable speech in which he said quite
openly that he was not deposing them because he wanted his own
son to succeed, far from it, but because the Turks had demanded that
they be deposed and he was afraid that, if he did not agree, they
would be killed by one of the soldiers. Taking revenge by executing
the soldier would not be a remedy because the princes' blood was
worth so much more than the blood of any soldier. In fact, it was all
for their own good. It was a curiously public admission of weakness
in the face of pressure from the military. Finally they kissed his hand,
he embraced them and they departed.

On 24 April Ahmad ibn al-Khasīb, Muntasir's vizier, wrote to
Muhammad b. Abd Allah b. Tāhir and no doubt to other governors
and officials, giving reasons for and details of the depositions. He
explained how the young princes had received oaths of allegiance
when they were under age and how, as they reached puberty, they
had come to realize that they could not exercise their rights.
Everyone was now released from their oaths of allegiance and the
two were to be considered people of the markets and commoners
(*āmma*). This last clause must have been especially hurtful. To be
part of the elite (*khāssa*) meant enjoying all the privileges of court life
and status. To be excluded from this would mark complete social disgrace. No members of the Abbasid family had ever been subject to
this sort of humiliation before. The document went on to order a sort
of *damnosa memoriae*: all mention of their names would be removed
from emblems and flags and from the markings on military horses.
Finally the governor was told that there was no one between him and
the caliph and he was responsible directly to him.

It was only a little over a month after this that Muntasir died of natural causes. He fell ill on 29 May and was dead by 7 June. There were rumours of poisoning – there always were – but they do not seem to have been taken very seriously.

Although he did have a son, he was probably too young to be considered a suitable caliph and Muntasir, having removed his brothers from the succession, had made no other arrangements. Presumably he thought there was still plenty of time. Muntasir had died on a Saturday, and on the Sunday the leading Turks gathered in the Hārūni palace. Leading the party were the two Bughās, the Elder and the Younger, and another Turk called Bāghir. On the advice of the vizier they made all the other Turks swear that they would accept whoever was chosen as caliph by these three. It was a straightforward military coup. The fate of the throne of Mansūr, Mahdi and Hārūn was now to be decided by a small group of Turkish soldiers. To emphasize the humiliation of the caliphs, all these were men who had been involved in the assassination of Mutawwakil, and they now seem to have made no attempt to deny or disguise their role in his death.

The clique had no intention of appointing Muʿtazz, or any of the sons of Mutawwakil. After all, they had killed their father and any new caliph would want to take his revenge. On the other hand they were clear that they wanted the caliphate to remain with the descendants of Muʿtasim, their patron, who had been responsible for the rise to power of the Turks in Sāmarrā. The question was which one. There was some idea of having one of Muʿtasim's own sons, Ahmad, a mature man of known ability. Bughā the Elder is said to have argued, perhaps with the wisdom of hindsight, 'We should appoint someone we fear and respect because then we will remain with him. If we appoint someone who fears us, then we will compete among ourselves and end up by killing each other.'[16] In the end, they chose a more malleable candidate, one of Muʿtasim's grandsons, and Bughā's prophecy, if such it was, was soon proved correct.

The new caliph, who took the title of Mustaʿīn, was twenty-eight but seems to have had no previous military experience. He was entirely beholden to the Turks for his elevation to the throne. He even appointed a Turk, Utāmish, as his vizier. This is the only example of a Turkish vizier in the history of the caliphate: normally the heads of the civil administration were Arabs or Persians, well trained in the arts of writing elegant official correspondence and supervising the complex financial administration. The appointment of Utāmish was an attempt by the Turks to dominate the government entirely, but he was obliged to rely heavily on Muntasir's old secretary, Ahmad ibn al-Khasīb, perhaps because he himself was illiterate. Experience was to prove that while the Turks might dominate the military, they could not dispense with the services of Arabs and Persians in running the administration.

On Monday, 9 June a formal procession was arranged to show the new caliph to the people. Before sunrise the guards had taken their places lining the route that led to the great public audience hall. The new caliph, dressed in his robes of office, and preceded by the ceremonial spear, made his way to the hall. Here he was to be greeted by all the leading people in the state, the Abbasids, including the sons of Mutawwkil, the Tāhirids and other high-ranking individuals. Suddenly the ordered calm of the occasion was disrupted by the sound of shouting coming from the main street. A group of fifty horsemen, non-Turks attached to Muhammad ibn Abd Allah ibn Tāhir, the governor of Baghdad, galloped through the streets attacking the guards. They were soon joined by a crowd of ordinary people, shouting 'Victory to Muᶜtazz'. It was a spontaneous protest against the Turkish military coup. The guard counter-attacked and drove the crowd back along the streets to a point where the road narrowed. Here the rebels made a stand, some shouting the traditional Muslim cry, '*Allahu akbar*', and the guard attacked them with arrows and then with swords. Meanwhile, in the public audience hall, the oath of allegiance was being sworn to the new caliph. By mid-morning they had finished and the new caliph and his supporters retreated to the Hārūni palace, down the hill towards the river.

On the street the Turkish guards were finding life difficult. They were driven back and the crowd pushed on into the public audience hall. Here, where only a couple of hours earlier the Abbasid elite had pledged allegiance to the new caliph, they set about pillaging. They entered the armoury and took all the swords, shields and coats of mail they could lay their hands on. Our bourgeois sources speak with disdain of spears and shields in the hands of the rabble, bath attendants and grocers' boys.[17] In central Sāmarrā, any Turks who were found were waylaid and deprived of their weapons by people described as 'sellers of barley-juice and dried fruits, bath attendants, water carriers and rabble from the markets', and prisoners escaped from the jails. It seems that matters calmed down after this, but the new regime was clearly deeply unpopular among many ordinary people and the Turks were unable to assert control over all the city. The position was made much more dangerous for the Turks because other elements in the military were prepared to join the civilian protesters against them.

The winter of 862/3 seems to have passed fairly quietly, but trouble erupted the next spring. The immediate cause was the death in combat of two veteran commanders of Muslim forces on the Byzantine frontier. Many ordinary Muslims were outraged that these people had perished while the Turks made no effort to support the frontier provinces. This opened the way for more widespread griev-ances. Tabari, who was in Iraq at the time, sums up the prevailing attitude.

> The Muslims' hearts were heavy because the two heroes had died so soon after each other. Moreover, they had already been appalled by Mutawwakil's death at the hands of the Turks and the way in which the latter had taken over the affairs of the Muslims. The Turks killed any caliph they wanted to and appointed anyone they liked in his place without any reference to religious authority or to the opinions of the Muslims.[18]

In March 863 trouble broke out in Baghdad. Popular opinion demanded action against the Byzantines and troops in the city demanded their pay. The prisons were opened and the files with their records thrown into the river and destroyed. One of the pontoon bridges was cut loose from its moorings and the other burned. The houses of two prominent Christian bureaucrats were sacked. Meanwhile popular enthusiasm for the *Jihād* was running high with volunteers coming from Jibāl, Fars and Ahwāz. Wealthy individuals in Sāmarrā and Baghdad made it their business to give money to support these people, partly out of the desire to endorse a pious endeavour but partly too, no doubt, to protect themselves from people who might turn nasty. Meanwhile the government did nothing to aid the holy war.

The atmosphere remained very volatile. On 14 May unknown people attacked the prison in Sāmarrā and freed everyone in it. A group of leading Turks, including Utāmish, Bughā and Wasīf, went out to find the perpetrators but were attacked with stones and Wasīf was injured by the contents of a boiling cooking pot. After this Wasīf gave orders to the fire hurlers (*naffātīn*) to torch the houses and residences in the area, and Tabari records seeing the burnt-out quarter with his own eyes.[19]

At the same time the financial position was worsening. Utāmish had been put in charge of the administration by Mustaᶜīn. Now he, his secretary and the queen mother seem to have combined to loot the treasury. The soldiers' salaries fell into arrears and Wasīf and Bughā were excluded from power. On Thursday, 4 June the troops mutinied. Utāmish was in the Jawsaq Khāqāni section of the palace with the caliph. He tried to flee but found himself surrounded. He threw himself on the caliph's protection but was rejected. On Saturday he was dragged out of the royal palace and slaughtered. The enraged troops went on to pillage his house and Tabari was told of enormous quantities of furniture, rugs and household items which were taken from it.[20] Needless to say, the killing of the vizier meant merely that the financial problems were passed on to his successor.

Financial problems certainly contributed to the growing rift between the leading Turkish officers, such as Wasīf and Bughā the Younger, and the rank and file. The officers, with their palaces in Sāmarrā and estates in the country, could maintain a grand and affluent lifestyle, but it was very different for the ordinary soldiers, trying to make do with irregularly paid salaries. They found their champion in the aggressive and charismatic figure of Bāghir. Bāghir had been one of the assassins of Mutawwakil and had done very well out of it. He had been given estates near Kūfa which were farmed out to a local Persian landowner, who paid 2,000 *dīnār*s a year to Bāghir's Jewish secretary. One day one of Bāghir's agents was assaulted. The outraged Turk demanded that the assailant be punished but the man had friends in the administration, especially someone called Dulayl the Christian, who was Bughā the Younger's secretary and was also in charge of paying the army. Dulayl refused to give him up and Bughā supported him. On 29 January 865 there was a confrontation. Bāghir, angry and very drunk, determined to confront Bughā. Bughā was in the bath and Bāghir waited for him to get out before demanding that he kill Dulayl. Bughā prevaricated, saying that he would hand Dulayl over to Bāghir but not until he had appointed someone else to fill his post. Bāghir meanwhile gathered his cronies, all men who had been with him at the assassination of Mutawwakil, and they renewed the oaths they had taken that night and promised to help him in killing the caliph, Bughā and Wasīf, 'who had taken every-thing and left us with nothing' – clearly an exaggeration, at least in Bāghir's case.

Palaces being what they are, this compact did not remain secret for long. Bāghir's divorced wife told the caliph's mother. The caliph sent for Bughā and Wasīf, imagining that they were in on the plot, and reproached them: he had not asked to be made caliph, but they and their friends had put him on the throne anyway. Now they wanted to kill him. Wasīf and Bughā decided to strike first. Bāghir was sum-moned and shoved into one of Bughā's bath houses and chains were ordered for him. Bath houses, having thick walls, no windows and easily secured doors, made ideal temporary prisons. Then they sent men with axes in to finish him off.

To Wasīf and Bughā, Bāghir was a loud-mouthed and obstreper-ous lout, a man who was getting well above his station. For many of the Turks, however, he was a hero, who supported their interests against the establishment. Rioting broke out in the Hārūni palace, the government stables were burned and the animals seized. Asked to disperse by some of their officers, the Turks defiantly replied 'Yok, yok,' which, as Tabari notes, is the Turkish, then as now, for 'No, no'.[21] Faced with this mutiny, the caliph, Bughā and Wasīf decided that Sāmarrā was too dangerous for them and slipped away by river, heading for Baghdad, where they could expect a friendly welcome from the governor, Muhammad ibn Abd Allah ibn Tāhir, and the general populace, all of them hostile to Turkish rule.

The mutineers were at first nonplussed by the caliph's departure but, after pillaging the houses of administrators, stealing the riding animals and looting wine cellars, they began to take action. They forbade anyone to go by river to Baghdad: one unfortunate sailor who had rented out his boat to would-be escapers was given two hundred lashes and hanged from the mast.[22] The fugitives soon arrived in Baghdad, probably on 5 February, and the caliph took up residence in Ibn Tāhir's palace. Other Turks close to Wasīf and Bughā began to leave Sāmarrā. When they arrived in Baghdad, they went to see the caliph and threw themselves on the ground with their belts around their necks to ask for his forgiveness and suggested that he should return with them to Sāmarrā. He started to reproach them for ingratitude given all he had done for them, including putting their young sons on the state payroll and subsidizing their daughters' marriages. Their suggestion that he should return with them was greeted with mockery: they did not know how to address a caliph properly and Ibn Tāhir and the Baghdad aristocracy made fun of them. Finally the caliph said that they could return to Sāmarrā, where their salaries would be paid, but he was staying where he was.[23] Angering the Turks like this, and essentially saying that they were going to be of no importance any more, was not a prudent or intelligent move, but the whole confrontation shows the contempt in which these barbarian soldiers were held. They were to have their revenge within the year.

When the group returned to Sāmarrā they told their comrades of their rejection and humiliation. They needed a caliph they could call their own and, amazingly, they turned to Muʿtazz, so long the figurehead of the anti-Turkish party. Equally surprisingly, he agreed, no doubt seeing it as his last chance to reach the throne. A long and eloquent oath of allegiance was written out, proclaiming that the oath was an oath to God Himself and that anyone who disobeyed would be punished in this life and the next. Muʾayyad, Muʿtazz's brother, was to be heir apparent. Anyone who violated the oath was to lose all his possessions, which were to be given to the poor, and all his wives would be considered divorced. How far the Turks understood this orotund prose we do not know, but events were to show how lightly their promises lay on their shoulders.

The taking of the oath to Muʿtazz meant that war between Sāmarrā and Baghdad was now inevitable. In Baghdad, Muhammad the Tāhirid acted with speed and determination to establish a blockade of Sāmarrā. He wrote to supporters in Mosul and the Jazira to prevent supplies coming from the north. River traffic from Baghdad was prohibited: a ship carrying rice was apprehended and the captain fled, leaving his vessel abandoned until it sank.[24]

The city of Baghdad was now fortified. At the vast cost of 325,000 *dīnār*s, walls were constructed enclosing the main inhabited areas on both the east and west sides. Gates were constructed with passages big enough to shelter a hundred men, and catapults were set up on the walls and towers. By 22 February, the work was completed. To the north-west of the city, the lands around Anbar were flooded by breaching the canals and the bridges destroyed to prevent the Turks attacking from that direction: no doubt this made military sense at the time but it also contributed to the long-term degradation of the agricultural landscape of Iraq.[25] At the same time, Abd Allah wrote to all the tax officials in the empire, ordering them to send their receipts to Baghdad, not Sāmarrā.[26]

Muhammad also tried to persuade commanders of troops throughout Iraq and beyond to join him and his caliph Mustaᶜīn in Baghdad, and many local commanders with small groups of men answered his call. As in the first siege of Baghdad, the common people of the city played an important part in its defence, but, in contrast with the first siege at the time of Amīn, this time they were armed by the government. At first they were simply given tar-covered mats to protect themselves and bags full of rocks and brick-bats.[27] In April they were put on a more organized footing. They were given clubs studded with iron nails and some had bows and arrows; there is no mention of swords or armour. Their names were entered into a register so that they could be paid, and they were allowed to choose their own commander.[28] On the first day they proved their worth defending the gates against the Turks, and they remained an important part of the defence of the city to the end of the siege. Hatred of the Turks and, no doubt, the desire to see their city once more the capital, with all the opportunities that would bring, mobilized a wide cross-section of society.

Despite the strength of popular support in Baghdad, it was the supporters of Muᶜtazz in Sāmarrā who took the initiative and forced the Baghdadis on to the defensive. On Saturday, 24 February 865 an expeditionary force of some five thousand Turks and two thousand allies from among the North African troops in the army was assembled outside Sāmarrā. In command was Abū Ahmad, son of Mutawwakil and brother to the Sāmarrā caliph Muᶜtazz. It may be remembered that Abū Ahmad had been with his father on the evening of his assassination but had conveniently disappeared to the lavatory at the time the murderers struck. He remained on close terms with a number of the Turks who had killed his father, especially Mūsā ibn Bughā the Elder, and he was the only member of the Abbasid family they really trusted. He was also the only member of the ruling family to embark on a military career.

He led the Sāmarrā troops down the east bank of the Tigris. Once again it was the people of the villages and small towns along the route who suffered: the population of the small towns and the remaining villages on the west bank 'fled for their lives, leaving farms and harvests behind. Farms were ruined, crops and furnishings looted, homes demolished and travellers on the roads were robbed.'[29] On Sunday, 10 March, three weeks after they had set out from Sāmarrā, the Turks set up camp outside the Shammasiya Gate on the north-east side of Baghdad.[30] There were never more than twelve thousand of them and they were constantly afraid of being surrounded in a hostile environment. The defenders of Baghdad were certainly much more numerous but they lacked the military skills and singleness of purpose of their enemies. Muhammad ibn Tāhir, directing affairs from the luxury of his palace, was a very different sort of leader from the tough and determined Abū Ahmad, sharing the camp of his men.

The Turks began to attack the newly constructed fortifications while the defenders retaliated by showering them with missiles from mangonels mounted on the walls. The irregular troops, defended by their mats, gave a good account of themselves. A second Turkish force of some four thousand was sent from Sāmarrā to attack the west side of Baghdad, but on 20 March they suffered a major setback when the defenders, both professionals and irregulars, drove them back, looting their camp in the process. The surviving Turks threw themselves into the river, trying to swim across to Abū Ahmad's camp on the west bank, but many were picked up by Baghdad troops stationed in river boats. Boatloads of Turkish heads were taken downstream to be displayed on the bridges of the city, while the Baghdad troops were rewarded with bracelets and other presents. The commanders were presented with lavish silk and brocade robes.[31]

It was a triumph for the Baghdadi forces but, despite the urging of his advisers, Ibn Tāhir refused to follow it up by pursuing the enemy and slaughtering their wounded. Throughout, he stuck to his cautious, defensive policy. Instead of military action, a grandiloquent account of the victory was prepared and read out to the people of Baghdad in the old Friday Mosque which Mansūr had built in the centre of his Round City.[32] It dwelt at length on God's support for the cause of Mustaᶜīn, on Mustaᶜīn's generous offer of peace to the attackers, on the reckless leadership of the 'page boy' (*ghulām*) Abū Ahmad, and on the crimes committed by the Turks against ordinary

Muslims. Ibn Tāhir's role as commander of the defence is stressed throughout.

Warfare settled down to a pattern of Turkish attacks and Baghdadi resistance. On one occasion an attacker got a grappling hook to the top of the wall and climbed up but he was not supported and the defenders cut off his head and used a mangonel to throw it back into the Turkish camp.[33] Unusual, even comic, incidents were remembered. On one occasion in the heat of battle, a defender, with whom readers of this book may well sympathize, became confused about which caliph he was supposed to be supporting and called out for Muᶜtazz rather than Mustaᶜīn by mistake. The poor man was killed on the spot and his head sent to Ibn Tāhir and displayed along with those of other enemies. In the evening, his mother and brother came with his body on a bier, crying out that they wanted his head. The authorities refused and the head remained on display for all to see.[34]

One of the archers defending the walls told how a North African bowman used to approach and bare his backside to them, farting in their direction and shouting abuse. 'One day I chose an arrow for him and shot it right up his arse. It came out of his throat as he fell dead and a group of men came out of the gate and hung him up for public display.'[35] There were also unlikely heroes on the Baghdad side. Tabari heard about a young boy who set out one day with a bag of stones and a sling. He would fire them at the Turks and their mounts, always hitting his mark. Four Turkish archers began to shoot at him but missed repeatedly while his stones hit their mounts and threw them. Finally the Turks were joined by four North African horsemen with lances and shields and they charged at him. He was too quick for them and dived into the river. They tried to follow but could not catch him, and he reappeared on the other bank of the river, taunting them from a safe distance.[36] No doubt such stories circulated quickly and raised the morale of the defenders.

From the beginning of the siege in February 865 until mid December there was effectively a stalemate around Baghdad. On some occasions the Turks managed to penetrate the defences for a while, as on 8 September, when they broke the fortifications by the Anbar Gate to the north-east and rampaged through the streets, burning the workshops of the water-wheel workers and hoisting their flags on the roofs of shops. Everyone fled before them. By the afternoon regular forces commanded by Bughā had counter-attacked, killing some and driving the rest out through the gates. The common people helped to get rid of them. By the evening it was all over; many Turkish heads were sent to Ibn Ṭāhir and orders were given for the Anbar Gate to be bricked up to prevent it happening again.[37]

When the end came, it was not military defeat but hunger and internal discontent which brought the siege to a close. As late as November, the Baghdadi forces were still able to launch a sortie that almost destroyed the Turkish armies and allowed the irregulars to pillage their camp. It was only the determination of their commander, Abū Ahmad, which rallied the Turks and enabled them to drive the undisciplined citizens back. On 24 November there was a major demonstration outside Ibn Ṭāhir's palace as people cried 'Hunger, hunger' and demanded food, complaining of the high prices and the hardship being caused. Ibn Ṭāhir held them off with promises, but he opened negotiations with Muʿtazz. While discussions continued, the common people demonstrated again, demanding that he either lead them into battle or make peace. There were riots; the women's prison (this is the only record we have of this institution) was broken into and the inmates freed. Only the deployment of armed regular soldiers stopped them from doing the same for the men's prison.

Finally, on 27 December, five ships loaded with flour and other food supplies sent by Muʿtazz from Sāmarrā arrived in Baghdad and the people heard that Ibn Ṭāhir had deposed Mustaʿīn and accepted Muʿtazz as caliph.[38] Ibn Ṭāhir ordered his commanders to take the oath of allegiance and robes were distributed. Ibn Ṭāhir may have been prepared to change his allegiance easily but he had not counted on popular opinion. Crowds gathered outside his palace, proclaiming their allegiance to Mustaʿīn. The outer doors were broken down and it was only with difficulty that three hundred armed soldiers drove the people back. Still they continued to abuse Ibn Ṭāhir. When they got round to insulting his mother, the usual way of being really offensive to a man, he asked one of his companions, 'How on earth did they find out my mother's name? It was only known to a few of my father's slave girls', and his companion was amazed by his easygoing attitude.[39] Finally, to appease the crowd, Mustaʿīn was produced. He appeared above the gate of the palace, clad in the mantle of the Prophet, holding the ceremonial spear, with Ibn Ṭāhir by his side. He said that he was still caliph, he was not under duress and he would lead the prayers on Friday.

By Friday the secret was out and the people were aware that Ibn Ṭāhir was not being honest with them. They accused him of being prepared to use force to ensure that the Turks and North Africans dominated the city. Once more Ibn Ṭāhir and Mustaʿīn appeared on the palace roof. The crowd tried to persuade their caliph to leave the palace: he said that he was in no distress there but that he would soon leave for the palace of Umm Habib, daughter of Hārūn. Mustaʿīn was still allowed to act as caliph at the Feast of the Sacrifice (2 January 866) when, accompanied by Bughā and Wasīf, with the spear of authority and the spear of Solomon carried before him, he led the public prayers.[40]

Despite this public confirmation of his status, Mustaʿīn's position was very vulnerable. Ibn Ṭāhir continued to play a devious game, telling the caliph he was simply negotiating peace while assuring his enemies that he would agree to Mustaʿīn's deposition. On 7 January 866, Ibn Ṭāhir opened formal negotiations with Abū Ahmad. Accompanied by two hundred cavalry, he awaited the Abbasid prince in a red pavilion that had been pitched just outside the city walls. Abū Ahmad arrived by boat. The negotiations were mostly about money; one third of the revenues were to go to Ibn Ṭāhir and the Baghdad army, two-thirds to the Turks of Sāmarrā. Mustaʿīn was to be responsible for paying the Baghdad army in the interim. The next day, Ibn Ṭāhir rode to Mustaʿīn and told him he was deposed. At first he resisted, thinking that Bughā and Wasīf, who had escorted him six days before at the Feast of Sacrifice prayers, would support him. He was soon disabused when they revealed that they were in on the plot. Ibn Ṭāhir sent a message to him that he had no choice but to abdicate and, anyway, 'if you take off the cloak of authority, by God it will not make matters any worse for it is already torn beyond repair. You will give up nothing by doing this.' Suddenly aware of the extent of the treachery that surrounded him, the young caliph simply said, 'Here is my neck, the sword and the execution mat.'

The end was not to be so quick. The deposed caliph was to be allowed to retire to the Hijaz, where he was to be given an estate, but allowed to travel only in the areas between Mecca and Medina. He remained suspicious and insisted that senior courtiers and members of the Abbasid family go to Sāmarrā to get Muʿtazz's signature on the document. On Saturday, 12 January, Ibn Ṭāhir arrived with judges, lawyers and jurists to witness the document of resignation and servants came to take away the caliphal jewels. The emissaries returned from Sāmarrā on 24 January with Muᶜtazz's confirmation of the terms and on Friday, 25 January Muᶜtazz was acknowledged as caliph in the mosques of Baghdad.[41]

The second siege of Baghdad was over and there was now only one caliph, Muᶜtazz, in Sāmarrā. Mustaᶜīn was banished, not, as had originally been stipulated, to the Holy Cities, but to Wasit in southern Iraq, no longer a threat. The problems of the caliphate were far from over. There was a continuing financial crisis. Long-term decline in agricultural revenues had been accelerated by the damage done in the wars – burned harvests and flooded fields as armies crisscrossed the fertile lands of Iraq, laying waste as they passed. The Turks of Sāmarrā were determined to secure a monopoly of the revenues that were received. The aggrieved garrisons of Baghdad and other areas sought to secure a share for themselves. The demands of the military were immediate and very pressing. Good government and stewardship of the land would have to wait.

Chaos at the centre led to the collapse of caliphal authority in the provinces. Just as civil wars in the early-fifth-century Roman Empire led to garrisons being withdrawn from Britain and the province slipping out of the empire, so the civil war in Baghdad meant Abbasid commanders and troops were withdrawn from outlying areas to help one side or another. In Rayy, the local inhabitants begged the Abbasid army commander to stay, but they had scores to settle in Sāmarrā and left the people to their own devices: Rayy, the strategic stronghold on the way to Khurasan and birthplace of Hārūn al-Rashīd, was never under the power of the caliphs again. Rebellions and secession movements became apparent in many provinces, and areas such as Syria, much of Jazira, Armenia and Azerbayjān, Egypt and much of Arabia soon slipped from caliphal control. These areas were easily lost but later caliphs would have to work hard to regain any of them. With the loss of territories went the loss of their revenues, adding another element to the vicious downward spiral.

The new caliph was just nineteen when the Turks acknowledged him as their leader. He was a tall man with white skin and thick dark hair. His eyes were beautiful and his face narrow and handsome.[42] He never stood a chance.

Some of his problems were of his own making. At the time when his father Mutawwakil had been murdered, he had been the candidate of the anti-Turkish party, but he allowed himself to be placed on the throne by those very same Turks who had opposed him so viciously before. They may have made him an offer he could not refuse, but they clearly had little long-term loyalty to their young sovereign. Other problems were ones he inherited, above all the continuing financial crisis, and it was this which turned his opportunity into a nightmare.

At first, the new caliph's reign was marked by a spirit of reconciliation. Ibn Tāhir was allowed to retain his position in Baghdad, and Bughā and Wasīf were restored to favour. Wasīf was helped by his sister Su'ād, who had been brought up by the caliph's brother Mu'ayyad. Through her, he sent 1 million *dirham*s he had prudently buried in his palace, and this smoothed the way for his restoration to power. Despite their differences, the rank-and-file Turks put pressure on Muʿtazz to restore both Wasīf and Bughā to favour, saying that 'they are our seniors and our chiefs'.[43]

However, the new caliph soon moved to rid himself of any rivals. The Abbasids never developed the sort of systematic fratricide that the Ottoman sultans of the late sixteenth and seventeenth centuries used to dispose of their brothers, with all the macabre trappings, the use of deaf mutes and the silken bowstring to execute the brothers or a new sultan, but Muʿtazz was certainly taking no chances. His first victim was his brother Mu'ayyad, his companion in many adversities. He was now arrested and put in chains in a small room in the Jawsaq palace. On 24 July 866, he was officially deprived of his position as heir apparent and on 8 August the judges and legal witnesses were summoned to see his body being brought out without any wounds or marks on it. The corpse with his shroud and funerary perfumes was carried on a donkey to his mother, and he was allowed a decent burial. Nobody believed he had died of natural causes but opinion was divided between those who believed that he had been wrapped in furs until he died of overheating and those who held that he was seated on a block of ice and covered until he froze to death.[44]

Mu'ayyad's place in prison was taken by his other brother, Abū Ahmad, the very man who had led Muʿtazz's forces so successfully against Baghdad. Immediately after the victory he had been given robes of honour and a golden crown studded with jewels in the form of a *qalansūwa* (it must have looked a bit like a papal tiara). Then,

seated on a throne with a jewelled sword, he watched as his commanders were given their robes. That had been on 9 February 866.[45] Now in
August he was confined in the same dismal dungeon in which his
brother had just died, and his life was saved only because of the regard
in which he was held by the Turkish troops he had commanded.

The defeated caliph of Baghdad, Mustaᶜīn, had no such powerful
supporters to save him. Despite the most solemn written guarantees,
he had not been allowed into exile in the Hijaz but had been kept at
Wasit. In October he was brought to Sāmarrā under heavy escort. A
Christian doctor called Fadlān who accompanied him recalled that
he was full of foreboding as he approached the capital. A group of
horsemen was seen coming towards them from the city. The ex-
caliph, who was travelling in a litter with his nanny on the other side,
asked Fadlān to go and find out who they were: 'If it is Saᶜīd the
Gatekeeper, then I am done for!' Fadlān came back with the news
that it was indeed Saᶜīd, and Mustaᶜīn replied with the ancient
Muslim expression of resignation, 'We are from God and to Him we
return'. As the horsemen approached, Fadlān wisely hung back from
the group and watched from a distance as the men forced Mustaᶜīn
to the ground and finished both him and his nanny off with their
swords. When he arrived on the scene he saw the corpse, now headless and clothed only in his drawers. Fadlān and his companions
brought earth from the nearby river bank and covered the corpses.
Then they went on their way. When the head was brought to
Muᶜtazz, he was playing chess. 'Put it over there,' he ordered, and
went on with the game. When he had finished he ordered that the
head be buried and Saᶜīd the Doorkeeper be given 50,000 *dirham*s
and a lucrative government post in Basra.[46]

Disposing of his rivals among the Abbasid family did not solve
Muᶜtazz's fundamental problems. Tabari explains the position quite
clearly: the payments required by the Turks, North Africans and
other soldiers every year amounted to 200,000,000 *dīnār*s, which was
the equivalent of two years' taxes for the entire realm. The position
was unsustainable but the military would stop at nothing to ensure
their economic survival. Everywhere provinces were taken over by
usurpers and warlords to whom the caliph in Sāmarrā was increasingly irrelevant. Baghdad was convulsed by unrest as different groups of
soldiers tried to force Ibn Tāhir to pay them and prowled around the
city, seeing what they could extort from the citizens. No money

reached Sāmarrā from Baghdad or from the once rich lands that surrounded it.

In Sāmarrā the angry and desperate troops turned on their own leaders. Relations between Wasīf, Bughā and the rank and file had long been difficult, and the reconciliation that had followed the end of the siege of Baghdad proved short lived. Wasīf was the first victim. On 29 October 867 there was a riot when the Turks and others confronted Wasīf and Bughā and demanded their pay. Wasīf's response was more blunt than tactful: 'Do you really think we have got any money? You'll have to take dirt!' Bughā and the others went off to consult the caliph and Wasīf was left on his own. Almost immediately he was set upon by the troops, dragged out of the house of one of his officers to which he had fled, and decapitated. They put his head on one of the sticks that people used to move bread around in the ovens and paraded it through the streets. They had hoped to pillage his houses but Sālih and his other sons were too quick and put the family residences into a state of defence.[47]

It was Bughā's turn next. He was increasingly unpopular with the rank-and-file Turks, and when he discovered that he had lost the confidence of the caliph too, he decided to escape from Sāmarrā. In November 868, he headed north towards Mosul. He had with him about a thousand men, including five hundred of his own *ghulām*s, and masses of money. They left in haste and failed to bring any tents to protect them from the early winter cold, and one evening his men sent an officer to complain. Bughā lost his nerve and slipped away, unarmed and almost alone, going downstream to Sāmarrā, hoping to take refuge with Sālih, son of his old friend Wasīf. The guards on the bridge intercepted the boat and a message was sent to the caliph saying that Bughā was in captivity. The caliph, who had slept in his clothes fully armed and had drunk no wine since Bughā had led his men out, ordered that his head be brought immediately. Fifteen of Bughā's children fled to Baghdad, where they were rounded up by the Tāhirid authorities and imprisoned in Mansūr's old palace in the Round City.[48]

Wasīf's son Sālih was still trying to find money for the Turks. He had made up his mind that the government secretaries were deliberately withholding and hiding money that was due to the troops. On Thursday, 19 May 869, matters came to a head. The caliph slept late and when he woke up at midday he summoned the secretaries to meet him in the palace. Sālih launched an attack on them and there was a furious row. The caliph fled to his private quarters as Turkish troops burst in and arrested the unfortunate ministers. They were beaten up and taken away and put in heavy chains, but all attempts to extort money from them failed: there was simply none to be had.[49]

As far as the rank-and-file Turks were concerned, a caliph who could not pay them was no use at all. They offered Muᶜtazz one last chance: if he would give them their pay, they would kill Sālih ibn Wasīf for him. It was a tempting offer but Muᶜtazz had no cash on the table. He sent to his mother, the formidable Qabīha, who replied, falsely as it turned out, that she had nothing to give. It was the end of the road for the young caliph. On 11 July 869 they came for him. Alarmed by the shouts of the approaching soldiers, he took refuge in his private quarters. They demanded that he come out. He replied that he had taken medicine the day before and it had given him diarrhoea. He had already been to the lavatory twelve times that day and was too weak to come out. If they did not believe him, they could send a representative in to see for himself. They were not interested in excuses. He was dragged out and probably beaten with clubs. When he emerged into the sunshine, his shirt was torn in several places and there were traces of blood on his shoulders. They stood him in the sun in the palace courtyard. It was high noon in Sāmarrā. In the pitiless summer heat, he attempted to ease his burning feet by lifting one and then the other from the baking surface of the court. The Turks continued to beat him around the head and abuse him. In the end they tired of their fun, and he was taken inside and a deed of abdication drawn up and signed. It proclaimed that Muᶜtazz had come to realize how unfit he was for the office of caliph and how much better it would be for the Muslims if he resigned. He now did this freely and without any compulsion.[50] It stipulated safe conduct for the caliph's sister, mother and young son, but none for the man himself. Despite the obviously false assertion that the caliph was acting voluntarily, the document was witnessed by the judicial establishment, spineless and ineffectual as usual in the face of military power. Then he was taken away and refused food and water for three days: even when he requested a mouthful from the well it was denied. Finally, on the evening of 16 July, he was taken, miserable and alone, to a small brick vault and the door was shut. The next morning he was dead. The usual cynical charade was then played out: members of the Abbasid family and army commanders came to witness that there were no marks on his body. Finally he was laid to rest next to his brother Muntasir in an out-of-the-way part of the Jawsaq palace.

A new caliph was soon found. One might imagine that after the terrible fate of Mu^{c}tazz men might be reluctant to accept this truly poisoned chalice, but the new man was determined that he could do better and restore the caliphal office to its former glory. Muhtadi, son of caliph Wāthiq, and so cousin to Muntasir and Mu^{c}tazz, was comparatively old, thirty-eight at the time of his accession. He was short, balding and stout with broad shoulders and a wide forehead. His eyes were dark blue, possibly inherited from his Greek mother, his beard long, and his face habitually wore a stern expression.[51]

We do not know why he was chosen from among the numerous Abbasid princes, but he may have put himself forward to deliver his programme for the caliphate. The court of Muhtadi was going to be very different from that of his predecessors. There was to be no wine, no musical instruments, no frivolities of any sort. Singers of both sexes were banished from Sāmarrā. The lions that were kept in the caliphs' palace were to be killed and the dogs driven out.[52] His family were to live a life of pious austerity. He boasted that, unlike Mu^{c}tazz, 'I have no mother who requires the sum of ten million *dirham*s every year as expenses for her slave girls, eunuchs and hangers-on. As for me and my children, we only want enough for food and something for my brothers who have fallen on hard times.'[53] He was also going to take the public role of the office seriously. He would sit in person every week in the *Mazālim* (Complaints) Court to hear the petitions of his subjects, a just and accessible monarch. He hoped and believed that this policy would build up goodwill among ordinary Muslims which would enable him to break free of the tyranny of the Turkish military. He might have succeeded given time, but financial crisis and the demands of the soldiery meant that his policy was overtaken by events.

There were a number of players in the drama that overwhelmed his caliphate during the autumn of 869 and the spring and early summer of 870. There were the rank-and-file Turks, based in the quarters of Dur and Karkh in Sāmarrā. They were only about five thousand strong but they were well armed and determined. Their main concern was to ensure that they got paid. They were deeply suspicious of any attempts to replace them with other troops, North Africans, for example, and they were quick to believe that they were being defrauded by the Turkish officers. The Turkish officers were led by second-generation sons of men who had originally served Muᶜtasim, notably Mūsā, son of Bughā the Elder, and Sālih, son of Wasīf; both men had been heavily implicated in the murder of Mutawwakil nine years before but had now acquired estates and large households of their own. Then there were the civil administrators, Persians and Arabs, whom the Turks, officers and rank and file alike, suspected of embezzling money that should rightly have been theirs.

Muhtadi became caliph on 11 July 869 and by early September his rule was already in crisis. In the last days of Muᶜtazz, the brutal and thuggish Sālih ibn Wasīf, desperate for money to pay the Turks, had seized the most senior figures in the bureaucracy and attempted to extort money from them. He now set to work torturing them. Unusually we have an account of what happened from the lips of the torturer himself, a man called Dūshābi, and pretty chilling reading it is too. What comes across most clearly is his ferocious delight in inflicting pain and his contempt for the lack of endurance shown by his wretched victims. His job was not to kill them, at least not yet, but to extort any remaining money they might have from them. He told the first object of his fury, Ahmad ibn Isra'il, that 'Death in this life and torment and ignominy in the next are your fate if you do not receive God's pardon and mercy and your caliph's pardon and forgiveness.' The only way Ahmad could do this was to give up any money he might have. When words were not enough, Dūshābi called for whips and ordered that Ahmad be stood in the sun. 'I assailed him with ferocity, though success might have slipped through my grasp if he had shown a little courage and fortitude.' Eventually Ahmad agreed to write a bond for 19,000 *dīnār*s, which he probably did not have, and was let off the hook for while. The next man, Abu Nūh (Noah), was a convert from Christianity and Dūshābi was able to accuse him of keeping to his old faith in private and violating Muslim women; 'Abu Nūh made no reply to this, weak and miserable man that he was'. The third man, Hasan ibn Makhlad, was 'already weak and humiliated' and Dūshābi taunted him, saying someone like him should never appear humble and impotent. Eventually he signed a bond for a large jewel worth some 30,000 *dīnār*s.

Their ordeal was far from over. Hasan was sent back to prison, but on 8 September the other two were brought before Ṣāliḥ ibn Wasīf at the public gate of the palace. Each received five hundred lashes, the floggers taking it in turns to give two lashes then stand aside while their companions gave the next two. Finally they were paraded through the streets on the backs of water-sellers' donkeys, facing the tails with their lacerated backs plain for all to see. Ahmad and Abu Nūh were both dead before the gruesome procession had finished.

The flogging of the secretaries made a deep impression: these were respected figures, well educated in the great traditions of Abbasid bureaucracy, and this barbarous assault showed both the power and the savagery of the Turkish leadership. The caliph could only lament, 'Is there no other punishment than the whip and death? Is imprisonment not enough?', and he repeated over and over again, 'We are from God and to Him we return.'[54]

After the destruction of the secretaries, Sāmarrā remained quiet for a few months, though Baghdad was in a state of constant turmoil. In December, however, a new crisis broke out. This was caused by the arrival of Mūsā ibn Bughā the Elder from Rayy. Mūsā had been sent to northern Iran to counter the menace posed by Alid rebels in the mountains south of the Caspian Sea. His men had had some success, but they were convinced that Ṣāliḥ ibn Wasīf and his friends were hogging the state funds while they foundered in this inhospitable terrain. They wanted to be back in Sāmarrā to safeguard their interests. Mūsā decided to abandon the campaign and return. The caliph was appalled: Mūsā and Ṣāliḥ were bitter rivals and the former's presence in the capital would certainly exacerbate an already tense situation. But there was more to it than that. Mūsā was abandoning an important strategic area to heretic rebels. Muhtadi lamented to God that Mūsā had betrayed the trust of the Muslims. He himself would have fought for the Muslims anywhere they were under attack as a good caliph should. But God would have to reward his good intentions, because he had no supporters to make his wishes a reality.

On 19 December, Mūsā and his troops entered Sāmarrā. He went straight to the caliph, who was sitting in the Complaints Court, and hauled him out and took him away, while the Turks plundered the palace. Muhtadi remonstrated with him and Mūsā swore by the grave of Mutawwakil that he intended the caliph no harm. It was not a reassuring message: Mūsā had, after all, been one of the Turks who had participated in Mutawwakil's assassination and everyone knew it. Meanwhile Sālih, finding his support among the Turks slipping away, had gone into hiding. From his place of concealment, Sālih wrote to say that he had substantial sums of money, some of it confiscated from the secretaries, and that they should all sleep on the matter. The caliph urged reconciliation, which made Mūsā and his followers even more suspicious of him, and some Turks began to talk of deposing him.

Muhtadi decided to confront them. The Turks assembled in the audience hall and Muhtadi came out wearing his sword, perfumed and wearing clean robes. 'I have come to confront you, prepared to die. This is my sword and I shall fight with it so long as I can hold it. And, by God, if one hair of my head is harmed, you will all surely die. Have you no religion? Have you no shame? Have you no respect for God? How long will this rebellion against the caliphs, this boldness and effrontery against God, go on for?' And he went on to stress that he and his family were poor and had nothing worth taking. If they wanted to find Sālih and kill him, then they could, but he himself did not know where he was.[55]

It was a bold attempt to appeal to the dignity of his ancient office, and for a while, at least, the Turks were prepared to give him the benefit of the doubt. The rank-and-file Turks now approached the caliph directly, complaining that their leaders, men like Mūsā and Sālih, had prospered, acquired great estates and lived in luxury while they were in desperate want. In effect they offered him an alliance against the officers, asking him to appoint one of his brothers to be their commander and their direct link to him. He wrote back, thanking them for their loyalty but stressing again that he simply had no resources to offer them. He would gladly have met their needs by impoverishing his own family but they were already so poor that there was nothing to be gained by this. When the Turks heard the reply, they again demanded that he take personal command (and pay them) and that the proper military system be restored. They wanted every nine men to be under a sergeant, and every hundred under a commander, as it had been in the old days, and they wanted to be paid regularly every two months. Women and other hangers-on should be removed from the payrolls and officers should no longer be granted fiefs. On 12 January 870 the caliph replied, agreeing to their demands. A settlement that would satisfy both the caliph and the rank-and-file troops seemed possible. The only problem was Mūsā ibn Bughā and the other officers, who were effectively being removed from their posts. There was stalemate as the officers gathered their followers and led them armed through the streets of the capital.

On 16 January news came that a party of Bedouin bandits had set fire to the small town of Balad, near Mosul. The caliph saw this as an opportunity to get the commanders to do something useful for a change and to remove them from the city. They refused to go, afraid, they said, that Sāliḥ ibn Wasīf would come out of hiding and make trouble in their absence. On Sunday, 28 January, the owner of a property opposite Sāliḥ's palace was sitting around chatting with his friends when they noticed a slave boy emerging from one of the alleys looking very scared. Before they had time to ask him what he was doing he had disappeared. Soon afterwards a henchman of Sāliḥ's appeared with four companions and disappeared into the alley. They soon reappeared, bringing Sāliḥ with them. It emerged that the boy had gone into a house in the alleyway wanting a drink of water when he heard someone say in Persian, 'Commander, hide quickly for a boy has come asking for water.' The boy heard these words and went to tell a henchman of Sāliḥ's, whom he knew. The man decided to betray his old master to his enemies. He found him in the house with a mirror in his hands, combing his beard. Sāliḥ rushed out of the room and the henchman was afraid he was going to get his sword, but when he followed him into the next room, he found him whimpering in a corner. He begged to be let go. His captor refused but made a bargain: he would take him past the residences of his family and supporters and if any of them came out to help him, he would let the prisoner go. The party set out, Sāliḥ barefoot with his head uncovered. No one came to his aid as the little party made their way 3 kilometres through the streets. When they reached Mūsā ibn Bughā's palace Sāliḥ found himself surrounded by his enemies. He was taken under escort to the caliph's palace, but as they passed the base of the great spiral minaret that still dominates the Sāmarrā skyline, one of the escort struck him from behind. After that, it was over very quickly.

The party, with Sāliḥ's head, dripping with blood and wrapped in one of the slaves' garments, was brought to the caliph at sunset, as he was praying. The next day, Monday, his head was paraded round the town and a poet was moved to compose a verse in which he said that Mūsā (Moses) had slain the pharaoh.

Mūsā ibn Bughā was now the only important survivor of the group of Turks who had killed Mutawwakil nine years before. But the blood-letting that had begun then was not yet over. After Sālih's death, Mūsā and his men had left Sāmarrā and marched north to fight the Bedouin who had burned Balad but, as before, they remained keenly interested in what was going on in the capital. There are a number of different accounts of what happened next[56] but the broad outlines at least are clear. According to some sources, the caliph tried to use Mūsā's absence to undermine his position. He wrote to a senior commander in Mūsā's army, called Bāyikbāk, ordering him to take over command and bring Mūsā to him in chains. He had misjudged his man: Bāyikbāk took the letter straight to Mūsā and they agreed to act together against the caliph. Bāyikbāk went to court, arriving at the Jawsaq palace on Saturday, 16 June. He pledged his loyalty to the caliph but made excuses for not tackling Mūsā. Muhtadi was suspicious, and the protesting Bāyikbāk was deprived of his weapons and arrested. His armed followers surrounded the palace. Among Muhtadi's advisers was a member of the Abbasid family called Sālih ibn Alī, a direct descendant of the caliph Mansūr. He urged his master to be more daring than his predecessors. He reminded Muhtadi how, in the early days of the Abbasid caliphate, Mansūr had executed Abū Muslim and how, when Abū Muslim's followers saw his head, they had dispersed peacefully even though many of them had regarded him almost as a god. The caliph should do the same with this obstreperous Turk.

A little history is a dangerous thing. Muhtadi was impressed and summoned a blacksmith who made tent pegs and poles and had become a trusted intimate of his. Bāyikbāk was killed by this man and his head thrown out to his followers. They did not disperse peacefully. Instead they rioted and killed the commander of the guard. The caliph summoned other army units and the rank-and-file Turks who had pledged their loyalty to him such a short time before. There was a confused mêlée.

Muhtadi then decided to make a personal appeal to the Turks, as he had done before to good effect. He went out to them with his adviser Sālih ibn Alī, who had a Koran tied around his neck, and urged them to come to the aid of their caliph. Instead, they answered the appeals of the dead Bāyikbāk's relatives and all the Turks put aside their differences and united against the caliph. He appealed desperately for help. Sword in hand, he ran through the city, crying out for ordinary people to support him. 'People, I am the Commander of the Faithful. Fight to defend your Caliph!' Nobody came. As he ran through the deserted streets, past the blank, unwindowed mud-brick walls and barred doors of the houses, he realized that his gamble had failed. Eventually he took refuge in a palace. He put away his sword and changed into a plain white robe and went up to the roof, where he could jump from one building to another and escape his pursuers.

His enemies were hard behind him: dashing up the stairs, they found him on the roof and he was wounded by an arrow and had to give himself up. He did not last long. The Turks reproached him, with some justice, for his bad faith towards Mūsā and the murdered Bāyikbāk, to whom he had given written promises. There were different stories about how he died, but it was commonly believed that they killed him by crushing his testicles. He was dead by Wednesday, 20 June, and the next day his body was produced, washed and ready for burial with his face uncovered.

Muhtadi had had a bold vision for the restoration of a caliphate that would appeal to Muslim sentiment and have a broad popular base. Given time, he might have succeeded. If he had been in Baghdad, with its vast population of scholars, merchants and common people, he might have attracted the support he needed. In Sāmarrā, where most of the population were in the military or other sorts of government service, there was no such source of mass popular enthusiasm that might have allowed his policy to work. From now on it was clear that the military were in charge: no ruler could survive unless he cooperated with them.

The death of Muhtadi at the hands of the Turkish military marked the end of the nightmare in Sāmarrā but it did not lead to the restoration of the caliphate as it had existed on the night of Mutawwakil's assassination. The nine years of anarchy had undone the caliphate that Mansūr had constructed and Ma'mūn revived. In the east, the chaos in Sāmarrā had been accompanied by the collapse of Tāhirid power in north-eastern Iran. Control of the original homeland of the Abbasid movement passed into the hands of local

Muslim rulers who sent the caliphs nothing more than polite letters and a very distant deference. When the people of Rayy had pled with Mūsā ibn Bughā to defend them against the wild Daylamites of the mountains to the north, he had rejected their pleas and abandoned them to their fate so that he could pursue his ambitions in the capital. In the west, the Abbasid-appointed governor of Egypt, Ahmad ibn Tūlūn, made himself the first independent ruler of the country since Cleopatra.

For the next sixty years the caliphs and their supporters struggled to renew and extend their power. At the height of this revival, at the end of the short reign of Muktafi in 908, the caliphs exercised a shaky control over all of Iraq and much of Syria, Egypt and areas of western Iran. The Abbasid caliphate was a substantial regional power. All of this was to be lost once more during the long and disastrous reign of Muqtadir (908–32). The caliphate, plagued by financial crisis and ruined by military disorder, was reduced to complete impotence and effectively disappeared as a political power in the 930s. The diminishing resources provided by the devastated agricultural lands of Iraq could not sustain the ambitions of the caliphs. The last great vizier of the caliphs, Ibn Muqla, was confined in a dungeon, his hands, which had created the finest Arabic calligraphy, cut off in spiteful revenge. By this time the army had taken matters into their own hands, the great palaces were pillaged and abandoned, much of Baghdad lay in ruins, the irrigation systems were damaged beyond repair, and the great Nahrawan canal, breached to help a military adventure, was never to be restored. Bedouin brigands had even stolen the sacred Black Stone from the Kaaba in Mecca and the Byzantines were on the offensive all along the frontier. The failure of the caliphs to wage *Jihād* and protect the pilgrims was plain for all to see. In 935 a military adventurer by the name of Ibn Rā'iq took power as *Amīr al-Umarā,* Prince of Princes, depriving the Abbasids of the last remnants of their secular power.

The passing of the Abbasid caliphate marked the end of an era in many ways. It signalled the demise of the unity of the Muslim world under a single sovereign: in 909 a rival Shiite Fatimid caliphate was established in Tunisia and in 969 the Fatimids took Egypt. In 931 yet another caliphate was established by the Umayyads in distant Spain and Portugal. But the debacle of the Abbasids marked the end of a much longer story. The Abbasid caliphate was the last polity to use the resources of Mesopotamia to support a great empire. Since the third millennium BC a succession of powers, Sumerian, Babylonian, Assyrian, Achaemenid Persian and Sasanian Persian, had used the fertility generated by the Tigris and Euphrates to create great civilizations and world empires. The Abbasids were to prove the last representatives of this ancient tradition. By the tenth century, the broken and desolate landscapes, exploited by corrupt and grasping administrations and ravaged by marauding bands of unpaid soldiers, could support nothing more than small-scale principalities. The real powers in the Muslim world were to be based in Egypt, Iran and, later, Turkey.

The memory of the caliphate survived to inspire later generations. Muslim revivalists throughout history have seen its greatness and sought to restore its power, prestige and unity. The recollection of ancient greatness is a potent inspiration for Osama bin Laden and his followers. The cultural legacy of the Abbasid court was immensely influential. The poets they patronized are still read and acknowledged as among the greatest in the Arabic language, and the translations they sponsored formed the basis of higher learning not only in the Islamic world but in the medieval West as well. The Abbasids defined the style and performance of Muslim monarchy: they showed how a caliph and vizier should behave, how to decorate a palace, how to compose a formal proclamation; the flowing elegant script itself was a product of the Abbasid chancery. For the descendants of the gentleman farmer of Humayma it was an astonishing achievement.

Notes

KEY

Aghāni = al-Isfahāni, *Kitāb al-Aghāni*, ed. Yusuf al-Biqā'i and Gharīd al-Shaykh, 25 vols. (Beirut, 2000)

Akbbār al-Abbās = Anon., *Akbbār al-Abbās*, ed. A. A. al-Duri (Beirut, 1972)

Bal., *Ansāb* = al-Balādhuri, *Ansāb al-Ashrāf*, vol. iii, ed. A. A. al-Duri (Beirut, 1978)

Bal., Futuh = al-Balādhuri, *Futūh al-Buldān*, ed. M. J. de Goeje (Leiden, 1866)

CHAL = Ashtiany, Julia (ed.), *Abbasid Belles-Lettres: Cambridge History of Arabic Literature*, vol. ii (Cambridge, 1990)

Fihrist = al-Nadīm, *Fihrist*, ed. Rida Tajaddud (Beirut, 1988)

Hadāya = Anon., *Book of Gifts*, trans. Ghāda Qaddumi (Cambridge, MA, 1966)

Jah = al-Jahshiyāri, *Kitāb al-Wuzarā*, ed. M. al-Saqqa et al. (Cairo, 1949)

Jāhiz, *Qiyān* = *The Epistle on Singing-girls by Jāhiz*, trans. A. F. L. Beeston (Warminster, 1980)

Jāhiz, *Rasā'il* = *Rasā'il al-Jāhiz*, ed. A. M. Harun, 2 vols. (Beirut, 1991)

Ibn Abi Tāhir = Ibn Abi Tāhir Tayfūr, *Kitāb Baghdād*, ed. H. Keller (Leipzig, 1908)

Ibn Khall. = Ibn Khallikān, *Wafayāt al-aʿyān*, ed. I. Abbas, 8 vols (Beirut, 1968–72); *Ibn Khallikān's Biographical Dictionary*, trans. M. de Slane, 4 vols. (Paris, 1842–71)

Khatīb = al-Khatīb al-Baghdādi, *Ta'rīkh Baghdād*, ed. M. A. Atā, 24 vols. (Beirut, 1997)

Lassner = Lassner, Jacob, *The Topography of Baghdad in the Early Middle Ages: Text and studies* (Detroit, 1970)

Mas. = al-Masʿūdī, *Murūj al-dhahab*, ed. C. Pellat, 7 vols. (Beirut, 1966–79). References are to paragraph numbers

Mas., *Tanbīh* = Masʿūd, *Tanbīh wa'l-shrāf* (Beirut, 1981)

Misk. = Ibn Miskawayh, *Tajārib al-umam*, ed. H. F. Amedroz, 7 vols. (London, 1920–21). References are to vol. i of the Arabic text

Sābi, *Rusūm* = Hilāl al-Sābi, *Rusūm Dār al-Khilāfa*, ed. M. Awwad (Baghdad, 1964)

Shābushti = Shābushti, *Kitāb al-diyārāt*, ed. G. Awad (Baghdad, 1966)

Tab. = al-Tabari, Muhammad ibn Jarīr, *Annales*, ed., M. J. de Goeje et al., vol. iii
   (Leiden, 1879–1901)

Yaq. = al-Yaᶜqūbi, *Ta'rīkh*, ed. M. Houtsma, 2 vols. (Leiden, 1883)

Yaq., *Buldān* = *al-Yaᶜqūbi, Kitāb al-Buldān*, ed. M. J. de Goeje (Leiden, 1892)

Yāqūt = Yāgūt al-Hamawi, *Muᶜjam al-buldān*, ed. F. Wustenfeld (Leipzig,
   1866–70) (references are given, sv = sub voce, that is to the entry in this alpha-
   betical dictionary)

FOREWORD

1 For a good introduction, see Robinson, *Islamic Historiography*.
2 Jāhiz, *Rasā'il*, p. 139.

I REVOLUTION

1 *Akbbar al-Abbas*, p. 196.
2 *Akbbar al-Abbas*, pp. 198–9.
3 al-Istakhri, *Masālik al-Mamālik*, ed. M. J. de Goeje (Leiden, 1927), p. 260.
4 Tab., p. 115.
5 Tab., p. 33.
6 Tab., p. 35.

II MANSŪR AND HIS LEGACY

1 Tab., p. 60.
2 Tab., pp. 391, 414.
3 Tab., pp. 250, 307, 362.
4 Tab., p. 398.
5 Tab., p. 411.
6 Tab., p. 423.
7 Tab., pp. 392–3.
8 Tab., p. 393.
9 Tab., pp. 426–33.
10 Tab., p. 402.
11 Tab., pp. 417–18.
12 Tab., pp. 325–6.
13 Tab., p. 435.
14 Tab., p. 398.
15 Tab., pp. 445–6.
16 Tab., pp. 405–6.
17 Tab., p. 406.
18 Tab., p. 408.
19 Tab., pp. 99–115; Mas., 2,392–4.
20 Īsā b. Nahīk al-Akkī. Tab., p. 110.

21 Tab., p. 111.

22 Tab., p. 117.

23 Tab., pp. 143–317; Mas., 2,401–13.

24 Tab., p. 169, p. 203.

25 Tab., pp. 241–2.

26 Tab., p. 223.

27 Tab., p. 167.

28 Tab., p. 168.

29 Tab., p. 168.

30 Tab., pp. 154–5.

31 Tab., pp. 172–80.

32 Tab., p. 172.

33 Tab., pp. 195–6.

34 Tab., p. 205.

35 Tab., pp. 223–4.

36 Tab., p. 217.

37 Tab., pp. 228–9.

38 Tab., p. 229.

39 Tab., p. 247.

40 Tab., p. 252.

41 Tab., p. 254.

42 Tab., pp. 126–7, 330, 375.

43 Tab., pp. 328–31.

44 Muhammad ibn al-Ashᶜath al-Khuzāᶜī. Tab., p. 72; Bal., *Ansāb*, p. 89.

45 Tab., p. 466.

46 Tab., p. 494.

47 Tab., pp. 262, 375.

48 Bal., *Ansāb*, pp. 276–7.

49 *Aghāni*, xiii, pp. 228–9.

50 Tab., p. 359.

51 Tab., pp. 616–17; *Aghāni*, xxiii, pp. 113–14.

52 Bal., *Ansāb*, p. 275.

53 Tab., p. 188.

54 Bal., *Futūh*, p. 386.

55 Lassner, p. 78.

56 See, for example, the household of Ubayd Allah ibn Jaᶜfar b. al-Mansūr in *Aghāni*, xxiii, pp. 112–15.

57 Kilpatrick, *Making the Great Book of Songs*, p. 246.

58 Ibn Tayfur, p. 19.

59 Yaq., *Buldān*, p. 252.

60 Jah., p. 116: Bal., *Ansāb*, pp. 243–4.

61 Tab., pp. 405–6, 408.

62 Tab., pp. 488–90.

63 *Aghāni*, vi, p. 232.

64 Tab., p. 609.

65 Tab., p. 638.

66 Tab., pp. 620–1.

67 Tab., pp. 699–70.

68 Tab., p. 692.

69 *Fihrist*, p. 366.

70 Tab., p. 738.

71 Tab., p. 1,065.

72 Tab., p. 529.

73 *Aghāni*, vi, p. 121; v, p. 115.

74 Tab., p. 684.

75 *Aghāni*, vi, p. 240.

76 Yaq., *Buldān*, p. 256.

77 *Fihrist*, p. 587.

78 Tab., p. 273; Jah., p. 100.

79 Jah., pp. 117–19.

80 Jah., pp. 101, 114.

81 Jah., pp. 99–100.

82 See his *Siyar al-mulūk*, ed H. Darke (Tehran, 1962), 218–20, English trans.,
    H. Darke, *The Book of Government* (London, Routledge and Kegan Paul,
    1960).

83 Tab., p. 32; Jah., p. 87.

84 Much the same story is also told of Khālid's son Yahya (Jah., p. 229).

85 Tab., pp. 381–4.

86 Jah., p. 138.

87 Tab., p. 367.

88 Jah., pp. 133, 149.

89 Tab., p. 384.

90 Tab., p. 599; Jah., p. 136; see Abbott, pp. 23–5, 63, for a full discussion.

91 Tab., pp. 497–8; Jah., p. 150.

92 Tab., p. 631.

93 For example, Jah., pp. 180–2.

94 Jah., p. 188.

95 Jah., p. 178.

96 Jah., p. 177.

97 Jah., p. 91.

98 Jah., p. 177.

99 *Fihrist*, p. 539.

100 *Fihrist*, pp. 826–7.

101 *Fihrist*, p. 710.

102 Yaq., *Buldān*, p. 246.

103 Yaq., *Buldān*, p. 243.

104 Yaq., *Buldān*, p. 248.

105 Tab., p. 620.

106 Tab., p. 479.
107 Tab., p. 240.
108 Lassner, *Topography*, pp. 55–7.
109 Tab., p. 131.
110 Tab., p. 495.
111 Tab., pp. 416–17.
112 Tab., p. 354.
113 Tab., p. 387.
114 Tab., pp. 456–7.
115 Tab., pp. 451–5.
116 Tab., pp. 537–8.
117 Tab., p. 460.
118 Tab., pp. 486, 520.
119 Tab., p. 530.

III HĀRŪN AL-RASHĪD: THE GOLDEN PRIME

1 Abbott, pp. 23–4.
2 Tab., pp. 494–9.
3 Tab., pp. 497–8.
4 Tab., p. 496.
5 Tab., pp. 503–5.
6 Tab., p. 505.
7 Tab., pp. 506–7.
8 Tab., p. 545.
9 Tab., p. 523.
10 Tab., p. 580.
11 Tab., p. 545.
12 Tab., p. 668.
13 Tab., pp. 523–6.
14 Tab., pp. 545–6.
15 Tab., p. 548.
16 Tab., p. 458.
17 Tab., pp. 572–3.
18 Tab., p. 574.
19 Tab., p. 571.
20 Tab., p. 571.
21 Tab., pp. 601–2.
22 Tab., p. 646 for Muslim year 181 for examples.
23 Tab., pp. 603–4.
24 Tab., pp. 646, 647.
25 Tab., p. 637.
26 Tab., pp. 640–5.
27 Tab., pp. 635–7.

28 Tab., pp. 642–4.

29 Tab., p. 635.

30 Tab., p. 609.

31 Tab., p. 610.

32 Tab., p. 629.

33 Tab., pp. 638–9.

34 Tab., p. 646.

35 Tab., pp. 651–2.

36 Tab., p. 701.

37 Tab., p. 604.

38 Tab., p. 646.

39 Tab., pp. 708–9.

40 Tab., pp. 606–7.

41 Tab., pp. 606–7.

42 Tab., p. 610.

43 Tab., p. 646.

44 See article 'Rakka' in Encyclopaedia of Islam, second edition.

45 Tab., p. 647.

46 Tab., p. 649.

47 Tab., p. 654.

48 Tab., pp. 610–12.

49 Tab., p. 647.

50 Tab., pp. 651–2.

51 Tab., pp. 664–5.

52 Tab., p. 653.

53 Tab., pp. 678–9.

54 Tab., pp. 683–4.

55 Tab., pp. 681–3.

56 Tab., pp. 667–8.

57 Tab., p. 669.

58 Tab., p. 676.

59 Tab., pp. 613–14.

60 Tab., pp. 623–4.

61 Tab., pp. 669–72.

62 Tab., pp. 670–1.

63 Tab., pp. 671–2.

64 Tab., pp. 676–7; Mas., 2,588–95; Tanūkhi, *Table Talk*, p. 257; Abbott, pp. 196–8 (see also Jahshiyāri on this).

65 Mas., 2,589–91.

66 Tab., pp. 700–2.

67 Tab., p. 709.

68 Tab. p. 710, quoting a poem of Abū'l-Ma'ālī al-Kilābī.

69 Tab., pp. 695–6.

70 Tab., p. 696.

71 Tab., pp. 709–10.
72 Tab., pp. 713–15.
73 Tab., p. 704.
74 Tab., p. 712.
75 Tab., pp. 716–17.
76 Tab., pp. 720–1.
77 Tab., pp. 733–9.

IV THE WAR BETWEEN THE BROTHERS

 1 Tab., p. 771.
 2 Tab., p. 781.
 3 Tab., pp. 784–5.
 4 Tab., pp. 785–6.
 5 Tab., pp. 786–7.
 6 Tab., pp. 793–4.
 7 Tab., pp. 792–4.
 8 Tab., p. 810.
 9 Tab., p. 818.
10 Tab., p. 818.
11 Tab., pp. 796–8.
12 Tab., p. 808.
13 Tab., pp. 796–8.
14 Tab., pp. 819–20.
15 Tab., pp. 821–2.
16 Detail added from Mas. 2,628.
17 Tab., pp. 823–4.
18 Tab., p. 802.
19 Tab., pp. 802–3.
20 Tab., pp. 830–1.
21 Tab., p. 803.
22 Tab., pp. 804–5, abbreviated trans. with some variations based on Fishbein trans., pp. 58–9, incorporating his reading of the text.
23 Tab., pp. 836–8.
24 Tab., pp. 840–1.
25 Tab., pp. 842–6.
26 Tab., pp. 846–51.
27 Tab., pp. 851–5.
28 Tab., pp. 855–6.
29 Tab., pp. 860–4.
30 Tab., pp. 885–6.
31 Tab., pp. 896-7, abbreviated; trans. Fishbein, p. 165.
32 Tab., p. 883.
33 Tab., pp. 883–5 trans. after Fishbein, abbreviated.

34 Tab., pp. 873–80. The text of the Leiden edition is problematic here and I have abridged Fishbein's excellent translation, which is in itself a new edition of the poem based on the collation of the Leiden and Cairo editions and other witnesses.

35 Tab., pp. 890–1.

36 Tab., p. 887.

37 Tab., p. 897.

38 Tab., p. 911.

39 Tab., pp. 908–9.

40 Tab., pp. 909–11.

V POETRY AND POWER AT THE EARLY ABBASID COURT

1 Gruendler, Beatrice, *Medieval Arabic Praise Poetry* (London, 2002), pp. 42–7.

2 Ibn Khall., i, pp. 221–2, trans. i, pp. 204–5.

3 *Aghāni*, iii, p. 109.

4 trans. A. H. L. Beeston, CHAL, p. 280.

5 trans. Julia Bray, CHAL, p. 286.

6 Tab., p. 508.

7 Tab., p. 538.

8 trans. Julia Bray, CHAL, p. 289.

9 trans. Julia Bray, CHAL, p. 292.

10 trans. Julia Bray, CHAL, pp. 294–5.

11 trans. Julia Bray, CHAL, p. 298.

12 trans. Julia Bray, CHAL, p. 298.

13 Farmer, Harold, *A History of Arabian Music* (London, 1929).

14 What follows is based on his biography in *Aghāni*, v, 111–17.

15 Kilpatrick, pp. 40–7.

VI LANDSCAPE WITH PALACES

1 Jah., pp. 281–8.

2 Tab., p. 273.

3 Yaq., *Buldān*, pp. 238–54; Khatīb, i, pp. 50–141, trans. with commentary in Lassner, pp. 45–118.

4 Khatīb, i, p. 9.

5 Lassner, p. 238, n.17.

6 Yaq., *Buldān*, p. 238.

7 Tab., p. 322; Khatīb, i, p. 9.

8 Tab., p. 352.

9 Tab., pp. 426–33.

10 Tab., p. 537.

11 Khatīb, i, p. 93; trans. pp. 52–3.

12 Ibrāhīm ibn Alī al-Khutabi (d. 951) quoted in Khatīb, loc. cit.

13 Hillenbrand, pp. 390–1.

14 *Amurath to Amurath*, Gertrude Bell (London, 1911), p. 140.

15 Creswell, p. 248.

16 Tab., p. 333.

17 Tab., p. 396.

18 Tab., p. 394–5.

19 Tab., pp. 581–2, 608–9.

20 Tab., p. 573.

21 *Aghāni*, v, pp. 202–3.

22 Tab., p. 332.

23 Tab., p. 586; Ahsan, pp. 30–1.

24 Ahsan, pp. 31–3.

25 Ahsan, pp. 42–3.

26 Tab., p. 622.

27 Tab., p. 463.

28 Tab., p. 585.

29 Tab., pp. 582–3.

30 Tab., p. 409.

31 Tab., p. 488.

32 Tab., pp. 608–9.

33 Tab., p. 415.

34 Tab., p. 525.

35 Tab., p. 472.

36 Tab., pp. 510–13.

37 Tab., pp. 417–18.

38 Ahsan, pp. 181–4.

39 Tab., p. 516; Sourdel, *Questions*, p. 129.

40 Tab., pp. 524–5.

41 Tab., pp. 752–3.

42 This discussion of the palaces of Sāmarrā is based on Alistair Northedge, 'The palaces of the Abbasids at Sāmarrā', in ed. C. Robinson, *A Medieval Islamic City Reconsidered: an interdisciplinary approach to Sāmarrā* (Oxford Studies in Islamic Art, xiv, 2001).

43 *Aghāni*, v, p. 138.

44 Shābushti, p. 170.

45 Shābushti, p. 161.

46 Tab., pp. 1,331–2.

47 See the tabulated lists in Northedge, pp. 251–2.

48 Shābushti, p. 96.

49 Northedge, pp. 39–41.

50 Yāqūt, s.v.; Northedge, p. 259.

51 Misk., p. 258.

52 Misk., pp. 53–5.

53 Khatīb, i, p. 117.

54 Khatīb, i, pp. 117–20.

55 Watson, pp. 48–50.

56 Lassner, pp. 269–70, n.14 for refs. Also Yāqūt, s.v. *Dār al-shajara*.

57 Misk., pp. 195–9.

VII THE HAREM

1 See, for example, the denunciation of the harem by the general Mu'nis in Misk., p. 189.

2 Sābi, *Rusūm*, p. 120.

3 Mas., 2,593.

4 *Aghāni*, v, pp. 173–5.

5 Lassner, p. 78.

6 Lassner, p. 80; Tab., p. 757.

7 Tab., p. 757.

8 Lassner, p. 78; Yāqūt, s.v. *Qasr Umm Habīb*.

9 Lassner, p. 85, with trans.

10 Misk., p. 193.

11 *Aghāni*, x, p. 145.

12 Abbott, p. 138.

13 Mas., 2,961.

14 August 847 to December 861 (Mas., 2,872).

15 Tab., pp. 423, 442; Abbott, pp. 15–16.

16 Tab., p. 442.

17 Daughter of Sālih b. Alī: Tab., p. 466; Abbott, pp. 39–40.

18 Tab., p. 580.

19 Tab., pp. 757–8.

20 Peirce, pp. 28–9.

21 Peirce, pp. 61–3.

22 Peirce, esp. pp. 109–12.

23 Tab., pp. 1,081–7; Mas., 2,752–3; Ibn Khall., i, pp. 268–71.

24 Abbott, p. 12.

25 Ibn Khall., I, 289; trans. I, 270.

26 Mas., 2,752.

27 Abbott, pp. 234–5.

28 Tab., p. 138.

29 Tab., pp. 753, 1,329.

30 Tab., p. 1,365.

31 Mas., 2,978.

32 Mas., 3,109.

33 Mas., 3,241.

34 Mas., 3,015.

35 Jāhiz, *Qiyān*, para. 53.

36 *Aghāni*, xvi, pp. 267–8; Abbott, pp. 144–5.

37 For the story of Inān, see *Aghāni*, xxiii, pp. 72–9; Abbott, pp. 146–7.
38 Khatīb, x, pp. 411–21; Abbott, pp. 148–9.
39 Tab., p. 590.
40 Tab., p. 836; Abbott, p. 209.
41 Tab., pp. 1,029, 1,102.
42 *Aghāni*, x, p. 138.
43 *Aghāni*, x, pp. 154–6.
44 *Aghāni*, x, p. 146.
45 *Aghāni*, x, p. 144.
46 *Aghāni*, x, p. 142.
47 *Aghāni*, x, p. 143.
48 *Aghāni*, x, p. 155.
49 Tab., p. 405.
50 Tab., p. 510.
51 Abbott, pp. 32–9.
52 Tab., pp. 543–4; Abbott, p. 32.
53 Abbott, pp. 38–9.
54 Abbott, p. 30.
55 *Hadāya*, caps. iii, 148.
56 Abbott, p. 140.
57 Abbott, pp. 154–5.
58 *Aghāni*, xviii, p. 234; Abbott, p. 152.
59 Lassner, pp. 72–3; Abbott, p. 238.
60 Abbott, pp. 236–7.
61 Abbott, pp. 242–7.
62 Yaq. p. 519.
63 See the account in Mas., 3,449–51, taken from Muhammad ibn Alī al-Misri al Khurasāni al-Akhbāri's oral account of the history of the caliphs given to al-Qādir.
64 Tab., pp. 610–12; Abbott, pp. 172–3.
65 Abbott, pp. 178–88.
66 Tab., p. 730, trans. Williams, p. 291.
67 Tab., p. 775.
68 Abbott, p. 299.
69 Mas., 3,451, trans., pp. 390–1; for this and other examples of cross-dressing, see E. Rowson, 'Gender Irregularity as Entertainment: Institutionalized Tranvestism at the Caliphal Court in Medieval Baghdad', in S. Farmer and C. Pasternack (eds.), *Gender and Difference in the Middle Ages* (Minneapolis, 2003), pp. 45–71.
70 Khatīb, iii, 433–4.
71 *Aghāni*, x, p. 182; xiv, p. 76; xix, p. 234.
72 *Hadāya*, caps. 141–2.
73 Tab., p. 1,718.
74 Tab., pp. 1,710–2.

75 Tab., pp. 1,718–20; trans., xxxvi, pp. 8–9.

76 Tab., p. 1,916.

77 Misk., p. 20.

78 Misk., p. 40.

79 Misk., pp. 24–5, 42.

80 *Hadāya*, p. 353.

81 Misk., p. 22.

82 Misk., p. 185.

83 *Hadāya*, p. 350.

84 Misk., p. 75.

85 Misk., p. 143.

86 Misk., p. 164.

87 Sābi, *Rusūm*, pp. 27–33.

88 Misk., pp. 41–4.

89 Misk., pp. 179–81.

90 Misk., p. 193.

91 Misk., p. 235.

92 Misk., p. 226.

93 Misk., pp. 243–4.

94 Misk., pp. 244–5.

95 Misk., p. 260.

96 Misk., p. 13.

97 Misk., pp. 189–93.

98 Misk., pp. 241–2.

VII MA'MŪN TO MUTAWWAKIL

1 Ibn Khall, i, p. 85.

2 Tab., pp. 1,027–8; Mas., 2,747; Abbott, pp. 224–5.

3 Tab., p. 1,030; Yaq, ii, p. 551.

4 Lassner, pp. 265–6.

5 Lassner, pp. 48, 66, 68, 251.

6 Tab., pp. 1,042–3.

7 Ibn Abi Tāhir, text 35–53, trans. 18–25, Tab., pp. 1,046–61; Bosworth, 'An early Islamic Mirror for Princes', *Journal of Near Eastern Studies*, xiv (1970), pp. 25–41.

8 Tab., p. 1,055.

9 Tab., p. 1,056.

10 Tab., p. 1,059.

11 Tab., p. 1,060.

12 Tab., p. 1,060.

13 Tab., pp. 1,030, 1,039.

14 Abbott, pp. 227–35.

15 Tab., p. 1,068.

16 Tab., p. 1,068.

17 Tab., p. 1,046.

18 Tab., pp. 1,080–1, quoting the Koran, xii, 92; see also the accounts in *Aghāni*, x, pp. 98–101, where Ibrāhīm's eloquence saves his life.

19 Ibn Khall., trans., i, pp. 16–20.

20 Tab., p. 1,103.

21 Tab., pp. 1,109–11.

22 Ref. to Koran, ix, 52.

23 Tab., p. 1,111–12.

24 Accepting the dates given in Tab., p. 1,140.

25 Ibn Tayfur, pp. 349–50, trans. pp. 157–8; Tab., pp. 1,134–5.

26 Mas., 2,780–1.

27 Tab., p. 1,137. The later political provisions of this will were probably elaborated after his death, but the details of his burial certainly ring true.

28 I owe this information to Michael Cooperson.

29 Tab., pp. 1,323–4.

30 Tab., p. 1,164.

31 Mas., *Tanbīh*, pp. 322–3.

32 Tab., pp. 1,183, 1324, trans. Bosworth, n. 617, quoting Mas., *Tanbīh*.

33 Tab., pp. 1,325–6.

34 Tab., p. 1,164.

35 Tab., pp. 1,181–3.

36 Tab., pp. 1,183–4.

37 Tab., pp. 1,183–4.

38 Tab., p. 1,181.

39 Tab., p. 1,180.

40 Tab., pp. 1,180–228.

41 Tab., pp. 1,230–2.

42 For the date see Bosworth trans., n. 270 quoting Mas.

43 Tab., pp. 1,234–56.

44 Tab., p. 1,236.

45 Tab., p. 1,256.

46 Tab., p. 1,249.

47 Tab., p. 1,249.

48 Tab., pp. 1,257–8.

49 Tab., pp. 1,249–50.

50 Tab., p. 1,261.

51 Tab., p. 1,265; Yaq., ii, p. 581.

52 Tab., p. 1,265.

53 Tab., p. 1,267.

54 *Uyūn*, p. 398.

55 Tab., pp. 1,308–13; there are brief accounts of Afshīn's arrest and death in Yaq., ii, p. 583, and Mas. 2,819–21.

56 Tab., p. 1,317.

57 Tab., pp. 1,317–18.
58 Tab., pp. 1,326–8.
59 Tab., p. 1,364.
60 Tab., pp. 1,351–7.
61 Tab., pp. 1,343–9. The leader was Nasr ibn Ahmad al-Khuzā'ī.
62 For the importance of this, see below, pp. 250–51.
63 Tab., p. 1,338.
64 Tab., p. 1,369.
65 Tab., p. 1,465.
66 See Kraemer's n. 631 in Tab., trans., p. xxxiv. My interpretation of the headgear is slightly different from his.
67 *zayy al-mukhanithīn*.
68 See Tab., trans. Kraemer, n. 244, for details of the use of this story by later authors.
69 Tab., p. 1,375.
70 Tab., p. 1,377.
71 Tab., pp. 1,411–12.
72 Tab., p. 1,421.
73 Tab., p. 1,407.
74 Tab., trans. Kraemer, n. 358, quoting Ibn Hawqal.
75 Tab., pp. 1,389–90. The full text of the decree is given in Tab., pp. 1,390–4.
76 Tab., pp. 1,413–14.
77 Tab., pp. 1,424–5.
78 Tab., pp. 1,435–7; Yaq., ii, 600; Mas., 2942.
79 Tab., pp. 1,438–9.
80 Tab., p. 1,459.

IX ABBASID COURT CULTURE

1 Mas., 2,857–68.
2 Mas., 3,043.
3 *Fihrist*, p. 66 (trans. pp. 131–3).
4 *Fihrist*, pp. 320–1 (trans., pp. 626–8); Mas., 3,316.
5 See D. Gutas, *Greek Thought, Arabic Culture* (London, 1998), pp. 54–60, for a full discussion of the evidence for the *Bayt al-hikma*. I have followed Gutas's conclusions although it should be noted that these remain controversial.
6 Yāqūt, *Mu'jam al-Udabā* (*Irshād al-Arīb*), ed. I. Abbas (Beirut, 1993), ii, pp. 545–6. I would like to express my gratitude to Letizia Osti who drew my attention to this passage. My translation is based on hers with minor modifications.
7 Yāqūt, *Udabā*, ii, p. 536.
8 For his lively and disreputable career, *Fihrist*, p. 67, trans. pp. 133–5; Ibn Khall., trans. iii, p. 37.

9 For his life, *Fihrist,* p. 163, trans. pp. 320–2. The surviving section of his *Kitāb Baghdād* was edited with a German translation by H. Keller (Leipzig, 1908).

10 *Fihrist,* pp. 378–9, trans. p. 742.

11 *Fihrist,* p. 170, trans. p. 335.

12 See G. J. van Gelder, 'Beautifying the Ugly and Uglifying the Beautiful: the Paradox in Classical Arabic literature', *JSS,* 48 (2003), pp. 321–51.

13 Tab., p. 165, n. 556, trans. (Kraemer) p. xxiv.

14 Sūli, *Kitāb al-Awrāq,* ed. A. Khalidov (St Petersburg, 1998), pp. 457–8.

15 Tab., pp. 1,557–8.

16 Tab., pp. 1,634, 1,641–2, 1,647.

17 Gutas, p. 138.

18 Ibn Khall., i, pp. 478–9.

19 *Fihrist,* p. 346, trans. p. 673.

20 *Fihrist,* p. 353, trans. pp. 694–5.

21 *Fihrist,* p. 304, trans. p. 585.

22 *Fihrist,* p. 331, trans. pp. 647–8.

23 Jāhiz, *Bukhalā* (Misers), pp. 81–93, trans. pp. 67–78.

24 See the list in G. N. Atiyeh, *Al-Kindi: the philosopher of the Arabs* (Rawalpindi, 1966), pp. 148–210.

25 Ibn Khall., v, pp. 162–3, trans. pp. 315–17.

X HIGH NOON IN SĀMARRĀ

1 Tab., pp. 1,394–403, gives the full text of the documents. See also Yaq., ii, pp. 594–5; Abbott, 'Arabic papyri from the reign of al-Mutawwakil', *ZDMG,* 92, 1938, pp. 88–135.

2 Tab., p. 1,497.

3 Tab., p. 1,542.

4 Tab., p. 1,543.

5 Tab., pp. 1,454–5.

6 Tab., trans. p. xxxiv (Kraemer), n. 589.

7 We can compare contemporary examples, such as Princess Diana's alleged premonition of her death in a car accident.

8 Tab., p. 1,462.

9 Tab., p. 1,471.

10 Tab., p. 1,472.

11 Tab., pp. 1,463–4.

12 Tab., p. 1,473.

13 Tab., pp. 1,481–5.

14 Tab., p. 1,484.

15 Tab., pp. 1,486–8.

16 Sūli as quoted in the Leiden edition of Tab., p. 1,502, trans. Saliba, p. 1,502.

17 Tab., p. 1,505.

18 Tab., p. 1,510.

19 Tab., pp. 1,511–12.
20 Tab., p. 1,515.
21 Tab., pp. 1,538–9.
22 Tab., p. 1,542.
23 Tab., p. 1,544.
24 Tab., p. 1,550.
25 Tab., p. 1,553.
26 Tab., p. 1,552.
27 Tab., p. 1,552.
28 Tab., pp. 1,586–7.
29 Tab., pp. 1,555–6.
30 Tab., p. 1,556.
31 Tab., pp. 1,563–4.
32 Quoted in full in Tab., pp. 1,565–76.
33 Tab., p. 1,578.
34 Tab., pp. 1,578–9.
35 Tab., p. 1,580.
36 Tab., pp. 1,592–3.
37 Tab., pp. 1,621–3.
38 Tab., p. 1,630.
39 Tab., p. 1,632.
40 Tab., pp. 1,638–9.
41 Tab., p. 1,645.
42 Tab., p. 1,712.
43 Tab., p. 1,659.
44 Tab., p. 1,669.
45 Tab., p. 1,657.
46 Tab., pp. 1,670–1.
47 Tab., pp. 1,687–8.
48 Tab., pp. 1,694–7.
49 Tab., pp. 1,707–8.
50 Tab., pp. 1,712–13.
51 Tab., p. 1,374.
52 Tab., pp. 1,736.
53 Tab., p. 1,720.
54 Tab., 1,722–4.
55 Tab., pp. 1,793–4.
56 Tab., pp. 1,813–34.

Bibliography

HISTORICAL AND GEOGRAPHICAL SOURCES IN ENGLISH TRANSLATION

Anon., *Book of Gifts and Rarities*, trans. Ghāda Qaddumi (Cambridge, MA, 1996)

Anon., *The Arabian Nights*, trans. Husain Haddawy (New York, 1990)

al-Balādhurī, *The Origins of the Islamic State*, trans. P. Hitti and F. Murgotten, 2 vols. (New York, 1916–24)

Jāhiz, *Nine Essays*, trans. William M. Hutchins (New York, 1988)

Jāhiz, *The Book of Misers*, trans. R. B. Serjeant (Reading, 1997)

Jāhiz, *The Epistle on Singing-girls by Jāhiz*, trans. A. F. L. Beeston (Warminster, 1980)

Ibn Khallikān, *Ibn Khallikān's Biographical Dictionary*, trans., M. de Slane, 4 vols. (Paris, 1842–71)

al-Māwardī, *The Ordinances of Government*, trans. W. H. Wahba (Reading, 1996)

al-Masᶜūdī, *The Meadows of Gold: the Abbasids*, partial trans. P. Lunde and C. Stone (London and New York, 1989)

Miskawayh, *The Eclipse of the Abbasid Caliphate*, trans. with continuation by Abū Shujā al-Rūdhrawārī and D. S. Margoliouth, 3 vols. (London, 1921)

al-Muqaddasī, *The Best Divisions for Knowledge of the Regions*, trans. B. Collins (Reading, 2001)

al-Sūli, *Customs of the Caliph's Palace*, trans. E. Salem (Beirut, 1977)

al-Tabari, *The History of al-Tabarī*, ed. Y. Yarshater, 38 vols. (Albany, NJ, 1985–2000)

al-Tabari, *The Early Abbāsi Empire 754–808*, trans. J. A. Williams, 2 vols. (Cambridge, 1989)

SECONDARY LITERATURE

Abbott, Nabia, *Two Queens of Baghdad* (Chicago, IL, 1946; reprinted London, 1986)

Agha, Saleh Said, *The Revolution which Toppled the Umayyads* (Leiden, 2003)

Ahsan, M. M., *Social Life under the Abbasids* (London, 1979)

Allen, Roger, *The Arabic Literary Heritage* (Cambridge, 1998)

Ashtiany, Julia (ed.), *Abbasid Belles-Lettres: Cambridge History of Arabic Literature*, vol. ii (Cambridge, 1990)

Bell, Gertrude, *Amurath to Amurath* (London, 1911)

Bloom, Jonathan, *Paper before Print: the history and impact of paper in the Islamic world* (New Haven and London, 2001)

Bonner, Michael, *Aristocratic Violence and Holy War. Studies in the Jihad and the Arab–Byzantine Frontier* (New Haven, CT, 1996)

Bosworth, C. Edmund, *The New Islamic Dynasties* (Edinburgh, 1996)

Bowen, Harold, *The Life and Times of 'Alī b. 'Īsā, the Good Vizier* (Cambridge, 1928)

Bulliet, Richard, *The Camel and the Wheel* (Cambridge, MA, 1975)

Bulliet, Richard, *Conversion to Islam in the Medieval Period* (Cambridge MA, 1979)

Bulliet, Richard, *Islam: the View from the Edge* (New York, 1994)

Cobb, Paul M., *White Banners: Contention in Abbasid Syria, 750–880* (Albany, NJ, 2001)

Cooperson, Michael, *Classical Arabic Biography* (Cambridge, 2000)

Creswell, K. A. C., *A Short Account of Early Muslim Architecture*, ed. James Allen (Aldershot, 1989)

Crone, Patricia, and G. Martin Hinds, *God's Caliph: Religious authority in the first centuries of Islam* (Cambridge, 1968)

Daniel, E. L., *The Political and Social History of Khurasan under Abbasid Rule* (Minneapolis, MN, Chicago, IL, 1979)

El-Hibri, T., *Reinterpreting Islamic Historiography: Hārūn al-Rashīd and the Narrative of the Abbasid Caliphate* (Cambridge, 1999)

Farmer, Harold, *A History of Arabian Music* (London, 1929)

Frye, Richard, *The Heritage of Persia* (London, 1964)

Frye, Richard, *The Golden Age of Persia* (London, 1975)

Goldziher, Ignaz, *Muslim Studies*, ed. and trans. C. R. Barber and S. M. Stern, 2 vols. (London, 1967, 1971)

Gordon, Matthew S., *The Breaking of a Thousand Swords: A History of the Turkish Military of Samarra* (A.H. 200–275/815–889 C.E.) (Albany, NJ, 2001)

Gruendler, Beatrice, *Medieval Arabic Praise Poetry* (London, 2002)

Gutas, Dimitri, *Greek Thought, Arabic Culture* (London and New York, 1998)

Heidemann, Stefan and Becker, Andrea, *Raqqa II: die Islamische Stadt* (Mainz, 2003)

Herrmann, Georgina, *Monuments of Merv* (London, 1999)

Hillenbrand, Robert, *Islamic Architecture* (Edinburgh, 1994)

Hourani, Albert, *A History of the Arab People*s (London, 1991)

Humphreys, R. S., *Islamic History: a framework for inquiry* (Princeton, NJ, 1991)

Irwin, Robert, *The Arabian Nights: A Companion* (London, 1994)

Irwin, Robert, *Islamic Art* (London, 1997)

Irwin, Robert, *Night and Horses and the Desert: An Anthology of Classical Arabic Literature* (London, 1999)

Jafri, S. M., *The Origins and early Development of Shi'a Islam* (London, 1979)

Kennedy, Hugh, *The Early Abbasid Caliphate: A political history* (London, 1981)

Kennedy, Hugh, *The Armies of the Caliphs* (London, 2001)

Kennedy, Hugh (ed.), *An Historical Atlas of Islam* (Leiden, 2002)

Kennedy, Hugh, *The Prophet and the Age of the Caliphates*, 2nd edn. (London, 2003)

Kilpatrick, Hilary, *Making the Great Book of Songs* (London, 2003)

Lassner, Jacob, *The Topography of Baghdad in the Early Middle Ages: Text and studies* (Detroit, MI, 1970)

Lassner, Jacob, *The Shaping of Abbasid Rule* (Princeton, NJ, 1980)

Lassner, Jacob, *Islamic Revolution and Historical Memory: An inquiry into the art of Abbasid apologetics* (New Haven, CT, 1986)

Le Strange, Guy, *Palestine under the Moslems* (London, 1890)

Le Strange, Guy, *Lands of the Eastern Caliphate* (Cambridge, 1905)

Le Strange, Guy, *Baghdad during the Abbasid Caliphate* (London, 1909)

Mez, Adam, *The Renaissance of Islam*, trans. Khuda Bakhsh (London, 1937)

Morony, Michael, *Iraq after the Muslim Conquest* (Princeton, NJ, 1984)

Mottahedeh, Roy, *Loyalty and Leadership in Early Islamic society*, 2nd edn. (Princeton, NJ, 2001)

Northedge, Alistair, 'The palaces of the Abbasids at Samarra' , in ed. C. Robinson, *A Medieval Islamic City Reconsidered: an interdisciplinary approach to Samarra* (Oxford Studies in Islamic Art, xiv, 2001)

Peirce, Leslie, *The Imperial Harem: Women and Sovereignty in the Ottoman Empire* (Oxford, 1993)

Petry, Carl (ed.), *The Cambridge History of Egypt*, vol. i, *Islamic Egypt, 640–1517* (Cambridge, 1998)

Popovic, A., *The Revolt of the African Slaves in Iraq in the 3rd/9th Century* (London, 1999)

Robinson, Chase (ed.), *A Medieval Islamic City Reconsidered: An interdisciplinary approach to Samarra* (*Oxford Studies in Islamic Art*, xiv, 2001)

Robinson, Chase, *Islamic Historiography* (Cambridge, 2003)

Roden, Claudia (ed.), *Medieval Arab Cookery* (Totnes, 2001)

Sharon, Moshe, *Black Banners from the East* (Leiden, 1983)

Sharon, Moshe, *Revolt. The Social and Military Aspects of the Abbasid Revolution* (Jerusalem, 1990)

Sourdel, D., 'Questions de cérémoniale Abbaside', *Revue d'Études Islamiques* (1960), 121–48

Stetkevych, Suzanne P., *Abū Tammām and the Poetics of the Abbasid Age* (Leiden, 1991)

Van Gelder, Geert, *Of Dishes and Discourse: Classical Arabic literary representations of food* (London, Curzon, 2000)

Waines, David, 'The third century internal crisis of the Abbasids', *Journal of the Economic and Social History of the Orient*, xx (1977), pp. 282–306

Waines, David, *In a Caliph's Kitchen* (London, 1989)

Williams, J. A., *The Early Abbasid Empire*, 2 vols. (Cambridge, 1988)

Zaman, M. Q., *Religion and Politics under the early Abbasids: The emergence of the proto-Sunni élite* (Leiden, 1997)

In addition the reader can refer to the two editions of the *Encyclopaedia of Islam*. The first edition, 4 vols. (Leiden, 1913–42) is complete but many of the articles are dated. The second edition (Leiden, 1954) is now almost complete. It is also accessible on CD-ROM. A third edition is planned. Many of the articles are of great scholarly value and general interest. Another important reference tool is the *Encyclopaedia Iranica*, ed. E. Yarshater (London and New York, 1985–), which contains more discursive articles on the history and culture of Iran and is still incomplete.

Index